BASEBALL

The Heroes of the Game and

GALAHAD BOOKS • NEW YORK

AMERICA

the Times of Their Glory

DONALD HONIG

Published in 1993 by

Galahad Books
A Division of Budget Book Service, Inc.
386 Park Avenue South
New York, New York 10016

Galahad Books is a registered trademark of
Budget Book Service, Inc.

Published by arrangement with The Macmillan Publishing Company.

Library of Congress Catalog Card Number: 84-25006

ISBN: 0-88365-817-8

Designed by Jack Meserole

Printed in the United States of America.

The title "Baseball America" is used under license from and with the consent of the publisher of
Baseball America Newspaper and proprietor of the trademark "Baseball America," American
Sports Publishing, Inc., Durham, North Carolina.

This book is dedicated to the memories of
RED SMITH
and
JOE FLAHERTY

BASEBALL AMERICA

ONE

BASEBALL LEGENDS have age and diversity. One of the grand old stories, which once upon a time serious men gave credence to, involved Abraham Lincoln. According to this story, a committee from the Chicago convention, which on May 18, 1860, had nominated Lincoln as the Republican candidate for president, arrived in Springfield, Illinois, to notify him formally of the event. When the distinguished deputation appeared at the Lincoln home they found the candidate not available. A messenger was dispatched to apprise Mr. Lincoln that he had visitors. This particular moment of American history, so the tale goes, found Mr. Lincoln out on the commons engaged in a game of baseball, standing at home plate, bat in hand. When the messenger informed the tall, muscular prairie lawyer that he had a living room full of politicos, Lincoln replied, "Tell the gentlemen that I am glad to know of their coming; but they'll have to wait a few minutes till I make another base hit." (The only thing missing from this little fable is that Lincoln then pointed to the center field chestnut trees and lofted the next pitch over the very spot; but that particular flourish was being reserved for another American original, in the next century.)

Whether Lincoln actually ever struck a pitched ball with a piece of one of those rails he was so famous for splitting is not known, but it is certainly true that baseball was played by the soldiers of North and South during the Civil War. The time spent between the heavy work at places like Chancellorsville, Gettysburg, and Cold Harbor could become tedious. Between battles of terrifying intensity and long marches were months of inactivity. The men lay on cots in Sibley tents or in winter huts and wrote letters, smoked their pipes, read and reread newspapers, or played checkers. They sang songs, encouraged their amateur musicians, cut wood, and had snowball fights. They also burned off the hours by engaging in competitions like foot racing, wrestling, leapfrog, quoits, marbles, and baseball. The last of these, known also as bass ball, was one of the most popular of these diversions.

Wearing their slant-visored forage caps or slouch hats, with a broad X of suspenders crossing their backs, they went to bat, swinging cut-down broomsticks or sawed-off fence planks at balls that may have been so many stockings or so much yarn held together by a piece of stitched leather, sometimes with some rubber from an old boot tucked in to make the ball livelier. Some Confederate boys in Virginia ran the bases after whacking a yarn-wrapped walnut with a roughly trimmed hickory limb.

The game was only recently out of the incubator in those days and there were many variants. One way of playing it saw a base-runner retired if one of the fielders was able to pink him with a thrown ball, implying that the ball was not as hard as the missiles they play with today. Nevertheless, some of those boys could throw even a soggy ball with impact. A soldier from a Texas regiment noted in his diary that "Frank Ezell was ruled out" of the game because "he could throw harder and straighter than any man in the company. He came very near knocking the stuffing out of three or four of the boys, and the boys swore they would not play with him."

The boys in the 1860s knew all about baseball fever. After the war, they scattered to all points of the national compass and, along with tales of cannon fire and bayonet charges, they talked about the new game and showed how it was played. Americans young and old took to it with alacrity, playing it in all its variants, skillfully and clumsily, but with an enthusiasm that guaranteed the contagion would continue to spread. It wasn't long before every community had its team and local rivalries were established. Teams sponsored by merchants or by politicians sniffing a popular craze go back to the 1860s.

The origin of the game is not known, but legends quickly sprang up to fill this gap in our knowledge. The most celebrated story is that Abner Doubleday invented it at Cooperstown, New York, in 1839. This highly varnished fish story received official propagation in 1907, thanks to a distinguished if credulous group known as the Mills Commission. The group was formed at the behest of Albert Spalding, one of the game's pioneer figures and founder of the sporting goods firm that still bears his name, and charged with the task of determining the origin of baseball (or "Base Ball," as they wrote it). The commission included A. G. Mills, described as "an enthusiastic ball player before and during the Civil War," and the third president of the National League; Arthur P. Gorman, a former United States senator from Maryland; Morgan G. Bulkeley, former governor of Connecticut and the first president of the National League; and four other gentlemen of varying distinction and impeccable pedigree.

After sifting through the available evidence, the group came to a unanimous decision, to wit:

That Base Ball had its origins in the United States.

That the first scheme for playing it, according to the best evidence obtainable to date, was devised by Abner Doubleday, at Cooperstown, New York, in 1839.

Bingo: instant mythology, particularly in the second assertion, a high bouncer of a story that remained airborne for decades. That the game as we know it today had its origins in the United States is true; but that Doubleday was its originating genius and that Cooperstown was the cradle for all runs, hits, and errors is malarkey of the purest brand. Nobody believes the tale today, but Cooperstown remains the game's symbolic home, and it couldn't have happened to a lovelier, more picturesque American village.

The commission closed its report (signed by Mills) with "evidence" as substantial as a butterfly's wing. In part it reads:

in the interesting and pertinent testimony for which we are indebted to Mr. A. G. Spalding, appears a circumstantial statement by a reputable gentleman, according to which the first known diagram of the diamond, indicating positions for the players was drawn by Abner Doubleday in Cooperstown, New York, in 1839. Abner Doubleday subsequently graduated from West Point and entered the regular army, where, as Captain of Artillery, he sighted the first gun fired on the Union side (at Fort Sumter) in the Civil War. . . .

In the days when Abner Doubleday attended school in Cooperstown, it was a common thing for two dozen or more of school boys to join in a game of ball. Doubtless, as in my later experience, collisions between players in attempting to catch the batted ball were frequent, and injury due to this cause, or to the practice of putting out the runner by hitting him with the ball, often occurred.

I can well understand how the orderly mind of the embryo West Pointer would devise a scheme for limiting the contestants on each side and allotting them to field positions, each with a certain amount of territory; also substituting the existing method of putting out the base runner for the old one of "plugging" him with the ball.

And so on and so forth. Doubleday went on to a modestly distinguished military career, rising to the rank of brevet major general. He commanded a division at the battles of Antietam and Fredericksburg and had a moment of glory at Gettysburg when he temporarily assumed command of a corps upon the death in battle of General John Reynolds. However, General George Meade, commander-in-chief of the Army of the Potomac, immediately gave that command to another because Doubleday was not considered aggressive enough. A reputation for deliberateness had earned for Abner the nickname Forty-eight Hours. Today, for those who think baseball is a slow-moving game, that remains Doubleday's only legitimate claim to its invention.

Doubleday died in New Jersey in 1893 at the age of seventy-three, fourteen years before the filing of the Mills Commission concoction, so we will never know what he would have thought about it. No doubt he would have been astounded. As far as anyone knows, he was as removed from the game as a Tibetan lama and didn't know a baseball from a kumquat.

Actually, the game began to take recognizable shape in New York City in the early 1840s. It was around that time that a group of young middle-class gentlemen began playing a very rudimentary game of ball in the open spaces of the Murray Hill area, what is today the East Side around Thirty-second Street. The area was considered uptown then. The heart of New York was still far downtown, with lower Broadway the city's teeming main artery, its pavement stones clattering with horse-drawn omnibuses, hackney cabs, four-wheeled phaetons, two-wheeled tilburies, and private carriages driven by liveried coachmen.

By one conveyance or another, the gentleman players got to the playing ground, and gentlemen they were, for the game as played in the 1840s bore little resemblance to the aggressive, sophisticated, highly competitive baseball of today. The game, an outgrowth of British cricket, was a placid, mannered diversion played purely for recreational purposes. The ladies watching sat on chairs, protected by parasols if the sun was too strong. Bouquets of spectators in their colorful silks and satins and ribbons and tassels, they were attended by their young men in stovepipe hats and grave chin whiskers who bent and gave whispered explication of some nuance of the quietly conducted game before them. The man standing some forty-five or fifty feet away and delivering a one-bounce pitch to a man with a stick? Why, he was the bowler. The man with the stick? He was the striker.

Nothing remained the same for very long in America, and certainly not in that big-shouldered age of growth and expansion. Whatever the country needed seemed to spring miraculously from the creative genius of its citizens. Samuel Morse provided instant communication with the telegraph. Charles Goodyear stumbled upon the secret of vulcanizing rubber. Elias Howe invented and Isaac Singer perfected the sewing machine. Cyrus McCormick constructed reaping machines to harvest the wealth of the prairies. Baseball? Baseball had a luxuriantly whiskered young man named Alexander Joy Cartwright. In the middle of the 1840s this enthusiast came along and began shaping the game into the one we know today. Through observation, calculation, and refining, Cartwright arrived at a design of nine men on a side, four bases, and ninety feet between the bases—those ninety feet being one of the most geometrically perfect concepts in all of sports.

While Abner Doubleday was off in Mexico fighting a war as captain of artillery, Cartwright was formulating the rules of the new game. When the twenty-five-year-old bank teller was finished finetuning on the diamond, the game was clearly distinct from any other. With a group of young men from the city's financial district, Cartwright in 1845 organized the Knickerbocker Base Ball Club, whose set of rules was strictly enforced. These included punctuality for the players, the appointment of an umpire whose job included keeping the scorebook, three strikes and out, three outs per side. One of Cartwright's more significant changes was the elimination of "plugging"—throwing the ball at a runner to put him out. "A player running the bases," the rules stated, "shall be out, if the ball is in the hands of an adversary on the base, or the runner is touched with it before he makes his bases; it being understood, however, that in no instance is a ball to be thrown at him."

This was baseball New York style, and it took a while for it to catch on in other parts of the country. It also took a while, a long while, for baseball to catch up with Alexander Cartwright. In 1849 he left New York and eventually ended up in Hawaii, where he spent the rest of his life, dying in 1892 at the age of seventy-two. It wasn't until 1938 that his contributions to the game were duly recognized and he was inducted into the Hall of Fame at Cooperstown.

After the Civil War, the masses took hold of the game and altered it to reflect a much broader common denominator. Baseball as a mere pleasant diversion was soon an obsolete concept, and baseball as a game that was fun, important, and for some, positively essential to win, became the norm. A pungent sense of competitiveness, spurred in part by the increasingly large number of spectators who came out to watch, began communicating itself to the players, leading them to play with more intensity. Professional teams were formed and traveled far and wide to play, representing their cities more than in name alone. As the professional leagues grew in popularity in the 1870s and 1880s, the players were demonstrating greater and more exciting skills, and crowds were responding in larger numbers and more enthusiasm, and civic pride began revealing itself to an ever intensifying degree.

TWO

WHAT AMERICA LACKED at the turn of the century were heroes, living, breathing heroes; men who could stand in the sunshine the way Washington and Lincoln towered in the shadows. Throughout the nation's brief history its pantheon consisted of soldiers and pathfinders and men of action: buckskinned, uniformed, plume-hatted earthshakers like Daniel Boone, Andrew Jackson, and Jeb Stuart; or they had to be embroidered and stretched a bit to fit the desired picture, like Davy Crockett, Wild Bill Hickok, and Buffalo Bill.

Admirable though these gentlemen were, they all had distance from their idolators in time, place, and drama; they were to be admired and revered and contemplated, but they could not—at least not realistically anyway—be emulated; for in the minds of the nation's youth, those fecund pastures where heroes take shape and legends assume proportion, they were stories in a book, pictures on a page, granite or cast-iron monuments on a village green. Unseen, unfelt, they had to be taken on faith.

The recent war with Spain had turned out a couple of splendid overachievers, one of whom was Admiral George Dewey, who, it seemed, had virtually singlehandedly pulled the plug on the Spanish fleet. This was certainly praiseworthy work, but the admiral had earned his garlands in Manila Harbor, a long cannon-shot from home. One homecoming, one gaudy parade of men and music, and the admiral was pressed between leaves. The other notable to emerge from that tropical little war was currently America's premier living hero, who happened to be a New World Renaissance man—a soldier, an adventurer of sorts, a writer, an ebulliently oversized personality; the throbbingly perfect character to usher the nation into its century of dominance. But Theodore Roosevelt was also president of the United States, a somewhat remote office in those pretelevision days, and for all of his bustling conquests, Teddy was a hero primarily

7

because of the office he occupied, and how many dreamy little boys could honestly hope to aspire to it?

Heroism being concomitant with virtue in those less unsettling days, it was not easy to lead a life worthy enough of inspiring sculptors. Along with brilliant achievement, there was a veritable obstacle course of qualities a man had to negotiate before he could earn his pedestal: manliness, honesty, fearlessness, resolution, fair play, moral purity, modesty. It was enough to make a man want to opt for obscurity. There were guidebooks that blueprinted the way to success, stories written by a Harvard-educated former minister named Horatio Alger that demonstrated how such bottom-of-the-rung youngsters as newsboys and bootblacks got to the top by being clean, pure, and virtuous. There were also stories about a sterling Yalie named Frank Merriwell, which first appeared in 1896. If each virtue had weighed as little as an ounce, Frank would have been too weighted down to move without wheels, much less hit his bottom-of-the-ninth home runs clear out of New Haven into Long Island Sound. The message of Frank Merriwell was simple: Be pure and decent and humble and you shall succeed, and never mind the robber barons who were pillaging the country and living in palatial splendor.

Given the ethics of American big business in those years, it probably would have been disastrous for any youngster to swallow unquestioningly the philosophy of success then being measured out for him yard by unrealistic yard. (In the end, even the stainless Alger hero got his brass ring by a stroke of providential luck or by marrying the boss's daughter.) It wasn't that the litany of necessary virtues was by any means objectionable; it was just that as yet no truly admirable hero had come forth who embodied them, no one whom man and boy, rich and poor, learned and unlearned, could esteem, marvel at, and try to emulate. But that was about to change.

Arguably, the most abundant suppliers of heroes in America have been its athletic arenas, with baseball turning them out more prolifically than all the other sports put together. Never mind profundity or social significance. We're not talking about Thomas Edisons, Guglielmo Marconis, or Jonas Salks; we're not talking about Charles Lindbergh, Alvin York, or Ernest Hemingway, or Douglas MacArthur, Dwight Eisenhower, Franklin Roosevelt, or John F. Kennedy. We're talking about heroes who were at once life-sized and out-sized, who showed up for work every day and who performed their wizardry before the eyes of thousands of witnesses. They were deities in knickered uniforms who hurled not thunderbolts but baseballs, Mercuries in spiked shoes, Thors who swung bats and not hammers; not statues but blood-carrying men sculpting their own figures inning by inning, game by game, year after year, until they were complete in memory and record book, hallowed and emblazoned. They were heroes who were all too often disappointingly and heartbreakingly human: living, breathing heroes who for a change had the history books open ahead of them, not closed behind, and who were performing their feats not in unpathed wildernesses or in distant lands, but who were out there in golden American sunshine, playing America's own game on the bright green grass of home.

The lure of baseball? The charm? The magic? Sociologists will tell you. So will symbolists and psychologists and maybe even anthropologists. The truth is, it is so basic and simple and primitive of appeal as to slip unscathed through the mesh of learned critique or analysis. Hold a ball in your hand and your instinct is to throw it; grip a stick in your hand and your desire is to strike that ball; be some distance away and your need is to catch that ball; and if you are a spectator, then you won't move a muscle or blink an eye until you have seen who wins the race—the ball plunging toward earth or the man who is trying to prevent that from happening. With unending renewal the ritual goes on and on, for there will be, in Carl Sandburg's phrase, "Always the young strangers" who will come to try it anew. Those are the rudiments that expand to shape a game and embrace all fanaticism. Are they symbolic of joy, aggression, man's eternal infantilism? It might be interesting to know, but much more momentous are these questions: Did the batter get a hit? Did the pitcher get him out? Did the fielder make the play? Who won? What was the score?

By the very nature of its design, a baseball game is timeless. No clock measures its beat. Before the installation of arc lights, only God could end a baseball game prematurely, by gradually dimming His sunlight. But artificial light has relieved the Almighty of what was surely a conscience-stricken act. The phrase "the game is never over until the last man is out" is in truth more than a weary, catchy slogan, as some startling ninth-inning rallies will attest. In other games we hear of "freezing the ball" or "eating up the clock." Not in baseball, where the outcome can still be in doubt though the game be twenty-six twenty-sevenths over. We have shaped our national game to be different.

Baseball provided camaraderie. It also gave a youngster a sense of independence, it gave him an arena that belonged solely to him and his friends (and to his goals and dreams, too), that was free of any parental authority. It was free-spirited, it was fun, it was exciting, and it was important. A boy could be a hero, he could share in the raucous, close-knitting exultation of a team victory. And it could be recorded in a scorebook, play by play, to be remembered for all time, just as it happened.

From the end of the Civil War to the beginning of the new century, America was at peace with itself and with the world at large. It went a third of a century without a major conflict, a luxury the nation would not enjoy in the next hundred-year cycle. The bright new game fit perfectly into the life of those summer days. The pacing was just right, and the machinery of the game was laid out for all to see. It could be as intricate as the timing between shortstop and second baseman making the double play, or as simple as a centerfielder waiting for a high fly ball. It could rise to moments of sudden tension—a full-count pitch with the bases loaded, a runner trying to score from second on a hit to the outfield—and then relax again into its measured rhythms. It gave the fans a unique opportunity—to be at one with their heroes, watch them grow, develop, and thrive, to know every nuance and gesture of their burgeoning legend. Where else but at a ball park could the masses watch their idols at work? For fans with the proper currents of imagination or longing or reverence, it was joy pure and sublime just to be able to stare at Honus Wagner crouched at his shortstop position, hands on knees, eyes riveted on the pitcher's delivery. For many, this was enough: to watch him cast his shadow on the field, or trot to the dugout, or sit on the bench with his legs crossed. All summer long you could see him, and for the rest of your life remember. For some old-time fans, their most vivid memories of Wagner were not of the great Dutchman digging out grounders or smashing line drives, but this: "I can still see him standing out there at shortstop." Merely being, posted where the adoring eye could comfortably and unhurriedly linger upon him.

Major-league baseball started in 1876 with the formation of the National League, giving the nation the nicest centennial birthday gift imaginable. And it is probably just as well that it took one hundred years to get around to it, since the 1982 edition of the *Baseball Encyclopedia* already runs to over twenty-two-hundred tightly packed pages of statistics. Think of a volume trying to compile all the leading batters and pitchers from 1776 on. Think of unscrupulous frontier rascals not only selling guns and whiskey to the Mohawks and Sioux, but also teaching them how to throw a spitball. Think of the havoc the British would have wrought on the schedule when they burned Washington in August 1814, even though the Senators would surely have been out of the race by then. Think of some of the splendid careers that would have been interrupted by service with the Union and Confederate armies.

So the National League came into being in 1876. The original eight teams were located in Chicago, St. Louis, Hartford, Boston, Louisville, New York, Philadelphia, and Cincinnati. Making all the necessary travel possible, and relatively comfortable, was the world's largest network of railroad tracks. More than half of the steel coming out of the nation's seething foundries was being stretched across the land as railroad tracks, binding one section of the country to another. Since 1869, with the driving of the final spike at Promontory Point, Utah, linking the Central Pacific and Union Pacific railroads, transcontinental rail travel had been a reality, the coast-to-coast trip taking seven days. Boston and Cincinnati were only forty shaky, rattling hours apart by rail. No jet lag there, but as one old pioneer National Leaguer said, "Baseball is fun; the travel is wearisome."

That was no ordinary year, that 1876. For its hundredth anniversary, the nation recorded events positive and negative. A series of financial scandals shook President Grant's administration, while out in the Dakota Territory a swarm of Sioux warriors wiped out General George Armstrong Custer and his force of 250 men. On August 2, one of the nation's top guns, Wild Bill Hickok, took an assassin's bullets in the back in Deadwood, South Dakota. On the sunny side, Alexander Graham Bell patented the telephone, and the National League came into being.

Great stars and popular players were always there, from the very beginning and on up into the 1890s, but while many of them were looked upon as ornaments of municipal pride, few were held up as models for American youth. Justly or not, baseball players were regarded as roughnecks engaged in a socially unacceptable profession. There were a lot of hard drinkers in the game then, some of them not averse to going out between the lines with smiles straight out of the gin bottle. There was heavy gambling on games and in those days the final score was sometimes determined by who had wagered how much on whom. There was rowdyism at the games, and an unpopular umpire often had to be escorted out of the ball park by the local constabulary. On one occasion, in Chicago in 1886, after several close calls had gone against the home team, a few disgruntled Chicago fans began swinging a noose from their seats behind first base, letting the umpire know it had been adjusted to his neck size. After that, one old-timer remembered, "The close ones began going Chicago's way, along with the ones that weren't so close."

The greatest team of its time was the Baltimore Orioles of the 1890s, many of whose players graduated from mere mortal status to that of rousing legend. Running down the lineup of the Orioles, and indeed of all the big-league teams of the day, one sees reflected the impact of the Irish immigration that began hitting the shores of the New World a few decades before: Hughie Jennings, Joe Kelley, Willie Keeler, Jack Doyle, John McGraw, skipper Ned Hanlon. Approximately one-third of the major-league players in the 1890s were Irish. This was a syndrome destined to repeat itself again and again in American history—those at the bottom rung of the social ladder (as the Irish were in the 1890s) look for the way up and out via jobs offering ready acceptance and good opportunity. Baseball, that beloved game but disreputable profession, asked for pedigree only that a man could play it well enough that people would pay money to watch him. For young Irishmen of ballplaying ability, seeing their elders mired in the most arduous and low-paying jobs, baseball was the American promise in glorious fulfillment.

Nowhere was that aggressive, hardscrabble Irish spirit more in evidence than in Baltimore, a city known in the early 1890s up and down the eastern seaboard for the quality of its seafood, but soon to have even greater renown for the quality of its baseball team. Guided by the innovative, sometimes unethical managerial genius of Ned Hanlon, they were a band of marauders, these Orioles, dazzling their partisans and outraging their opponents, who were still locked into the game's conservative tactics, with such avant-garde maneuvers as hit-and-run executions, backing-up throws, and positioning men to take relays from the outfield. Those Orioles were tough, devious, relentless, and allegedly immune to pain, giving rise to the bromide that a man who played through an injury had "the old Oriole spirit." How much of this was primitivism and how much good old Irish malarkey now belongs to the windblown dust of history. But there is no question that they were the best of their day, winning pennants in the twelve-team National League (at the time the only major league) in 1894, 1895, and 1896, with a three-year team batting average of .332.

They were known, too, for giving the hip to opposing baserunners and for going from first to third via the middle of the diamond when the then sole umpire's back was turned. Long drives that fell between Oriole outfielders would reappear with miraculous rapidity from the tall grass, holding the startled batter to a single or double when more had been his apparent due. The miracle was later discovered to have been wrought by the Orioles, who had secreted several baseballs in the grass, to be retrieved upon demand. In those days balls fouled into the crowd were often pitched back onto the field. When an opposing batter nicked one into the stands in Baltimore, a prepared Oriole lackey hurled out a little sphere of mush, which when whacked solidly did little more than roll sheepishly into an infielder's glove.

Although these tactics were, in spirit, well within the book of American business ethics of the day, they were definitely not bruited as standards for upright American boys to aspire to. Nevertheless, the Baltimore diamond was the incubator for many a managerial brainstorm of the future, with an impact destined to be felt across the nation's ball yards for generations. The most astute student of Ned Hanlon's machinations was his slim, young, tough-as-flint third baseman, John McGraw, who absorbed it all and then later brought his own varnish to the application as manager of the New York Giants from 1902 to 1932. John J. in turn was studied by one of his own players, an outfielder named Casey Stengel, and Stengel was scrutinized by a young infielder named Billy Martin. Hanlon to McGraw to Stengel to Martin: ninety years of winning.

THREE

As FOR many later residents of cities scattered around the league, New York meant the hated McGraw and his arrogant Giants or the awesome Ruth and his lordly Yankees, so in the 1890s Baltimore meant the Orioles, baseball's most successful team and its most despised. The primary target of grandstand vituperation was the club's feisty, acidulous third baseman, John McGraw.

John McGraw was born in upstate New York in 1873, in the village of Truxton, about twenty miles south of Syracuse. But no small town of late-nineteenth-century America was going to contain the spirit of a John McGraw. No town where the loudest noise was a farmer's wagon crossing a wooden bridge or the iron beating of a smith's hammer was going to satisfy a youngster born to hear and to provoke the roars of thousands.

It was placid, rural country that McGraw grew up in, and as a youth he earned money as a cow drover for the neighboring dairy farms, tending horses at the local hotel, and hawking candy for the railroad. With little formal education but with sharp innate intelligence, he focused an irrepressible drive and spirit on baseball. Having made a name for himself on the Truxton town team, by the age of sixteen he was being paid for playing, earning two dollars a game pitching for a team in East Homer, five miles away.

By the time he moved into professional baseball in 1890, McGraw was a case-hardened young man who had already endured more than his share of life's shocks and lacerations. In 1885 the boy had lost his mother, two sisters, and two brothers to a diphtheria epidemic. Those tragedies no doubt laced some tabasco into a personality that was already highly seasoned.

As military tactics were to Napoleon, so the maneuvers of a baseball diamond became to the youngster who would grow up to be known as the game's Little Napoleon, though more for his tyrannical nature than for his abundant tactical skills. McGraw took to baseball the way an eagle takes to the blue sky, and not only played the game avidly and well but also became an expert on its rules, which he later learned to blur and finesse as adroitly as any man who ever played. Posterity remembers McGraw mainly as a fiery and successful manager, but John J. was also an outstanding third baseman who had a .334 lifetime batting average, including a .390 season in 1899, facts he always took immense pride in. (In the early 1920s he had a good-looking young third-base prospect in his spring training camp. The skipper took the lad out early one morning to personally show him how it should be done around the bag. "This is the way I played it," John J. said. "Oh," said the youngster, "did you play ball, Mr. McGraw?" The clouds instantly crossed the skipper's face and he stalked away. Word of the incident got around. That night McGraw was dining with several sportswriters. The generally voluble manager was moodily quiet. One of the writers winked slyly at the others and then in a country bumpkin's falsetto piped up, "Oh, did you play ball, Mr. McGraw?" John J. looked up with a scowl, then struck the table with his fist and bellowed, "Can you imagine that son of a bitch!" The third-base prospect never made it to New York.)

If John McGraw was later to become the epitome of intolerance of mistakes, as many of his players sullenly claimed, then as a boy he apparently had not very far to look for his model. During one of those long summer days he spent as a youngster on the makeshift diamonds of Truxton, McGraw either hit or threw a ball that took unexpected flight and entered a neighbor's living room through a closed window. The attendant shattering sound is one that is known to the ears of every youngster who has ever swung a bat. It is a thrilling, paralyzing, not-to-be-missed moment that brings the game to abrupt termination and clears the premises quicker than a charge of cobras could. When he heard what happened, McGraw's father, a sour-blooded railroad worker and Civil War veteran, drained the occasion of its giggles by giving his son what must have been a memorable hiding. McGraw senior, like most parents then and for decades to come, frowned upon the playing of baseball as a waste of time. If his intent was to beat baseball out of his son, the old man would have had better luck trying to drop a lampshade over the sun; and if he meant to discipline the lad, then this intention was equally without hope. The very thought of *anyone* putting bruises on John J. McGraw is barely thinkable, like goosing William Howard Taft or slipping a whoopee cushion under Woodrow Wilson. The beating must have been a terrific one, for it drove the boy from his home and he took up residence with a neighbor where, by his father's agreement, he continued to live. If one is moved by Freudian motivation to examine the later dictatorial, insensitive, sometimes irrational behavior of McGraw, the murky loam is available.

John McGraw, however, let it be known he was interested in results, not motives. In later years, when he was building both winners and a personal legend as manager of the Giants, any player who tried to explain the error of his ways by saying, "I thought . . ." would find himself brusquely cut off by his skipper snarling, "With what?" There was one pope in Rome, one president in the White House, and one manager on the New York Giants' bench, and as long as none tried to impinge on the other two there would be tranquillity in the land.

By the summer of 1891 McGraw was playing for the Baltimore Orioles. A year later Ned Hanlon took over as manager and began assembling the first Greatest Team of All Time. A few years later, while Edison was laboring in his laboratory up north in New Jersey, and the Wright brothers were gazing challengingly up at midwestern skies, and Henry Ford was hearing putt-putt-putt in his sleep, McGraw and Keeler were perfecting the hit-and-run play, with McGraw doing the running and Wee Willie the hitting. The Brooklyn-born Keeler, who uttered the line, "I hit 'em where they ain't" to account for his remarkable success with the stick and thereby became one of America's most oft-quoted sages, was a tough, sharp-eyed customer who left behind a radiant .345 lifetime batting average for a nineteen-year career that included a truly Olympian .432 joyride in 1897. Willie also, more than any other man who ever played America's game, demonstrated its pure democratic aspect by proving that size meant nothing, and that anybody could play and excel as long as given the opportunity: at five feet four-and-one-half inches, Willie was the last man on the field to know when it began to rain.

A hero at home, McGraw on the road was the embodiment of unabashed villainy. Never averse to roiling the emotions of hometown fans, John J.'s natural enemies were those symbols of on-the-field authority, the umpires. Umpires were not then the sacrosanct, inviolable figures they later became. There was only one umpire running a game, and this fellow had to be quick and agile, with eyes in back of his head, and with an unerring sense of where the exits were in the event of a wrathful crowd streaming onto the field. Crowds in the 1890s were much more obstreperous and prone to violent display than their counterparts a century later, whose wont was to redesign ball parks (often out of sheer joy) rather than dismember umpires. The 1890s saw a generation with frontier experience still very much a part of their ethos—Jesse James and Billy the Kid, those demigod princes of American outlawry, had been gunned down and set to ballad a little more than a decade before.

Life in the cities could be hard and unrewarding. The work week was endless and management answered to no one. (The life expectancy of the average American male was a little over forty-six years, a statistic that could have put the late-stage careers of such 1980s luminaries as Pete Rose and Phil Niekro in severe jeopardy.) But still it was a free country and that meant its citizens could, when the occasion arose, be volatile and irreverent, and no occasion then better suited the baser expressions of freedom than a baseball game, with its tough-nut athletes in zealous competition and an umpire who could spoil everything for the home crowd.

The game's democratizing values were emphasized with pride by its adherents. The fact that paunchy merchants in expensive suits and derby hats could sit together and for several hours share the same tension, exhilaration, and excitement with some bimbo from the wrong side of creation said more about American democracy than any election ever could. The ball park was a convening point for every element of society, a place where sweatshop drudges could feel sudden and sustaining bursts of exaltation, and arrogant merchant princes forced to sit in despair and dejection.

McGraw may have seemed merely a nasty, ill-tempered son of a bitch to many; but on a ball field he was as wily as a hunted feline. He knew that antagonizing the opposition could throw their game off balance, and he knew that an abusive crowd could intimidate an umpire. And so, like another big rouser of the day in a different arena— William Jennings Bryan orating an audience into a frenzy—McGraw learned how to work the customers. The invective and antagonism that he deliberately drew down upon himself was part of the combative world he had to live in. So it was only natural that McGraw, the tough little boy who had moved out of his father's house when the old man's intractable authority became unendurable, should be contemptuous of any authority, and in the realm in which he chose to stride, that authority was the umpire. But McGraw did not stop with the man in blue; this relentless, innovative soul of defiance went on to exchange shots not only with umpires but also league presidents and fans, as well as his own and opposing players.

"Thought? With what?" Not for John McGraw was steel magnate Andrew Carnegie's suggestion for his own epitaph: "Here lies the man who was able to surround himself with men far cleverer than himself." Success alone was not enough for McGraw; it had to have been schemed and devised out of his own head and no other. And when it could not be done entirely his way, when some decisive element that shaped his world changed, John McGraw could not tolerate it and had to move on.

The man who brought the lash of discipline to major-league baseball was Byron Bancroft Johnson, known to the world at large as Ban, and to his enemies, who probably outnumbered the cornstalks of Iowa, by names that would have made a family newspaper blush. The entire ambience of baseball was rough in the 1890s, not just on the field. In order to rein in the gamblers and the drunkards and the all-round scoundrels who were throwing the game into disrepute, a man was going to have to be tough, autocratic, unforgiving, and braced with the grim rectitude of a zealot. This is a fair description of Ban Johnson, a man who looked as though he might have been weaned on an icicle. This humorless, austerely self-confident man burned night and day with a single obsession: to create a second major league, one to rival the monopolistic National League, which was then so self-assured it had invoked a $2,400-per-year salary ceiling on its employees, whether they batted .220 or .400.

Johnson was in the 1890s the president of the Western League, the strongest of the minor leagues, with teams scattered through the Midwest. Sensing baseball's spirited appeal as well as its potential for growth and expansion, and at the same time seeing the dangers posed to it by rowdyism and gambling, Johnson became at once reformer and dictator. He forbade the sale of liquor in his ball parks, discouraged the use of profanity on the field (not that choice expletives would have bruised the ears of the existing clientele, but it was a better class of paying customer that Ban was after), and insisted the authority of umpires be respected. Upon this last, Johnson was adamant. In order for the game to flourish and gain respectability, the umpires had to be recognized as pillars of integrity and command. As far as Johnson was concerned, the officials not only embodied these qualities, they also symbolized them. Consequently, to abuse or try to intimidate an umpire was a direct attack on baseball. In the Western League, umpire-baiting was frowned upon and dealt with harshly through fines and suspensions. The chain of command in the league began with Ban Johnson's left hand and ended with his right. But no one could deny that the clubs in his league were prospering and that games were increasingly becoming a more pleasant afternoon's diversion.

By the turn of the century the nation, with Manifest Destiny long since an accepted, unquestioned, almost scriptural part of its doctrine, had grown to a mosaic of forty-five states and included as well the offshore outposts of Hawaii, Guam, the Philippine Islands, American Samoa, and Puerto Rico. For Ban Johnson Manifest Destiny had a special ring, a highly personal one. It included not just territory, but aspiration and recognition. And like the parent doctrine, it meant aggrandizement, high-handedness, and uncompromising self-righteousness.

When Johnson in 1901 declared his operation a major league, the move was greeted in the true spirit shown by any monopoly: The National League bombarded Johnson and his club owners with snarls, threats, insults, and lawsuits. But Ban Johnson and his new league had come to play and to stay.

In 1900 the National League cut back from twelve to eight teams. One of the cities dropped was Baltimore. When Johnson organized his American League, he included Baltimore, to be managed by its twenty-eight-year-old third baseman, John J. McGraw.

At first Johnson was delighted to have the notable John McGraw bringing his special brand of prestige and excitement to the fledgling league. But the two men were like a couple of locomotives started from opposite directions along the same track. When Johnson began enforcing his edict against umpire baiting, McGraw rebelled. John J. no doubt felt deprived and persecuted; making an umpire's afternoon miserable was almost as much fun as winning. McGraw's antics upset a lot of people, particularly certain members of the press who were trying to convince their readers that baseball was a patriotic and immensely uplifting game. One writer described John J.'s belligerence as McGrawism and insisted it must be done away with. But John McGraw was not going to go away, nor was he going to change. Neither was Ban Johnson. Ban told John to stop bullying the umpires, and John stopped—until the next time. First there were fines and then suspensions. In July 1902 McGraw's behavior became so contemptuous that Johnson suspended the Baltimore skipper for an indefinite length of time.

Well, John McGraw wasn't going to live like this. Unable to stay within the bounds as defined by Ban Johnson, McGraw soon showed that he could be as devious off the field as on. He helped engineer a deal whereby John T. Brush, president of the Cincinnati Reds of the National League, bought into the Baltimore Orioles of the American League. The fox was in the hen coop; but instead of having himself a meal, this fox opened the front door. Brush issued unconditional releases to the cream of his roster, including first baseman Dan McGann, catcher Roger Bresnahan, outfielders Cy Seymour and Joe Kelley, pitcher Joe McGinnity, and third baseman–manager John McGraw. McGann, Bresnahan, McGinnity, and McGraw quickly signed with the New York Giants, John J. as manager. Why did Brush deliberately wreck his own team? He was planning to buy the Giants, which he soon did, for around $125,000. So he tore down the team he was leaving in order to build up the one he was buying. Unethical? Unfair to the fans? Yes, of course. Unequaled in baseball history? Well, a half century later the owners did even worse—they took the whole team out of town, bats and balls and home plate included. For every teardrop there's a smile somewhere.

That is the tale of how John McGraw at the age of twenty-nine became manager of the New York Giants. It is not a tale that Ban Johnson recited to his grandchildren at bedtime. The story was not without ramifications, however. Determined to keep the depleted Baltimore club functioning for the rest of the season, Johnson used his authority to pluck players from other American League clubs to fill out the Orioles roster. The following year, Johnson achieved a long-desired coup—he placed an American League team, the Orioles, in New York where they became known first as the Highlanders and then as the Yankees. The New York Yankees would slowly grow from poor-cousin status to dominate their league, their city, and then all of baseball, leaving John McGraw fuming in the dust. But that all happened a quarter-century later.

McGraw quickly made the National League his own personal domain. League president Harry Pulliam clashed with the Giants' manager, but Pulliam was no Ban Johnson and was unable to control McGraw.

McGraw wasn't just tough, belligerent, outrageous, and devious, of course. He also carried in his emotional baggage that most admired, revered, and cherished attribute that man or woman can bring to athletics, the attribute that makes acceptable and forgivable all but the most abominable sins and outrages: He was a winner.

McGraw's snappily drilled Giant teams were exciting to watch. They were virtually always at the top or spiritedly in contention. John J., with the soul of a drill instructor, a fungo bat his swagger stick, demanded that his men be the best, nothing less. Those clubs were known as McGraw's Giants, not just in homage to the notoriety of their skipper but to his baseball-playing philosophy; not just winning, but his style of winning. McGraw saw to it that his players carried with them the pride and the arrogance of champions. The Giants became New York to the citizens of Cincinnati and Pittsburgh and St. Louis, and an image of the style and burgeoning hustle of the big city was fostered by those crisply efficient players. (Decades later, in 1930, rookie catcher Al Lopez entered the National League with the Brooklyn Dodgers and was awed by McGraw's Giants: "When they threw the ball around during infield practice, they really fired it; that's the way he wanted them to do it. When you watched that Giant team on the field, you could always feel McGraw's hand everywhere. He was all business on a ball field, and so were they. There was never any clowning on that club.")

It was one of McGraw's players, second baseman Larry Doyle, who summed up those intoxicating days in one of the loveliest of all baseball lines: "Oh, it's great to be young and a Giant." Despite the manager's sandpaper disposition, any ballplayer worth his salt wanted to play for McGraw, because that's where the best baseball was being played, that was where the money was (McGraw's players, at his insistence, were among the highest-paid in the game), and that was where the pride was—that ineffable, incalculable pride that puts the overdrive into the engine of any good athlete, makes him excel and dominate, makes him special. Not too many managers have been despised by players who would stand in line to play for him; among the handful, the most prominent was John McGraw.

And so we had a new century. The two major leagues grudgingly settled their differences and began living in harmony with one another. It was at that moment that there appeared by way of the serene and leafy campus of Bucknell University a young pitcher destined to become America's first genuine sports hero, one whom a

Horatio Alger boy could want to grow up to emulate, one who was as electrifying as Frank Merriwell and who might well have emerged from the same unlikely pages, for he was handsome, intelligent, heroic, modest, and virtuous, admired by fans of every age and station, men and women alike. His name was Christy Mathewson. His team was the New York Giants. His manager was John McGraw.

FOUR

NOW AND THEN there appears an athlete who seems to be the product of a collaboration between the Almighty and a writer of fiction. In baseball there have been several of these landmark figures—among them the colossally outsized Babe Ruth and the fiery crusader Jackie Robinson. Further back in time, too far now, in fact, for his social impact to be appreciated, was another player who remains a watershed figure in the game, straddling history and sport as man, personality, and performer. In addition to everything else—and he seemed to possess everything—Christy Mathewson's timing was perfect.

In his memorable collection of reminiscences with old-time ballplayers, *The Glory of Their Times*, Lawrence Ritter quotes turn-of-the-century outfielder Davy Jones on the social standing of baseball players: "I was going with a girl at the time and after I became a professional ballplayer her parents refused to let her see me any more. Wouldn't let her have anything to do with me. In those days a lot of people looked upon ballplayers as bums, too lazy to work for a living." Today, the best hotels vie for the prestige of catering to big league teams; back then, Sam Crawford told Ritter, "Baseball players weren't too much accepted. . . . We were considered pretty crude. Couldn't get into the best hotels and all that. And when we did get into a good hotel, they wouldn't boast about having us. Like, if we went into the hotel dining room—in a good hotel, that is—they'd quick shove us way back in the corner at the very end of the dining room so we wouldn't be too conspicuous." Some of this notoriety was of course well earned. A group of Detroit Tiger players once returned to their hotel in St. Louis after a night on the town and started an impromptu crap game on the carpet at the end of the corridor. Soon the rattle of dice and the accompanying chanting of the players reached the ears of one of their teammates, a catcher named Charley Schmidt, who had been asleep in a nearby room. Roused from slumber by the action, Charley took some money from his pants pockets, and clad only in an ankle-length white nightshirt, went out into the corridor and crouched down and joined the game. The dice were cold for Charley that night, and in a little while the catcher had lost his stake, whereupon he straightened up and walked away—leaving behind on the carpet a tidy little pile of turds.

The public's dubious regard of professional baseball players— "You're all right, but please don't try and join the family"—continued for the better part of the century's first two decades. It revealed a curious ambivalence in the country's attitude toward its favorite game. The game was an entity unto itself, part of the American ethos, exemplifying cherished national virtues and qualities, but paradoxically divorced from its most gifted practitioners who were to be cheered, applauded, admired, and fussed over, but not invited to dinner. It pointed up the sharply differing areas of fantasy and reality that, in other contexts, the game still occupies in the minds of its devotees.

The man who more than any other began to force a modification of the public's opinion of its favorite athletes was Christy Mathewson. In his youthful photographs, with his pressed suit, tie, white shirt with batwing collar, his frank, open face with its full lips and wide, intelligent eyes, and parted hair lying neatly, Christy Mathewson looks like a medical student or a budding young attorney destined for the United States Senate; looks anything, in fact, but what he became—a superbly gifted righthanded pitcher who would dominate with class and style a realm of social pariahs.

Mathewson was born on August 12, 1880, in Factoryville, a small town in northeastern Pennsylvania that lay in the heart of the state's anthracite coal region. Unlike many of his friends, young Christopher did not head for the mines as soon as he was of age. Son of a gentleman farmer and a mother described as monied, Mathewson, oldest of five children, attended Keystone Academy, a junior college founded by his grandmother. Here the studious young man was lacquered with poise and purpose and sent on to Bucknell University. At Bucknell, Mathewson made the invention of Frank Merriwell superfluous. His good looks were at once sturdy, distinguished, and boyish. He excelled at baseball and football; indeed, he was called "the greatest drop-kicker in America" by Walter Camp, the most celebrated football coach of the era.

In contrast to some latter-day college athletes, Mathewson found diversions other than athletics available on campus and took advantage of them: things like opening books, taking exams, and thinking. But of course that was to be expected back then. Today, college sports are an industry and the public image of a star athlete is that of someone being led around the campus on a chain. Mathewson, however, was a born overachiever. In addition to being a star athlete, he was also class president, a member of the glee club (the only time, apparently, he was known to raise his voice), active in several literary societies, a member of the Phi Gamma Delta fraternity, and a champion checker player. A nice boy to have around. Overlooking nothing, he even found himself a campus sweetheart, whom he married a few years later. Naturally, the marriage was a happy one. This was America's first golden boy and for a long time nothing was going to go wrong; it simply would not be allowed, because America needed Christy Mathewson, baseball needed him, New York needed him, and John McGraw needed him—four natural forces that in conjunction could roll back tidal waves and paralyze tornadoes.

Today, however, it would all be stored and dust-laden in some ancestral attic if not for the young man's uncanny way with a baseball. There is no record of what Matty's family said when their young prince announced he was opting for a career as a professional baseball player (apparently his mother had been hoping he would take up a career in the ministry, but the closest he came to this was a promise that he would never play ball on Sunday, a promise he seems never to have broken). The family was probably so mesmerized by him that they assumed anything Christopher did was all right. Or they may have tried to stop him, but history tells us there is no use trying to stop a legend-to-be from hacking out its niche with those golden hammers and chisels. So, almost like a missionary from the gardens of the true and the good, he set forth, converting by deed and not word.

If Mathewson had pursued a different career and become, say, a United States senator or the most successful physician in Scranton, Pennsylvania, he might well have been marked down as a snob. Part of the Mathewson legend is the very fact that Christy was bred differently from the vast majority of his ballplaying colleagues; like another American objet d'art whose appeal approached canonization, Joe DiMaggio, he could be aloof and reserved. His teammates, as Emerson said of Thoreau, would as soon have taken the limb of a tree as the arm of their mighty star. He once refused to greet the friends of a teammate who had traveled a long distance to see him pitch. When the train carrying the Giants pulled into a small-town depot he was known to lower the window shade where he was sitting so as to conceal himself from the view of those on the platform. To the sportswriters, those instant historians whose fervent bouquets of prose helped create and perpetuate much of the Mathewson legend, the great pitcher was only as cordial as he had to be. These are the behavioral patterns of royalty, and the citizens of Matty's democratic land loved him for it. They had enthroned him because of his reserve and his dignity, and any deviation from the image on his part would have been viewed as an act of *lèse majesté*.

The image was so without blemish that some sportswriters felt compelled to point out that Matty, while indeed perfect, was also human. He took a sip now and then—in moderation of course—and did occasionally smoke a pipe or cigarette, and when properly aroused could and did let fly with some language not found in McGuffey's readers. He loved to gamble at cards and now and then at dice. Once when McGraw caught Matty rattling the bones with some teammates, the irate skipper fined the mere mortals ten dollars each, while Matty was drenched with a hundred-dollar fine, because, as McGraw explained, "With your intelligence you should be setting a good example for those guys." The responsibilities of a legend were onerous, and the price could be high. When Mathewson's image began growing dangerously marmoreal, Mrs. Mathewson felt impelled to say that while Christy was a good man, "he was not a goody-goody."

The Mathewson legend began modestly. He started pitching when he was eleven years old, diagraming his future on the playing fields of Factoryville. When he was a teenager he was getting a buck a game to silence the bats of older boys, doing it with his healthy fastball and a roundhouse curve, of which he was very proud. In the summer of 1896, when John McGraw was giving the hip to opposing baserunners, the man who was going to make him famous was sixteen years old and pitching semipro ball in Scranton, a few miles down the road from Factoryville. While at Bucknell, Matty continued pitching semipro for a couple of hundred a month—in those days college athletes were allowed to earn money without jeopardizing their amateur status. (They still are today, except that it's more fashionable to pretend otherwise.)

Mathewson started his professional career in 1899 in Taunton, Massachusetts, a small industrial city in the New England League, about thirty miles south of Boston. It was here, laboring for ninety dollars a month, that he began perfecting the pitch that was to make him famous. Already gifted with a smoking fastball and a good curve, and with masterly control of each, the addition of the new pitch was another case of the rich getting richer and the poor not being able to buy a base hit.

As with many momentous discoveries, there remains a residue of uncertainty as to just when Mathewson stumbled upon his famous "fadeaway" pitch. Whenever or wherever, he was definitely throwing it at Taunton in 1899. The fadeaway, so called because it broke suddenly and sharply and was no longer there for the batter to whale at, was today's screwball. Basically, the pitch is a reverse curve, thrown by twisting the thumb toward the body. Since the ball curves in the direction in which it is spinning, this pitch, when thrown by a righthander, drops and breaks in on a righthanded batter and away from a left. Today the pitch is thrown by a number of pitchers; back in the age of innocence it was considered exotic. Also, very few pitchers could control it. Mathewson's mastery of this "freak delivery" made him preeminent among pitchers. And it added to his mystique, for he alone had full command of it; but because its delivery put so taut a strain on his arm, he seldom threw it more than ten or twelve times a game.

A year later, in 1900, Christy Mathewson served notice. He was a formidable figure now, with his prepossessing manner that exuded a mature strength, dignity, and self-confidence. He was full grown now, six feet one-and-one-half inches tall and 190 muscular, well-proportioned pounds. He was considered tall for his time—six-footers were thought to have snow on their heads in those days. He was working the mounds of the Virginia League that year, pitching for Norfolk and having the time of his life. The perfect man was the nearly perfect pitcher in that summer that broke the seal on the new century. By the end of July his record was 20–2. They were coming from all over the Norfolk area to see the young man pitch, coming on horseback and by wagon and one-horse shay, because they knew a pitcher this good wasn't going to be theirs for long. They knew there were big leagues, big cities, and big money beckoning, and that their gifted athletes, like their gifted young in any activity or profession, were sworn to a dream and were marking time and listening for the train whistle and their journey to glory and success.

Twenty wins and two losses by the end of July was as good a ticket out of town as an affair with the police chief's daughter, and for

Matty the ticket was punched for New York, that bustling, hustling, cavernous jaw of opportunity and temptation that another small-town boy, O. Henry, would soon label Baghdad-on-the-Subway. Mathewson's contract was bought by the New York Giants. The purchase price was around $2,000.

John McGraw was picking up ground balls in St. Louis that summer, and managing the Giants was one George Davis, also the club's shortstop. On a warm afternoon in late July, Davis's new recruit showed up at the Polo Grounds. Built in 1889, the field lay in uptown Manhattan, at 155th Street and Eighth Avenue, in the shadow of Coogan's Bluff, a broad, steep-faced cliff. Davis asked the new man to throw batting practice, with the skipper taking first cuts. Davis approved of Matty's fastball, told him to forget the roundhouse curve that had been wowing 'em since Keystone Academy days, and liked the overhand curve (called a drop back then). When asked if he had anything else, Matty shyly conceded he had "a sort of freak ball." Ordered to throw it, he did. Davis, a perennial .300 hitter, had trouble putting wood on the pitch. Supposedly it was Davis who named the pitch by saying, "It sort of fades out of sight. A fadeaway." This is as forthcoming as mute old history is about the christening of baseball's most famous delivery.

Nevertheless, the young man was not quite ready for the big push. Used sparingly during the final two months of the season, Mathewson logged an 0–3 record and did not pitch impressively. By season's end the Giants were disenchanted and returned him to Norfolk. But this is how it should be, how any good scenarist with an eye on the coming cheers and trumpets would have it—"Too bad, kid, but I guess New York ain't Norfolk," and the legend-to-be, with the first bitter taste of failure on his palate, packs his straw suitcase and heads dejectedly toward a lonely train ride, shaking a figurative fist at the big city and vowing to return and make good. Return and conquer he did, of course, but how Christy Mathewson returned to New York is in itself a story of the ethics then prevailing in America's favorite game.

The Cincinnati Reds drafted Mathewson from the Norfolk club for $100 and almost immediately traded him to the Giants for right-handed pitcher Amos Rusie, something of a flaming legend himself. Rusie was one of those pitchers who threw so hard people wondered his arm didn't come flying in after the ball. His quickie earned the Indiana-born Amos the nickname Hoosier Thunderbolt. Pitching for

New York, Rusie helped make the nineties gay in the big city, winning over thirty games three times and leading in strikeouts six straight years. He also led in bases on balls five times, which meant that, like most thunderbolts, his rarely struck twice in the same place. Connie Mack, a most reliable witness who seemed to have entered the game at about the same time as the round ball, described Rusie as fearsome. And fearsome the big fellow must have been, for he forced a rules change for which all hitters are to this day grateful, even though most of them never heard of Amos Rusie. Up until 1892 the pitching mound was a neighborly fifty feet away from home plate, giving a wallbreaker like Rusie what was finally deemed an unfair advantage. Accordingly, in 1893 the mound was hauled back to its present sixty feet six inches. The National League's collective batting average promptly jumped from .245 in 1892 to .280 in 1893 and then to .309 a year later, when a good time was had by all except the pitchers. (To this day psychological studies of pitchers come up with persecution disorders, dating back to 1893.) Today, the thought of a Nolan Ryan or a Goose Gossage pitching from fifty feet would be enough to make big-league batters perspire unto dehydration.

In those days pitchers were little more than dray horses, harnessed to the mound. What they started they were expected to finish. Rusie had for five straight years burned it in for over 400 innings, three times over 500. By 1898 the toll was beginning to show on the twenty-seven-year-old pitcher's powerful right arm. Following that season, when he posted a 20–10 record (fancy doings by today's standards, but fourteen National League pitchers won more than Amos that season), the Giants decided to cut his salary from $3,000 to $2,000. This action struck Rusie in the pocketbook and in his pride, and the twice-wounded pitcher went home to Indiana where he sat out the next two seasons.

In 1901 the Cincinnati Reds decided the inactive, one-time Thunderbolt was just the man for them. Or so it seemed. The truth of the matter is less savory. Running the Reds was the devious John T. Brush, who already knew he was going to New York to assume ownership of the Giants. In order to get the brooding Rusie off of New York's hands (and thus, soon, his own), he agreed to swap them Christopher Mathewson of Factoryville, Pennsylvania, Bucknell University, and future resident of Mount Olympus.

So Mathewson returned to New York in 1901 and this time made it stick. (Rusie pitched three games for Cincinnati, was 0–1 and took a hike back to Indiana, his thunderbolts turned to cabbage. Mathewson went on to win 372 games for the Giants. So when out-of-towners voice their suspicions of the machinations of big-city folk, pay heed.)

If a legend may be said to be a thing woven, then Matty went right to the loom his first full year in New York. For a seventh-place club he won 20 games and lost 17, completing 36 of 38 starts. That complete-game statistic is impressive today, but back then it was the norm. While America may have had lots of unfinished business in 1901, that state of affairs had nothing to do with the pitching mound, although it should be stated that only two pitchers in the league, Cincinnati's Noodles Hahn and Matty's teammate Dummy Taylor completed more games than the imminent legend. Note, if you will, those nicknames—Noodles and Dummy. This was a more homespun, less refined society that these boys sprouted up from. Nicknames could be brutally literal—Luther (Dummy) Taylor, for instance, was a deaf-mute. Another of Matty's teammates was Charley (Piano Legs) Hickman, which gives us a fairly graphic mental snapshot of Charley, at least from the waist down. Looking around the National League during that 1901 season we find Bones Ely, Ginger Beaumont, Jiggs Donohue, Klondike Douglass, Cozy Dolan, Snags Heidrick, Daff Gammons, Cupid Childs, Topsy Hartsel, Brickyard Kennedy, Snake Wiltse, Wild Bill Donovan, as well as a number of Kids and Docs. The American League had its own crowd of colorful handles, like Nixey Callahan, Zaza Harvey, Socks Seybold, Farmer Steelman, Boileryard Clarke, Crazy Schmidt, and Pink Hawley. The Detroit Tigers were the champs in the identity-crisis sweepstakes, their starting lineup including two Docs, two Kids, one Pop, and one Ducky. Nicknames have, of course, always been a colorful adjunct to the game, as latter-day saints rechristened Dizzy, Yogi, Harry the Cat, and Mark the Bird can attest, but nothing like the plethora and apparent literalness that obtained back then. Special players, if not tagged with some pedestrian nickname like Lefty, were later accorded an approximation of knighthood with alliterative titles like Larrupin' Lou (Gehrig), Joltin' Joe (DiMaggio), The Splendid Splinter (Ted Williams), Rapid Robert (Feller), Hammerin' Hank (Greenberg or Aaron), or Pistol Pete (Reiser).

They called Mathewson Big Six, and the origin of the name is somewhat in question. Some say it was in tribute to his imposing height, others that it was after a famed New York City fire wagon of the day that was noted for its efficiency in speeding to the scene of the fire and dousing the flames. In any event, the nickname was unique and had dignity. No Boileryards or Klondikes would do for Christopher Mathewson of the New York Giants.

Mathewson must have been a perfect, unoffending mix of aristocrat and regular guy. His cultured, slightly standoffish ways gave affront to no one. To the opposition he was an Olympian who scaled heights loftier than a mound and was to be respected. His teammates worshiped him. Pitcher Rube Marquard: "What a grand guy he was!" Catcher Chief Meyers: "How we loved to play for him! We'd break our necks for that guy. If you made an error behind him or anything of that sort, he'd never get mad or sulk. He'd come over and pat you on the back. He had the sweetest, most gentle nature." Outfielder Fred Snodgrass: "He was a wonderful, wonderful man, too, a reserved sort of fellow, a little hard to get close to. But once you got to know him, he was a truly good friend." To all who played with or against him during the first decade of the century, he was, without reservation, the greatest pitcher they ever saw. Reminiscing about Mathewson, Marquard, a year or two before he died in 1980, said, "Sitting on the bench watching him pitch, I often forgot I was a ballplayer, a pitcher myself. I became a fan. That's how good he was. I've seen every pitcher you can name for the last seventy years, but Matty was the only one who ever made me feel like a fan."

By 1903 Mathewson was a 30-game winner (30–13). A year later he was 33–12. In 1905 he was 31–9. It was that October that he applied the seal of flawlessness to his achievements, crowning them with an autumnal splendor to match America's color-drenched landscape. As a great athlete must, he did it in the glare of his sport's most conspicuous event, the World Series. In 1905, the Series was being played for only the second time, but it had already laid its grip upon the national imagination and become, as it still is, the most momentous athletic clash of the year, sports' most supple springboard for fame and notoriety. Most of baseball's great pitchers have worked in a World Series; none have come close to Mathewson's performance against the Philadelphia Athletics in 1905.

The Series opened on October 9, in Philadelphia. Mathewson shut out the A's on four hits, 3–0. On October 12, celebrating Columbus Day in his own fashion, he again allowed just four hits in shutting down the A's, 9–0. Taking one day of rest, he came back on October 14 at New York's Polo Grounds and, allowing six hits, completed his lamination of the Athletics by a 2–0 score, locking up the title for the Giants. (In fact, every game of that Series ended in a shutout, Joe McGinnity winning the Giants' other game 2–0, while Chief Bender won the A's lone game by a 3–0 score. In that Series, score first and the game was yours.) In the space of six days Mathewson had—in a World Series—pitched twenty-seven innings of shutout ball, allowing just fourteen hits and one base on balls. With that kind of performance, you become an empyrean one-man fraternity, and everybody wants to join you.

The *New York Times*'s account of the day's events began:

Two neatly dressed, ruddy faced athletic looking young men, grinning broadly; one a giant in contrast to the squattiness of the other, walked along the veranda of the clubhouse at the Polo Grounds about 5 o'clock yesterday afternoon. Below them was a sea of 10,000 faces, wildly emitting a thunderous eruption of enthusiasm. The two young men looked down upon the reverberating ocean of humanity for a moment, and then walked to a point directly in front of the plaza, where they were in view of all. The ten thousand throats bellowed forth a tribute that would have almost drowned a broadside of twelve-inch guns.

The two smiling athletes stopped, one of them drew forth a long sheet of yellow paper rolled under his arm. As the crowd pushed and fought and cheered he unwrapped an impromptu banner and let it flutter on the breeze. The multitude pressed forward like a wave to read this inscription:

THE GIANTS, WORLD'S CHAMPIONS, 1905

Geological records show that Vesuvius disturbs the earth and that seismic demonstrations are felt by the greater number. But if that doctrine had been promulgated in the vicinity of the Polo Grounds yesterday, as Christie Mathewson and Roger Bresnahan of the New York Baseball Club unfurled their victorious banner, it would have been minimized. For, as volcanoes assert themselves upon the earth's surface surely must that deafening, reverberating roar have lifted Manhattan's soil from its base.

The story went on to proclaim "Christie Mathewson, the giant slabman, who made the world's championship possible for New York, may be legitimately designated as the premier pitching wonder of all baseball records." At the conclusion of this tumultuous ceremony, the *Times* went on, Mathewson responded with "a half-suppressed smile and bow." Nobility's acknowledgment of the crowd.

This was Mathewson's sublime moment. At twenty-five he had it all, as only a revered athlete can have it all. Monarch of the mound, he was as royal as a democratic people can allow, a hero to his peers, a model for American youth, an example cited from the pulpits of the land. But it was dangerous to sit so loftily, to be so enviably perfect, for the gods, they say, are jealous, and the panegyric from the Polo Grounds that day must have rattled the shutters of other realms, for little more than a decade later the vipers would begin to gather around his feet and a miasma drift toward him.

But that would come later. The glories had to mount before the tragedy could match the man, before the pure gold became as fragile as crystal. In 1905 he seemed as mighty, as invincible, and as abundantly blessed as a man could hope to be. Not even the irascible, bullying John McGraw could disturb this obelisk of splendor. The fact of the matter is, the two men regarded each other warmly and affectionately.

The relationship between John McGraw and Christy Mathewson fascinates. Antagonism between the two seemed inevitable. But the flinty soul of John McGraw melted before the radiance of his ace. McGraw demanded his players be tough and combative and disciplined, and Mathewson surely delivered these qualities, but with a distinction that made him as unique a person, in his element, as his right arm made him a pitcher. Mathewson exemplified a credo of sportsmanship and fair play his skipper disdained; yet McGraw never tried to roughen the edges of his great pitcher. Of course there was no need to, for Mathewson won, consistently and effectively, in his own way. Mathewson was too vast, complex, and mysterious a machine for even McGraw to try to tinker with. It was a case of both sides of the tracks conjoining to produce the desired result, for if McGraw never tried to influence Mathewson, neither did the pitcher object to his manager's sarcasm, vulgarities, and uncompromising demand for discipline, for those relentlessly drilled, hard-driven, tongue-lashed teams were scoring the runs and making the plays that Mathewson needed. Mathewson had the highest regard for McGraw, whose baseball acumen impressed him immensely. In a book he authored in 1912, *Pitching in a Pinch*, Matty wrote: "Around McGraw revolves the game of the Giants. He plans every move, most of the hitters going to the plate with definite instructions from him as to what to try to do." Mathewson was an extremely competitive man, very passionate about baseball, proud of his ability, and himself a sharp student of the game and its players. But McGraw knew even more and was willing to take chances based on the cutting edge of his intellect, and this fascinated and intrigued his great pitcher. Matty was in awe of his manager's constantly clicking and evaluating and devising mind. McGraw's concentration during a game was so intense, Matty wrote, that it induced his players to speak in whispers around him, if they spoke at all. "He was the game," said Mathewson.

For the McGraws and the Mathewsons, husbands and wives both, it was a lifelong friendship, warm and affectionate. The two couples even shared a New York apartment one summer, a unique arrangement, since many players find it difficult to share even the dugout with their boss for a few hours each day. For the childless McGraw, Matty was the son he never had, and until the day he left his post as Giants manager in 1932, Mathewson's was one of just two photographs that hung on the wall of his Polo Grounds office (the other was of Ross Youngs, a Giants outfielder of the 1920s and another McGraw favorite, who also died before the old man).

The only other manager of the day whose dugout brainpower was said to be the equal of McGraw's was in every conceivable way John J.'s antithesis. Connie Mack, eleven years older than McGraw, was tall, gentle, considerate, fatherly, placid. Recorded occasions of Connie staining the air with a cussword are most infrequent, occurring only when he was provoked beyond endurance. Like the time in 1931 when he really gave it to his incomparable lefthander, Robert Moses (Lefty) Grove, he of the dour and choleric disposition and almost invisible fastball. Stalking off the mound after completing a less than successful inning's work, the muttering Grove heard from his sixty-nine-year-old manager a mildly phrased suggestion about how to improve things out there. Lefty sidled him a glance, said, "Oh, go take a shit," and sat down at the far end of the bench. No one, but no one, spoke to Connie Mack like that. No one even called him Connie or Skipper. It was Mr. Mack, from presidents of the United States on down to batboys. To suggest in public that Mr. Mack, the game's most venerated gentleman, go and empty his bowels was heresy of the first rank.

So a visibly angry Mr. Mack lay down his scorecard, rose to his full six feet one inch of ramrod height and began marching the length of the dugout floor, each face he passed turning to follow this one-man procession to its destination. Connie stopped in front of Grove and confronted him. Leaning forward slightly for emphasis, Connie delivered what was for him a tirade: "*You* go take a shit, Robert." Whereupon with dignity and honor intact he returned to his seat at the other end of the dugout while his squad of Philadelphia Athletics tried to avert grinning faces and stifle gagging laughter.

Ramrod he was, a ramrod of integrity. At six feet one inch and a trim 150 pounds he looked as though he might have been a stake driven into the soil by a sovereign destiny that said, "I hereby proclaim this baseball territory." For he became the game's patriarchal image, as singular in his way as McGraw, Mathewson, Cobb, Ruth, Dean, DiMaggio, and Jackie Robinson were in theirs. For fans who grew up following the game in the 1920s, 1930s, 1940s, and early 1950s, he was there, an indomitable monument, and always an old man, benign of face and reputation, a cornerstone of the national game, grandfather to every pitched ball and base hit, with billing above his team, for they were "Connie Mack's A's" the way they were "McGraw's Giants"; tributes paid no other managers, for no others had such longevity nor held so decisive a dominance. Yes, he was always there, part of our spring and summer and sometimes our autumn, too, for he put together some mighty ball clubs.

He was born in East Brookfield, Massachusetts, in 1862, during the Lincoln administration, and survived until the Eisenhower administration, from bayonet charge to nuclear age, from Gettysburg to Pork Chop Hill. He was a contemporary of everybody from John Wilkes Booth and Nathaniel Hawthorne to Marlon Brando and J. D. Salinger. And marvelously enough, from 1884 to 1950, he was employed in professional baseball, a record to be admired but more to be envied. In the context of certain American fantasies, it is pure Arabian Nights to get into pro ball at twenty-one, the big leagues at twenty-three, and at thirty-one become a manager and thereafter to remain on and on and on, as manager and then as owner-manager, deriving your livelihood from hanging around with the likes of Eddie Collins, Rube Waddell, Chief Bender, Home Run Baker, and later on Al Simmons, Jimmie Foxx, Lefty Grove, Mickey Cochrane; sitting in the dugout shade every summer's afternoon and watching the ballplaying artistry of every American Leaguer from Cy Young, Ty Cobb, and Walter Johnson on through Babe Ruth, Lou Gehrig, Joe DiMaggio, Ted Williams, and Bob Feller. What are four or eight years in the White House compared to that, or even twenty years as a Hollywood idol?

Connie Mack. In American folklore the name is synonymous with age, white hair, and grandfatherly benevolence. A year or two before his own death in 1978 at the hearty age of ninety, another of baseball's managerial titans, Joe McCarthy, was entertaining an inquisitive writer with tales of the days when mighty trees were mere saplings. He began a Connie Mack story by saying, "This happened when Connie was a young man . . ." And then he paused, reading the inquiring look on the writer's face, nodded, and smiled with that tolerance age must occasionally show for imperfectly informed youth, and said, "Oh, yes. Connie was a young man once." He was indeed. In fact, he was not even Connie Mack then, but Cornelius McGillicuddy, a name he shucked when he went public in baseball, thereby earning the eternal thanks of linotype operators everywhere.

Like most parents at the time, McGillicuddy senior frowned with disapproval when he heard his tall young pencil of a son was interested in professional baseball. "Why don't you get into something more lasting?" the old man asked. But try to talk a kid with a good arm and a quick bat out of it. Connie may have looked like a candidate for village pharmacist or kindly old ticket seller down at the depot, but like McGraw, he had been hand-picked by destiny to help build and personify our national narcotic. If McGraw, the small-town kid, was born to become baseball's image of the roaring big city, then Connie, that impeccably erect New Englander, carried with him always a quality of Main Street politeness, something summery and gently paced, a courtly pillar-of-the-community integrity.

The images could go awry, of course. McGraw, with his predator's eye for talent, was willing to hire black players in the first decade of the century. Devious as ever, he tried to palm off his prospects as Cubans but couldn't get away with it. Not even baseball's most powerful personality could batter down that particular barrier. Connie? Well, when Jackie Robinson was enduring his maiden voyage with the Brooklyn Dodgers in the spring of 1947, the club had an exhibition game scheduled with the Athletics. When some of the Philadelphia writers convened with the eighty-four-year-old repository of baseball history the day before and made mention of tomorrow's game, Connie reportedly said, "I'm not putting my team on the same field with that nigger." Later, when the writers had retired to refresh themselves from out of ice-tinkling glasses, they agreed that "the old gentleman had spoken out of turn" and decided not to print the story—quite a commentary on journalistic mores of the day. Connie saw the light overnight and the game went on as scheduled.

Connie got into pro ball in 1884 with Meriden in the Connecticut State League. From the very beginning he was something of a character. He did not smoke or swear, nor did he drink heavily, an anomaly among his peers. This young fellow, built like a fungo stick, was a catcher and a crafty one, apparently. Getting into the spirit of the game as much as his stainless character allowed, he had a reputation for chattering at batters to distract them and even on occasion tipping the bat just before the hitter swung, which probably accounts for the many twinkle-of-the-eye photographs we have of the old gent. A saint of venial sins.

He got to the big leagues in 1886 with Washington, then a National League outpost. In 1889 the beanpole batted .293, his best mark ever as a big leaguer. By 1894 he was managing the Pittsburgh club. Two years later he was canned for finishing sixth in the twelve-team league. He managed for another fifty-four years without seeing a pink slip. Of course fifty of those years were spent with the Philadelphia Athletics, where he had part or full ownership, and never, not even after seven straight last-place finishes from 1915 to 1921, did Owner Mack find it in his heart to rid himself of Manager Mack. In 1897 Ban Johnson, then running the Western League, asked Connie to skipper the Milwaukee club. Ban, as ever looking to polish the image of his circuit, felt that the dignified Connie was just the man to take on board. Mack managed the Milwaukee outfit for four years, and then, in 1901 when Johnson waved his wand and turned his minor league into a major one, he awarded the Philadelphia franchise to Connie. With backing from Benjamin Shibe, a moneybags from the Reach Sporting Goods Company, Mack was able to bite off a 25 percent interest in the team that was to become his personal dominion for half a century.

Very early on, Connie decided to wear civvies on the job and manage from the bench, thereby becoming the game's only day-in-and-day-out deity who did not appear in public. But they knew he was there, in a uniform all his own—neatly creased suit and tie and stiff white collar (on hot days he might remove his jacket and brainstorm in vest and gartered shirt sleeves), on his head a derby or straw hat, as style or time of year determined. He was not the type to disturb an umpire's disposition and was never thrown out of a game, though he did occasionally debate with an umpire, signaling the man in blue and asking him to please approach the dugout. Once he engaged in the following colloquy with umpire Bill McGowan, who had called an Athletics runner out on a close play at third base.

"That man looked safe to me, Mr. McGowan," said Mr. Mack.

"No, Mr. Mack," said Mr. McGowan, "he was out." Feeling the patriarch's keen blue eyes contemplating his judgment, the umpire felt constrained to add, "I wouldn't lie to you, Mr. Mack."

"No, you wouldn't, Mr. McGowan," said Mr. Mack. "Thank you."

So there he sat, in his hand one of the most vivid appendages of his legend—the scorecard with which he wigwagged his fielders to the defensive positions where the next ball was sure to be hit. Sometimes Connie's foresight bordered on the magical. Outfielder Doc Cramer, then a rookie, recalled the old man waving him to what Cramer deemed a dangerously shallow center field for power hitter Goose Goslin. Goslin nailed the next pitch with a resounding crack, but on a low line that stayed up just long enough for Cramer to glove it in short center. When Doc reached the dugout he asked the boss to explain this wizardry. "Just a hunch, boy," Connie said. "That's all it was. Just a hunch."

It was more than that, of course. Connie was too much the practical logician and tactician to trust entirely to psychical agencies. He was one of the first managers to keep charts and records on opposing hitters. Not only did he record how a man might hit the curve ball, Connie refined it to how the man might hit Chief Bender's curve ball, or Eddie Plank's, or Jack Coombs's. So Connie instructed his pitchers how to work the hitters, and if in the course of the game the old gentleman saw that his chucker was spotting his pitches accurately, then it would be the wise thing to adjust his defensive alignment accordingly. No mystery, no magic, no clairvoyance; just some sequential perception and hard work paying off, though a young outfielder might think the old man was getting messages from upstairs.

As a manager who wanted to win ball games, and as an investor whose livelihood depended on the success and general health of this free-spirited young industry, Connie was in accordance with Ban Johnson that baseball's image needed some uplifting: less spit and more polish. He preached sobriety to his players and urged them to curb their profanity. He insisted they wear business suits on road trips and to maintain a high standard of decorum. As a device of trying to establish this discipline (Connie called it pride and self-respect), the owner-manager made it a point not to socialize with his employees; outside of the ball park, the only places they saw him would be on the train and in the hotel dining room. If he needed to snap the whip, Connie had established the distance in which to do it. And snap it he did. Those players unfortunate enough to have incited his wrath (usually by some error of omission on the field, like missing a sign or throwing to the wrong base) said that Connie could read you out with the best of them. Unlike McGraw, however, Connie never embarrassed a player in public. Usually twenty-four hours would pass, and then the player would be summoned to the boss's office to listen to a candid, sometimes irate disquisition on the finer points of the profession.

Looking for what he believed would be a higher-caliber athlete, Connie was in the vanguard of the recruitment of college-educated ballplayers. He believed that, all things being even, a player who possessed intelligence would learn more (and more quickly) and forget less and be a more effective performer. So the A's skipper began patiently (he seemed always to be patient, as if he knew he was going to live right up to the frontiers of forever) looking for talented college boys and enticing them into pro ball. Among some of them who, as Connie said, were "boys who knew their Greek and Latin and their algebra and geometry and trigonometry" and who "put intelligence and scholarship into the game," were Eddie Collins of Columbia University, Jack Coombs of Colby College, Eddie Plank of Gettysburg College, Chief Bender of the Carlisle Indian School, and Jack Barry of Holy Cross.

While Connie preferred brainy athletes to those who were in danger of suffering a concussion every time they sat down, the thing that still quickened his pulsebeat faster than anything else was a big package of raw, brimming talent, the kind of talent that was its own intelligence, its own primitive instincts. One never knew when one of these ballplaying milestones would show up, nor what manner of eccentric baggage it might be packing. When it came along, this baseball equivalent of a Keats or a Mozart sprung fully armed into the world, it had better be recognized and seized with both hands and no questions asked. Intelligence evokes appreciation and nods of recognition; we all speak this language or conjure those harmonies, at whatever level of response. The Noble Savage in all its glory, however, generates crudities of excitement that rush from a mold that is broken at birth.

There haven't been too many of these noble creatures in baseball history, nor should there be. Their myth is enhanced by their infrequency. They are comparable to sightings, like comets hyphenating vast realms of the universe or giant splayed footprints at rarefied

snowy heights. They are originals, sprung from primary chutes, up-
roariously singular, wonderfully ingenuous, joyously uninhibited,
with every justification for their being concentrated in a peerless talent for baseball—the perfect game for them in that it emphasizes the
solitary exploit. Since eccentricity of personality is a prerequisite for
entry into this select unit, such uncomplicated naturals as Walter
Johnson, George Sisler, Joe DiMaggio, Mickey Mantle, and Willie
Mays do not qualify. But Babe Ruth was a member and so was Dizzy
Dean. The first of the diamond's genius-eccentrics, however, was
George Edward Waddell, whom they called Rube (again, notice
those singular nicknames; no plain Walters or Willies for this breed).

Waddell was born in Bradford, Pennsylvania, in the centennial
year, 1876, on October 13, six days before another notable pitcher,
Mordecai Peter Centennial Brown, whose parents gave him the extra
name to observe the nation's birthday, but who was called Three
Finger because of a childhood accident that mangled one of his digits. But while Brown seems to have been a plain old regular guy with
few tales spun about his persona, Waddell was a gravitational center
for the lovably odd episode. An ungovernable child was at loose in his
big, powerful body to the day he died, which happened with sad
prematurity in 1914, before his thirty-eighth birthday. He was distinguished, then and now, for his eccentricities and for the air-
burning fastball he turned loose, maybe the fastest of all time. That
old-timers nominated him as candidate for fastest ever is enough
to know.

He might have leaped full-blown from the imagination of Mark
Twain, at the time the only artful contriver liberated enough to have
spun him out. Surely the tales of Waddell have the whiff of folklore
about them, but since we have seen the later fables of Ruth and Dean
documented by reliable witnesses, why not Rube's? He did have the
necessary résumé for an American original—raised on a farm by poor
parents, no formal education, and a big outgoing personality without
a bit of meanness. He also must have possessed in abundance that
cardinal American virtue, optimism. How else to explain the reck-
lessly self-destructive byways he pursued all his life? The small-town
boy epitomized, he loved parties, parades, fire engines, fishing,
pretty girls, and red neckties, and could eat ice cream by the quart.
Grass roots American baseball needs an infusion of Rube Waddell at
least once every decade or so: a man with an electrifying talent, a
big, happy, foolish heart, and a mind as placid as a mushroom.

The most memorable Waddell stories concern his passion for fishing and for chasing fire engines. It is said that more than once Rube jumped off the bench during a game at the sound of a horse-drawn engine clanging past the ball park and in full uniform gave chase, jumping aboard if he caught up. In a little boy this is charming; in a grown man, it is suspect; in a little boy who is a grown man and also a great pitcher, it is folklore.

Fortunately, Connie Mack, for whom Rube turned in his greatest years, knew how to handle his wayward star. Realizing Waddell's fondness for fishing—the country boy loved fishing almost as much as he did fire engines—Connie would promise him that if Rube won a certain game he could take off a few days and drop his line in the water. Thus inspired, Rube was mightier than ever, firing what he called his Thunderball relentlessly and tirelessly inning after inning, his quaint mind savoring the pot of gold at the end of this particular rainbow—several days sitting under a sycamore at the side of a stream, rod in hand, breathing the scented country air, his Huck Finn soul at peace. Fire engines? Well, Connie knew that he might be able to stop a man from drinking or gambling, but from chasing fire engines? Never. That was much too esoteric a foible. "The only thing I worried about," Connie said years later, "was that he might fall off of one of those engines and get hurt."

A baseball-conscious country was filled with town teams and semipro teams in the late 1890s. While pitching for a semipro outfit in Franklin, Pennsylvania, in 1897, Rube's accomplishments were so sensational they rattled the ears of Fred Clarke, manager of the Louisville club, then in the National League. Clarke offered the twenty-year-old southpaw $500 to perform his magic for Louisville, and Rube came hand over hand down the vines to Kentucky. He arrived at two in the morning and went straight to Clarke's hotel, woke the skipper up, and announced his arrival. Fred made it known that he would have been just as happy to receive the news a few hours after sunup.

Clarke soon realized he had a free spirit on his hands and decided he would tame the beast. Consequently, when after pitching two games for Louisville Rube went on a bender, Clarke hosed him down with a fifty-dollar fine, figuring he would give the pea-green kid a dose of authority. Rube's thinking was very clear on this matter: The team was supposed to pay you money, not take it away. So he jumped the club and Fred Clarke became the first man in professional baseball to come up with an empty halter when it came to trying discipline on Rube Waddell.

For the next couple of years Rube worked his trade in Ban Johnson's Western League. One of his teammates on the Grand Rapids club was Sam Crawford, future Hall of Fame outfielder who earned his niche by denting baseballs with shuddering regularity for the Detroit Tigers. "They never made another like him," Sam said, affectionately recalling his old teammate. Rube would sometimes caution that he had so much speed he was in fear of burning up the catcher's glove, and in order to avoid a sudden fire at home plate, he would go over to the water barrel, lower the dipper, and pour ice water over his left shoulder and arm to cool himself down a bit. "You had to notice him," Crawford said. "First, because he was such a big kid. Then, because of that fastball. And once you started noticing him, you found you never took your eyes off of him. He was always laughing out there on the mound. That's because the other side tried to keep him in good humor, even when he was striking them all out. They figured he was tough enough to hit against when he was happy; get him mad and there was no telling."

Among the Western League clubs Rube stood on their collective ears was the one in Milwaukee, then managed by Connie Mack. Rube's fast one burned mental impressions upon Connie's mind like grooves laid by a blowtorch. And what a swiftie Rube must have turned loose! To the end of his life, Connie claimed Rube to be the fastest lefty he had ever seen, quicker even than Grove, the Mount Olympus of left-handed fastballers. Later, the generations would line up opposite each other to claim Koufax was faster than Grove, and vice versa. (Waddell was no longer a party to the discussion, the summer afternoons he had blistered long, long gone now, vanished with their witnesses.) The fastest left-hander? Wherever Connie was, he must have been smiling benignly: He knew.

These opinions or prejudices are by no means frivolous. We must, in this competitive society of ours, know just who or what is the biggest, the greatest, the best. The judgment determines our yardsticks, our aspirations, our goals, our achievements. To attain greatness and a brand of immortality, one must have someone or something to be measured against. The case for Waddell's fastball can be made with some conviction, for Rube's strikeout totals, in an age when the choke-hitters did not fan nearly as often as the free-swingers do today, are most persuasive. In leading American League pitchers in whiffs for six straight years (1902–1907), Rube set records. He burned out 301 batters in 1903 and a record 349 a year later, a major-league high until 1965, when Koufax struck out 382. (Eight years later Nolan Ryan rubbed out that mark with 383. Rube's record had stood for sixty-one years.) What tells us something about the swift in Rube's fastball are the comparative strikeout figures we see in the league during his heyday. In 1902 he had 210 strikeouts, the only man in the league to go over 160; in 1903 he had 301, with the next highest being 176; in 1904 he broke the bank with 349, more than 100 over the runner-up; in 1905 his 287 were almost 80 more than the next man.

Rube was back with Louisville in 1899, and when the franchise was shifted to Pittsburgh a year later, he went along with it. But it was still no go between Rube and skipper Fred Clarke, no matter how refreshing Fred found the breezes that rushed from the lefty's fast one that hot summer. With a wealth of pitching talent on the staff (Clarke's Pirates would take pennants in 1901, 1902, and 1903), Fred decided to rid himself of the headache named Waddell and traded him to the Chicago Cubs. Rube put in a .500 season in Chicago, and in 1902 turned up pitching for Los Angeles in the Pacific Coast League. He did well there and became a popular fellow— even back then southern California had the reputation for being hospitable to oddballs.

Rube might have stayed in southern California forever had not the memory of his lightning continued to crackle in the mind of Connie Mack. During his travels, Rube had stopped off in Milwaukee in 1900 and pitched part of the season for Connie. Mack decided he would be able to handle this wayward genius. So he dispatched a couple of Pinkerton detectives to Los Angeles with instructions to bring Rube back alive. What inducements the flatfoots were authorized to make is not known, but time off for fishing and visiting firehouses were no doubt among them.

So Rube Waddell arrived in Philadelphia in 1902, and this time it was for keeps and for glory. Connie employed every artful dodge in his saintly bag of tricks to keep his ace primed, happy, and available. He coaxed, wheedled, cajoled, bribed, praised, humored, lectured, and when necessary, overlooked. Rube responded to the gentle touch and rewarded Connie with win totals of 23, 21, 25, and 26 during the first four of the six years he whooped it up in Philadelphia.

And whoop it up he did. Slightly cracked, like the town's other main attraction, the Liberty Bell, he became an adored local hero.

They knew him in the saloons, where he would often step behind the bar, tie on the white apron, and begin serving and drinking at the same time, while all the world that he could see or cared about laughed and cheered him on. They knew him on the playgrounds where he sometimes joined in games with youngsters or got down on all fours to shoot marbles with them; and in the firehouses where he would sit for hours, still in thrall to whatever that fascination had been that had begun back in Bradford when he was a child. He could also, upon occasion, be found in a local jail, for this prodigious man married and unmarried three (or maybe four, the record is not clear) wives and was wont to shoot his alimony payments across mahogany bar tops instead of where the law had commanded they go. Connie would have him bailed back to freedom and Rube would issue a battery of promises: to stop getting married, stop getting divorced, honor his obligations, and stop drinking so much. No doubt he meant it all at the moment he spoke, for he was an honest man—it was innocence that did him in, not deceit. But for Rube the next moment might arrive carrying such fresh, enticing, irresistible cargoes that the previous was forgotten.

In baseball nothing is mightier or more compelling than the arm of a great fastballer; at the same time neither is anything more fragile. When that arm went, and it could go suddenly, it seldom left behind anything but memories, as well as a maddening sense of unanswerable and inexplicable loss.

To hang such an arm to the shoulder of a Mathewson or a Walter Johnson was to create an icon; to append one to Rube Waddell was almost like playing a practical joke on the baseball fraternity; it was guaranteed to provide teeth-gnashing, hilarity, and much raucous entertainment. It was like filling a balloon with air for the sole purpose of watching it dart and dive and snort and finally collapse emptily back to earth.

Naturally, Waddell stories began to proliferate. Like their progenitor, they had a character uniquely their own, a zany charm, an impetuousness, a quality foreshadowing self-destruction. Rube's roommate, catcher Ossee Schreckengost, found the big lefty a wonderful guy to room with, except for one thing: Rube insisted on eating animal crackers in bed. (In those days, two players often shared the same bed when the club was on the road. The reasons were economic. It was a less sordid age, too; today, two players sharing the same bed would be a sensational story.) Tired of sleeping on those pesky little crumbs, and unable to talk his roomie out of bringing crackers to bed with him, Ossee, so history tells us, demanded that the club write into Rube's contract a clause forbidding the consumption of crackers in bed.

And there was his taunting of the most revered mound star of the day, Cy Young. Early in the 1904 season Rube screwed his head on tight and fired an overpowering one-hitter against Cy's Red Sox. It was a near perfect game, Rube allowing a bunt single to leadoff man Patsy Dougherty and then knocking the bats out of the hands of the next twenty-seven men in a row. It was a five-game series and Rube's turn came up again before the A's left town. He drew as his opponent the thirty-seven-year-old Young, who had already achieved enough in his long career to have an award named after him. Before the game, Waddell walked up to Cy and said, "I'm going to give you the same thing I gave Tannehill the other day." (Jesse Tannehill had been the victim of Rube's one-hitter.) Young eyed the brash farm boy, only in his third season in the league, and said nothing. "I knew who he was all right," Young said later. "I'd been watching him. He was a damned fine pitcher, but he ran his mouth quite a bit. I figured he was calling me out and I had better do something about it." Cy did more than something. He shot down Rube and the A's with a perfect game, allowing just six balls to be hit out of the infield. "I had good speed and stuff," said Young modestly after the game.

And then there was the story of Rube and the alligator. This one tells us that one time when he was in Florida, Rube was among the spectators watching a professional alligator wrestler hauling the big, snap-jawed reptiles out of the water and going to the mat with them. Entranced by the spectacle, Rube asked if he might give it a go. Moved by the inherent possibilities—a big strapping fellow gulped down by an alligator—the crowd encouraged Rube and the professional gave him the go-ahead. In the great tradition of Davy Crockett, Paul Bunyan, and other American folk heroes real and made up, Rube Waddell, twenty-game winner, strikeout artist, whiskey drinker, and all-around Promethean, pressed his slippery opponent in no time flat.

Rube was never a thirty-game winner, nor did he ever pitch in a World Series. Like everything else, it was his own fault. The year was 1905, the time early September. Rube had already racked up his greatest win total, 26, on his way to pitching the Athletics into that brand-new institution, the World Series. The club was traveling from

Boston to New York when some hijinks broke out on the train. Teammate Andy Coakley appeared wearing a hard straw hat. Straw hats,
for some reason, seemed to bring out the animal in certain ballplayers, especially after Labor Day when these hats, symbol of summer,
were considered passé. Players were known to take hold of an offending skimmer and bite pieces out of the brim, or seize the brim firmly
and pull it down over a man's eyes, sending the top of his head bust-
ing up through the crown, or simply grab the hat and send a fist
through it. Rube spotted Andy's lid, and Andy spotted the gleam in
Rube's eye. Rube made a grab for the hat and Andy tried to fend him
off. The two men began wrestling in the aisle, and Rube soon found
that a man defending his straw hat made a much more formidable
opponent than an alligator.

The two men fell to the floor, Rube landing heavily on his left
shoulder. "Goddamn," the big man said, not because Coakley's
boater had escaped demolition but because he felt pain in the only
thing that lay between him and oblivion—his left arm. The arm hurt
the next day and continued to hurt for the rest of the season, depriving Rube of the six or seven starts that might have made him a thirty-
timer as well as an opportunity to work against Mathewson in the
World Series. It would have made for a fascinating match-up: the
uninhibited whirligig Waddell and the staid, dignified Mathewson. It
was the Series in which Matty spun out his three shutouts; Waddell
could throw blankers as prolifically as anyone, and under World
Series inspiration might have done the same. It was another baseball
might-have-been that never was, thanks to Rube's insatiable appetite
for a straw hat.

The thud that Rube gave his left shoulder was the beginning of
diminishing returns for the great pitcher. First of all, it threw a little
dirt on his reputation. There was talk that the gamblers had reached
Waddell and paid him to fake a sore wing in order to stay out of the
Series. There was probably no truth in the canard; Rube's arm
seemed legitimately out of action. Nevertheless, when the A's
dropped the Series in five games there was some muttering by teammates about the big guy's irresponsibility and the special treatment
he was being accorded by Mack, who continued to be fascinated by
his prodigal ace.

But even for Connie, much of Waddell's charm lay in the way the
lefty burned out the opposition with his fastball and a curve that the
old-timers say was just as lethal. They say it exploded from the shoul-

ders to the ankles and was just as searing as his full-throttle pitch. And even if it is true that the venerable sometimes remember more with pride than accuracy, even if the curve broke only from the shoulders to the knees, it still must have been a nightmare for batters to anticipate.

As Rube's effectiveness on the mound began to wane, so did the sorcery of his bad-boy charm, and so did Mack's patience with him, a patience that had been laced with a lot of purposeful tolerance and philosophical sighs. (There is a telling difference in worrying that a man might fall off a fire engine and hurt his left arm, and worrying that a man might fall off a fire engine, period.) It's a painful lesson that must eventually be learned by any rule-breaker who does one thing better than anyone else can do it. This unhappy educational process applies most saliently and rudely to athletes, of course, because their endings are preordained, doomed by clock and calendar, be they ordinary mortals or Mount Rushmore types like Waddell, Ruth, or Dean. Rollicking souls in other fields of endeavor, like, say, F. Scott Fitzgerald, can sober up and pull it back together and attempt or actually achieve a comeback; athletes seldom can. The strongest, best-conditioned, cleanest-living athletes are fated to professional expiration in the prime of manhood. The Rube Waddells carry their destinies about in eggshells.

Rube won 15 games in 1906, 19 a year later; decent seasons, but not enough to cover the shenanigans. The midseason fishing expeditions, the pursuit of fire engines, the heavy drinking, the overall irresponsibility—they were wearing thin, along with Mack's forbearance. After the 1907 season, Rube was sold to the St. Louis Browns for a reported $5,000. No doubt it hurt his pride. On July 29, 1908, Rube geared up for a start against his former club, and the stars must have pierced the blue heaven that afternoon to watch him pitch. He set a strikeout record that soft, long-ago summer's day, fanning sixteen of his old buddies, setting a one-game mark that stood for decades. But he was on the downhill side now; the merry-go-round was slowing down, the brass rings fewer. Early in the 1910 season, aged thirty-three, he was back in the minors, the fastball and the awesome snapping curve no longer intimidating. He never made it back to the bigs.

We are a forgiving people, but in turn we demand to be entertained, amused, have our heartstrings tugged, our magnanimity massaged. Rube no longer had a talent for doing any of those things. The pranks were no longer redeemed by strikeouts and shutouts, no longer vindicated by crowded grandstands throbbing with shouts of "Hey, Rube!" That artless, unmingled mind must have been a turmoil of loss and confusion as the breezes of a big-league summer blew by without him. Gone were the adulators who had crowded around his big shoulders to stand him drinks. If he chased a fire engine now, he looked like a buffoon. If he hied himself off to sit somewhere beside a forest stream with his fishing rod, no one cared. If he wrestled an alligator now and the beast snipped off that left arm, what would it have mattered? In the bustling big cities and out where the train whistles died on the rimlands of America, they no longer talked about him. The circus was over, the tents had been struck, and all had gone home but George Waddell.

Abandoned by the game, by the mighty fastball that had always seen him through, on and off the field, that had made him special, pampered, wanted, and needed, he no longer was who he had been, and since that was all he had ever been, there was nothing left. Most likely he would have tied on a white apron and gone and stood behind a bar somewhere, dispensing drinks and being stared at, soaking in the dregs of his legend. But there wasn't time for that any more. The spool was spinning rapidly into emptiness now. In 1912 Rube pitched for the Minneapolis club, and after the season the manager, Joe Cantillon, took Rube home with him to Hickman, Kentucky, for safekeeping over the winter. In the spring there were heavy rains, then the melting snows came rushing down from the mountains, and suddenly an avalanche of water came roaring through the levee not far from Cantillon's home. Rube joined hundreds of volunteers and stood deep in icy waters helping stack bags of sand. Rube's action has been described as heroic, though surely not any more so than that of the others, but not any less either. And anyway it's the demise of a legend we're talking about here. From the experience he emerged with a chill that penetrated to the bone and never left.

That summer, 1913, he pitched for Virginia of the Northern League, saw minor-league batters teeing off on his once-vaunted pitches and left in midseason, mortally ill. Cantillon paid Rube's way into a sanitorium in San Antonio, and there the great pitcher lay, waiting to die of tuberculosis, his weight falling from a once robust 200 pounds to almost half that, thinking heaven only knows what thoughts about a life that had been so hilariously wonderful and so naively taken for granted. In the spring of 1914, the man who had been one of the game's most adored and enchanting performers died at the age of thirty-seven. The date was April Fool's Day. Make of that what you will.

Decades later, taking one of those interminable train rides between American League cities that partitioned his life for a half-century, Connie Mack sat watching the landscape fold into twilight from the window of the speeding train. One of his younger players had coaxed the old man into reminiscing. In slow litany the old names were recited, each attended by some awakening memory. Plank. Collins. Baker. Bender. Lajoie. Waddell. Ah, yes. Rube Waddell. Connie's eyes showed a mellow twinkle. "He gave me fits," the old man said affectionately. "But that fellow could pitch. He could really pitch." And that, finally, was all that mattered.

⚡IVE

AMERICA in the first decade of the twentieth century was a synthesis of drowsy rural idylls and galvanized activity, of endless tracts of unspoiled land, and cities throbbing with creative energy and industrial might. Most Americans lived on farms or in small towns, where home was the center of their world. Summer evenings were spent on the front porch in rocking chairs or languidly swinging gliders, watching the unhurried world before them. Home was insular, was family; there were few distractions from outside. There was no television, no radio, no phonograph, and thus the old formalities and inhibitions were slow to die. Young ladies still attended picnics dressed in ankle-length skirts and ruffled blouses, while the men remained jacketed, straw-hatted. At the beach or lakeside, a lady's swimsuit exposed only her face and hands. Many of the country's song hits—sold in sheet music in those days—reflected the rural life in names like "In the Good Old Summer Time," and "Shine On, Harvest Moon."

That was one side of the American sphere. The other was an America roaring up through a structure like an inverted pyramid, bulging with energy, ideas, ambition, and daring. J. P. Morgan's newly organized United States Steel Corporation was the nation's first billion-dollar corporation. A massive oil strike had been made at Spindletop, Texas. The twenty-story Flatiron Building on New York's lower Fifth Avenue was the world's tallest building. The Wright brothers had made their historic flight in the sea wind at Kitty Hawk, North Carolina. The first motion picture to tell a complete story, a twelve-minute epic called *The Great Train Robbery*, had been shot in a freight yard in Paterson, New Jersey, so captivating its viewers that within a few years nearly ten thousand small theaters, called nickelodeons, had opened across the country, luring Americans from their living rooms and front porches in ever increasing numbers. In 1906 an Iowa-born Yale graduate named Lee De Forest invented a tube that would lead to a tireless and ubiquitous sound called radio. The General Motors Corporation had been formed, and so had the Ford Motor Company, which in 1908 was selling its Model T for $850. Three American cities—New York, Chicago, and Philadelphia—already had populations in excess of one million and were growing steadily with the influx of European immigrants and restive Americans departing from country lanes and sycamore-shaded main streets. For those who became nostalgic for that rural life or for the shadows of their own boyhoods, there was baseball, a three-dimensional time-warp right smack in the middle of a big city, oblivious of steel, concrete, industrial smoke, and the passage of time; for there the game was, in the midst of a growing, shouldering-out metropolis, just as the boy had left it, with its green grass and rituals redolent of old summer afternoons. Those rituals had caught meticulously and miraculously the patterns of those pastoral days of the unmoving clock so that youth could be re-created every afternoon at the ball park. It was all a most uncomplicated and accessible dream world, perforated at the edges for easy detachment and filing.

We were hurtling into the modern age, a time ripe for the making of myths, and of these none was mightier than Wagner at shortstop. Of all baseball players, he alone dominates a position so illustriously that the question of who is second-best is irrelevant. At no position is any man so automatically and indisputably the first and only choice. An all-time outfield without Cobb or Ruth could still include DiMaggio, Speaker, Williams, or Mays. All other positions have enough titans lined up behind them that distinctions become blurred But try your all-time team without Wagner at shortstop, and you have Elizabethan playwrights without Shakespeare, you have the American Revolution without George Washington, you have Melville without *Moby Dick*.

He did not have the aloof elegance of a Mathewson, the zany charm of a Waddell, the intensity of a Cobb, the majesty of a Ruth, the aristocracy of a DiMaggio, the lethal perfectionism of a Williams, the breathless excitement of a Mays. But for many witnesses, including John McGraw, who watched him close-up for twenty years, Wagner was the greatest of ballplayers, with Cobb the only other candidate in the running for the title. Only once did those two matchless contemporaries find themselves shaking the earth at the same time on the same field. The backdrop for the confrontation was the 1909 World Series between Cobb's Detroit Tigers and Wagner's

Pittsburgh Pirates. From out of the encounter came one of the game's most enduring vignettes, one that has served to mark indelibly the image of the fiery Cobb and the indomitable Wagner.

Cobb is on first base and he cups his hands around his mouth and shouts at Wagner, "I'm coming down on the first pitch, krauthead!" Wagner accepts the challenge silently. The pitcher works into his delivery and, sure enough, here comes Cobb. Wagner moves to cover the bag, the catcher's peg is on the money, and Honus takes it and gives Cobb a teeth-jarring tag. A chastened Cobb lies in the dirt listening to chimes as a nonchalant Wagner flips the ball back to the pitcher.

Thus a baseball fable, the antelope and the buffalo. And that is exactly what it is, a fable. Who first wrote it is not known, but it has received sanction from virtually everyone who has set out to tell the tale of Cobb, Wagner, and the 1909 World Series. A play-by-play examination of that Series shows that at no time did Wagner tag Cobb out at second. What the story does prove, however, is that both Cobb and Wagner were transcendent enough figures to have myths tailor-made for them.

The greatest shortstop in the history of the planet was born in 1874 in Carnegie, Pennsylvania, just a line drive from Pittsburgh. Actually, the town was called Mansfield when Honus was born, later changed to Carnegie in homage to the steel magnate. (If they had waited a while longer they might well have changed it to Wagner.) Wagner was one of nine children of a Bavarian immigrant who made his living in the coal mines. At the age of twelve, the husky young John Peter took what seemed the inevitable route to a livelihood by going into the mines and loading a ton of coal a day for $3.50 a week. It was backbreaking work, but this fellow had a back that would not break. Altogether he was a magnificent physical specimen, but in his component parts looked as though he had been put together in a dark room by people who didn't speak the same language. His bland, pleasant face was adorned by a doorknocker of a nose. His powerful five-foot-eleven-inch, 200-pound frame featured a massive chest that might have come from a barrelmaker's shop and shoulders broad enough to serve dinner on. His arms were extremely long ("the only man who could tie his shoelaces without bending over," it was said), with enormous hands, and fingers so long they could barely fit into the raggedy gloves of the day. His most prominent feature was his bowed legs, a veritable pair of parentheses in spiked shoes. He looked ungainly until he began to move on a baseball diamond, and then all those disparate parts coordinated into smooth, graceful agility and remarkable speed. Running out a triple, he was described as looking like a hoop spinning around the base paths.

Wagner afield must have been impressive. A thicket of tales about his fielding prowess has grown tall with the passing generations, but maybe not so tall, for after all, we in our time have seen with our own eyes the everyday magic of a Mays or a Brooks Robinson, which our grandchildren will listen to with tolerant skepticism when we try to tell them just how it was. In trying to convince their own young skeptics, Wagner's admirers described how their man could plunge deep into the hole and through the astonishing alchemy of those long arms, quick hands, and strong pegs turn a base hit into an out. The most famous image of Wagner at shortstop is that of Honus picking up not only the ball but what bits of unattached real estate happened to be around it at the moment of entrapment and then throwing the lot across to first base. Many teammates and opponents have sworn to the truth of this, and one wonders just what kind of burrowing pick-ups Honus made; or was it simply that his hand was *so* large it was like a scoop shovel, his fingers *so* long that they had to scrape the ground before closing upon the ball? The way Wagner's pegs to first are described, they must have resembled hurtling planets surrounded by satellites of dirt and pebbles. They say his deceptive speed could send him charging to his left, where he would intercept aborning singles on the outfield grass, and through another burst of Wagnerian magic turn them into outs. They ("they"—those many, emphatic, anonymous witnesses whose testimony posterity ignores at its peril) say his overhand deliveries were cannon-shots, his sidearm pegs were bullets, and that when he had to charge a slow roller with only time for a snap underhand throw, that ball, too, came to the first baseman humming a tune. In those mighty hands, a baseball was a model of behavior.

Considering his unusual physique—those arms hanging like a pair of elephant trunks, that wine cask of a chest, those ludicrously bowed legs—his speed afoot may have been his most remarkable attribute. But, really, we should ignore what he looked like, for inside of that body was an athlete, a marvel of grace and coordination, one of the noblest of the Lord's beasts. Yes, he could run, leading the league five times in stolen bases and racking up 722 lifetime. And hit. He stood deep in the box, a no-nonsense figure with that bat cocked back behind his right ear, gazing intently over his large hooked nose at the pitcher, ready to take a full stride into the ball and wheel the bat with a short, powerful swing that sent line drives through the baseball sound barrier, delivered to all fields with the same ruthless impartiality. He took eight batting titles, and at one time or another led in hits, doubles (eight times), triples, runs batted in, and slugging. He batted .300 or better his first seventeen years in the National League, and not until he was almost forty did the habit leave him.

A buoyant destiny floated young John Peter up out of the mines and steered him toward baseball, abetted by older brother Albert, who played in the bigs for one year, and by Papa Wagner, who was, of all things, a baseball fan and encouraged his boys to play. The practical young man was contemplating becoming a barber when professional baseball beckoned him into its ranks in 1895. Wagner spent that season earning around thirty-five dollars a week and playing for four different teams in four different leagues in Ohio and Michigan. When he came home that fall he was a free agent.

The man who "discovered" Honus Wagner was Edward Grant Barrow, then a twenty-seven-year-old fledgling baseball executive who was running the Paterson, New Jersey, club in the Atlantic League. It isn't that Ed Barrow is without his own well-earned fame—he was the Red Sox manager who in 1918 switched Babe Ruth from the mound to the outfield, and although every peanut vendor in Fenway Park probably had the same idea, Ed was the man who did it. He is also the man who, as general manager, helped build the Yankees into baseball's greatest dynasty. Nevertheless, anyone who is on the spot when some budding titan is beginning to make whitecaps on the lake is assured of a special carriage ride all the way to sundown. There have been quite a few since, but Ed Barrow is probably baseball's first Balboa, and how that happened is by itself a homey vignette of folklore.

Barrow's trip through the portals of history occurred on a raw autumn day in 1895. Having heard flattering reports about this Wagner fellow, the young executive decided to take a hike out to Mansfield and try to sign him to a Paterson contract. When he arrived in town and began inquiring about John Peter Wagner, Barrow was directed to the railroad tracks, having been told he might find Wagner down there with some of the boys. So Ed buttoned up his overcoat and began walking along the ties. Soon he began hearing some resounding booms echoing hollowly. A little farther along he came upon a half-dozen sports firing chunks of coal at an empty hopper car. Barrow stopped and watched them for a while—a baseball man is easily mesmerized by the sight of someone throwing something, be it a baseball, an apple core, or chunks of coal. He watched the group of young men picking up the coal and going into elaborate windups and firing the missiles against the side of the hopper, their topcoats whirling around them, their derbies shaking gently. He did not know which one was Wagner, but he quickly had a notion, because there was one rather awkward but yet compelling young man whose arm swung with a slow but decisive snap and from whose hand the pieces of coal flew in blurs and struck the side of the hopper with deep bellowing reports. A baseball man would neither sleep nor eat until he had spoken to the owner of that arm. Ed Barrow knew he was seeing talent, more talent, in fact, than by his own oft-stated assertion he would ever see again, though he spent another fifty-two active and bountiful years in baseball. (Interestingly, Barrow, whose long big-league experience was all in the American League, always maintained that National Leaguer Wagner was the greatest ballplayer of all.)

It was, in retrospect of course, a sublime moment in Barrow's life. For young Wagner, it was something else. "When we took notice of him standing there eyeing us," Honus said later, "we sized him up as a railroad cop and ran like the dickens." But Barrow caught up to them, or to Wagner anyway, and signed him to a contract with the Paterson club, on the simple reasoning that anyone with an arm like that *had* to be a ballplayer.

Honus did not disappoint Barrow. The new man batted .349 for Paterson in 1896 and was clipping away at a .379 pace in midseason 1897 when Ed sold him to the Louisville club, then in the National League. The rookie got into 61 games and batted .344. After the 1899 season, Louisville dropped out of the big leagues and most of the roster, Wagner included, was tranferred to Pittsburgh, a move that delighted Honus because it brought him home. (The Honus nickname derived from "Johannes" or "Johann," both German equivalents of "John.")

Interestingly enough, the greatest shortstop ever corralled didn't appear at the position until his fifth big-league season and didn't become a full-timer at the spot until his sixth year up. Wagner had been playing the outfield, third base, and first base and doing it so superbly at each position that there was no thought of putting him at short. When Barrow, McGraw, and the others said Honus was the greatest of ballplayers, they were bearing in mind the big man's versatility. While Wagner's defensive skills at shortstop are legendary, it is forgotten that he performed with similar brilliance at three other positions.

How great was he? Well, the consensus among those who played with and against him—really, the only witnesses worth listening to— is that the legend of Honus Wagner is a mosaic of truths large and small. To understand the significance of the consensus, one must understand something about big leaguers, for if there is a constant among big-league ballplayers from the beginning on up to the present, it is that they are not easily impressed. To achieve special rank with them, a man must not only perform the extraordinary but he must do it game after game, year after year, otherwise his marquee lights dim one by one, as has happened to so many outstanding players.

There is a particular undiminishing pride big-league ballplayers carry about with them, right to the lip of the grave. It derives not only from the pride they take in themselves as having been among an uncommonly gifted group, but also from the importance of baseball in America. Inculcated from childhood with the game's unique place in the national consciousness, both symbolic and real, they regard big-league status as entry into an exclusive fraternity and the sense of conferred privilege never leaves them. For these hard-bitten professionals to unanimously elect a small handful to represent them at the summit of all achievement speaks for itself. And none have been so readily chosen as Wagner.

But in one respect, Wagner was no different from his diamond contemporaries. In 1900, his first year with Pittsburgh, Honus won the first of his eight batting titles with a .381 average; he also led in doubles, triples, and slugging. That added up to a lot of mayhem at home plate, but no satisfaction at the paymaster's window, for the league had its $2,400 salary limit. While this is, quite literally, a day's wages for many of today's spiked-shoe capitalists, back then it was not exactly the sort of wage that breeds anarchy; it was, in fact, well above the norm. Unskilled laborers earned around $600 a year, while clerks took home on the average of $700. In addition, the work week in those good old, bad old days was around sixty hours, a massive amount of time compared to what the ballplayers put in, especially in those days of ninety-minute games. And of course the baseballers were only working seven months a year, enabling them to spend the hot-stove months subsidizing their incomes, which many of them did working as bartenders or back on the family farm (in 1900 one of every three members of the work force was employed in agriculture). Ballplayers were paid better than teachers, college professors, and any biologists, chemists, or other scientists that might have been working to cure mankind's ills. In certain respects, some things haven't changed very much.

But the dollar, as they said when George Washington hurled his silver one across the Potomac, went further in those days. A gentleman could go into a decent restaurant and have himself a dinner of half a canteloupe, chicken fricassee, corn on the cob, raspberries and cream for dessert, and a cup of coffee to make it all float lightly, for just sixty cents, not counting tip. Beef was ten cents a pound, eggs twelve cents a dozen, coffee fifteen cents a pound. A Saturday-night suit cost maybe nine bucks, a good hat just two. On a salary of $2,400 a year, plus what he chose to pull in during the off-season, Honus Wagner could enjoy life with gusto.

But money never seemed to interest Wagner very much; in fact it seemed almost to embarrass him. When the American League began its forays upon the National League rosters, Wagner was one of the prime targets. But while such luminaries as Nap Lajoie, Ed Delahanty, Jimmy Collins, and Cy Young succumbed to the seductions of a flapping checkbook, Honus remained steadfast. Reportedly, he turned down an offer of $20,000 to jump to the new league, and then refused to use this as a bargaining chip to try and pry a better contract out of his boss, Pittsburgh owner Barney Dreyfus. Why this folksy American hero did something as un-American as turning down proffered wealth, we cannot be sure. Perhaps Honus simply did not want to leave the Pittsburgh precincts where he felt so comfortably at home. The most money he ever earned was $10,000, and he did not attain this figure until 1909, after twelve years in the big leagues and six batting titles. Once he had got to $10,000, Honus deemed it fair and adequate and never asked for a raise, routinely signing the same contract year after year.

Wagner's on-the-field credentials by themselves, impressive though they are, do not fully explain why the man achieved such popularity during his career, nor why he remains in permanent orbit as a genuine American sports hero. One of his contemporaries, Napoleon Lajoie, second baseman from 1896 through 1916, may well have been Wagner's equal on the field; he in fact outhit Honus life-time by 11 points—.339 to .328. He won four batting titles, including one with a .422 average in 1901, which is still the American League's highest. His fielding was impeccable. The word invariably used by his contemporaries to describe him in the field was *graceful.* The Rhode Island–born Frenchman was tall and darkly handsome and perfectly proportioned, unlike the ungainly looking Wagner. He certainly did not lack acclaim nor fall short of idolators; in his heyday he was one of the most admired of baseball players, but though his sterling gifts demanded it, he never quite caught the public imagination as did Mathewson or Wagner, with all three careers running parallel. "Graceful," and line drives that could break an infielder's shinbone—that was what we heard from his peers fifty years later. That was the arrived consensus, and today it is not enough, nor was it, apparently, enough then. That sanctum sanctorum where we keep the most revered of our treasures—those impressions and those memories that define the perimeters of our personal quests—is not large enough to include "graceful," even though the grace includes a .400 batting average and bone-breaking line drives.

The difference between Wagner and Lajoie on the field might have been as fine as the difference between a Walter Johnson fastball and one coughed up by Bob Feller or Nolan Ryan. Wagner, however, brought another dimension onto the field with him, and still another away from it. Honus was a "character," one who touched a responsive chord in the public. Unlike a Lajoie, whose grace was indigenous to his every movement, Wagner seemed especially endowed. The grace that flowed from that unlikely physique had an endearing quality. Never taken for granted, it never ceased to marvel. And he was indeed a character, though not like Waddell. Hardly. Wagner was shy, modest, unpretentious. By mid-career he had already formed the benevolent, foxy grandpa look and bearing that would settle classically as he grew older: the beer-drinking front-porch philosopher and spinner of tall tales.

"One time I was going for a ground ball," Honus would say, "and a rabbit ran across my path. In the confusion I picked up the rabbit and fired it to first base." Pause. The mischievous old face grins slyly. "I got the runner by a hare."

"When I was just a rookie breaking in," Honus would say, "they sent me up to pinch-hit in the bottom of the ninth with the score tied. I got ahold of one and drove it over the left-field fence. I became so excited that I started running the bases the wrong way, heading up the third-base line and running to second, to first, and then home. When I touched home plate the umpire subtracted a run and we lost."

Sometimes, if the game in New York hadn't burned off enough energy, he would walk all the way from the Polo Grounds back to the Pirates' hotel, a distance of eighty or ninety city blocks. And he was quite a sight, too, walking casually along the sidewalks of New York in the twilight of a summer's day, hands in pockets, broad body weaving slightly, derby hat pushed back on his thick hair. A man could get thirsty on a walk like that, especially in warm weather, and when he did, Wagner would step into a neighborly looking saloon, take an old silver dollar from his pocket and bounce it on the bar so it rang out. Naturally, everyone looked around, and inevitably someone recognized him and of course had to have the privilege of buying Honus Wagner a beer. Honus would drain the stein, run the back of his hand across his mouth, thank his benefactor and leave, the silver dollar still intact in his pocket, ready to be rung again at the next stop.

He could drink prodigious amounts of beer; he never touched hard liquor. He indulged in cigars but frowned upon cigarettes, to the extent that he created a legacy for a handful of baseball card collectors decades after his death. The collecting of baseball cards is a venerable hobby, going back to the 1880s. After the turn of the century it became widespread. Fans could not only see their heroes live, but could also collect their likenesses on the small, colored cards issued by tobacco companies in cigarette packages. The winged dreams of farm boys and city boys alike were here embodied in those manly faces under their team caps. No dubious Droeshout engravings for Cobb or Mathewson or Lajoie, but the real thing, faithful icons for pious contemplation. There was a Wagner cigarette card, but when Honus saw it he became angry and demanded it be withdrawn—he would not be associated with cigarettes. So the company withdrew and destroyed the Wagner cards—all but a few. Today, in the burgeoning collector's market, those cards are worth upwards of $15,000 apiece.

His aura never left him. He retired after the 1917 season. In 1933, nearly sixty then, he rejoined the Pirates as a coach. Occasionally he would be lured by some old siren call and pick up a glove and go out to shortstop during batting practice. "He didn't do it often," one Pirate player remembered, "but when he did, it was something to see. First you'd see the other infielders move away from him, far away, almost as if they didn't think they belonged out there with him. Everybody would go on with what they were doing, but they were watching him out of the corners of their eyes, and as soon as a ball was hit his way, by God, everybody froze and watched him pick it up and arc a soft, lazy throw over to first base. Then we'd look back at each other and everybody had a little smile on his face. Something special had happened. In our world, anyway."

Wagner was the most prominent representative of another large-sized ethnic immigrant group that took avidly to the national game. Although not as numerous as the Irish in the game, every big-league roster in the early part of the century featured its share of Germanic names, like Schmidt, Unglaub, Hoffman, Thielman, Schreckengost, Steinfeldt, Zimmerman, and Kruger. It took a while for the sons of Italian and Eastern European immigrants to break into baseball, but as their numbers increased upon these shores, so they did in the big leagues.

Of the larger immigrant groups, the one that contributed the fewest players was the Jews. Whereas many immigrants came from farm or peasant backgrounds, the Jews had been living largely in urban areas, and when they came to the big cities of America they were able to adapt more easily than the others. They brought with them, too, a tradition of business skills, a reverence for study and education (both secular and religious), and a tight, highly disciplined family unit. While some of the other immigrant boys were encouraged to go out and find work as soon as they were old enough to lift a pay envelope, the Jewish boys were made to sit, study, learn, and generally to wise up in order to know how to survive what was going to be a difficult world under the best of circumstances, and especially so for them. Difficult world it surely was, and even if a Jewish kid was agile enough to escape the books and get out to play ball, and even if he was gifted enough to make it to the big leagues, it was seldom with the added burden of a name like Cohen or Goldberg or whatever the giveaway label might have been, for those were much more rattle-headed times and life was tough enough.

Early on in its history, baseball began cultivating a genius for propagandizing itself, a process that continues unabated to this day.

The game was artfully canonized, Americanized, and quickly put beyond the pale. If many of the players were looked upon as social undesirables, well, that was irrelevant, because nothing could pollute the game itself. It was as if baseball were self-purifying, a shining water despite some of the odd fish that swam in it. The game's advocates preached that it had no equal when it came to assimilating and Americanizing the crowds of foreign-born youngsters with their funny clothes and English-mangling tongues. While their fathers might be shut out of jobs and refused entrance to certain restaurants ("No Jews or Irish" were common signs to be seen posted in those days, while anti-Negro attitudes were so pervasive signs were not even needed), their sons were allegedly imbuing the spirit of Washington, Jefferson, and Lincoln merely by whacking soggy, misshapen balls with scarred bats. Well, maybe there was a shadow of truth in the contortion, baseball being, like any other sport, highly competitive and America a country that has always thrived on competition.

§IX

A CURIOUS GEOGRAPHIC LACUNA existed in the national game in the early years of the century. There were hundreds of players who had been born in the Northeast and the Midwest; there were big-leaguers who had been born in Canada, Germany, Ireland, and Switzerland; but just a mere fraction who came from what had once been known as the Confederate States of America. In the American League in 1905, out of 203 men who broke into games that year, just seven were born in the one-time Confederacy—three from Texas and two each from Virginia and Georgia. Explanations for this paucity must be purely speculative. Perhaps, with the major leagues centered in distant cities to the north, insufficient attention was paid to southern talent, despite there being minor leagues in the South, the Southern Association, for one, having been organized in 1885. There were no farm systems in those days and virtually no scouting as we know it today, making it quite possible for raw young talent to be left withering on the vine. Not to be overlooked either is the fact that big-league baseball was a northern industry, by location and control, and the Civil War was still a fact of living memory. For years a common nickname for southern players was Reb. But whatever, the situation was about to modify itself, beginning with a ballplayer unlike any seen before, or for that matter, since.

One of the two Georgians in the American League in 1905 joined the Detroit Tigers late in the season, purchased from the Augusta, Georgia, club of the South Atlantic League for $750. And southerner he was, from the top of his head to the tips of his mercurial toes. Unreconstructed, utterly and forever, from day one unto the last rush of purple under the last trumpet call, as a southerner, as a man, as a genuine, mold-shattering American phenomenon. The rebel yell embodied. Six feet and three-quarters of an inch and 175 pounds of concentrated mercury and dynamite in spiked shoes, turned loose upon the big cities of the North, where he caused more havoc and consternation than Lee's gray legions ever dreamed of achieving. Forty years after Appomattox came the Confederacy's revenge.

Tyrus Raymond Cobb, in person. The record book says he was, by far, the most unstoppable man who ever came to home plate. Sometimes a decade or more will go by before a single major-leaguer achieves the .367 batting average that Cobb *averaged* throughout twenty-four big-league seasons. The story of Cobb, however, is more than mere statistics, if one may be so impertinent as to breathe the word *mere* near the word *statistics* in a sentence that includes the name "Cobb." All right. There is the .367 lifetime figure, the twelve batting championships (including nine in a row), the 4,191 lifetime hits, and all those other facts and figures, until they numb with redundant splendor. It is under the compulsion of those statistics that Cobb has more frequently than any other player been declared the greatest of all time. The year-by-year recitations of his accomplishments in the record book are baseball's nearest approximation of Scripture. There is majesty in a .367 lifetime.

Yes, he did more of this and more of that than anyone who ever lived. To say that he was less than *numero uno* would be like saying the record book lies or does not count. Cobb *adds up* to the greatest of all players. But was he? When heavyweight baseball intellects are gathered in convocation and the matter of the greatest, or purest, or most natural hitter comes up, the names most vehemently put forward are those of Babe Ruth, Rogers Hornsby, Joe Jackson, and Ted Williams. As a defensive outfielder, Cobb's exact contemporary in center field, Tris Speaker, is accorded the highest mark. Tyrus's throwing arm? Adequate. Where Cobb stood alone among his peers seems to be running speed and his audacious employment of it. Slippery as a lathered eel, he seems to have gone around the bases with the same devastation with which Sherman marched through Cobb's native state. But while he stole 96 bases one year, he was also thrown out 39 times that same year, meaning he was swift and daring but also reckless. He was probably not as abundantly gifted as Wagner, Ruth, DiMaggio, or Mays. But if Cobb was indeed the game's premier player, it was because of a certain intangible he brought with him to the diamond: He was almost certainly psychotic. His drive to excel has been described as frightening. Each time at bat for Cobb, said a teammate, "was like a crusade." He was incensed every time he made out, and since throughout a long career that ran from 1905 to 1928 he made out some 7,238 times, Ty had an inordinate amount of irritation to deal with. But then again, if one listens attentively to accounts by his contemporaries, not even a batting average of 1.000 would have made Cobb a happy man. The man who had every-thing—number-one status in his chosen profession, a strong body, a good mind, a large family, millions of dollars (he was an early inves-tor in Coca Cola stock)—seemed wretchedly unhappy, always. He was tough, aggressive, unforgiving, contentious, mean-spirited, bigoted. And that, according to the evidence of some, was his sunny side.

Ty also had something else cherished by southerners—a distin-guished lineage that included lawyers, doctors, Revolutionary War heroes, politicians, and two Civil War brigadier generals. Accom-plished gentlemen all, but destined to be remembered, if at all, only because of their descendant's uncanny way with a baseball bat.

He was born on December 18, 1886, in the rural community of Narrows in northeast Georgia, near the town of Royston. By all ac-counts, he had a placid, secure boyhood growing up in the small town of large-roomed old antebellum houses, spending hot summer afternoons playing baseball, listening to his elders discussing those two prime southern topics, crops and politics, and hearing tales of a war whose banners he would carry forever. And there were those cosmically still southern nights when a boy would lie abed with his eyes on the stars and his thoughts on the future.

For Tyrus Cobb, that future was being mapped for either a ca-reer in medicine or the military. The cartographer of the boy's future was his father, William Herschel Cobb, one of the solid citizens of Royston, being at one time or another mayor, state senator, school teacher, country school commissioner, and editor of the local paper. William Cobb was tall, physically strong, stern, strict, and a discipli-narian. Nevertheless, he and his strong-willed, firebrand son were devoted to each other, their relationship one of mutual love and re-spect. (Perhaps in the light of recent historical events, there was a certain tolerance for rebellious southern boys.) As far as is known, with no one else did Ty Cobb ever have such a relationship, not with his mother, his younger brother or sister, either of his two wives, or any of his five children. The clues to Cobb's aberrant behavior are sparse and slight. There is one story that we know, however, and it could well have had a lasting, unhinging effect on him. It is a story that has never been fully explained, rife with rumors and innuendos. The only certainty is that it ended in tragedy.

It took place on the night of August 8, 1905, when the eighteen-year-old Ty was playing ball with the Augusta club, in his second year of pro ball then, pursuing the profession his father had opposed; but the elder Cobb had finally given the boy his mixed blessings and sent him off with the admonition, "Don't come home a failure." How many points those words from a worshiped father can add to the batting average of a murderously competitive boy, there is no telling, but on that August 8 Cobb was leading the league in batting and was just a few weeks away from joining the Detroit Tigers.

On the night that was to forever cloud the sunshine for Ty Cobb, his father ate supper, then went out to the barn and hitched up his buggy, telling his wife he had business to attend to in a nearby town. He said he would return either very late that night or early the next morning. With her younger children spending the night with friends, Mrs. Cobb was alone in the house. At around 10:30 P.M. she went to bed. Some hours later she was awakened by a noise at her bedroom window. She got out of bed, took a revolver from a bureau drawer, and went to investigate. Through the curtains she saw the silhouette of a man trying to gain entry. She raised the revolver and fired twice, blowing aside the curtains and shattering the glass. The man fell back, struck in the head and stomach. The roar of gunfire brought a neighbor running to the scene. He examined the body, then shouted through the window to a dazed, incoherent Mrs. Cobb that she had shot her husband.

Why William Cobb was poking around the bedroom window was never satisfactorily explained, but there was some lurid grinding of the town's rumor mill. The most persistent bit of speculation was that he suspected his wife of infidelity and that his trip away from home had been a ploy to enable him to slip back to discover what he might discover. Indeed, the *Royston Record* said that "sensational developments" would follow in the wake of the investigation of the shooting. Nothing followed, however. Time passed and the case was quietly dropped.

How much of an impact did this family tragedy have on the psyche of young Tyrus? He once said, in defense of his fiery style of play, that he felt as if his father was always watching him. If William Cobb was indeed bearing witness from some celestial box seat he certainly would have been impressed, and proud, sometimes bemused and amazed, and at times would have had to turn aside and cough in his hand. What was unleashed upon American League basepaths for nearly a quarter of a century was more than competitive ardor, more than hustle, more than winning spirit; it was baseball played with evangelical fervor, with an unrelenting single-minded obsession not only to excel but to dominate and demoralize. That this obsession was dangerous and abnormal is evident when one considers that it was sustained without slack through twenty-four years, 3,033 games, 11,429 official at bats. Those satanic batting averages bear it out—twenty-three consecutive years over .300, eleven consecutive years of .368 or better. That's something more than just sharp hitting. There is a terrifying, almost unreasonable quality to such protracted, undeviating superiority. What motivated the pure rage that drove him we cannot know; but never, never did he attempt any restraints upon those seething furies, and his lifetime achievement of nearly 3.7 hits for every ten times at bat is as near perfection as any hitter has ever come.

Anyone who was ever on a ball field with him agreed that Cobb possessed, along with his blinding speed, a quick, hyperactive mind that seemed always thinking ahead, daring his body to keep pace; it was as though he were dichotomized—the evil-genius brain taunting, goading, and enraging the lightning-reflexed body toward ever more distant and daring goals. At bat he could be subtle and devious, dropping bunts, slapping the ball to all fields with his split-handed grip, moving his feet in the batter's box and changing his stance even as the pitcher was delivering. These were tactics, shrewd and controlled. It was on the basepaths, unleashed, that he seemed to lose this control, sending himself hurtling on audacious, sometimes hopeless missions. Washington Senators third baseman Ossie Bluege was a rookie in 1923 when he encountered the thirty-six-year-old Cobb on the base paths.

"Ty's on first," Bluege recalled years later, "and Harry Heilmann hits a line-drive single to right field. Well, Cobb seldom stopped at second. He just kept on going and you had to throw him out, that's all there was to it. On this particular play Sam Rice picked up the ball in right field and fired it in to me, and now I've got the ball at third base just as Cobb is rounding second. And he doesn't care; he's coming. I'm thinking to myself, this is going to be interesting! Instead of waiting at the base, I took a few steps out to meet him, in a little bit of a crouch, waiting to tag him. Well, this is no exaggeration now. He didn't slide. He just took off and came at me in midair, spikes first, about four or five feet off the ground, so help me just like a rocket. He hit me in the upper part of my arm, just grazing the flesh but tearing open the sleeve. I made the play. I tagged him out, but I was so mad I was going to konk him with the ball while he was lying on the ground. But Billy Evans, the umpire, pulled me away. Then he threw Cobb out of the game for making such a vicious slide.

"The next day I was standing around the batting cage waiting my turn to hit when up walks Mr. Tyrus Raymond Cobb. Just as sweet as apple pie. He's apologizing.

" 'Son,' he said, 'I hope I didn't hurt you.'

" 'I'm all right,' I said.

" 'Good,' he said. Then the look in his eyes changed just a little, his face got mean, and he said, 'But remember—never come up the line for me.'

"But that wasn't what had got him mad. I'll tell you what got him mad—he knew he was going to be out. That was like waving a red flag in a bull's face. When he knew you had him, it seemed to make him a little crazy, like a cornered animal. That's when he was most dangerous."

A little crazy. A cornered animal. Dangerous. Not words ordinarily employed in putting a baseball player in perspective. Was it only because his mother had shot his father to death? Well, it was that, and more. Reportedly, he had always been brash and hot-tempered. Coming to the big leagues when he did hardly helped his disposition. Rookies were not made welcome; they were, after all, out for somebody's job, and that somebody had friends on the club (and jobs were fewer—big-league clubs only carried seventeen or eighteen players when Cobb broke in). Nor did being a rookie from the Deep South help. The old sectional animosities, the rancor from a war that left a half-million men dead, had not yet settled. The North may have forgiven, but not forgotten, and if a southern boy's ears were sensitive and his temper a bit fine, he was going to have trouble. No one was immune when this particular boy blew up, not even the venerated Cy Young, a long-established legend when Cobb came into the league. The young Georgian once provoked the great veteran into shouting down at him from the mound, "It's too bad Sherman didn't do more to Georgia when he was down your way. He left too many corncobs lying around." And Tyrus shouting back, "I'm going to drive the next one down your throat and they can cart you off to the cemetery."

His talent for collecting base hits was equaled only by a perverted genius for alienating people. So to hear Cobb described by so many of his peers as the game's greatest player is a most telling tribute, because most of the encomiasts despised him, and usually with evidence in hand, because Ty had at one time or another spiked them, run them down, slugged them, bedeviled them, insulted them, intimidated them, humiliated them, or otherwise unsettled their digestive tracts. When stepping out of the batter's box to get some dirt on his hands, he always made sure when bending to show his backside to the pitcher, in effect telling the man on the mound where he could kiss old Tyrus, or young Tyrus (there was no difference between the two; his disposition was as constant as his batting averages).

His calculating mind never stopped, never relaxed, not even when it refined itself down to the barely perceptible, the minute. Some people thought that Cobb's kicking at the bag when he reached first base was an absentminded habit. But this mind was never absent on a ball field. What he was doing, he conceded years after his retirement, was trying to kick the sack a few inches closer to second base, to give him this extra sliver of advantage on a close pick-off throw by the pitcher. And even when he was not in the game, he was capable of having an impact on it, if you let him. In 1911 he boarded the train in New York that was taking the Giants to their World Series rendezvous with the Athletics in Philadelphia. Anxious to talk hitting with the great Cobb, Giants outfielder Josh Devore sat down next to him and the two had several hours of engrossed conversation.

"Gee," Devore said to one of his teammates when they got off the train, "that fellow Cobb knows a lot about hitting. He told me some things about the American League pitchers just now, and he didn't know he was doing it." One of the pitchers discussed was Philadelphia's starter, Eddie Plank. Filled with Cobb's inside information, Devore went confidently to bat four times against Plank and four times struck out, not realizing until later that the wily Tyrus, who liked Plank, had actually laced him with misinformation about Eddie's stuff and style. Cobb no doubt sat in his seat chortling as he watched the confused Devore stir the breezes around home plate.

He was one of the most fearsome athletes ever turned loose in any arena anywhere, and surely the most lethal uncoiling ever seen on a baseball diamond. He should have been a manager's delight, but Hughie Jennings, for fourteen years his skipper at Detroit, would have traded him at a moment's notice, if he could have received equal value in return. But where, ever, was there equal value for Ty Cobb?

Ready or not, baseball and America now had Ty Cobb, a hero with bloodlines, real and symbolic, going back to the frontier, a bridge between the untamed wilderness and a future now accelerating and rushing in faster, it seemed, than any twenty-four hours could carry it. Cobb's silver-streak spikes hit the highways of the diamond almost simultaneously with the arrival of the automobile culture. Magazines were featuring gentlemen sitting behind long-shanked steering wheels in caps and goggles, their ladies next to them in wide-brimmed hats tied down with scarves knotted under their chins. In 1901, a Henry Ford buggy could hurry along at more than ten miles an hour. In order to publicize the new industry and enhance its appeal, Ford encouraged and promoted the building of racing cars. His ace driver, Barney Oldfield, became a national hero, winning race after race, climbing to one new speed record after another, hitting a dazzling 83.7 miles per hour at Daytona Beach in 1904.

Like him or not, Cobb was a symbol of America on the go, unstoppable, audaciously self-confident, innovative. Ty was a shock and a revelation, personifying a nation soon to burst its seams in its rush to outdo itself and all contenders. The latent fire had reached the surface and the need to be first, to be the best, was there for all to see and try to defy. Wagner may have been as good as Cobb; Honus may have been better; but it was Cobb who won championships year after year; it was Cobb who fascinated and outraged, who set the standards for a following century of players to pursue. In his brain, his personality, his performance, he was alone. It was Cobb against the world, until finally it became the world against Cobb. As far as Tyrus was concerned, an even match.

If Cobb was for many a disturbing dose of reality, transcending the orderly world of baseball and giving it new dimensions, his only rival for preeminence in the league was cut from a more comfortable pattern, one of pleasing American homespun. He was a Kansas farmboy with the plain old country name of Walter Johnson. A photograph of Cobb can be misleading; one of Johnson, never. The Cobb pictures—the early ones especially—show a pleasant, absolutely bland face under thin hair and a high forehead. There are no compelling features, no hint of personality. A perfectly deceptive mask. Look at a Walter Johnson photograph, however, and you are seeing the man, a man you would intuitively like and trust. The face suggests friendliness, gentleness, modesty, character, as well as a paterfamilias strength and dependability. There is an early photograph of Walter spiffed up in his Sunday suit, with jacket and tie, slightly baggy trousers, and brightly polished shoes. And a derby sitting square on his head without the least degree of tilt. The set of the derby is the giveaway; positioned as it is, there is almost an invitation to some roughneck to knock it off, make the big boy scramble after it. But right under the lid of that hat is an open, uncomplicated face and a pair of eyes with a fixity of gaze that seem to be daring the roughneck to step up and take his chances.

He did not have the polish or elegance of a Mathewson, nor the folksiness of a Wagner, but he became a folk hero of equal stature, and today only Ruth has a legend of strength to match his. And the reason that Ruth and Johnson remain unchallenged, almost mythic, in what they were and did, is because each was in all likelihood a "one-time only" model, the mold immediately broken upon delivery; each in his way physically unique. The power of Caruso's lungs, the complexity of Einstein's brain, and the cobra swiftness and bricklike impact of Joe Louis's fists were analogous to the length, strength, and durability of Walter Johnson's right arm. The most awesome and methodically working piston ever on a mound. When he stood at his ease, that arm hung far down toward his kneecap. When he slung it back in his low sidearm, almost underhanded delivery, the motion seemed effortless, but the ball he shot up to home plate was the greatest disappearing act in baseball history.

Johnson is one of the very few larger-than-life figures in baseball history, a member of that exclusive galaxy that is looked up to with an almost fanlike pride by their peers. There are old-time pitchers who describe with relish the mammoth proportions of a home run they fed to Ruth, as though this was assurance of being footnoted into history. There was the same sense of exhilaration and historical participation—in retrospect anyway—in being whiffed by Walter Johnson. Walter surrendered nearly 5,000 hits in his career, but no one seems willing to come forward and claim any of them. Talk to the men who faced him and the nearest any of them ever came to putting the slug on Walter was a loud foul. They knew then and they knew later that part of the stature they enjoyed as big-leaguers lay in having faced the incomparable Walter, and to tarnish him in the least would therefore diminish them. There are not many pitchers described with such awe. Johnson is foremost, along with Grove, Feller, Koufax, and Ryan.

The Johnson legend carried tremendous impact, because speed and power are the two most exciting and captivating elements in baseball. (Johnson-Ruth confrontations in the early 1920s, when Ruth was young and Walter still had plenty of swift left must have been spellbinding, similar to Feller-Williams hookups twenty years later.) In 1932 Johnson, then close to forty-five years old, was managing the Senators. Before a spring training game against Cincinnati, he took the mound to throw some batting practice. The Cincinnati players closed in around the batting cage to get as near as possible to a Walter Johnson pitch, even a middle-aged Johnson. Among them was Babe Herman, a .393 hitter just two years before with Brooklyn. Heinie Manush, a Washington outfielder and an old friend of Herman's, was about to step in and take his licks. He saw the little-boy-at-the-circus expression on Herman's face and invited Babe into the cage. Herman eagerly accepted.

"Johnson threw four or five balls that I just couldn't get around on," Herman said. "When I got out of the cage I asked Manush for cripe's sake why Johnson was retired. Heinie laughed. 'You've seen all he's got,' he said. 'A half-dozen pitches and then it's gone. In another few days he'll crank it up again. But it's something to see, isn't it?' " (Yes; almost like stepping into a time-warp for a few moments.)

If it was something to see in 1932, what must it have been like twenty-five years before, when the big, shy youngster came almost literally out of nowhere to dazzle the American League? The first time Cobb saw the nineteen-year-old rookie warming up in 1907, Ty reported back to his teammates, "That busher throws the fastest pitch I ever saw."

Of all the mythic stars, none was more intimidating, none less colorful. He came, he saw them, he struck them out, he left. What he left behind were records and a myth of near-invincibility. His absence of temperament and his simplicity were admirable, but they left him at the brink of dullness. He neither smoked nor drank, and "Dad gum" was about as close to profanity as he got. He was probably closer to the prototypical American hero than Mathewson or Wagner—the man of might and power, modest and humble in his ways, dangerous only when in contention. He would console teammates who erred behind him, telling them the batter should rightfully have been struck out. He refused to throw at a batter. He would occasionally, when the game was safely won, let up and allow an opponent to get a hit. But his disposition was a blessing. Put the least bit of tartness in him and he could have been a menace.

They said that with his low, sidearm delivery it looked as though he "buggy-whipped" the ball up to the plate. He had two nicknames: The Big Train (the epitome of speed at the time), and Barney, after Barney Oldfield. Buggy whip. Big Train. Barney. Walter was of his time and place.

Was he the fastest ever? That grand old question. Try not asking it. It's as irresistible as it is unanswerable. If you come flat out and say that Walter Johnson was the fastest pitcher of all time, no one can really dispute you; they will just want to know how you know. And how *do* you know? Well, you can cite the statistics, namely that he led in strikeouts twelve times, including eight years in a row, and that he was fanning them in droves (over 200 for seven straight years, including over 300 twice) at a time when batters struck out at about two-thirds the rate they do today. And you can say that Walter kept the air between home and the mound simmering just about all the time—his curve was a real lollipop and he seldom threw it. In other words, the batters came up to the plate knowing just what was on the menu and still went away hungry. It is important to emphasize again that it was an era of contact hitting, when the batter choked far up on the handle and just poked at the ball. To illustrate the point with the meat and potatoes of any baseball devotee, statistics: from 1913 through 1925 only seven American League pitchers fanned more than 150 batters in a single season, and they were all named Walter Johnson.

This prime cut of Americana was right out of the national heartland, having been born in Humboldt, Kansas, on November 6, 1887. Walter's father was a farmer, and it was here amid the blowing wheatfields of Kansas that the youngster helped his father work the soil and began developing the mighty physique that would unleash the most fearsome pitch ever seen. In 1901 Walter's father felt the siren call of California and moved the family westward, stirred by the dream of striking oil in that land of endless allure, not knowing that one of the continent's greatest natural resources was before him all the time, swinging from his son's right shoulder. The Johnsons did not strike oil in California and ended up earning a living by supplying mule teams to oilmen.

In 1907 the nineteen-year-old Walter was helping bring the twentieth century to western Idaho. He was working in Weiser, for the Weiser Telephone Company, digging postholes. When he wasn't crunching the Idaho earth with pick and shovel, the young man was pitching for the phone company's baseball team. Now grown and splendidly proportioned, he was in full possession of the pitch Cobb was soon to say was the fastest he ever saw. What the hapless amateurs of western Idaho had to say about it hasn't been recorded; but one captivated spectator had plenty to say. This was a traveling salesman, a gentleman who lives anonymously as part of the Johnson legend. This fellow must have been a Washington Senators fan, because he kept a steady stream of letters and telegrams flowing eastward to Washington manager Joe Cantillon that fairly quivered with superlatives about the young pitcher. The missives stressed two things above all: Johnson's speed and control. "He throws the ball so fast it's like a little white bullet going down to the catcher," the salesman said in one communiqué. In another: "He knows where his pitch is going. Otherwise, there would be dead bodies scattered all over Idaho." Now, from Mountain Man Jim Bridger onward, the Old West was known as fertile ground for tellers of tall tales, and traveling salesmen in particular were known to dabble in hyperbole. Much as Bridger himself was disbelieved when he began describing the spectacular sights he had seen in the place that became Yellowstone National Park, so were the salesman's insistent and persistent reports crumpled up and pitched into the wastebasket. In those days before formal scouting was done, it was quite common for big-league clubs to receive excited reports from small towns or backwoods enthusiasts convinced they had stumbled upon the eighth wonder of the world.

In that same summer of 1907, the Washington club was interested in an outfielder named Clyde Milan who was playing for Wichita of the Western Association. So the club dispatched catcher Cliff Blankenship, who was injured and not playing, to go out west and check out Milan. And while he was there, he was told, he might as well go and have a look at the kid pitcher in Idaho, just to pacify the salesman.

Well, Blankenship liked Milan, who became a mainstay of the Washington outfield for fifteen years, and his eyes popped when he saw Walter. The catcher won Johnson's allegiance with a $100 bill and promise of $350 a month for the rest of the season. And so Walter went to Washington, where he became, along with Presidents Andrew and Lyndon, one of the three most celebrated Johnsons to reside in the nation's capital. Years later, a Washington sportswriter recalled his first glimpse of the new man:

Here, they quickly realized, was everybody's country cousin, a big, handsome, modest hick. Even the rube in him, that was brought into bolder relief by the high-button shoes and celluloid collar that were high fashion in Idaho, couldn't obscure the rare nobility of his facial features. Sandy hair with a reddish tint bristled generously, if somewhat wildly, atop his strong-looking face. He knew little of the pomades that were advertised. The eyes were blue, naturally. The jaw a good one, firm and square cut, if on the shallow side. The nose, a straight one that was to be a model for later-day plastic surgeons. If there was a gimmick to the strength of the Johnson countenance—well, it registered the blush more readily than the smile.

Here he was, just a few years behind Mathewson, another flawless hero, though cut from a different bolt than Matty, who was, after all, polished, well-educated, and a true aristocrat of the diamond. Walter, in his rough-hewn nobility and simple dignity, is made to sound almost Lincolnesque. If Mathewson was what baseball needed at the time, then Johnson was what America, at its storybook best, turned out.

He was a different style of pitcher than Matty, of course. Mathewson probably had the most potent arsenal of any pitcher— good fastball, crackling curve, and that inscrutable fadeaway, all of it meticulously controlled. Walter had his own style, like the man, simple and direct—fastball, fastball, fastball. "It ran in on a right-handed batter and then sank," said the fine old pitcher Ted Lyons, and added, in his voice the strains of admiration, wistfulness, and perhaps the least drop of envy: "His ball did so much." And there you have it—that movement on the ball. Speed alone, as any hitter will tell you, is not enough. Hear a big-league hitter describe somebody's fast one as "being straight as a string" and you are hearing a hungry man describing a steak dinner. The ball must have movement, for it is this that makes the best-laid schemes of a batter *gang aft agley.*

So picture Johnson's lightning bolt as a right-handed batter might. The abbreviated windup—Walter got down to business quickly—and then the big body wheeling and pivoting with the right arm flung back so you can see the ball in his hand far behind him, and then he is coming back toward you, the entire mass of him, his right arm sweeping, and then the buggy-whip snap and the ball is rocketing through thin air and you have to stand there knowing that the merest fraction of error in that smooth yet ferocious delivery can turn a pitch into an assassin's bullet. And not just the speed of course, but that movement, too. Not merely is it coming at you with such sublime speed that you can hear it go by (as some batters swore), but it is also breaking in on you and sinking at the same time, while you have all of two-fifths of a second at the most to time its velocity, decide whether it is a ball or a strike, and move your bat out to meet it.

Cobb? Cobb merely crowded the plate on Johnson, to get as close to the comet as he could, trusting Walter's control, and knowing the big fellow would not throw at him to drive him back. Ever the tactician, Tyrus stacked the odds in his favor before going to war. He came to bat 245 times against Johnson—more than any other pitcher he faced in his career—and connected safely 82 times for a .335 batting average. Sixty-four of the hits were singles, and those that weren't bunts probably all dropped into left field.

Cobb and Johnson. Speed and speed, but different, as different as were the men. Cobb's speed was human; he was the psychotic, driven man, expelling his fury and trying to placate his ever-recycling demons. There were probably psychoanalytic reasons for Cobb's speed, or for that raging edge of it, anyway. Johnson was like a force of nature, and nature reveals no reasons why a man, long arms or not, marvelous physique or not, can throw a baseball to the point of near invisibility. Cobb played with his emotions raw and in full gear, and those of us who are not professional analysts are at least self-assured amateurs and so can finally deal with Tyrus, rightly or wrongly. But Johnson? He fascinates in a way that only Ruth can, and not because of personality but because of that force of nature that he not only possessed but harnessed to his command. If Cobb symbolized the verve and speed of a burgeoning America, Johnson was the demonstration of the strength and power and what it would be when brought to control. Ruth of course would soon become the greater, more graphic symbol; where the modest Johnson was home plate–oriented, the untamable, gregarious Ruth would be sending booming messages in all directions, strength and power and this time, distance.

No, Walter had little personality. He was bland, shy, modest, stoic, and it was this last quality he was going to need in abundance,

for it was a dismal Washington Senators team that he joined, a team
that flailed and struggled ineptly for him through all but the waning
days of his career. Tirelessly and uncomplainingly he whipped in
those fastballs, a most comfortable hero. He did not turn in bravura
performances as a rule; it didn't seem to fit the man's personality.
None of the strikeout records for a game or for consecutive batters
belong to him. Indeed, most of the significant strikeout records belong to later-day pitchers—Koufax, Seaver, Ryan, Carlton. In
Walter's day the single-game strikeout record was Waddell's 17, and
there is no evidence that Johnson ever strove to challenge it. He did
pitch one no-hitter (against the Red Sox in 1920); and in 1908, his
first full season in the bigs, he fired shutouts against the Yankees on
September 4, 5, and 7. He did have his 55²/₃ scoreless innings in 1913.
But generally he was a quiet, unassuming Hercules on the mound,
pouring it on when he had to, letting up when he judged it permissi-
ble, which probably wasn't too often. His teammates worshiped both
the man and the pitcher ("My little tin god," said Ossie Bluege), but
there were no doubt times when Walter would have traded a bit of
adulation for a base hit, for The Big Train more often than not was
hauling a string of cabooses. Overall, he won 416 games, more than
any other twentieth-century pitcher. He also lost 279 games, more
than any other twentieth-century pitcher, and this with a lifetime
earned-run average of 2.17, meaning that with even some modest
hitting he might well have won another 100 games. From 1910
through 1916 he never won fewer than twenty-five games a season,
despite a lineup that bordered on the harmless. Only twice during his
first seventeen big-league seasons did his team rise as high as fourth in
the league in batting average, and only five times did they rise as high
as fourth in runs scored. He was a titanic winner for a chronic loser.
Walter Johnson and the Washington Senators: as close to a baseball
oxymoron as one can get.

Whether or not he was indeed the fastest ever, he remains the
symbol of speed, just as Ruth and not Henry Aaron is the symbol of
the home run. Once, only once, was his American League supremacy
challenged, and it led to what is probably the most dramatic fastball
shootout in all baseball history.

Yes, for one year, 1912, when most sumptuously in his prime,
Walter Johnson had a bona fide rival, an equal. His name was Joe
Wood and they called him Smoky Joe because that's what a sports-
writer who saw him warming up one day said the youngster threw.

And youngster he was, spectacularly precocious, with a tough, boyishly handsome face and a rocket arm that for one year was as good as Johnson's ever was. Youngster he remained, remains, to this day, to whatever day hears the dying sunset trumpets of baseball; for Smoky Joe was destined never to grow old on a mound, never doomed to that inevitable long, slow decline that is the tribute time exacts from its proud, young athletes; he never struggled with slow curves or knucklers, never had to pack his suitcase and ride the sleepers to yet one more stop with that ballplayer's unslakable thirst for one more draught from an arid fountain of youth.

No, Joe Wood did not die at the age of twenty-two after the 1912 season; he in fact pitched effectively but sporadically for three more years. But what froze him on the mound of Boston's Fenway Park forever young, potent, and lethal in the minds of those who conjure the game's legends was the arm injury he suffered in the spring of 1913 that fixed the legend in full furious motion, left it in classic sculpture, unaged and undiminished, immune to decline or compromise. Because the injury was sudden and definitive, it left him prematurely completed and therefore tantalizingly so, unwitting progenitor of what some later writers would come to call the Smoky Joe Wood Syndrome to give historical definition to those careers of lush promise that had been cruelly aborted by injury. The group is small; the austere keepers of this particular flame will tell you there are just three genuinely haunting members: Wood, Brooklyn's Pistol Pete Reiser, and Cleveland's Herb Score. These were the ones with the dazzling natural gifts who were sent once around the carousel, and when next it wheeled about, their seats were empty.

Star of the 1912 World Series when he won three games, including the finale over Mathewson, Joe Wood, still giving interviews ninety-four years after his birth, said he could remember when there was no such thing as a World Series, which is a long and startling piece of remembering. But there was always baseball, at least where young Joe Wood was anyway. When the family decided to relocate from the Midwest to Colorado in 1899, they went by covered wagon, and Joe remembered that when he sat up on the front seat of the wagon next to his father he was wearing his baseball glove. "That," he said, "showed anybody who was interested where *I* wanted to go." The nomadic American is hardly a recent phenomenon; the wagon wheels were always grinding, Wood said. "Wherever you went, you met people going in the opposite direction." New Englanders heading for the Midwest, midwesterners heading for the Pacific Coast, farm boys aiming for the big cities. Back and forth, forth and back, like tides in a bathtub; Americans trying out their great, prodigious country, looking for their special place, their patch of land, their destiny. It was always thus, right from the beginning, from those first Eastern Shore beachheads; an ambitious, energetic people with an astonishing and bountiful continent to explore, conquer, and possess: trapping beaver, leveling forests, hacking trails, slaughtering buffalo, scattering Indians, building settlements, villages, towns and cities, and making the earth yield its bottomless plenty.

Like Walter Johnson's, Joe Wood's father also heard the American El Dorado calling on the wind. Walter's went to California to try and strike oil, but Joe's left the family behind, went north to Alaska to dig for gold along the Yukon River, and came back with frozen feet, "lucky to get out alive," Joe said. Frozen feet or not, the gold fever remained a swelter on his brain and he kept on the hunt in California and then Nevada before giving up. But young Joe understood his father, because the youngster knew about obsession: He had one of his own. Even out in Ouray, in western Colorado, nearly eight thousand feet above sea level, in those glorious ermine-crowned mountains, even out there, in 1903, "those people were crazy about baseball. They used to have town teams," Wood recalled, "and they'd cross the mountains to play each other. Everybody made a great hullabaloo out of those ball games. That was the center of it as far as we were concerned; we just didn't pay much attention to baseball anywhere else."

Imagine, a fourteen-year-old baseball-crazy boy who had worn his glove on the front seat of a covered wagon—to show anybody who was interested where *he* wanted to go—had never heard of John McGraw, Honus Wagner, Christy Mathewson, or Cy Young. But it didn't matter, because even in that insularity, where winters bore the wrath of the gods and deadened the world with what seemed like biblical finality, baseball flourished, as natural a national resource as gold, silver, wheat, and timber, and wherever the game was played was the center of the universe. That fastball was somehow going to get through those mountains or over them, and its owner was going to follow it and play out his own special destiny.

We will never know how many fastballing youngsters became "mute inglorious" Miltons here resting, but the thunderbolts hurled by Walter Johnson in Weiser, Idaho, and Joe Wood in Ouray,

Colorado, were simply too explosive to be missed. By 1908 Wood was pitching for Kansas City in the American Association, and by then he had heard of McGraw, Mathewson, Wagner, and all the rest, and in a moment they would be hearing about him. In August he was sold to the Red Sox and was suddenly a teammate of Cy Young, forty-one years old, big-bellied, and a 21-game winner that year. "For a long time it was said he was the greatest pitcher who ever lived," Wood said; but as far as Joe was concerned, speaking from his ninety-four-year perspective now, "Walter Johnson was the greatest pitcher that ever lived." (And in 1912, Walter answered one of those irresistible questions thusly: "Can I throw harder than Joe Wood? Listen, mister, there's no man alive can throw harder than Smoky Joe Wood.")

Tough, a flashy dresser (see him in his porkpie hat, three-button suit, celluloid collar, and stickpin), perfectly handsome but with no-nonsense eyes that had seen the world from a covered wagon, Colorado peaks, and major-league mounds, carrying himself with the pride of the fireballer. The toast of Ouray was soon the pride of Boston, and it was all so different and yet the same, because it was still baseball, and the thrall of winding up and the excitement of whipping one past a paralyzed batter was the same whether that batter was a miner wearing overalls and a flannel shirt on some hard-scrabble surface of the Rockies or was Ty Cobb or Napoleon Lajoie in the baseball mansions of Detroit or Cleveland. And in 1912 he out-pitched them all, Eddie Plank, Chief Bender, Big Ed Walsh, and yes, even Walter himself, who was 32–12 that year and had to settle for second-best.

Johnson was at his peak then, the unassailable Everest of pitchers, sunlit and glorious on every side. From July 3 through August 23 he was unbeatable, winning an American League record-setting 16 straight games (that's close to a win every three days), topping Jack Chesbro's old mark of 14. But The Big Train hardly had time to savor his achievement, for coming up the tracks behind him was the sleek new locomotive named Joe Wood, winning steadily and insatiably. He began on July 8, already carrying a record of 16–4. By September 6 he was gunning for his fourteenth straight. His opponent that day at Fenway Park? The newly crowned record holder, Walter Johnson. According to one contemporary newspaper account, it was Walter himself who suggested the confrontation, since Joe's regular turn was not due until a day later. Walter, said the account, approached his younger rival and said, "Joe, if you want to beat my record, you will have to beat me." "All right, Walter," said Wood. "I'll see you tomorrow and we can settle it." Spoken like the two true products of the frontier they were, only in this more genteel setting it was to be baseballs instead of six-shooters, and a big-league ball park under blue New England skies instead of some O. K. Corral under a white-hot Southwestern sun. The exchange between Johnson and Wood was amicable; the mutual respect was genuine. But for the unassuming, self-effacing Johnson to have suggested the confrontation allows us a brief, intriguing glimpse into the cylinders of that great competitive engine he kept so finely tuned.

Naturally, Red Sox management acceded to the idea of the match-up. The Boston newspapers, as excitable as newspapers anywhere, went booming with the news. The world was informed with headlines: WOOD AND JOHNSON IN PITCHING DUEL TODAY. Beneath their headline, one paper added: "One of Greatest Battles of Boxmen in Years To Be Fought at Fenway Park."

"The newspapers publicized us like prizefighters," Wood told Lawrence Ritter years later, "giving statistics comparing our height, weight, biceps, triceps, arm span, and whatnot. The champion, Walter Johnson, versus the challenger, Joe Wood."

It was high noon at Fenway Park, Louis and Dempsey in spiked shoes, a classic American duel, two buzzballing thirty-game winners as quick on the draw as any two men that ever lived. Christy Mathewson versus Three Finger Brown, Carl Hubbell versus Dizzy Dean, Sandy Koufax versus Juan Marichal, Tom Seaver versus Bob Gibson: None of them ever engaged in so monumental a measuring of swords or worked under such emotional voltage as Wood and Johnson at Fenway on September 6, 1912.

Sensing yet another moment of history about to break in the historic old city on the Charles River, over thirty thousand Bostonians, straw-hatted George Apleys and cloth-capped Honey Fitzes alike, poured into Fenway that afternoon, poured, filled, and finally overflowed. Those who could not be seated were given standing room on the playing field behind ropes in front of the outfield walls, while others spilled out along the foul lines. Wood warmed up in front of the Boston dugout hemmed in on all sides by fans whose eyes bulged as Smoky Joe began popping his swifty into the catcher's mitt. The living theater that is baseball, with its unforeseeable final acts, was never at more perfect pitch.

Resolute, determined, incomparable, the two leading men gave the crowd what one supposes had to have been inevitable—a 1–0 game. Walter was involved in 64 of them during the often crushing frustrations of his career with the Washington Senators, winning 38 and losing 26. This was one of the latter, because this was Joe Wood's sunlight, his year, the one bright and matchless year that was to be his portion, and nothing was going to stop him, not even the monumental Walter Johnson, who at his gentlemanly twenty-four years seemed like age compared to the dashing twenty-two-year-old Joe Wood. Beat Joe Wood in 1912? *"Listen, mister . . ."*

Fittingly, it was Wood who had the hairbreadth escapes that day, surviving a bases-loaded threat in the third and leaving men in scoring position in the sixth, eighth, and ninth innings, usually escaping with the élan of a strikeout. The lone run was scored in the bottom of the sixth. With two out, Tris Speaker (Wood's roommate and closest friend) hit an opposite-field double into the crowd in left. A moment later, Duffy Lewis did the same, belting an opposite-field two-bagger into the crowd in right, Washington rightfielder Danny Moeller leaping and barely scraping the ball with the tip of his glove (notice those two fine hitters swinging late on Walter). Had the crowd made way for Moeller, one newspaper said the next day, he would have caught the ball "and the game might have gone on until darkness called a halt." But this was a Red Sox crowd, a Joe Wood crowd, and so the ball fell into it and history vibrated.

In winning his fourteenth straight, Wood fanned nine, walked three, and gave up six hits. Walter whiffed five, walked one, gave just five hits. The game was played in one hour and forty-six minutes.

Oh, flair he had, this twenty-two-year-old Joe Wood. Hours after his pulsing victory over the greatest pitcher he ever saw, he announced his engagement to his sweetheart, Laura O'Shea; or, as a Boston paper unblushingly put it: "He also was winning a game far better than the Washington-Boston baseball struggle in which he beat Walter Johnson—and this great game was love." A young lady of classic beauty, Miss O'Shea had some verve of her own. "I don't like to hear anybody call him 'Smoky,' " she told a reporter. "He's just plain Joe to me, and always will be, although I will admit he has some speed—both on and off the diamond."

"Just plain Joe" went on to win his next two starts and made it 16 in a row to tie Johnson for the league record before finally losing. He finished the season with a 34–5 record, 10 shutouts, a storm of strike-outs, a .290 batting average ("I wasn't just a pitcher," he said. "I was a *ballplayer*"), and then three more wins in the World Series including the seventh-game triumph over Christy Mathewson. (And what did a 34-game winner earn in 1912? Oh, around $4,000.)

So he had taken on the world and won, conquered it from the Colorado Rockies to Brahmin Boston. He had beaten Johnson and Mathewson, set records, won the World Series, won the hand of the beauty he loved, and just twenty-two years old, his prime still to come.

And then it was over. The following April he slipped while fielding a ground ball and broke his thumb. When the cast was removed several weeks later he found he could not throw a ball without feeling terrific pain in his shoulder. He tried. He tried harder. There was not too much consideration for injuries in those bare-knuckle days of baseball, not even for thirty-game winners. "I don't know whether I tried to pitch too soon," Wood said, "or whether maybe something happened to my shoulder at the same time." The pain did not go away. "It remained, like a little tooth chewing inside my shoulder."

He was a crashed comet now, pitching when he could, and most of the time winning when he pitched. But his win total over the next three years added up to just 33, one fewer than in his year of glory, and finally the pain became too unbearable for even this tough customer to endure. So he became an outfielder and played several years for Cleveland, where his buddy Speaker was playing and managing. He hit tolerably well, averaging close to .300 before retiring in 1922. He coached baseball at Yale for several decades, and then went on and on into his nineties, indulging an endless flow of enchanted pilgrims who came to his door to talk about baseball games that were played in the age of antiquity. An old man defying a certain romance of mythology that says he died in the spring of 1913, age twenty-three.

"My fastball never came back," he said. Not to Joe Wood, no; but in that mythology it travels yet, undiminished, forever vibrant and free, a comet sighted by all who study the firmament of baseball.

$EVEN

FOR DECADE AFTER DECADE there was heard a certain inevitable litany when any good-old-fashioned baseball bull session came to its summit—the selection of the all-time all-star team. However divisive and inconclusive the debate might be at other positions, the pitching was set. There were always three pitchers; three, it seemed, because no team about to be verbally bronzed for eternity would have looked right if any one of the three had been omitted. They were Mathewson, Johnson, and Alexander, in name and sequence as constant and inseparable as a classic vaudeville act or venerable Wall Street law firm, though the truth was they really did not see that much of one another. Mathewson had only a few years left when Alexander came into the league with the Phillies in 1911, and Johnson of course was employed in the American League. Alex made an immediate and indelible impression on Matty, who wrote about the new man in his book, *Pitching in a Pinch*, published in 1912. Pitching for the first time against the Cincinnati club, Alexander was being harassed by the sharp-tongued Clark Griffith, Cincinnati's manager. In a tense situation with several Reds runners on base, Griffith yelled at the rookie pitcher, "Now here is where we get a look at the 'yellow.' " According to Mathewson, Alexander walked toward Griffith and shouted back that he was "going to make that big boob up at the bat" show such a "yellow streak that you won't be able to see any white." Alex then returned to the mound and struck his man out. "Griffith," wrote Matty with evident satisfaction, "had tried the wrong tactics."

When baseball fans talk of the year of the Golden Rookies, they most frequently genuflect to 1936, when Bob Feller and Joe DiMaggio invaded the American League, each a conquering force come to stay and prevail. The accolade for 1936, however, is mostly for the coincidence of arrival, for despite the glamor of their blazing talents, Feller, a late starter that season, won but five games and DiMaggio batted .323. It was their subsequent careers that made 1936 significant. For high-style freshman achievement, however, 1936 is a mighty thin slice compared to 1911; for that was the year when rookie outfielder Joe Jackson batted .408 in 147 games for Cleveland, while a new man in the National League, twenty-four-year-old right-hander Grover Cleveland Alexander, was 28–13 for a fourth-place Philadelphia Phillies team that was seventh in runs scored. For astonished Philadelphia fans who might have spent the winter of 1911–12 wondering if their young world-beater was really that good, well, they had these win totals to look forward to for the next six years: 19, 22, 27, 31, 33, 30. Overall for his first seven years, Alex was 190–88, a winning percentage not far from .700. The three straight thirty-game seasons tied a Mathewson record set from 1903 to 1905.

So again, one of those questions that lurk in the baseball under-brush: Who was better, Alex or Matty? Well, it seems that history itself couldn't decide between them, each of these pitchers finishing their careers with identical win totals of 373, the National League record, and one of the most intriguing statistics in all of baseball. The personal advocacy is hardly surprising, breaking down this way: Those who played against Mathewson in his prime think he was the premier pitcher; those who played against Alexander think he was. Among the latter is Burleigh Grimes, himself a Hall of Fame right-hander who won 270 games in his career.

"If anybody was ever a better pitcher than that guy," said Grimes, "I wouldn't know what his name was. It was just a pleasure to watch him work, even though he was beating your brains out most of the time. Smooth and easy—always smooth and easy. He threw a sinker and a curve. Always kept them down. He was fast, too. I'll say he was! That thing would come zooming in and then kick in about three inches on a right-handed hitter. He'd throw you that fastball and that curve, and you couldn't tell which was which because they didn't do anything until they were right on top of you. And once they showed you what they were going to do and where they were going to do it, your bat was someplace else. Yeah, he's my pitcher, Alex."

Alex or Matty. Who was better? For an answer, perhaps we should take a clue from the elementary school boy who was asked by his teacher which city was closer to the equator, Honolulu or Rio de

Janeiro. After pondering the question for several moments, he replied, "Neither."

Grover Cleveland Alexander occupies a unique niche along the corridors of American legend. Equal in glory with Mathewson and Johnson, he outdid them in drama and tragedy. His is the most poignant superstar story in all of baseball, a story that began with matchless talent and beguiling innocence and kept going through an ever-deepening and darkening abyss of horror, illness, and self-degradation. We, who prefer our heroes to be luminous with purity, cannot condemn the fall from grace of the one known, inevitably, as Alexander the Great, because he became suddenly a prototypical victim of a world and a time he never made and was utterly unprepared for. Named for a sitting president, he was later to have a future president portray him on the screen in a movie based on his life (*The Winning Team*, starring Ronald Reagan, made in 1952, two years after Alex's death).

Alexander was born on February 26, 1887, on a farm near St. Paul, a small town in the Nebraska sandhills that was a shipping point for the surrounding agricultural communities. He grew to be a tall (six foot one inch), lanky, shy, freckle-faced, good-natured youngster with, naturally, that zest for baseball that always seems to come with the talent. There must be a self-propelling drive in that talent, a drive that will brook neither resistance nor obstruction, a drive that demonstrates its own mindless reasoning with implacable forward motion. It was there from inception in all of them, McGraw, Mathewson, Cobb, and Joe Wood, a passion that by itself compels baseball to be important. And they all have their early, folksy stories upon which later tales of grandeur are built. Alex? Well, supposedly the Nebraska farmboy hunted chickens and turkeys with rocks; even then, we are told, possessing control uncanny enough to stun or brain his prey, the same control that would later enable him to fire a baseball from the mound into an opening no larger than a tomato can. Should we believe it? Why not?—in 1923 he pitched 305 innings and walked just 30 men, or slightly less than one every ten innings. With Alex, the legend looks suspiciously like fact.

So once more, Grover Cleveland Alexander in Nebraska, far from the madding crowd, as were Walter Johnson in Idaho and Joe Wood in Colorado, pumping baseballs with uncommon speed and accuracy, waiting for the call to glory, and for Alex, the weighted drop to tragedy, his indissolubly compounded destiny. For in contrast to the eternal prime of Joe Wood, Alex grew wearily and sadly old; but from out of that length of years was to come one final sunburst so brilliant it left his twilight sky with a permanent glow.

Alexander began pitching his way eastward on the rough-surfaced diamonds of Nebraska, deadening the bats of semipro teams with enough emphasis for the word to start spreading. In 1909 he was pitching for the Galesburg, Illinois, team in the Illinois-Missouri League, earning a modest $100 a month and posting a 15–8 record. His season ended prematurely when he suffered a serious injury. Going into second base standing up on a double play, he took the full force of the shortstop's relay square in the head. Carried from the field, he remained unconscious for two days. When he finally came to he was unable to focus his eyes and was afflicted with double vision. Baseball being a tough business in those days, Galesburg sold his contract to Indianapolis, omitting the fact that the young pitcher was pitching to two batters at once. When Alex arrived in Indianapolis the skipper there decided to have a first-hand look at the new recruit in batting practice. Alex promptly caved in the man's rib cage with a steaming fastball and earned himself passage back to St. Paul.

Continuing to be plagued with double vision, Alexander refused to give up. He threw to whoever would catch him, somehow convinced that the only way to solve his problem was to throw a baseball, for a man of his compulsions a naive but understandable bit of reasoning. He said later that if he had stopped throwing he "would have gone to pieces." Obviously that live, unappeasable snake of a right arm was not in communication with his head and was wondering where all those batters had gone, and so it refused to die, working up and down like some stubborn, independent pump handle in tireless reflex. In whatever backyard or empty lot he could find in St. Paul, Nebraska, to whoever would, and could (yes, could: Remember who it is we're talking about here), hold up the glove to him, he kept pitching and pitching, in his pain and his anguish like some fanatical supplicant calling on the one agency he believed in, performing day in and day out his ritualistic act of faith. And who are we to say that the grimly repetitive ritual, the faith, did not enact restoration, for suddenly and for no logical reason, in the midst of pitching to a friend in the St. Paul schoolyard, his plural world abruptly flashed singular again, and the tall, lanky Nebraska farm-

The Polo Grounds, 1886.

Connie Mack.

Rube Waddell.

John McGraw.

Christy Mathewson.

Honus Wagner.

Ty Cobb.

Grover Cleveland Alexander.

Joe Wood and Walter Johnson.

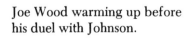

Joe Wood warming up before
his duel with Johnson.

Joe Jackson.

Lefty Williams and Eddie Cicotte.

Buck Weaver.

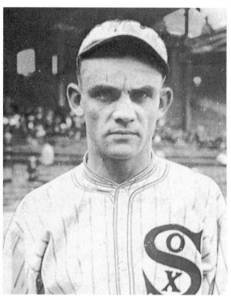

Happy Felsch.

Fred McMullin.

Kenesaw Mountain Landis.

boy was heading east once more, to become part of the mighty litany: Mathewson, Johnson, and Alexander.

As Galesburg had done unto Indianapolis, so did Indianapolis do unto Syracuse—suavely pass along the contract of an impaired pitcher. But this time the pitcher was not impaired. In 1910 Alex worked for Syracuse and won 29 games, one fewer than he would win a year later for Philadelphia, to whom he was sold for $500.

They called him Old Low-and-Away because that's where he threw the ball, slicing off corners of the plate with knee-high fastballs and short, sharp-breaking curves that were probably ancestral to today's sliders. Statistics? Yes, right up there with those of his partners in the triumvirate. Along with those three thirty-game seasons there are the 1.22 earned-run average in 1915, 16 shutouts (the major-league record) in 1916, four one-hitters in 1915, and five times the leader in strikeouts, shutouts, wins, and complete games in his first seven years—those masterful Philadelphia years, which he always said were the happiest of his life, the years when he built the brighter side of his legend, before the torments of an incomprehensible world came storming at him.

In 1917, that watershed year in American history, Alexander's manager, Pat Moran, said about him, "Not only is Alexander great because of his pitching work, but he's an invaluable member of the team because of his splendid character. He is the easiest star pitcher to handle I have ever known. He is willing to work out of turn, no matter the weather, no matter if he is feeling fit or not. He is always ready for the call of duty. He is a model athlete and one of the cleanest, manliest fellows I have ever known."

Yes, he was always "willing to work." He surely proved that on September 23, 1916, and again on September 3, 1917, when he pitched and won both ends of a doubleheader, trying to carry his team to a pennant, as he had done in 1915 when his 31 wins brought Philadelphia its first National League championship. (They are an all but extinct species today, these thirty-game winners; but once they stalked the land, great mythic creatures, pitching and winning doubleheaders.)

He won the opener against the Red Sox in the 1915 Series, the only game the Phillies were to win (nor would they win another World Series game until 1980), holding Tris Speaker hitless and retiring a pinch-hitting rookie pitcher named Babe Ruth in the ninth, while sore-armed Joe Wood watched from the bench. ("Sometimes," the old man named Joe Wood said nearly seven decades later, "I'd be sitting on the bench during a game with my arms folded and all of a sudden realize my left hand was working its fingers into my right shoulder like it was trying to find something.") Would he have liked to pitch against Alexander? Wood was asked. "Lord, yes," said the man who had matched serves with Cy Young, Rube Waddell, Walter Johnson, and Christy Mathewson. "I would have loved to pitch against Grover Cleveland Alexander. I think it would have been a good match."

Alex's opponent that day was Ernie Shore, a tall North Carolinian who recalled not only Alexander's mound mastery but his "sweet, likable nature. He seemed utterly delighted by the most foolish antics or the merest jokes, giving out an easy unforced laughter like a boy at the circus. Great pitcher or not, he was still a country boy pure and fresh, and all our fellows thought he was tops, even though we knew he was going to stand us on our heads."

Well, there were a lot of country boys pure and fresh, and along with the genially smiling and uncomplicated Grover Cleveland Alexander they were about to go by the tens of thousands across the Atlantic in troopships to help attend the savage birth of a new world, coming out of it—if they came out at all—abruptly matured and forever changed, the world they left behind suddenly a quaint scrapbook of nostalgia.

For decades America had been striving toward stage center, and finally we were there, making it in the way of nations, not with moral grandeur or with scientific or cultural daring, but through blood and conquest. Amazed and fascinated, an ocean away, we watched it happen, an unveiling of monstrosities as madness built upon madness until the last plaintive cries of reason had been smothered. In the summer of 1914 we read the line scores as they were chalked onto the blackboards of neighborhood saloons—a gimmick to attract patrons—watching the Boston Braves become a "miracle" team by climbing from last place on July 4 to win the pennant and then dispatch Connie Mack's A's in four straight in the Series. Meanwhile, other chalkboards of 1914 were reporting this:

July 28: Austria-Hungary declares war on Serbia.
August 1: Germany declares war on Russia.
August 3: Germany declares war on France.
August 4: Great Britain declares war on Germany.

August 6: Austria-Hungary declares war on Russia.
August 23: Japan declares war on Germany.

Not to be outdone, major-league baseball found itself in a war of its own that year. A brand-new big-league concoction called the Federal League anointed itself, placed teams in Chicago, Brooklyn, Pittsburgh, St. Louis, Baltimore, Kansas City, Buffalo, and Indianapolis, and began stocking its clubs by the old tried-and-true way—the sound of a flapping checkbook. There were outcries, curses, threats, denunciations, and litigation. It was 1901 all over again, and if a fulminating Ban Johnson saw the irony of the situation, he didn't let on.

Some big names succumbed to the fatal lure of the long green— Detroit's George Mullin, Chicago's Three Finger Brown and Joe Tinker, Philadelphia's Eddie Plank and Chief Bender—but they were all near the end of the road anyway. Cobb, Speaker, Johnson, and the other glory names were tempted but held in place by grudging salary increases. The closest to jump was Johnson. Walter had just finished averaging 32 wins a season from 1912 to 1914 when the Chicago club of the new league offered him a $16,000 contract, plus a signing bonus of $10,000. Walter, earning $12,000 for Clark Griffith's Senators, was sorely tempted, especially after receiving an astonishing letter from Griffith. In it the owner pointed out that Walter's win total had dropped from 36 in 1913 to "only" 28 in 1914, and therefore Walter had no business asking Griff to meet the Federals' offer. (Griff sounds as though he had studied diplomacy at the feet of some of his highly placed contemporaries in Europe.)

The letter set a fuse burning in the normally saintly Walter, and he was about to reach for his suitcase when Griffith came to his senses and agreed to meet the $16,000 figure. But what about the $10,000 signing bonus, which Walter was also demanding? Well, they called Griffith The Old Fox, and it was not without reason. Unable (or unwilling) to ante up the ten grand, Griff slyly pointed out to Chicago White Sox owner Charlie Comiskey how bad it would be for Charlie's club to have Walter Johnson pitching in Chicago for the Federal League competition. Comiskey could throw a half nelson on a dollar bill as well as anyone, but he was also a realist. So he cut a check for ten big ones, shut his eyes and handed it to Griff, who handed it to Walter, and The Big Train continued to make stops only at American League depots.

Cobb was offered a three-year contract for $100,000 if he would bring his grainy disposition and .400 bat to the new league. Tyrus, then earning $12,000 a year for Detroit, turned it down. Detroit owner Frank Navin rewarded Cobb's loyalty with an increase to $20,000, making the game's greatest player also its highest-paid.

Though it was well-heeled in spots (Federal League entrepreneurs included oil tycoon Harry Sinclair and Robert Ward of the Ward Bakeries), the Federal League lasted but two years. In its second and final year, 1915, some of its clubs were selling tickets for ten cents and not finding many takers. The upstart league remains little more than a blur upon the history of baseball. If the Federal League achieved anything besides increasing salaries for star players and providing headaches for American and National League club owners, it was to establish once and for all the unchallengeable position of the two big leagues. Just as *Homo sapiens* was equipped with two arms, two legs, two eyes, and so forth, so America required just two major leagues and no more.

Baseball's example of settling a war relatively quickly and bloodlessly made no impression on the foreign ministries of Europe. Thanks to stalemated armies, unimaginative commanders, suicidal frontal assaults, and an advanced technology for killing, Americans were hearing such incomprehensible things as sixty thousand men being killed or wounded in one day at the Somme River. Tanks, machine guns, poison gas, long-range artillery, and bombs dropped from airplanes—they rattled the headlines like events taking place on another planet. For Americans, there was no last, somnolent drowse of peace to be shattered, nothing comparable to that pastoral prewar summer of 1914 that England had enjoyed, that summer of sunlit Edwardian idylls that was actually the twilight of an era. American innocence was being eroded by degrees, by that other new weapon, the submarine, which the Germans were employing with indiscriminate terror under the Atlantic waves. British shipping was going down, including liners carrying American citizens, 124 of whom died in the sinking of the *Lusitania* in 1915. There were others in 1916 and 1917. Isolationist sentiment in the country was rapidly melting, and on April 2, 1917, the inevitable occurred when President Woodrow Wilson asked Congress for a declaration of war on Germany.

So America was finally part of it, and it wasn't just this European conflict, but that we had at last broken the walls of our fortress America and reached deeply and irretrievably into the concerns of the world. But despite the solemnity of the occasion, despite the tight-lipped Presbyterian firmness and eloquence of our president, there was still an ingenuous quality to it all. Fight? Fine. But with what? United States Army regulars numbered just under 100,000, a total the Western Front abattoirs could consume in just a few days of engagement.

The only way to raise an army in a hurry was through conscription. Accordingly, the draft was enacted into law, and early in June 1917 nearly ten million American males between the ages of twenty-one and thirty-one began signing up at their polling places. Resistance to the draft was scattered and minimal. The country had not been involved in a major bloodletting since the Civil War, now more than a half-century in the past and highly romanticized in word and song anyway; and so patriotic fervor ran high.

Baseball got through the 1917 season virtually unscathed, only a handful of players going off to war, with Boston Braves catcher Hank Gowdy the first major-leaguer to enlist. (Twenty-five years later, the fifty-three-year-old Gowdy did it all over again, getting himself a captain's commission in the army.) In 1918, however, the rosters took a beating. In late May the provost marshal of the armed forces, General Enoch Crowder, issued a "work or fight" order that stipulated that men in nonessential industries either find themselves work related to the war effort or be drafted. Baseball—and this might have come as a shock to some—was deemed a nonessential occupation (it is doubtful if the fans in Brooklyn were ever completely convinced). With rosters being depleted and fan interest diverted by the European bloodbath, the owners decided to terminate the season on Labor Day, trimming the season by twenty-five to thirty games per team. The Cubs–Red Sox World Series began on September 5 and wound up on September 11. A quarter of a century later, baseball was so deeply a part of the national ethos that, not even with a bigger, more devastating, terrifying, and threatening war, would anyone monkey around with the baseball schedule.

Among those who went off to war were Cincinnati's thirty-eight-year-old manager Christy Mathewson, and stars like Grover Cleveland Alexander, Herb Pennock, Sam Rice, Harry Heilmann, Eddie Collins, Dutch Leonard, Wally Pipp, Jimmy Dykes, Bob Shawkey, Ernie Shore, Urban Shocker, Red Faber, Eppa Rixey, Casey Stengel, Rabbit Maranville, Jack Barry, and many others. Unlike World War II, however, when some players had three or four years gouged from their careers, most of the game's World War I fighting men lost only part of the 1918 season and were back home soon after the November armistice. Ironically, of all the major stars, it was those two pitching marvels of the National League, Mathewson and Alexander, who suffered the longest-lasting effects of their military service. Matty inhaled some poison gas in the trenches in France, causing severe and lasting damage to his lungs.

When he boarded a troopship as part of General John J. Pershing's American Expeditionary Force, Alexander was a sergeant in the 342nd Artillery Battalion of the Eighty-ninth Division, an outfit made up largely of Kansas and Nebraska farmboys. (He was also lately an employee of the Chicago Cubs. The previous November the Phillies, fearing their ace was going to be drafted, had dealt him to the Cubs for two nondescript players and $60,000. Alex won two of three decisions for Chicago and then went off to war.) A photograph of him on the deck of the troopship shows the thirty-one-year-old pitcher in overseas cap, knee-length overcoat with sergeant's chevrons on the right sleeve, canvas leggings, and ankle-high boots. He is squinting in the sunlight, in his face still some of the guilelessness of the Nebraska farmboy. He knows he is going to cross an ocean and fight a war, he has heard of the new weapons and the awesome slaughter; still, he is a portrait of the unsuspecting. There are other doughboys in the picture, and they are staring not at the camera but at Grover Cleveland Alexander, at that moment a treasured and unsullied demigod in khaki, fresh off of three thirty-game seasons, in the prime of his life and at the peak of his fame, who might have been squinting at a red sun setting behind the Nebraska sandhills.

A few months later that freshness of expression was gone, for Alex, for all of them, along with whatever illusions they might have brought with them. Units of Alex's battalion were caught in the trenches by a roaring bombardment from German howitzers hurling forty-six-pound shells. He huddled protectively against the unoffending earth of France, the ground shuddering around him, the exploding shells loosening every rock and stone and earthen clod, throwing them into the thundering concussive air, and then hurling them back down like disintegrating mountains. The experience left Alexander deaf in one ear, his soul shaken into epileptic seizures that plagued him for the rest of his life, and with a desperate helplessness that only whisky could exorcise.

A dozen years later Alexander was sitting on the bench during spring training. "Some kids up in the grandstand started shooting off fireworks," teammate Bill Hallahan recalled. "A few of the guys gave a little start with each burst. But Alex never budged. He just sat there stiff as a board, teeth clenched, fists doubled over so tight his knuckles were white, staring off into space like he was hypnotized. When finally somebody came and chased the kids off and the noise stopped, he turned and looked at me with a sad little smile."

EIGHT

THE WORLD may have gone to hell for four years, the doughboys may have returned with far fewer illusions than they took away with them, and the victors may have been in the process of fumbling away their victory at Versailles; there may have been race riots in northern cities, the Ku Klux Klan may have been stirring their caldrons of hate with impunity, and a radical labor union called the Industrial Workers of the World (known as Wobblies) may have been having its members beaten, jailed, and murdered; the responsibilities of a world power and the surging maelstrom of a modern era may have been shaking the self-assurance of some Americans reluctant to discard comfortable old values; the war may have literally and figuratively torn the world apart, burying forever the old decayed European dynasties and giving birth to the Russian Revolution with its black night of unforeseeable horrors: all of those things and countless others. But for those Americans who sought to slip into something more comfortable, still available to them was the escape to the timeless and unchanging rhythms of the national game, that dependable old ritual that was as immune to change as a Sabbath ceremony.

More dependable than an heirloom watch, as true as sunrise and moonbeams, forever planting the seedlings of its own continuity, as logical as appetite and indulgence, it was there, almost part of nature, encompassing the four seasons with spherical symmetry. It rose in the spring, stretched its length across the summer, culminated with a crowned champion in the fall, and then was endlessly recalled and debated through its wintry hibernation, binding together all the divisions of nature like some benignly overarching fifth season: the special, magical, undying season of baseball.

Baseball remained above reproach, the unassailable democratic institution, the mighty leveler, the most equitable of all breeding grounds, where the short man could best the tall, the dull be swifter than the wise, and the poor humble the rich. If black could not play

94

with white, well, prejudice and stereotyping were still too indelibly part of the national fabric to make it seem wrong.

Despite the roughnecks and the drunkards who had passed through its ranks, the game's image had remained unstained. This secular religion and its apostles like Mathewson, Johnson, Wagner, Alexander, and those others who could be unreservedly admired, were the beneficiaries of the game's relentless propaganda machine that was tirelessly churning out a dogma that amounted to an American ideology in action: fair play, good sportsmanship, teamwork. The blend with the larger American dream was seamless.

Helping to color and popularize, romanticize and mythologize the players and the game were the sportswriters, a hearty brand of fellow travelers who were infected with the prevailing virus that baseball and America were synonymous, each redolent with the virtues of the other. It was a case of partial truths being shrewdly woven into a convincing tapestry. The players, the crown princes of this empire-within-a-republic, were protected by the writers who ignored stories their professional descendants of a later day would have framed in headlines. Things were reported in an arch, ingenuous style in accord with recording events that were played out in some cozy wonderland. On April 19, 1910, President Taft and Vice-President Sherman attended a game in Washington. One writer's report of this visit from high up read:

President Taft went to the Base Ball game to-day, saw Washington beaten, 8–4, by the Boston Americans, was initiated into the mysteries of the "spit ball," shared a five-cent bag of peanuts with Vice-President Sherman, wished hard for Washington to win and said sadly that he hoped he was not a hoodoo.

Mr. Sherman kept a detailed score of the game, supplying the President with such statistical information as he asked for, and caused some one in the party to remark that if he ever lost the job of Vice-President, he might get a place on Ban Johnson's scoring staff. [Then, as now, vice-presidents were delegated crucial assignments.]

The President was the center of interest up to the sixth inning, when Washington got the bases full, with no one out. Then the ruling passion put the chief executive temporarily in eclipse and the faithful rooters nearly yelled their heads off for Delehanty to "Hit 'er out!" and for Charley Street to "Biff it in the eye!"

Mr. Taft was as interested as all the rest. He knows Base Ball thoroughly and is up on all the finer points of the game. The day was ideal for the national game.

It's all there. Even the president gets into the leveling process. He comes to the ball game and is a regular guy, eating peanuts and rooting for the home team. But not even the president of the United States, not even one that weighs 300 pounds, can remain the center of attention when the home team loads the bases. The president "knows Base Ball thoroughly." The equation is important. Even President Wilson, who probably cared as much for baseball as he did for the measles, showed up for the 1915 World Series. Wilson, however, gave himself away; he was twenty minutes late, causing the start of the game to be delayed. That would not happen today, on two counts: no politico would dare be late for a World Series game, and the start of no World Series game would be held up for a president. The balance of power has shifted.

There was a lovely fairy-tale quality to it all, but there was a darker side, too.

With the kind of fan enthusiasm the game engendered, gambling upon it was natural and inevitable. Baseball provided a new and fertile enchantment for the sporting crowd, whose investment opportunities had hitherto been pretty much limited to horse racing and prizefighting. And since gambling is often equated with corruption, corruption was not long in being equated with baseball. With all that money being wagered on the outcome of a game, it seemed to make perfectly good sense to certain people to arrange the outcome. As far back as 1877, when the National League was in its second year, founding president William Hulbert was compelled to expel from the league and ban for life four players on the Louisville club for throwing games.

In a photograph taken in 1884 showing a game in progress at the Polo Grounds (then located in New York City at Fifth Avenue and 110th Street), a painted warning is clearly visible along the front of the rightfield grandstands: NO BETTING ALLOWED ON THESE GROUNDS. The injunction was no doubt sincerely meant, but its impact was decidedly negligible. Betting on ball games was as indigenous to a day at the ball park as green grass and fresh air. Gamblers circulated through the stands quoting odds to whoever was interested, with nothing furtive or circumspect about it.

Gambling was so widespread in the country that many of its higher-rolling practitioners were looked upon as respectable men. Indeed, before baseball became more discriminating about who it let through its executive turnstiles, ball clubs were occasionally controlled by men euphemistically known as sportsmen. Frank Farrell, one of two partners who were the first owners of the New York Yankees franchise, was one of the city's best-known gamblers. His partner, William (Big Bill) Devery, was long remembered as New York's most corrupt police commissioner, quite a heady status to have achieved in those rip-roaring gas-lit days.

Gambling at the ball parks became so flagrant after the turn of the century that some clubs began circulating private detectives through the stands to stop the practice and eject the gamblers. While this gave the game a cleaner appearance, it did not prevent betting on games in pool halls, barber shops, taverns, and other places where venture capitalists gathered. Now, not every man who drew on a big-league uniform in those days was immune to the thrills of temptation. A ballplayer knowing that little mounds of money were being exchanged because of his performance on a given day could get to indulging in seductive reveries. Many did, and some began acting them out—how many, we cannot be sure. The sportswriters of the day certainly weren't telling; they had taken a vow of silence when it came to staining the image of the fantasy world Americans found so clean-limbed and inspiring. Those writers who did mention their suspicions to their editors were told to let it pass. Apparently there was enough corruption in the political wards, the police department, and other municipal byways to suffice. A cynical populace accepted it as integral to the system. But baseball? Its blemishes were better glossed over. The escapist dreams of apple-piety Main Street had to be protected.

In his book of memoirs, *Baseball As I Have Known It*, veteran baseball writer Fred Lieb recalls an episode that occurred in 1913. Yankees manager Frank Chance disgustedly told Lieb and another writer that his first baseman, Hal Chase, was "throwing games on me." When Lieb reported this to his editor, he was told to "pass it up." Lieb suggests that Chase's shenanigans were common knowledge around the American League, but that nothing was done, except for Chase soon being dealt away from New York to the White Sox.

The notorious Hal Chase was a scintillating talent, so magical around first base that one team after another was willing to risk hiring him, probably figuring that a Hal Chase that gave you his all even 80 percent of the time was preferable to anybody else. This is another way of emphasizing how rare and how prized exceptional talent is. If you're temperamental, eccentric, abrasive, alcoholic, ethically dubious, but you can hit or pitch, your continued presence will be rationalized.

For those who saw him play first base, Hal Chase was forever the standard, sometimes approached, never equaled. He seems to have had mongoose qualities when it came to fielding bunts. Lieb claims Chase was quick enough to pick up bunts on the third-base side of the mound and nab runners at any of the three bases. Remember now, this is in the dead-ball era when the bunt was an important offensive weapon, and a first baseman (who, admittedly, did not play as deep as they do today) who could squash these little squigglers before they became hits or successful sacrifices was a blue-ribbon item. Chase must have possessed remarkable agility (for fielding bunts and for staying out of jail, too). He was also something of an innovator in the field, being one of the first to play wide of the bag and one of the few who could execute the 3–6–3 double play with unerring skill. He was apparently good enough, too, to dump a game and leave behind suspicions that were clouded with doubt. You've got to be pretty damned adept at what you're doing to deliberately fluff a play and not leave your teammates squinting too sharply at you. Roger Peckinpaugh, then a young shortstop with the Yankees, recalled one of Chase's dubious maneuvers:

I remember a few times I threw a ball over to first base, and it went by him to the stands and a couple of runs scored. It really surprised me. I'd stand there looking, sighting the flight of that ball in my mind, and I'd think, "Geez, that throw wasn't that bad." Then I'd tell myself that he was the greatest there was, so maybe the throw was bad. Then later on when he got the smelly reputation, it came back to me, and I said, "Oh-oh." What he was doing, you see, was tangling up his feet and then making a fancy dive after the ball, making it look like it was a wild throw.

Like many notable rogues, Chase could be a charmer. He was, by all accounts, witty, intelligent, and personable, eminently likable. He was also described as having a "corkscrew brain." Given his apparent inability to think straight, New York, where he began his big-league career in 1905, was probably not the most ethically healthful place for Chase. The twenty-two-year-old Californian hit the sidewalks of the big city running; along with his unprecedented glides and whirls around first base and an engaging personality that was animated by a winning smile, Prince Hal (yes, they did call him that) knew how to box, was a virtuoso with a pool cue, and a dead shot with a rifle. This suggests that whatever education he had included some time spent on the other side of the tracks, places where, if discussions of ethics ever came up, they centered on how best to live one's life around them.

So this was no ingenuous rookie hitting the big time, no gullible bumpkin unstrapping his suitcase in the big city. Chase soon became a drawing card by dint of his spectacular glovework. And the young Californian with the bright smile but guarded eyes soon revealed his penchant for gambling. As a baseball celebrity and as one of the pets of high-stakes gambler and club owner Frank Farrell, he was made welcome. What intrigued the boys around the dens where optimism blows forever hot was Chase's predilection for betting on ball games, including some in which he was a participant. Now, it would take a man with the moral fiber of a saint to whack out base hits and spear crucial grounders and pegs in a game in which his money was riding on the other team, as Chase's sometimes was. Occasionally, it was said, Hal shored up a sure thing by giving a teammate a piece of the action and then letting the man decide for himself where his best interests lay. Some teammates cooperated, some did not. Among the latter was a young right-hander named Jimmy Ring, a rookie team-mate of Chase's on the 1917 Cincinnati Reds. When before a game that Ring was starting Chase offered to increase the weight of Ring's wallet if Jimmy would dilute his best efforts, Ring told him, "If you ever say anything like that to me again, I'll beat the livin' shit out of you." Jimmy was one tough bruiser from the hard-fisted precincts of Maspeth, Long Island, and so Chase just smiled and walked away.

That Hal Chase's machinations were no secret was amply borne out later. After Frank Chance sent him to the White Sox, Hal jumped to the Federal League, and when that foredoomed enterprise folded up, joined Cincinnati in 1916. He led the league in batting that year with a .339 average and continued on as the Nijinsky of first base, when he felt like it, as teammates sighed, sportswriters chuckled or shook their heads, and fans went on buying tickets and going through the turnstiles with the faith of churchgoers. This time, however, Chase was performing his capers in the lengthening shadows of Judgment Day. The first of these shadows was cast by his Cincinnati skipper, none other than the game's first genuine icon, Christy Mathewson himself. Hal was about to get his head caught in a couple of slamming Sinai tablets.

When George Stallings, Frank Chance's predecessor as Yankee

manager, came right out and accused Chase of throwing games, Ban
Johnson chastised him for staining the name of a top drawing card.
When Frank Chance said the same thing, he was ignored. (Indeed,
when Chance traded Chase to the White Sox Frank Farrell was so
outraged he soon canned Chance.) But when Christy Mathewson
questioned Chase's honesty, people had to listen. Demigods speak in
thunder. By 1918 the demigod had seen enough and reported to
National League president John Heydler that Chase was throwing
games. Hal got a reprieve on this occasion, however, for just as
Heydler began his investigation of the matter, Mathewson joined the
army and went overseas. With his chief accuser in the trenches of
France, Chase was able to survive for another year. Baseball writer
Fred Lieb reported that in an off-the-record conversation with
Heydler, the league president said he believed Mathewson but lacked
the proof to make the charge stand up.

Interestingly enough, Chase's final big-league year, 1919, was
spent playing for John McGraw. Why McGraw decided to hire the
shady rascal is a mystery, particularly in light of Mathewson's
charges. It's true that the Giants needed a first baseman, and perhaps
McGraw, with his sense of omniscience, felt that his mere presence
would be injunction enough to intimidate Chase into honesty. But
even John J. must have felt at times that having Chase on the team
was like carrying around a parcel handed to you by an anarchist. As a
reformer and a deterrent, McGraw failed. Not only was he unable to
stop Chase from "funnying" up a game, but Hal's virus was apparently infectious. In mid-August the Giants announced that both
Chase and third baseman Heinie Zimmerman had been suspended
indefinitely. "Indefinitely" in this case meant permanently. Neither
Chase nor Zimmerman, whom Hal may well have cajoled into some
dubious investment opportunities, ever played in organized ball
again, though no formal charges were ever filed against either man,
nor did either man try to get back into the game.

Chase continued playing baseball, semipro, in Mexico, Arizona,
and New Mexico until well into his forties, and those dazzling skills
began to fade. One can only speculate what thoughts went through
that "corkscrew" brain as he moved from one dusty town to another,
being Hal Chase, Prince Hal, incomparable darling of New York
fans, upon the rocky, hard-surfaced diamonds of mining towns and
waystations, performing his 3–6–3 whirligigs for a few dollars under
the broiling white sun of the Southwest. If he had any regrets, he left

them unrecorded. He died on May 18, 1947, in Colusa, California, age sixty-four, leaving behind a legacy of smiles, charm, wizardry, and deceit—the Benedict Arnold of baseball.

Had baseball been more vigilant and decisive when it came to dealing with the Hal Chases in its midst, the greatest scandal in the history of American sports might never have happened. By studiously ignoring Chase and others of his kind, big-league baseball was allowing small fires to burn freely in its basement, with the naive hope that they would put themselves out. This approach was perhaps a remnant of that prewar America that believed if things went wrong they at least would never go dangerously so, that a country so in control of its own destiny would, when irregularities threatened to become unmanageable, easily slip them back into place. But it wasn't happening like that anymore, not in baseball, not in the country at large.

The war that Americans had fought and supported so ardently and enthusiastically was leaving a sour, cynical, and bitter taste in the aftermath of victory. Race riots that struck northern cities in the summer of 1919 were fomented in part by black war veterans who offended whites by seeking something of the better life they had ostensibly been fighting for. The Boston police force went on strike, and in September Massachusetts Governor Calvin Coolidge became a national figure when he sent the state militia to patrol the streets of Boston, declaring that there was "no right to strike against the public safety by anybody, anywhere, anytime." An anti-Communist hysteria suddenly swept the land, leading to "Red Raids" ordered by Attorney General Mitchell Palmer that saw the illegal jailing of many American citizens. And with a last surge of nineteenth-century morality, Congress was stirring an unrealistic brew called Prohibition that would soon become the law of the land and lead to bootleggers, speakeasies, widespread corruption of the police and judiciary, and finally to the institutionalization of organized crime. Even one of the few positive acts of the year, Congressional adoption of the Nineteenth Amendment (women's suffrage), was looked upon in certain quarters as another sign that the old verities were in a state of collapse.

For the plain folk who wanted to consider only the basics, there was this: We had won the war, the boys were home, and we still had baseball, and to hell with riots and strikes and Communists. With their usual fine feel for the national pulsebeat, the major-league club owners scheduled a 140-game season in 1919, fearing the country might have lost interest in the game during two years of war. It was neither the first time nor the last that these gentlemen would demonstrate their lack of understanding of and appreciation for the magical game of which they had ownership. Big-league turnstiles spun like windmills in a gale all summer long, with several clubs setting new attendance records. Good old dependable baseball soothed the troubled air that summer, especially in the American League, where the Chicago White Sox fought off challenges from the Indians and Yankees to take the pennant. In the National League, it was Cincinnati winning over the Giants, thanks to some pastings the Reds handed McGraw's club late in the season, Giant losses that John J. later grumbled were abetted by some questionable ballplaying by Chase and Zimmerman.

This was one very fine team, these 1919 White Sox, probably one of the best ever assembled. It included Eddie Collins, the game's top second baseman; Shoeless Joe Jackson, second only to Cobb as a hitter; and solid men like Chick Gandil at first base, Swede Risberg at short, Buck Weaver at third, Happy Felsch in center field, and Ray Schalk behind the plate. The pitching was first-rate, led by right-hander Eddie Cicotte, a 29-game winner that year; Claude (Lefty) Williams, a 23-game winner; southpaw Dickie Kerr, and righty Red Faber.

"They were one hell of a team," a contemporary said. "They could go out there and beat you just about anytime they felt like it." Didn't they always feel like it? Frankly, no.

"We'd play them one series and they would look terrible," Roger Peckinpaugh, then with the Yankees, recalled; "we'd play them the next time and they'd look like the best club in the world. I remember one time we went into Chicago and little Nemo Leibold came up to me. He was on the White Sox but wasn't part of the shenanigans, but he smelled a mouse. 'Listen,' he said, 'something screwy is going on here. I don't know what it is, but it's something screwy all right. You guys bear down and you ought to take all four games.' You just never knew when they were going to go out there and beat your brains out or roll over and play dead. Somebody was betting on those games, that's a cinch." Indeed they were. Baseball was going to pay dearly for the years of averting its glance from Chase and his cohorts, for advertising its integrity via "No Gambling" signs posted on its walls while ignoring the shady operators on the field. We will never know how many players picked up tainted money with impunity for giving fate a hand in deciding the outcome of a game, but that the practice had reached epidemic proportions within the family of the 1919 Chicago White Sox soon became evident. The fire burning freely in the basement of the house of baseball was about to become a conflagration heading right through the roof.

Eight Chicago White Sox players conspired to throw the 1919 World Series to Cincinnati. Their motives were probably multilayered, but chief among them was that old reliable: money. When White Sox owner Charles Comiskey heard what had taken place, he was shocked; he no doubt thought that his boys were adequately paid. Anyone as self-righteously parsimonious as Comiskey was *had* to think his employees were well paid.

There are a handful of Founding Father names that resonate through baseball history, first as players, then as managers, and finally as club owners. Connie Mack and Clark Griffith are two, Charles Comiskey is another. Born in Chicago in 1859, Comiskey was sucked into baseball's orbit as a youngster. He began playing pro ball in 1877 in Elgin, Illinois, a tall, well-proportioned pitcher–first baseman. What Hal Chase later perfected, Charlie had revolutionized— playing deep and away from the bag. Like the invention of the paper clip, it was no great shucks, but somebody had to do it first. In 1882 he was playing for St. Louis of the American Association, a circuit claiming big-league status for itself. A year later he was first baseman and manager. As a first baseman, he was average; as a manager, he was sensational, winning four pennants in a row. He soon became known as The Noblest Roman of Baseball, a nickname later boiled down to The Old Roman. (He was also known, in deference to his last name, as Commy, an ironic nickname for a tough-nosed old conservative.)

Comiskey played for Cincinnati in the early 1890s. Later in the decade he was owner-manager of St. Paul in the Western League, headed by his close friend Ban Johnson, with whom Charlie sat up many a night in midwestern hotels shaping the contours of their dream of forming a second major league. When the dream became a reality with the birth of the American League in 1901, the owner of the Chicago franchise was Charles Comiskey.

So he was the epitome of the self-made man, having made all the waystation stops, a survivor and an achiever in a chancy, rugged environment. The country had a lot of them in that wide-open time of far-flung opportunity, and the glorious view from the top was not one that inspired fiscal generosity. Like any lad who had taken the rough-and-tumble route upstairs, Charlie had a jealous lover's attitude toward his money. He figured that the joy of playing baseball and the adulation of the crowd should be sustenance enough for any man, and he supplemented this spiritual intake with ground-level salaries. To those players so bold as to debate their contracts with him, The Old Roman would say, "Look, I started at fifty dollars a month in 1877 and look where I am now." The story may have been inspirational, but not if you were on Charlie's payroll.

When it came to improving the club, however, Comiskey could be a liberal spender. He sank a half-million pre–World War I dollars into building Comiskey Park, a veritable palace when it opened in 1910, and it remains today, functioning heartily as the game's oldest ball park. In 1915 he bought Eddie Collins from the Athletics for $50,000, a mountain of money in those days. But when it came to adding some meat and potatoes to his athletes' income, Charlie's hands rolled up into clenched fists, a reflex action he shared with fellow Founding Fathers Mack and Griffith.

Of course Comiskey was no different from most employers of the day. Meager paychecks, execrable working conditions, endless workdays, management tyranny—they were the standard lot for labor then. And while ballplayers were earning, generally, an income above the national median, ownership was earning a whole lot more; and then there were comparative salaries to consider. Stars on other clubs, like Cobb, Speaker, Wagner, Johnson, and others, were being paid in five figures. Charlie's were not, with the exception of Collins, whose $14,000 contract had come along with Eddie from the Athletics. Joe Jackson was earning around $6,000, ace pitchers Cicotte and Williams, outfielder Felsch, and infielders Gandil, Weaver, and Risberg were getting less. On the road, the best team in baseball had the lowest daily meal-money allotment—three dollars. And what could they do about it? Nothing, because of the reserve clause that was hung to every contract like a ball and chain, giving the club unconditional rights to a man's services until the club put termination to them or until Judgment Day, whichever came first. For the owners, the reserve clause was a shrine at which to worship; for the players, a noose they played under, or a guillotine if they tried to get out from under.

It is easy to say that of all teams, the 1919 White Sox were ripest for corruption, because they were the one to fall from grace. But the susceptibility was surely there. The smug, portly, penurious Charles Comiskey was reason enough to make a man swindle his own ethics; but there were other factors.

Harmony is not essential to winning teams. Joe Tinker and Johnny Evers of the famed double-play combination barely spoke to one another; Ty Cobb was a one-man clique on three Detroit pennant winners; even Ruth and Gehrig had a temperature drop in their personal relationship in the Babe's waning days; and in more recent times Don Sutton and Steve Garvey had a celebrated no-decision punchout on a successful Dodger club. The 1919 White Sox, however, were probably the all-time champions of intrateam disharmony. The club was broken into two distinct factions. On one side was the cockily self-confident, Columbia-educated, highly intelligent and highly paid Eddie Collins, Ray Schalk, and pitchers Dickie Kerr and Red Faber. On the other side were Chick Gandil, Swede Risberg, Happy Felsch, Joe Jackson, and Lefty Williams. Their sympathizers were Eddie Cicotte, Buck Weaver, and utility infielder Fred McMullin. No unnecessary conversation passed between the two sides, though on the field they performed with a deadly, close-knit efficiency. The prime ingredients of this internecine conflict were Gandil's brooding hatred of Collins, of Eddie's mannered ways and sumptuous wages. Collins, for his part, looked down upon Chick, and in fairness to Eddie, who had learned his baseball in the Connie Mack school of team spirit and good fellowship, there was quite a bit to look down upon.

Chick Gandil was the probable ringleader of the 1919 Series fixers. The thirty-one-year-old first baseman was a rough customer. A runaway from his Minnesota home at the age of seventeen, Chick rode the rails down to the Southwest, where he played semipro ball, did some heavyweight fighting in the border towns, and worked in the copper mines as a boilermaker. He had enormous hands, "heavy as anvils," it was said, and a glowering face that reflected a sullen disposition. Tough, mean, suspicious, a product of the broiling inertia of a dying frontier, Chick was just the man to swap recipes with the likes of Comiskey and Collins.

Seven other players, in addition to Gandil, made up the gang of dumpers who became known as the Black Sox. They included the club's two ace pitchers, Cicotte and Williams, whose participation was essential. Eddie was the big winner, basking in the brilliance of a trick pitch he threw, called a shine ball. Then there was Happy Felsch, the centerfielder, and one supposes his nickname ought to speak for itself, but obviously there were things Happy was not happy about, his salary chief among them. And there was Swede Risberg, the team's shortstop, considered one of the finest gloves in the game.

Utility infielder Fred McMullin was surely no world-beater. Fred actually got into the mess by accident. Supposedly, he overheard Gandil discussing the caper with Risberg and demanded to be cut in. If star pitcher Cicotte was being paid less than $6,000, one can imagine what the seldom-playing handyman McMullin was drawing. Of all the players involved, Fred was the most superfluous. He batted only twice in the Series and is best described as a guilty bystander.

Third baseman Buck Weaver was a special case. Buck knew about the fix, didn't participate, but observed an honorable tradition by refusing to squeal on his buddies. This posture may have been considered laudable in some quarters, but when the unholy crew faced the music two years later, Buck was drummed out of the corps with the rest of them.

The eighth man is Joe Jackson, called Shoeless because he allegedly played that way once or twice on the playgrounds of his native South Carolina when his feet hurt. For many, the nickname conjured up an image of a poor, ill-educated country boy, and Joe was all of that. He was said to have been illiterate, to the extent that when he went out to dinner with the boys he would hold his menu in front of him and order last, listening to what the others were ordering and select his dinner from what he heard.

Raised in the small town of Brandon Mill, the thirteen-year-old Joseph went to work in the cotton mill, same as his father and brothers, putting in twelve hours a day amid the endlessly whirring machinery, and there he would have stayed if not for his truly God-given ability with a baseball bat. Once more we hear mighty things of prowess at bat and splendor afield, and this time we listen with awe, for the verdict is unanimous. Ty Cobb on the basepaths, Walter Johnson on the mound, Honus Wagner in the field—Joe Jackson at home plate is part of this mythic assembly. They—again those unimpeachable witnesses, those baseball people who saw all and forgot nothing—said he was the greatest natural hitter that ever lived, with the possible exception of Ted Williams. Even Cobb paused to admire the poetic purity of Joe's lash at the plate. Like the unique network of muscles and fibers of Walter Johnson's right arm, nature occasionally turns out these athletic objets d'art to establish a standard, to show the striving masses how wondrous it can be. Into the lean, strong body of Joseph Jefferson Jackson of Brandon Mill, South Carolina, it concentrated all the timing, coordination, and judgment a hitter could want, and then wound it all as tight as a hairspring and programmed it to attack a pitched ball.

There was no way to pitch to him, except Joe Wood's way: "You tried your best and hoped it wasn't his day." When Jimmy Dykes asked the crafty Chief Bender how the Chief pitched to Jackson, all he got in return was a wise old Chippewa Indian smile. "Made me feel like an ass," Jimmy said. When Jackson hit the ball to you at second base, Dykes recalled, "it came roaring, the only bouncing line drive I ever saw. It could eat your hand off."

Jackson was the rookie who swatted .408 in 1911, .395 a year later, .373 after that, and in 1920, just before he was banned from organized ball, .382. Because he played in the dead-ball era, his home-run totals were low. Unlike most hitters of the day, Joe was down at the handle of his black bat and took a full swing, yet seldom struck out—10 times in 1919, 14 in 1920. And everything he hit was really kissed. "He could break bones with his shots," pitcher Ernie Shore recalled ruefully fifty years later. "Blindfold me and I could still tell you when Joe Jackson hit the ball. It had a special crack."

Ill at ease when he first came to the big leagues—Connie Mack originally had him at Philadelphia, but a homesick Jackson kept going back to Brandon Mill until Connie finally gave up on him— embarrassed by his nickname, his country ways, and his illiteracy, Jackson gradually adjusted, became a flashy dresser, taking care always to buy the most expensive shoes. The darling of the rabid Chicago fans, he was a mild-mannered, unoffending country boy whose naivety left him with little immunity from the contagions of the big city. Joe, it seems, "went along" with the fix, uneasy about it but cajoled by the stronger personalities of Gandil and Risberg, apparently the most dominant of the crew. But Joe was so good a hitter that even when he wasn't trying, allegedly in the 1919 Series, he still stroked twelve hits and batted .375.

The reputation of this team has grown and grown with the passage of time. Their contemporaries remembered with awe the 1919 White Sox, and with increasing awe as the decades rolled on. Whether the outfit and its component parts were truly that outstanding, or whether we are listening to the allure of the unsavory, we cannot be certain. Evil always casts a special, mesmeric spell, and while the Black Sox can hardly be described as evil (especially given the competition they have in the twentieth century), in the context of baseball there is nobody who out-Herods them.

The throwing of a World Series seems today a barely conceivable adventure, but in the atmosphere in which the 1919 Series was played, it was indeed believable. Given the impunity with which games had been thrown, and the purblind attitude of the game's authorities, sabotaging an event as august as the World Series was merely the crescendo climax to all that had gone before. Gambling had so thoroughly insinuated itself into the game's mechanisms, it seemed inevitable, merely awaiting the ripening of the right combination. The players involved no doubt saw nothing terribly wrong in what they were doing; some of them had done it before, and some of them in fact went right on doing it the next season before the scandal finally erupted. There was probably a sullen self-righteousness involved, too. They were the adored heroes of a large, baseball-mad city; but an abundance of glory and a paucity of cash can make a mockery of the loudest cheers. These were heroes who were underpaid and unfairly dealt with, and any authority dishing out this kind of treatment to its subjects must expect to reap a harvest of evanescent loyalties and outright rancor. Another band of players of a later date, the three-time world-champion Oakland Athletics of the early 1970s, were forged together by dislike of their owner (Charles Finley) and in their anger perhaps gave more than they had in battering the opposition. The 1919 White Sox, infused with similar feelings toward their owner, gave less. It was a gigantic, defiant, contemptuous thumbing of the nose not only of Charles Comiskey but also of those exuberant fans whose applause made their heroes feel at once uplifted and hollow.

That the scandal didn't break until September 1920 is a tribute to baseball's determined refusal to believe what it had seen and what it was hearing. The rumors had been flying almost as soon as the scheme had been dreamed up, flying, as someone put it, "like a wind strong enough to blow an egg back up a hen's ass." Eight men sharing a secret with any number of high- and low-grade gamblers soon gives that secret the currency of a daily newspaper. The gamblers knew, their friends knew, certain newspapermen suspected but were afraid to print it, though after the White Sox had dropped the first two games to the Reds and were entraining to Cincinnati, they heard the acidulous Ring Lardner walk through their coach car singing, to the tune of "I'm Forever Blowing Bubbles," "I'm forever blowing ball games." The White Sox, prohibitive favorites before the Series, dropped to even money and then slight underdogs by the time the charade got underway, thanks to all the "smart" money piling up on the Reds.

With baseball experimenting with a five-out-of-nine Series, the agony was prolonged until the Reds won their fifth game in the eighth played. Dickie Kerr—he was "square" (the word had different connotations then)—won twice for the Sox, while Cicotte for some reason won one game (for the sake of his 1920 contract, cynics said later). Risberg proved to be the most devoted of the fixers, batting .080 and fielding with a palsied glove, while Felsch contributed a .192 batting average and some shoddy fielding. Gandil batted .233. Cicotte lost two games, but Lefty Williams was truly spectacular in deceit, starting three and losing three. Subtle in his first two losses, Williams was blatant in the eighth and final game, letting the Reds tattoo him for four runs in the first inning before Sox skipper Kid Gleason gave him the hook. Williams's money pitch was a back-breaking curve, but in that inning all he laid over the plate were batting practice–type fastballs, no matter what signs catcher Ray Schalk hung out.

The choice inning of the Series, however, had to be Cincinnati's top of the fifth in Game Four, in which they scored the two runs that gave Jimmy Ring his 2–0 victory. It was a one-man display of malefaction by Cicotte that must have had the gamblers winking at each other in the box seats. With one out, Cicotte fielded Pat Duncan's grounder and his peg to first became a souvenir for someone in the box seats. Duncan went to second. A moment later Larry Kopf singled to left. Joe Jackson's throw home had Duncan beaten, but Cicotte cut it off in front of an astounded Ray Schalk. Kopf scored a moment later on another hit. With the game safely tucked away for the Reds, Cicotte showed the world what he could really do, limiting the Reds to one single over the last four innings.

"That's when we knew for sure there was some horseshit going on," Jimmy Ring said, "when Cicotte cut that ball off. Up till then we'd heard a lot of talk which we tried not to pay any attention to. I'll never forget Schalk standing there in front of home plate staring at Cicotte. Eddie went back to the mound and was standing there with his back to the plate, staring out to center field and rubbing the ball up very slowly, like he didn't want to turn around and face Schalk."

The smell left behind by the 1919 World Series made the Chicago stockyards seemed aromatic in comparison. In addition, the whole scheme had been planned and executed as sloppily as the White Sox had performed on the field. Outside of agreeing to throw the first two games, the players had never really sat down and coordinated the swindle among themselves. And in the end most of the players, basically decent, gullible small-towners, saw very little money from the gamblers, who had been jollying them along with promises from game to game. Gandil, the liaison between the shady world and the sunlit, and himself the worldliest of the players, profited most, pocketing $35,000. Risberg received $15,000 and Cicotte $10,000, while around $20,000 was divided among Jackson, Williams, Felsch, and McMullin. They had all been promised much more. "The joke was on us," Felsch admitted sadly.

In retrospect, it seems everyone knew about the sellout except the fans, who came pouring out in record numbers during the 1920 season while the scandal simmered. For baseball, the scandal was like having an alcoholic uncle in the family—everyone knew he was there but nobody wanted to talk about him. Indeed, when newspapermen like Chicago's Hugh Fullerton wrote some scathing pieces about the White Sox performance in the Series, J. G. Taylor Spink, publisher of "Baseball's Bible," *The Sporting News,* fired a salvo aimed at Fullerton and beyond, a salvo that dripped with barely containable racial vitriol: "Because a lot of dirty, long-nosed, thick-lipped, and strong-smelling gamblers butted into the World Series—an American event, by the way—and some of said gentlemen got crossed, stories were peddled that there was something wrong with the way the games were played." Note that juxtaposition of Semitic stereotyping—some of the more notable gamblers were Jews—and an *American* event. (Spink's mole's-eye view of things remained consistent: A quarter-century later he would inveigh against the dismantling of baseball's color barrier.) This insulting, near-hysterical broadside against those who dared suggest baseball was not beyond reproach smacks of jingoism, bigotry, and ignorance.

By trying to ignore the mess, or by launching half-hearted investigations, official baseball was fighting a hydra of a slightly different sort: Shut one mouth and two more opened. Gamblers were talking, some big "inside" bettors were talking, newspapermen were talking, ballplayers were talking, and inside of all that smoke, were roaring, inextinguishable flames. When the names of ex-featherweight champion Abe Attell, an unsavory Broadway character, and Arnold Rothstein, "King of the Gamblers," came into the story as an entry, the malodorous brew was given another stir.

For Charles Comiskey, the months after the Series were one prolonged agony. The Old Roman was too good a baseball man not to have known the truth. But he was also too good a businessman not to have known that revelation of the scandal would be ruinous for him, his club, and all that he had built during more than forty years. Comiskey's dilemma was a brutal one: investigate and try to confirm what he knew was true, and thereby risk the destruction of his franchise and perhaps bring down with him the entire structure of major-league baseball; or pretend the whole thing never happened. Adding to the weight of Charlie's burden was the fact that he had a championship team, one that seemed certain to take another flag in 1920 and add to the stacks in the Comiskey vault.

Well, it ended up with Charlie having it both ways. He dithered and he sulked, he raged and he scowled, and in 1920 his club (minus Gandil—that crafty pirate didn't report in 1920) fought the Indians and Yankees throughout the summer in one of the American League's most sizzling pennant races. The fans filled Comiskey Park in record numbers all season—incontrovertible proof of their unsuspecting natures, their unacceptance of the rumors.

When the story finally hit the fan—and the fans—it came at a most inauspicious time, a week or so before the end of the season, with the Sox in a virtual tie with the Indians for first place. It meant the destruction of Comiskey's club, for immediately suspended were Cicotte, Williams (both twenty-game winners again), Risberg, McMullin, Felsch, and Jackson. Weaver, with innocent hands but guilty knowledge, remained for the moment unscathed. With the heart cut out of it, the team fielded some phantoms in its final games, predictably faltered, and finished second to Cleveland by two games.

The first to crack was Cicotte. Guilt-ridden, remorseful, threatened with exposure at any moment, Eddie flung off his hair shirt and spilled to a Cook County grand jury in Chicago. Other players soon followed. The grand jury listened solemnly, the Illinois judicial system began crackling, witnesses were subpoenaed, lawyers hired, testimony taken, and the headlines roared the biggest news since the signing of the armistice. Baseball was launching the nation into the most uproarious, corrupt, and irresponsible decade in its history, dur-

ing which it seemed that every sacred edifice tottered on its founda-
tions. Organized crime, bred by the well-meaning but cracked-brain
imposition of Prohibition, was soon making an art form of bribing
municipal, state, and federal officials. In a few years the highest corridors in Washington would rumble with a scandal called Teapot
Dome, involving government oil leases. Not even that sanctuary of
American morality, the small town, was spared, as Sinclair Lewis
(*Main Street*) and Sherwood Anderson (*Winesburg, Ohio*) wrote
books that parted once and for all the polite curtains and exposed the
boredom, sanctimony, and heavy breathing within. It was the last
decade that America would be untroubled by disturbances from
abroad, which was just as well, for nothing short of another world
war could have diverted the nation's involvement with itself during
that dancing decade.

America's stunned, hurt, incredulous reaction to the swindle of
the 1919 World Series and the larger blot on the national game was
best encapsulated in a poignant but apocryphal story. Supposedly
when Joe Jackson was exiting from a Chicago courthouse, a dirty-
faced little boy in a cloth cap separated himself from the crowd,
tugged on Jackson's sleeve and, looking up at the great slugger with
moist eyes, uttered plaintively, "Say it ain't so, Joe." Apocryphal or
not, it was a plea that rang from the hearts of the nation's baseball
fans.

Editorial writers were saying that baseball was now in the same
class as boxing, horse racing, and politics. By American standards of
morality, this was quite an indictment.

Frightened for the very survival of their game and their investments, the club owners, desperate to restore public faith in baseball,
decided, somewhat belatedly, they had better do something to not
only clean up the sport but also police it. Heretofore, the game's supreme ruling body had been the three-man National Commission,
comprised of the two league presidents and a club owner. They had
proven ineffective. So the owners went outside of baseball and hired
themselves a commissioner and invested him with absolute powers.
In making their necessary but almost masochistic appointment, the
owners swung in a 180-degree arc from a lax, irresolute administration to virtual dictatorship. Judgment Day had come to baseball, and
there it was in person, carved with biblical severity into the stern,
scowling, unforgiving face of the man empowered to summon, decide, judge, and, if necessary, execute: Kenesaw Mountain Landis.

NINE

WHAT A NAME! What a character! Egomaniac, reactionary, bully, dictator, hypocrite. He could pose and pontificate as blatantly as a third-rate jingoist; he could showboat like a vaudevillian (he wanted to bring the Kaiser to Illinois to be tried for murder because a Chicago resident had gone down with the *Lusitania*); and he could sentence a man to jail for years for violating the Prohibition Amendment, and then go home and sip bootleg liquor and not recognize the contradiction.

The club owners didn't just hire a commissioner, they reached back into the supposedly virtuous nineteenth century for him, for a symbol of the dependable old piety and morality, not for what people trusted or respected, but for what they feared. Baseball, at the beginning of the hellfire decade, resurrected a forbidding manifestation of all that seemed to have gone forever and gave it limitless authority. The universe of baseball was one of the few places in America where authority received total obeisance in that debauched decade. With poker-playing Warren Harding hiding girl friends in White House closets, with Prohibition virtually a license for the country to run amok, only in baseball was there unquestioned law and order, hammered down with such relentless finality that the game was, by sheer terror, purified forever.

Kenesaw Mountain Landis. The name itself bespeaks American history. Kenesaw Mountain is an eighteen-hundred-foot elevation in northern Georgia. In June 1864 it was the site of a battle between Union and Confederate forces. The future commissioner's father was a surgeon with Sherman's bluecoats. During the battle, Dr. Landis's leg was shattered by a cannonball. The affair must have made a profound, almost mystical impression on him, because when his son was born two years later, in Millville, Ohio, Dr. Landis named him after the battle. Kenesaw Mountain. Well, considering there were also battles at Spotsylvania and Yellow Tavern, it could have been worse.

The game's most prominent nonplaying hero was brought up in Logansport, Indiana. There he chased through a boyhood Horatio Alger might have novelized. Landis sold newspapers, worked in a general store, was a hustling errand boy for the railroad, and played a little baseball. Despite his lack of formal education (he was a high school dropout), he decided to study law. Always with a flair for the dramatic—in his later years he came to resemble, with his white hair, baggy eyes, and grim mouth, a Victorian thespian portraying a judge—he made a name for himself in midwestern courtrooms. In 1905 President Theodore Roosevelt appointed him federal judge in northern Illinois. Two years later Landis blew to national prominence when he fined John D. Rockefeller's Standard Oil Company $29,240,000 in a freight-rebate case; quite a resounding kick in the wallet. The fact that the Supreme Court later threw out the fine on appeal did not diminish Landis's luster.

No great intellect, he had an adamant sense of his own rectitude, and he brought into his courtroom the old rural and frontier values, adorning these rugged simplicities with thundering rhetoric as well as—when out of earshot—an unabridged cussword vocabulary. Any man so inflexibly convinced of his own mission must be narrow of vision. Hardened by the granite patriotisms of his origins, the judge was murder on anyone he deemed to be following an aberrant course—any course but that of pure, hard-working, God-fearing, honest Americanism. The old trust-buster had little sympathy for, understanding of, or patience with, the Socialists and "Bolshevik" labor leaders who came before him on charges of obstructing the war effort. Back a generation or two, he would doubtless have been a "hanging judge" on the frontier. There was more than a little of Roy Bean in Kenesaw Mountain Landis.

The commissioner was little different from the judge. For the corrupt there was instant retribution. Tinkering with the integrity of the game meant quick and permanent expulsion into a veritable American Siberia. But the shock treatment worked. Landis's draconian measures ended corruption in baseball so decisively, striking so compelling a terror into everyone connected with the game that a tradition of honesty was established that became the pride of baseball. Not even the abundance of wild money and easy scruples that cascaded through the 1920s could penetrate the game's newly erected palisades of integrity, leaving it lastingly free of scandal.

On November 12, 1920, the sixteen big-league club owners met with Landis in Chicago to offer him the position of dictator over their game. After accepting, the judge made some remarks to Washington's Clark Griffith, an old personal friend. Alone with Griffith in his office, Landis took him over to the window. "Griff," the judge said, "I'm going to tell you just why I took this job. See those kids down there on the street? See that airplane propeller on the wall? Well, that explains my acceptance. You see, that propeller was on the plane in which my son, Major Reed Landis, flew while overseas. Reed and I went to one of the World Series games at Brooklyn. Outside the gate was a bunch of little kids playing around. Reed turned to me and said: 'Dad, wouldn't it be a shame to have the game of these little kids broken up? Wouldn't it be awful to take baseball away from them?' Well, while you gentlemen were talking to me, I looked up at this propeller and thought of Reed. Then I thought of his remark in Brooklyn. Griff, we've got to keep baseball on a high standard for the sake of the youngsters—that's why I took the job, because I want to help."

Granted, cornball; but he meant it, it was part of his makeup, and when it wasn't, he adapted it and the pose always worked because symbols of incorruptible authority are irresistible. The judge played his role to perfection, because he knew exactly where in the hearts of Americans baseball lay. The autocrat of the federal bench knew where his constituency lay, too. He ran roughshod over the men who paid him—many club owners came to regret the sweeping powers they had given him—but the players idolized him and the fans respected him, and any attempt to remove him from office might well have been interpreted that something, again, was amiss with the game.

There is no way this one-man committee of vigilance could operate today. As managers can no longer impose authoritarian rule upon their players, so no commissioner can be as high-handed with the club owners as the judge was. But today is different. And anyway, he isn't needed today, because he was hired to solve a specific problem and solved it so well that the standards he set down generations ago still prevail. He remains a ghostly, menacing threat to any who would try to subvert the sanctity of the old ball game.

Landis was not long in establishing baseball's own special moral orbit. In the summer of 1921 the eight accused White Sox players were brought to trial. And they were the only ones—neither Abe Attell, Arnold Rothstein, nor any of the other gamblers who had purportedly strewn the path to temptation with thousand-dollar bills had been indicted, nor were they called to testify. The boys were on their own, and it did not hurt their case, for an already predisposed jury of twelve Chicago baseball fans could hardly feel it was fair that eight basically decent, albeit gullible, ballplayers should be in the dock while those big-time eastern gamblers who actually pocketed the money were spending the sweltering summer in the mountains or on the beach at Atlantic City.

In the middle of its presentation, the state had to admit that confessions and waivers of immunity signed by Cicotte, Jackson, and Williams had disappeared. This, along with the shady penny-ante gamblers and middlemen the prosecution put on the stand to incriminate the defendants, the absence of Rothstein and the other bankrollers, and the jury's evident sympathy for the ballplayers, gave the defense attorneys a feeling of confidence. It was not misplaced. On the evening of August 2 the jury filed out of the courtroom to begin deliberations. Two hours later they were back with a blanket verdict of not guilty. A loud, raucous celebration of approval broke out. The players and their attorneys and the jury congratulated each other, then all went out to a nearby Italian restaurant and ate and drank and celebrated jubilantly far into the night.

Who knows with what dreams of vindication and gratification the eight ballplayers finally went to bed that night. The ordeal was over. Or so they thought. But it was to be otherwise, for the avenging angel had risen with the morning and issued this statement:

Regardless of the verdict of juries, no player that throws a ball game; no player that undertakes or promises to throw a ball game; no player that sits in a conference with a bunch of crooked players and gamblers where the ways and means of throwing games are planned and discussed and does not promptly tell his club about it, will ever play professional baseball.

That was the judge, serving notice that the old ways were done and gone forever and the new here to stay, just as surely as today's flowers grow through last year's leaves. Swede Risberg responded: "I am entirely innocent and the jury has proved that." And Happy Felsch: "The jury has cleared my name." And normally, so it should have been. But not in this case, not under these circumstances. Landis had anticipated an acquitting jury and ruled it out of order. Further in his statement was this sentence: "Just keep in mind that, regardless of the verdict of juries, baseball is entirely competent to protect itself against crooks, both inside and outside the game." *Regardless of the verdict of juries.*

Here the old frontier throwback was ruling irrelevant this most sacred of democratic institutions and replacing it with his own outraged common sense and stern cracker-barrel dogma. An erring jury might be able to free murderers and other malefactors and send them back into a helpless society. Well, too bad for society. But the judge was dealing with something else, an innocent wellspring of joy, fun, excitement, and inspiration called baseball, something as dear to the nation as the flag itself, and no one—misguided juries included—was going to pollute it. What the judge was telling any who cared to listen was that baseball possessed a unique status and that those who made their living at it were going to be held to a higher moral standard. What Landis had done, in effect, was to pronounce special legislation to uphold and protect a sport that was a talisman American males carried with them from boyhood.

Today, one might snicker at the judge's theatrics or be appalled by his unappealable one-man edicts. But it all must be placed in context, and when it is, Landis towers above his own rigidity, his hypocrisy, his bigotry. When one considers the depth of baseball's importance in the lives of millions of Americans, one must concede the judge the wisdom of his ways and grant him a quirky greatness. In a large, swaggering, pluralistic society that insists on pedestals for its ballplaying heroes, where licit and illicit opportunity abounds in reality and breeds in the imagination, there is no telling how many scruples were loosened by the black magic of a fixed World Series nor how many more knots of integrity may have come undone had the swindles been allowed to continue unchecked and unpunished. But now the youngsters in the playgrounds and meadows of a freewheeling America knew they were playing an honest game, knew it because at the very top was a stern old man with white hair and Old Testament scowl to protect it.

Having pronounced, the judge now disposed. The eight White Sox players (forever tarred as the Black Sox) were not only banished from organized ball, but they were also doomed to carry with them guilt-by-association labels. When some of them banded together to try and find work as semipro players, they found themselves denied the use of ball parks and were often shunned by other players who were hoping one day to break into pro ball. The stigma of the Landis curse was upon them. Petitions of reinstatement made to the judge were brusquely denied. The most pathetic of the crew was Buck Weaver, guilty only of not reporting on his mates, but in the eyes of the judge it was guilt by infection. Distinctions were blurred; one was as guilty as the next.

Curiously, none of the eight contaminated players ever spoke publicly about the 1919 World Series. They endured their penance in silence and to the grave with them went the secrets, the guilt, the shame. So unique was the stain they left upon the game that behind them rose their own enduring legend. The greatest of them, Shoeless Joe Jackson, depicted always as a cornpone illiterate, who lived out his years with great personal dignity, was the first to die, in his native South Carolina in 1951, adored and respected by his fellow townsmen, who always believed the old slugger had somehow been taken in and wronged by the city slickers. Fred McMullin died in 1952, Buck Weaver in 1956, Lefty Williams in 1959, Happy Felsch in 1964, Eddie Cicotte in 1969, Chick Gandil in 1970, and the last of them, Swede Risberg, in 1975. Preceding them all to the grave was Kenesaw Mountain Landis, dying in office in 1944 (by this time to the relief of the big-league club owners, tired of his czarist ways but still too timid to unseat him). But even from the beyond, the old judge never relaxed his grip on those players; his successor, A. B. (Happy) Chandler, ignored a plea in 1951 from both houses of the South Carolina state legislature for Jackson's name to be cleared.

In October 1975, a few days after Risberg's death, a writer was interviewing Roger Peckinpaugh at the old shortstop's home in Cleveland. The conversation rambled through the sweet bygone years, invoking the names of Cobb, Speaker, Walter Johnson, Joe Wood, and Babe Ruth and all the other cornerstone legends. Then a wistful, distant look came into Peckinpaugh's eyes and the conversational tide came to a halt for a few moments.

"They're all gone now, aren't they?" he said.

The writer waited.

"Risberg died the other day," Peckinpaugh said. "He was the last of them."

"Yes," the writer said. The reference to "them" was clear.

"A helluva team," the old man murmured.

"Just how good were they?" the writer asked.

Peckinpaugh thought for a moment, then laughed heartily, a marveling, wondering laugh.

"With those guys, well . . ." He laughed again. "Who knows?"

So there sat Kenesaw Mountain Landis, upon as near a judgment throne as America has ever known, a benign despot with godlike power over his fiefdom. He had lifted the game from its polluted waters and held it aloft in the purity of the sunshine in which it was played, keeping it free of what he deemed a contaminating society.

Was he the game's savior, as the legends now avow? Well, none can deny the game was in a tottering state when it brought him upon the scene. If baseball legend requires a savior, then Landis is a prime candidate for the halo. The judge, however, could not do it alone. Help he needed, and help he got, from where it counted most—the field.

Simultaneous with Landis's arrival on the baseball scene came the greatest explosion of baseball-playing talent ever poured into a single man. Ironically, the reactionary Landis was in his opening years in office to preside over the revolutionary days of a new ball game, a game driven and inspired by a lively ball, a game made over in the image of an altogether new hero so colossal that he transcended it by dint of his unprecedented slugging; a rollicking, charismatic, uninhibited, rules-breaking character who was the perfect complement for the stern, frosty-faced godfather at the top.

MEN

IF BABE RUTH had not been born it would have been impossible to invent him. The reality is hard enough to accept. He was not just the premier left-handed pitcher of his time and the greatest home-run hitter ever corralled, but it was all packaged into a booming, fun-loving, perennially adolescent personality that would have brought tears to the eyes of P. T. Barnum. He was a one-man circus, born and molded to entertain, dominate, captivate, and altogether flourish in the imagination. The man and the career stand as examples of impeccable timing; they came crashing through baseball like a tidal wave across the placid face of a mountain lake. Everything about Ruth was big, big, big, from the statistics to the personality to the impact. He was Moby Dick in a goldfish bowl. To write about him is to drain your vocabulary of superlatives. To whatever engaged him he was the mightiest: hitter, pitcher, womanizer, drinker, eater. He was the greatest player on the greatest team in the greatest stadium in the greatest city. He was power. He was the Yankees. He was New York. He was baseball.

Like it or not, the country found itself possessing world-power status after the Great War. Despite Warren Harding's call for a "return to normalcy" in his 1921 inaugural address, there could be no turning back. A victorious army had returned to a proud people, and from sea to shining sea America had become a land of voracious appetite. Though its finest young writers may have been in Paris cultivating their cynicism and making art of their disillusionment, back home their fellow citizens were buying automobiles and building highways to speed across, and General Billy Mitchell had emphatically demonstrated the strength of air power by sinking several of the navy's sacrificial battleships. Speed and bigness and power and an insatiable appetite for its own flair and dramatics, and rushing along with the national energy was the world of sports, creating its own Golden Age with heavyweight champion Jack Dempsey, running back Red Grange, tennis champion Bill Tilden, golfer Bobby Jones, and the Hercules of all sports, the big man in Yankee pinstripes, Babe Ruth.

New York though he was, Ruth's charm was homey, appealing at once to the hurly-burly of Broadway and the somnolence of Main Street. This symbol of crushing big-city power entered the imaginations and won the hearts of the towns and villages in every corner of the land; his name and his record-busting feats swept across the prairies and the farmlands with a special magical electricity, because he was doing something majestically new to the game that grew out of the very grass roots of America, and he was doing it with the strength and bravado people everywhere admire, and because, despite the big automobiles he drove at reckless speeds and the big cigars he smoked and the women he chased and the bottles he emptied, he was neither slick nor sophisticated; he conveyed a grand spiritual innocence. People could love Babe Ruth because, in spite of the towering place he occupied in the national ethos, they could identify with him. They sensed the exuberant uncomplicated love flowing back from him— for the life he led to all its joyous fulfillment, for the cherished game he played so well, and for the children who surrounded him wherever he went and for whom he would stand tirelessly for hours, cheerfully signing their scraps of paper even as they jostled him and pawed at him and stained his clothing with squirting pens. People could love him because he could shed tears of genuine remorse when publicly chided by New York's Mayor Jimmy Walker for the raucous life-style that was "letting those little kids down." He was a lovable, rebellious, irreverent Santa Claus whose dynamic bat was discovering new heights for those little kids to aspire to.

Ruth had a natural informality that people found irresistible. He could greet Marshal Ferdinand Foch when the dignified French war hero visited the United States, with, "I hear you were in the war." He could, on a broiling day at Griffith Stadium, be introduced to President Harding, and say, "Hot as hell, ain't it, Prez?"

"There was never anything like him," said pitcher Waite Hoyt, most sophisticated of his Yankee teammates. "I tell you, there was never anything like him."

Those teammates stood in absolute awe of him. No one, not Mathewson or Cobb or Johnson or Wagner or any of the others, so totally overwhelmed and dominated his fellow big-leaguers. It wasn't just the hitting; it was the whole package. Daily, they were living, traveling, and playing with a phenomenon, with as close to a god as American sports can produce. And the god was a regular guy, one of the boys. He joked, he kidded, he ate hot dogs, chased women, was generous with his time and his money. There was one aspect of Ruth that perhaps impressed teammates and opponents more even than his hitting: his impact on people. Yankee centerfielder Earle Combs: "The effect he had on people is almost impossible to describe. Wherever he went, from the big cities to the small towns we barnstormed through on the way home from spring training, they came at him and surrounded him like flood waters. If they couldn't touch him, then they had to see him. We'd be on a train speeding through the backwoods somewhere and we'd go through a small town and suddenly there would be a knot of people standing alongside the tracks. They'd heard Ruth was on the train and they were willing to stand there hoping to catch a glimpse of him." Teammate Joe Dugan: "One time we were walking down Fifth Avenue and I happened to turn around and damn if we weren't being followed by a couple of hundred people. He was like a magnet picking up iron filings. They weren't saying anything or doing anything; just following us—following Ruth, that is—until we went into the building where Babe had some business to attend to. I said to him, 'Babe, do you suppose if we walked into the East River they'd follow right along?' "

The myth so completely blankets him that it seems to have obscured the inner man. An interior, subjective Babe Ruth is difficult to contemplate. He was so extravagantly public and external that he seems at times, paradoxically, like the most private of men. If he had doubts, fears, or insecurities, they were thoroughly obliterated by what he appeared to be and by what people wanted him to be. The public perception of Babe Ruth has become the definitive Babe Ruth.

As befits any genuine American legend, Ruth's origins were humble, ruggedly so. He was born in a frame house, number 216 Emory Street, in Baltimore, Maryland, on February 6, 1895. Emory Street was not far from a very active waterfront, Baltimore proudly calling itself The Liverpool of America. Though the fleets of the world may have brought to the Baltimore wharves the trade of nations, when Ruth was an infant the city was best known for its Orioles, the team of John McGraw and Wee Willie Keeler, artisans of the style of play the robust infant of Emory Street was destined to make passé.

His father was a saloonkeeper who died after a brawl with an obstreperous customer in 1918, when his son was lighting up the baseball skies as a star left-hander for the Boston Red Sox. Babe's mother, Kate, was a petite, sickly woman who died in 1911 when young George Herman was sixteen.

The mischievous, hell-bent, soaring free spirit that baseball fans came to idolize in the 1920s was just the Baltimore youngster in full size, unchanged and unchangeable, for from the very beginning this was an unbreakable force loose in the universe. A slippery customer, he was off and running as a youngster to convert the world to his purposes, contriving to escape the authority of his parents, as any boy can if he is willing to accept the consequences. But consequences are equated with tomorrow, and that equation never quite meshed in this fellow's mind—his todays were always too sumptuously enjoyable to raise thoughts about tomorrow. Headstrong, rebellious, he roamed with his like-minded buddies through the waterfront's lively streets. With his father occupied trying to make a living and his mother sweating out pregnancies (she gave birth eight times; only young George and a sister survived to adulthood), the future home-run king had it his own way, despite the heavy muscle his exasperated father sometimes laid on him.

Neither parents nor school could throw a yoke over the tough, unruly kid who was a chronic truant, and the parents finally conceded defeat. In 1902 the recalcitrant youngster was shepherded by his parents to St. Mary's Industrial School for Boys of the City of Baltimore, an institution established by the Maryland legislature in 1882 for boys who had proved themselves difficult to handle. Though run by Xaverian Brothers, St. Mary's was a secular institution, welcoming boys of all denominations (though not colors—the legislature stipulated "white male" minors), and, indeed, one of Ruth's predecessors at the school was America's future "greatest entertainer," Al Jolson, who spent a few months there in 1898 when he was still known as Asa Yolson.

It was at St. Mary's that Ruth came under the influence of "the greatest man I ever knew." This sobering benefactor was Brother Matthias, at six-feet-six and 250 muscular pounds a mountain of a man (and a spectacular sight in those pre-NFL days), who commanded first the youngster's obedience by an intimidating presence, and then respect by a firm, gentle, fair-minded concern and interest. Ruth may have been belligerent raw material, but as a street-wise kid he had developed certain survival instincts, and after contemplating the bald-domed, shrewd-faced Brother Matthias—St. Mary's well-chosen "prefect of discipline"—the youngster knew enough to apply the brakes.

One of Brother Matthias's methods of handling the wild colts who came his way was to locate their skills and interests and offer guidance and encouragement. Ruth evinced some talent for carpentry and sewing shirts, but there was no doubt about where his special gifts lay.

The Ruth of legend is big-bellied and hardly athletic-looking. The prelegend stripling was board-flat, hard-muscled, fluid. Sports were an important part of the St. Mary's curriculum, and Ruth starred at basketball, football, and especially baseball. Those reflexes and that coordination and strength, that ineffable grace when that body was at work at games, must have appealed to a Xaverian's belief in the divine. Brother Matthias worked at disciplining the athlete, and gradually, through this approach, the boy. It must have been quite a sight, too, the huge man in the black cassock whacking fungoes and grounders to the agile, eager, quick-handed youth. "Brother Matthias made me a fielder," Ruth said. "I could always hit." Surely. You don't teach a Babe Ruth to hit. That sort of gift comes from elsewhere, and Brother Matthias no doubt would have concurred.

By the time he was seventeen, Ruth, still in residence at St. Mary's, was the superstar of the school's active baseball program. He could send a ball on four-hundred-foot journeys, and he was a dazzling left-handed pitcher with a smoking fastball. The volcano was rumbling, about to split open on all sides.

Word was getting around. The youngster's booming bat was sending tom-tom messages all through the immediate environment, which happened to be one feverish with the baseball malady—Baltimore had a team in the International League.

Running the Orioles—he was both manager and owner—was Jack Dunn, a veteran baseball foot soldier who had served with modest distinction in the trenches at Brooklyn, Philadelphia, Baltimore (when it was briefly in the American League), and New York, His big-league career ran from 1897 through 1904 and was unmemorable. But we remember Jack Dunn today because he was one of the depots at which the Great Ruth Express paused on its way to the Valhalla terminal. Dunn was the man who brought Ruth into professional baseball, which, metaphorically speaking, is similar to having had a hand in the splitting of the atom. Note that we do not credit Dunn with "discovering" Ruth. Ruth was too vast a natural force for anything as mundane as "discovery." It's the same as Balboa "discovering" the Pacific Ocean; one gets the feeling that sooner or later someone would have noticed it. Nevertheless, it was Jack Dunn who came to St. Mary's on a cold February day in 1914 to discuss with the Xaverians—Ruth's legal guardians—the future of the now nineteen-year-old George Herman Ruth, skilled at shirtmaking, pitching, and hitting. Dunn was not inquiring about the shirtmaker.

Once upon a time there were people who derived their living from very peculiar sources, like driving stagecoaches, piloting Zeppelins, and owning minor-league baseball teams. At one time, in 1914 for instance, most minor-league teams were independently owned, with the owners making a living from gate receipts and from the sale of players to big-league clubs. Minor-league organizations and more sophisticated scouting were soon to come, but not yet, and the big-league teams were still largely dependent for acquisition of players on tips, word of mouth, good luck, traveling salesmen in Weiser, Idaho, and other scientific methods. Most of the ground-level development of players was left to men like Dunn, and Jack was one of the ablest of the lot.

The Xaverians, knowing Dunn as a good and decent man, agreed to release Ruth to his care. Dunn signed the young man to a contract calling for $100 per month, or $600 for the season. It is said that the naive Ruth was amazed to learn that someone would pay you money to play baseball. This noble bozo of the diamond would have gone at his specialty without thought of monetary return, so passionate was he about the game. Coronado and his eager adventurers may never have found the Seven Cities of Cibola in the New World, but American boys were to discover their own astonishing largesse all over the continent—payment for playing baseball. And nobody was going to earn more of it in his time than the rascal from St. Mary's.

The phenomenon of America's most widely beloved hero since George Washington (Lincoln's appeal, remember, thinned out somewhat below the Mason-Dixon line) was not just his prowess with a bat. What writer of fiction would have dared to get away with inventing a ballplayer who not only had the game's most thundering haymaker swing but was also the top left-handed pitcher of his day? Forget it. That kind of sliced delicatessen belongs in Greek mythology. But look out. He was on the way. World-power America was about to prove itself with a strength, spirit, and bravado that turned loose an aviator who flew the Atlantic in solitude, a world-class

novelist who banged down lions in Africa for recreation, and George
Herman Ruth.

Probably Jack Dunn himself, who knew better than Coronado
where to go prospecting, didn't know just how good his prodigy was.
(Observing his promise to the Xaverians to take care of the headstrong youngster, Dunn looked after him with parental care, leading
the Orioles players to calling Ruth Dunn's Baby, which was the origin
of the famous nickname. It wasn't original; Pittsburgh's ace pitcher
was Charles [Babe] Adams. It's one of the few things about Ruth that
wasn't original.) No, sir; if Jack Dunn had realized how good his
baby was he wouldn't have sold him to the Boston Red Sox in July
along with catcher Ben Egan and pitcher Ernie Shore for around
$25,000. In the 1920s Dunn kept Lefty Grove with Baltimore for five
years, finally commanding a record price for this superb pitcher—
$100,600, from Connie Mack. But then again, the summer of 1914
was a financially bruising one for Dunn. The Federal League had
placed a team in Baltimore and the presence of a self-proclaimed big-
league club in town was draining attendance from Dunn's minor-
league club. So, in order to raise needed cash, Dunn began selling his
players.

Among the Orioles for sale was Dunn's Baby, who hadn't been
long in establishing his credentials. At midseason the rookie lefty's
record was 14–6, most impressive for a young man who was jumping
from St. Mary's Industrial School to one of the fastest of the minor
leagues. So young Babe Ruth was for sale, which meant, unbe-
knownst to anyone at the time, history was about to be made, and in
the world of baseball a most earth-shaking piece of history. (Only
Jackie Robinson in 1947 could match the rousing Halley's Comet furor surrounding Ruth's important arrivals and departures.)

Of course, we know what happened. He ended up in New York,
where they built a stadium for him (or maybe it was the other way
around) and he launched a sports dynasty that lasted for more than
four decades before finally sputtering out in 1964, a dynasty that he
helped sustain long after his retirement. How many hard-swinging
huskies signed with the Yankees because they wanted to play where
Babe Ruth had played and nowhere else? How many even became
slightly metaphysical about it, wanting to stand out there in right
field wearing pinstripes just as he had, on the very ground, as though
hoping it would secrete something of the mighty spirit that had
paused there? And then there is that other intriguing exercise: what

might have happened. Dunn first offered Ruth to Connie Mack, but Connie, in 1914 on the way to a fourth pennant in five years, was not interested. But if he had been, then add Ruth's name to the lineup Connie fielded in the late 1920s, one that included Jimmie Foxx, Al Simmons, Mickey Cochrane, Bing Miller, and Mule Haas. But Connie said no, and John McGraw never got the chance to say yes. McGraw, who had a divining rod of a nose when it came to sniffing talent, had heard about Dunn's young leviathan and was interested. Dunn, however, had borrowed some money from Red Sox owner Joseph Lannin that spring and felt an honorable man's obligation to give Lannin an inside shot at the Baltimore roster.

McGraw was furious when he heard that Ruth had been sold to the Red Sox. Not only had *he* lost a crack at the promising youngster, but the indignity was compounded by Ruth's going over to that other league. (McGraw's feelings about American Leaguers were those of a patrician for people who arrive by steerage.) If John J. was irate at losing an unknown pitcher of promise, one can only guess at the permanent temperature rise he suffered when less than a decade later that unknown and his Yankees had dethroned McGraw and his Giants as lords of New York baseball. And when Ruth soon began drawing more people than a dozen meteor showers, McGraw, a skipper who paid equal attention to scoreboard and box office, must have really felt cursed. Owning Babe Ruth in the 1920s was the same as having a license to print money.

But baseball is replete with what-ifs. What if Joe Wood had not hurt his arm? What if Walter Johnson had worked for a winning team? What if the 1919 White Sox had been a club of saintly virtue? Add to them one more most intriguing what-if: McGraw and Ruth, side by side on the Giants, manager and player, choleric martinet and unbreakable natural force? It would have been a grand show.

So it was to begin in Boston with the Red Sox. On July 11, 1914, Ruth, along with Shore and Egan, reported to Bill Carrigan, catcher-manager of the Red Sox. He was in the big leagues now, probably the only stage in America large enough for him to perform on. But not quite yet. Carrigan had a surfeit of pitchers, and after posting a 1–1 record, Ruth rode the bench until the middle of August, when he was sent to Providence, Rhode Island, of the International League, returning to the Red Sox at the end of September. Pitching for Baltimore and Providence, he posted a combined 22–9 won-lost record. For the Red Sox he was 2–1. He came to bat ten times for

Boston, got two hits, one a double. Carrigan used him once as a pinch hitter. "I liked the way he swung the bat," the manager modestly stated years later.

But Carrigan wasn't able to get a handle on the nature of this big, happy, irrepressible beast that had come trampling out of the wilds. The manager kept turning to Shore, who had come up from Baltimore with Ruth. Shore was an impressive man, six feet four, educated, intelligent, and serious. "They had never seen a rookie like him," Shore said. "I don't mean just his ability; it was his attitude. You see, away from the ball park, in a restaurant or in a hotel, he was awkward and unsure of himself. But on the field, well, he just bustled over with self-confidence. He wanted to take batting practice with the regulars. Well, a rookie doesn't do that, much less a rookie pitcher. But he pushed himself in whenever he could. I don't think Speaker or Wood cared much for him. But it didn't bother Babe, if he even knew about it. It was like the ball field was his natural domain, more than Speaker's or anybody else's. And, hell, I guess it was. Carrigan got a big kick out of him. Bill was a tough man himself and he admired spunk in somebody else, especially a rookie. Babe wasn't arrogant or anything like that. He was comfortable, that's all, and when he was comfortable everything came out of him, that whole personality, the mischief, the laughter, the whole business. Carrigan said to me, 'Is he always like that?' 'Yes, sir,' I said. 'Then I guess that's the way he is,' he said."

So the grandest career of them all was underway, and it was beginning, it must be emphasized, in a city that had as unrelenting a case of baseball fever as any in the country. The city that had loved and admired and popped its vest buttons over Cy Young, Jimmy Collins, Joe Wood, and Tris Speaker lost its composure completely over Babe Ruth. Harvard professors and the boys from the corner saloon alike were impressed with his hitting and his pitching and taken with the ingenuous charm that was as natural as the rest of it. Those who came through the wickets of the recently built Fenway Park and sat on the wooden seats were enthralled by the noblest savage of them all at work on the mound and at the plate, where his bat was becoming ever noisier. They knew full well what they had out there before them, and the lack of education and social polish defined it even more sharply, gave it more clarity. They were having a rare glimpse of an athlete transcending his immediate environment and demonstrating new, unprecedented levels of achievement. There were combined qualities of performance and magnetism here that not even their beloved Speaker or the deadly Cobb could match.

It was the pitching at first, of course. In 1915, his first full year, he was 18–8, helping the club to the pennant. A year later he was the ace, with a 23–12 record and league-leading figures in earned-run average (1.75) and shutouts (9). In 1917 he was 24–13, with a 2.01 ERA and 35 complete games in 38 starts. He also batted .325 that year, and by now the power of that swing could no longer be locked away for three or four days at a time. In 1918 the Red Sox manager was Ed Barrow, the same man who had signed Honus Wagner after watching the Dutchman banging chunks of coal against a hopper car. The Red Sox were woefully short of hitting in 1918 (they won the pennant, but their .249 team batting average was sixth-best in the league). If you are in need of hitting and you have Babe Ruth on your team, do you let him sit on the bench three-quarters of the time? You do not.

So Ed Barrow gets credit for the move that made history. On the mound Ruth was just 13–7 in 1918, while breaking into 59 games in the outfield and 13 at first base. And now the lightning was out of the bottle and the thunder was beginning to rumble over Boston. He popped 11 home runs that year, good enough to tie for the lead, and before you yawn at what seems a paltry total, hear this: The rest of the Red Sox hit only 4, the Indians hit 9, the Senators hit 5, as did the Browns, while the White Sox hit 9. It was the first of his even dozen home-run titles.

A year later, pitching with less frequency, playing 111 games in the outfield, Ruth put on what Boston fans must surely have thought was a miracle once-in-a-lifetime show. He broke all single-season home-run records, spectacularly and emphatically, riding 29 out of the park, leading in runs batted in, and slugging. If one wants some idea of just how big he must have looked to his teammates and the Boston populace, meditate on this for a moment: he hit 29 home runs; the rest of the team hit just 4. The Red Sox players must have felt like pebbles at the foot of the Washington Monument. The war in Europe was over; the cannonading was about to begin in America.

In the World Series of 1916 and 1918, Ruth had bettered Mathewson's record by pitching a total of 29²/₃ consecutive scoreless innings against the Dodgers and the Cubs. So he had gone from a glamorous record-setting pitching performance to establishing a new standard for power hitting—in a year's time. This sort of thing simply was not done in the big leagues, where, supposedly, a network of highly skilled checkers and balancers were charged with keeping things in reasonable order. But this fellow was barely getting started; what lay immediately ahead, in 1920 and 1921, would make everyone forget the pitching and make the monumental slugging of 1919 look positively anemic. A sign of the grandeur of things to come occurred during an exhibition game in Tampa against the Giants in the spring of 1919. At bat against a beanpole right-hander named Columbia George Smith, Ruth took his full circle at the plate and connected with such terrifying impact that he sent a baseball on as endless a journey as one is likely to be sent. Players on both benches automatically came to their feet, stunned, for they were being given a jolting look into the future, and not a future of just another mundane and predictable tomorrow either but one that was going to be new and different and explosive. It was a moment of clear and awesome revelation, and for that moment they were Stone Age tribesmen sighting their first low-flying airplane.

"I came to attention with everybody else," said Red Sox outfielder Harry Hooper, telling it to a writer in August 1974 while sitting on a rocker on the back porch of the Otesaga Hotel in Cooperstown, a few months before his death at the age of eighty-seven. He was describing a ball he had seen hit fifty-five years earlier. The experience had lit up his memory with a flash that had never dimmed. "You watch the outfielder," he said. "He tells you how far it's going. Well, I looked up once at that ball and then I watched the rightfielder. It was Ross Youngs. He was running and running into right-center. Getting smaller and smaller. There was no wall or grandstand out there, just a low rail fence, way, way out. Youngs finally stopped at the fence and put his hands on his hips and stood there and watched that ball come down. Then he turned around and looked back toward the infield."

Everyone remained frozen for a few moments, as though it would have been irreverent to sit down too quickly after what they had just witnessed. Then the Red Sox players sat down en masse, wordlessly watching their young teammate trot around the bases, while Columbia George Smith stood motionless on the mound, a blank expression on his face, not quite sure whether he had been honored or humiliated. A couple of instant historians later measured the clout. Barrow claimed it had traveled 579 feet. He also said the home run removed any lingering doubts he might have had about converting Ruth to an outfielder.

Fifty-five years later Harry Hooper laughed. "I don't think anybody even went over to shake his hand when he came back to the bench. But then after a few minutes we started going over to him, one by one. Babe? He didn't think he had done anything wonderful. To him it was just another wallop."

In baseball, as in many of life's adventures, few things are inevitable. There was, however, one conspicuous exception to this doctrine of chancy tomorrows: Inevitably, Babe Ruth would play his game in New York. Now, Boston is a fine city, secure in the glory of its history and the renown of its sires. But as the mighty celestial architect designed the shark for water and the eagle for flight, so was George Herman Ruth dynamically and merrily shaped and endowed to play baseball in New York. With the Statue of Liberty posted inspiringly at the city's harbor approach and Babe Ruth swinging explosively uptown in the Bronx, New York was heroically bracketed, the home of the free and the brave and the home run.

Enter Harry Frazee, for some the original Boston strangler, the most disastrous dose of medicine ever applied to a major-league franchise, but down deep really a likable fun-lover who had simply wandered through the wrong door. A native of Peoria, Illinois, the portly, round-faced Frazee was a hustling, ambitious fellow with a buccaneer spirit that belied his nondescript appearance. Harry had a passion for the theater, a malady for which medical science has yet to find relief. He could also diversify adventurously, having had a hand in promoting the Jack Johnson–Jess Willard heavyweight championship fight in Havana in 1915, a fight that the unpopular black champion Johnson was alleged to have thrown to the lumbering Willard in order to be allowed to live unmolested in the United States. Harry later confided to some of the Red Sox players that the fight had indeed been a tanker, and that he, Frazee, being on the inside, had raked in some lucrative wagers. But for Frazee the most enjoyable and exciting way of making money was producing Broadway shows, which he did with some initial success, enough to buy a couple of theaters and look around for other worlds to conquer.

In January 1916, the thirty-six-year-old Frazee bought the Red Sox from an ailing Joseph Lannin. In the beginning, Frazee sought to improve the club, shelling out large sums of money for talented players like Stuffy McInnis, Joe Bush, Wally Schang, and others. His efforts were rewarded; then as now, the Red Sox were a profitable franchise, with fans whose loyalty and devotion were laced with relentless fervor. There was a pennant and world championship in 1918, the fourth time in seven years the Sox had made their fans kings of the hill.

Pennants and world championships were great fun, but the principal stars in Frazee's eyes were those of the Broadway variety. Even as Ruth was making the Fenway turnstiles spin like dervishes, Frazee was producing a string of musicals that were hitting the New York stages like so many wet cabbages dropped from the roof of the Flatiron Building. Baseball profits notwithstanding, Harry was soon feeling the chill winds of debt, certainly not a unique sensation for a Broadway producer. In order to raise cash, he began putting his players on the train and sending them to New York. In 1918 and 1919 he swapped for cash pitchers Carl Mays, Ernie Shore, Hubert (Dutch) Leonard, and outfielder Duffy Lewis. But Harry was just warming up for the big one.

By December 1919, Frazee was in need again, looking for capital with which to feather yet another Broadway turkey. At the same time, his biggest star and drawing card, the idolized and noisesome Babe Ruth, who earlier that year had signed a three-year contract calling for $10,000 a year, was demanding a doubling of his salary. Original in almost everything else, Babe might have been the first to seek a renegotiated contract. He even had an agent, one Johnny Igoe (people had names like that in the twenties). So here we have a man desperately wanting to raise cash being badgered for money by another man whose contract was worth a fortune. Frazee did what any red-and-cold-blooded Broadway shark would have: He sold Babe Ruth. It's quaint to think of a theatrical man selling The Greatest Show on Earth. But the man from Peoria was more mesmerized by leggy chorus girls than by woolen-uniformed baseball players, and there are no doubt those who will empathize. When Frazee said to a city shaken as it had not been since the Battle of Bunker Hill, "I believe the sale of Ruth will ultimately strengthen the team," he struck a level of hypocrisy that could have qualified him for political office.

The destiny that works the levers of inevitability was more than obliging in this instance, having situated Frazee's New York offices on Forty-second Street, practically next door to those of the New York

Yankees. In that Yankee office sat the owners of the club, most notably Colonel Jacob Ruppert. The "colonel" had been dropped on him by a New York governor. Lacking shots at lordships and dukedoms, democratic America has had to settle for bogus colonelcies. But we do have aristocrats, and Ruppert was one of those. In manner, mien, wealth, and lifestyle, the derby-hatted, Chesterfield-coated, mustachioed Ruppert was an aristocrat. A lifelong bachelor who squired elegant ladies with discretion, Jake was heir to a thriving New York brewery. He lived in a twelve-room Fifth Avenue apartment staffed by a butler, a maid, a valet, a cook, and a laundress; raised thoroughbred horses and showed pedigree dogs; collected objets d'art; and was a distinguished member of New York society. He had also been a four-time member of the United States House of Representatives. But as far as history is concerned, it all amounts to peanut shells; for despite a life as ornamented as a Christmas tree, he is remembered today as the man who owned the New York Yankees and Babe Ruth—as Frazee is dismally remembered, despite his checkered achievements, as the Man Who Sold Babe Ruth.

In partnership with a gentleman with the resounding name of Tillinghast L'Hommedieu Huston, Ruppert in January 1915 had purchased the Yankees for $460,000. The natty little Ruppert had always been a baseball buff—further evidence of the game's leveling propensities. Like any true aristocrat, Ruppert could not abide anything less than excellence, which in baseball translates into an intolerance for losing. The odor of defeat was repugnant to him, and it was an odor he was determined to wave away with his checkbook.

On January 6, 1920, New Yorkers awoke to learn they had been handed a New Year's present of gargantuan proportions. For $125,000 Babe Ruth had been sold to the Yankees. Since it involved Ruth, the transaction naturally was the largest ever, the previous single-player-for-cash record having been $50,000 swaps, Tris Speaker from Boston to Cleveland in 1916, and Eddie Collins from Philadelphia to Chicago in 1914. Because the Yankees were then playing as tenants of the Giants in the Polo Grounds with its neighborly rightfield wall, the *New York Times* speculated that "it would not be surprising if Ruth surpassed his home run record of twenty-nine circuit clouts next summer." Indeed.

And let us remember now that all of this, the big money, the furor, the expectations, was built on just one full season as a regular, during which he batted .322 (seven others in the league did better). It was those astonishing 29 home runs that had elevated him suddenly into a pantheon apart from Cobb and Speaker. Tyrus had just captured his twelfth (and, significantly, last) batting title with a .384 average, but alas, just one home run. But it wasn't just this new weapon—the Phillies' Gavvy Cravath had busted 24 melon-breakers in 1915—it was the gusto with which this most theatrical of athletes performed his feats.

Ruth and the beginning of the roaring decade were a perfect match. Ruth in New York brought high sheen to the match. America needed a big, big hero to fit the swaggering, expansive contours of the 1920s, and in the Babe it got one it could barely contain. Walter Johnson was beginning to slow down, as was Alexander. Wagner was through, Jackson was in disgrace, and Tris Speaker and Eddie Collins were quiet men who did not burn in the imagination. Cobb was for the moment still the game's reigning king, but Tyrus's pinched personality did not evoke splendor nor provoke love, and despite a .401 batting average in 1922 he was being phased out. Cobb found himself in a world he never made; he was a still deadly gunfighter caught in a suddenly paved frontier, surrounded by rails and highways and electronic miracles, watching Ruthian missiles sail over his head. The bunt, the well-placed single, the stolen base—Cobb's way—was being replaced dramatically by the long-distance clout and the home-run trot, as personified by the new young dynamo in New York. What it took Cobb craft and guile and stealth to do, Ruth was accomplishing with one mighty whale of the timber. The crown had been passed in the middle of the night and Ty Cobb awoke to find it resting on the big, homely head of George Herman Ruth, who had not only a roaring bat as scepter but with it an insatiable riptide of Henry VIII appetites that a boomtown America could identify with.

ELEVEN

RUTH STARTED IT in 1920, his thunderclaps in New York launching the most explosive and prolific decade of hitting in baseball history, a decade that culminated with so many bullet line drives in 1930 that the game's establishment felt compelled to drain a bit of juice from the ball. Home of so many cultural, social, and political ideas, innovations, and philosophies, New York might just as well take credit for if not inventing the home run, then for lending it grandeur and majesty. In New York it became the most exciting attraction in sports, with a veritable superman performing seemingly inexhaustible miracles, blasting those home runs not only breathtaking distances but doing it with wondrous frequency. If he had dazzled and intoxicated the imaginations of the baseball constituency with 29 in 1919, consider what 54 must have done in 1920. But forget that. What about 59 in 1921—in two years more than doubling the record he had set in 1919? Think of *that* feeding into the self-image of a people already proud of its galvanizing brawn as it rushed and jazzed and Charlestoned into its most vigorous decade.

No sir, Cobb, McGraw, the bunt, the stolen base, and "inside baseball" would not have done for the twenties. What good was the McGravian genius of thieving a run via subtleties when it could be retrieved with a single swing of the bat? Ruth's game quickly became America's game, for the big bat had touched some latent, or maybe not-so-latent, chord. The fans showed fervent delight in the big-bang, hit-'em-for-distance game. In his first year in New York, 1920, Ruth doubled the Yankees' attendance to over 1,280,000.

No, there was nothing subtle about him. He went at the record book like a kid with a brick at a plate glass window, rewriting it in his image like a tyrant imposing new legislation upon the land. Before the 1921 season ended he had already, at the age of twenty-six, hit more home runs than any man in the game's history, burying in the attic the old lifetime mark of Roger Connor, a nineteenth-century slugger who had rung up 136 long ones. Also in those two years, he set new records for not just home runs but runs batted in, slugging average, total bases, runs scored (the last three are still in the books, surrounded by moats and barbed wire, for as close as anyone ever comes to them). These are man-sized records, the heavyweight records of baseball. And here was the one man sweeping them all in, all at once, with nothing gradual about it. It was as if in 1920 he had landed in New York from another planet, product of a bigger, stronger, more monstrous species than we knew about. His 1921 season stands apart as the single most sustained work of devastation ever committed from a batter's box, by anyone, anywhere, anytime. The numbers: 59 home runs, 16 triples, 44 doubles, 204 hits, 177 runs scored, 171 runs batted in, 457 total bases, .846 slugging average, .378 batting average. (And remember, four years before, he was a 24-game winner.)

No athlete was ever more perfectly confluent with his time. He brought his home-run swing to New York just as the lively ball was being introduced, and the pitching repertory was being emasculated. Lively ball? What lively ball? If you want to believe the baseball establishment, the emblem of its game has never been changed or modified in the least, that it is the same soggy spherical bag of yarn it has always been. It's almost as if they believe that the baseball itself is a symbol of morality, that the game's mystique exists tick-tock like a tiny heartbeat inside of the ball, and that to tamper with it would be akin to taking liberties with the Almighty's handiwork. In 1910 a cork-centered ball had been introduced, giving the little round charmer a bit more bounce; but hitters weaned on a certain style of play were not ready to start blasting off. In 1919 the A. J. Reach Company, manufacturer of major-league baseballs, began using a more efficient yarn-winding machine that wound the yarn more tightly and gave the ball greater resilience. Batting averages went up, runs began pouring across the plate, pitchers became shell-shocked, and attendance went up.

Not only did the moguls give their employees a livelier ball to play with, they also conspired to make it easier to hit by outlawing the spitball and other trick deliveries. (Not wanting to deprive anyone of his livelihood, exceptions were made for active pitchers who relied heavily on the spitter, thus creating a soon-to-be-extinct species: the legal spitballers. The last of these dinosaurs, Burleigh Grimes, left the big leagues in 1934, since which time the spitball has continued to flourish, but under darker auspices.) One of the reasons given for the banning of the spitter was hygiene—a baseball lathered with saliva was suddenly considered unseemly. But Roger Peckinpaugh had his own interpretation of the ruling. "It wasn't the spitter exactly they wanted to bar," the old shortstop said. "They wanted to get rid of all those phony pitches. All of those pitches were in the disguise of the spitter. You see, the pitchers went to their mouths, but then they might throw you a shine ball or a mud ball or an emery ball. So as I understand it, the only way they could stop them fooling with that baseball was to bar the spitter, not let the pitcher go to his mouth. If a pitcher didn't go to his mouth and still threw one of those freak pitches, the umpire would know damn well that guy was doctoring the ball. That's how they stopped it."

Also at this time, the practice of removing scuffed balls from the game was begun. The pitchers—in the 1920s they needed shinguards, mask, and chest protector almost as much as the catchers did—had a harder time gripping smooth, fresh baseballs, while the batters had a much easier time sighting them. One statistic: Before 1920, the highest the American League had ever collectively batted was .277, in its 1901 shakedown season. From 1920 through 1929 the league *averaged* .285 per season. The National League's best average between 1901 and 1919 was .272, in 1912; from 1920 through 1929 the league averaged the same as its little brother, .285 per season, before going berserk in 1930 with a .303 average.

The various concomitants, plus the inspirational arrival of Ruth, made for a unique situation in baseball, one that will probably never happen again. The lusty hitting continued on through the 1930s, but not with the same ferocity as before, and from that 1920s cannonading we learned one thing as well as we are likely ever to learn it: Baseball, in all probability, established forever in the 1920s the highest frequency with which its good batters could hit safely. The consistency with which the leagues, teams, and individual players put the slug on the ball has never been approached.

Ruth, the man who virtually invented the home run, or at least the home run as a piece of theater, remained the big bonker, setting a new home-run record three years running with his totals of 29, 54, and 59 in 1919, 1920, and 1921. The National League also broke its long-ball record three times, but it took three different men and nine years to do it. In 1922 Rogers Hornsby hit 42 long ones to break Gavvy Cravath's 1915 standard of 24; in 1929 Chuck Klein stepped one rung higher with 43, and a year later Hack Wilson raised the ante to 56, where it remains.

Any man who broke home-run records with the gusto and emphasis of a Ruth, who lived with such generosity of spirit and lack of inhibition, who seemed one of the generators of the national maelstrom within which speeding roadsters and bathtub gin and flagpole sitters and buying on margin whirled, a man who ate a dozen (or was it two dozen?) hot dogs after a game and washed them down with a gallon of soda pop, cleared the lot away with fortissimo belches, and who used sunset and sunrise as parallel bars upon which to swing as he hunted and insatiably clocked women too numerous to count or remember ("He'd stick his thing into anything that had hair on it," a teammate remembered), and then reappear on the field the next day as fresh and ebullient and thundering as ever—such a man was a law unto himself. Or so it seemed.

Inevitability and Ruth. Again. One supposes it was the way the man ran his life. He rushed through rules and regulations like a sprinter through the tape, breaking them with the same free-swinging insouciance with which he broke home-run records. But records, as one of the game's nobler clichés goes, are made to be broken. Rules, no. Especially rules laid down, propagated, and enforced by Kenesaw Mountain Landis. Inevitably, the Ruth express would barrel through one of those rules and the judge would burn the bridges ahead.

The confrontation between the game's brace of "saviors" came after the 1921 World Series (in which McGraw whipped the Yankees after the latter had taken their first pennant). Since 1911 there had been a rule in effect forbidding World Series participants from barnstorming after the Series. The rationale for the rule was that these exhibition games would rub some of the gloss from the Series, which the game's moguls realized was already a national treasure only eight years after its inception. The rule was a foolish one, depriving players of some extra cash, and was in fact violated from time to time without penalty. When Ruth announced that he and several Yankee teammates were planning to barnstorm after the Series, Landis warned them not to. The judge, in his first full year in office, was seeking to consolidate his power, and what better way than to go nose to nose with the game's greatest natural force?

Ruth, the old waterfront truant, remained in character. "Tell the old guy to go jump in the lake," he said when Landis reinforced his warning. "If Ruth breaks the rule against World Series players engaging in such contests," the judge intoned, "then it will resolve itself into an issue between the player and myself." Get that—"the player." The commissioner had reduced the magical young demigod to a mere "player," thus making him beholden to the rules.

Ruth played his exhibition games and Landis bided his time. The canny judge was toeing the turf around him, trying to determine how solidly he stood. He soon found it very solid. Yankee co-owners Ruppert and Huston issued a statement that noted the unjustness of the rule, but went on to say "as long as it exists it should be obeyed." The press generally took the same approach, with one paper saying that "Judge Landis is absolutely correct in his attitude. Baseball made Ruth, and not Ruth baseball. . . . Baseball needs a Landis more than it needs a Ruth." This attitude tells us two things: that even a free-wheeling emperor of the home run does not have a blank check, and that there were still enough jitters about the game's moral health left over from the Black Sox scandal to give the blank check to Landis. The rest of the country might have begun spinning off its axis, but baseball still remained that special universe, and not even Babe Ruth could flaunt its rules and get away with it. Ruth had given the new commissioner a golden opportunity to solidify once and for all the totalitarian impact of the office.

Eary in December, Landis announced his decision. Ruth and teammates Bob Meusel and Bill Piercy, who had accompanied him on the tour, were fined the amount of their World Series checks ($3,362) and suspended for the first six weeks of the 1922 season.

Case dismissed.

TWELVE

ANOTHER MEASURE of Ruth's dominance of the game was the fact that he overshadowed Rogers Hornsby, his exact contemporary. Being a diamond hero in the era of Ruth was not easy; the colossal Babe seemed to occupy just about all of the available room. Hornsby should have matched Ruth as a folk hero, surely in the National League, where he dominated with the same crushing might as Ruth did in the American. Hornsby may not have hit as many home runs as Ruth, but he hit the ball as hard (none of Ty Cobb's defrosted ropes here), and if not as far, then with more frequency; for a time, with more frequency than anyone who ever lived, Cobb included. But the wintry-souled Hornsby seemed almost willfully to reject the hero's mold. If Ruth the slugger was the symbol of the new American might, and Ruth the personality the image of the hedonistic decade (the lively ball and the lively dollar), then the blunt-speaking, frosty-eyed Hornsby was a bit too redolent of times past.

He endeared himself to no one. Interestingly, neither of the two highest lifetime batters (Cobb, .367, Hornsby, .358) had much teddy bear in him. Cobb was mean, ferociously competitive, and psychotically driven, and Hornsby was cold, aloof, fiercely independent, and brutally frank. Handsome, with a bright smile that pressed engaging dimples into his cheeks, he was an intriguing character, the prickly personality probably a defense for some psychic injuries he sought to keep private.

And private they remain, as they do with all of our baseball heroes. Of all the members of our mythology of mortals, and we're talking here of statesmen, creative artists, lords of industry and commerce, even those insubstantial shadows known as movie stars, the subterranean depths of our athletes seem to have been the least violated. We seem not to be interested in whatever torments or neuroses might have helped propel those exquisitely coordinated bodies—further proof of the fantasyland they occupy in our collective unconscious. One assumes that Christy Mathewson had psychic disturbances every bit as interesting as Woodrow Wilson's, but because they did not impinge beyond the ball field and because Mathewson, real or not, existed then largely as a romantic notion and exists today as an unambiguous and irrefutable set of statistics, he has been permitted to lie undisturbed with his ghosts. Not even such earthshakers as Cobb and Ruth have been victims of psychobiography. Emily Dickinson, secluded in her room in Amherst, has had her soul dissected more clinically than the uninhibited Ruth who sped like a locomotive across the landscape, or the maniacal Cobb, who had a vortex that was no doubt as turbulent as the gentle Emily's. After years of superficial infringements upon their privacy, athletes are permitted to depart with all inner secrets intact and unprobed, as pure as the game they played and the memories they bequeathed.

Of course even if Hornsby had been subjected to the most penetrating psychoanalysis it would not alter in the least, no matter the conclusions, history's judgment of him as the greatest right-handed batter that ever lived. There is no one remotely close to him. A quick check of the twentieth century's high-average kings shows that of the top six, all but Hornsby swung from the left side, and of the top ten, the only righties are Hornsby and Harry Heilmann, who is seventh with .342.

He was born on April 27, 1896, in the small Texas town of Winters, a name that fits his disposition perfectly (five miles away was the town of Maverick, which would have done nicely, too). An older brother, Everett, pitched in the Texas League. Everett got Rogers a tryout with Dallas, making Everett roughly the equivalent of whoever it was that told young Will Shakespeare to go down to London and swing his quill. Dallas shipped the skinny (140 pounds then) eighteen-year-old shortstop (that's what he was then, and aren't you dream-team makers glad he moved over—what would you do with Wagner and Hornsby *both* at the position?) to the Hugo, Oklahoma, club of the Class D Texas–Oklahoma League. Hugo, which is in southeastern Oklahoma, about ten miles northwest of Frogville, couldn't stand the prosperity of a pro ball club on its acres, and the team folded after six weeks, whereupon Hornsby was sold for $125 to the Denison, Texas, club in the same league. (Four-hundred hitter or not, Hornsby has to take second place in the Denison pantheon, for that was where Dwight Eisenhower was born, in 1890. They were both rookies in 1914; Eisenhower was about to graduate from West

Point.) Rogers batted .232 that year, .277 the next—neither mark worth more than a yawn, but the enchantment of that swing must have been unmistakable, because by the end of the 1915 season he was in St. Louis with the Cardinals, playing 18 games and batting .246. Never mind where the ball is going; in the beginning it's the stroke of a Jackson, a Hornsby, a Williams, that narrows the eyes of the knowing beholder. If baseball is your business, the flawless geometry of that swing is in accord with your most fantastic daydreams. It is positively sensual. The sound of line drives cannot be far behind, and in Hornsby's case they began ringing in 1916 with a .313 batting average. Playing with a shaky glove at short, he did not become a second baseman until 1920, the year his averages began climbing like a thermometer in boiling water.

Rogers (the uncommon first name was his mother's not uncommon family name) smote them dead throughout the 1920s with batting averages that were as unreasonable as Ruth's home-run totals. But Babe outshadowed him, then and now. The reasons are obvious: Ruth was master of the most charismatic rocket in sports, the home run, and he had the personality to go with it. Hornsby, whose batting averages ran through the decade as rampant as the stock market, was primarily a line-drive hitter (there is little glory in decapitating infielders), with a personality that made him seem like a man campaigning vigorously in an unpopularity contest. Yet Hornsby, in spite of himself, through the first-magnitude dazzle of his batting averages, and yes, partially because of that cactus personality, fascinates. He possessed an ultimate quality, one that no great athlete can do without: He was special in the eyes of his peers. They all recognized and acknowledged his faults, and many had been burned by his sarcasm. "But when Rogers Hornsby picked up a bat," said a contemporary, "he was perfect." Rogers Hornsby with a bat in his hand and his feet planted deep in the batter's box, was the preferred image, outweighing, even making a bit eccentric, the other Rogers Hornsby, the one who told the world to go to hell, the one whose initial response upon hearing of the death of his son in a plane crash was, "I always told that kid that if he kept going up in those things he'd come down in one the hard way someday."

He was too at ease with his incomparable gifts to realize just how rare they were, how inimitable. In later years as a manager, he could not understand why his players, after a few lessons from the master, did not hit better. He was under the impression that the reason other men did not hit .400 was only because they did not listen to Hornsby. He showed them how to do it. He would show anyone, literally. When he was managing Cincinnati in the 1950s a few Philadelphia Phillies players approached him before a game to talk hitting. The Rajah (as he was regally known) was soon giving them tips. "I couldn't believe it," said Cincinnati third baseman Grady Hatton, watching from the dugout. "He was standing out there giving batting tips to guys on the team we were about to play." But that was because Hornsby, the batting purist, recognized no barriers when it came to imparting the holy wisdom of bashing a baseball. Hitting was his obsession (except for playing the horses, his only one), his *raison d'être*, his very religion, and it transcended frontiers, languages, and opposing uniforms. Improve everyone's hitting and you made the world a better place (except for pitchers). He probably wouldn't have realized it, but in a world of .400 hitters, Rogers Hornsby would have hit .500.

Hornsby's God-given artistry at home plate was supplemented by his theories. He would not go to the movies for fear they might hurt his eyes (Ted Williams would go to two or three a day), nor would he read anything more than the racing form for the same reason. He enjoyed the ladies, but put limits to it: "If I can't get it between seven P.M. and midnight, the hell with it," he said, because a man could not hit .400 without getting proper rest, nor could he if he smoked or drank. But if Hornsby was a puritan, he was a narrow one. The nonsmoker and nondrinker was a compulsive gambler, to the extent that he had a pinball machine installed in the Chicago Cubs clubhouse when he was managing there in the early 1930s and would gamble on it against his players. (And anyway, his puritanism, such as it was, was for the benefit of the body, not the soul.)

"He was a very cold man," said Billy Herman, who broke in with the Cubs under Hornsby. "He would stare at you with the coldest eyes I ever saw. We never knew what the hell he was thinking." This can be said of any man, but with a man who never read a newspaper, a magazine, or a book, it could be eerie and unnerving. With those coldest eyes he watched those baseballs from deep in the batter's box, and what he saw must have lit up his insides and set the bells to ringing just as they did inside his beloved pinball machine as he stepped into those baseballs and sent them on air-scorching line drives in every direction. And the young Hornsby could do more than hit. "I never saw a man go faster from home to first," said teammate Les

Bell. "And to watch him stretching out a triple was a sight to see." And at bat? "Once he stepped into that batter's box," said Bill Hallahan, "he was in another world. His concentration was so intense you could have shot off cannons around him and he wouldn't have heard it." The man who could tell the world to go to hell never argued with an umpire, was never, they say, thrown out of a game. If a pitcher had the audacity to knock him down—and they became fewer in time—he did not say a word, merely stood right back up and resumed his stance, that icy concentration unbroken. "He was never casual at home plate," said Hallahan, "not even in batting practice."

We can believe he was never casual while standing in that modest-sized rectangle of ground next to home plate, for here was his domain, to be possessed and defended, from where he sent forth his ferocious messages to all corners of that unique universe known as baseball. The averages are terrifying. From 1920 through 1925 he took six consecutive batting titles with averages of .370, .397, .401, .384, .424, and .403. The .424 is the twentieth century's summit of man and bat versus a baseball thrown from sixty feet six inches away. From what we have seen transpire in the more than six decades since that .424, it is simply impossible for a human being to do better. That batting average becomes more remote and mystical, like a mountain peak being shrouded by more and more layers of cloud.

No, not a hero of the Ruth mold, but yet there was something fundamentally American about him. Moody, a loner, he was like a character left behind by the receding frontier; he probably belonged in the first decade of the century rather than the one in which he set his fearsome records. He was an indefatigable exponent of an old, now passé baseball pastime: lobby-sitting. Those were the days of daylight ball and modest salaries. After dinner, most players retired to the lobby, took a seat, and, with legs crossed and arms folded, watched the lobby traffic pass to and fro until bedtime. For Hornsby, a man who did not drink, would not go to the movies, and chose generally to be friendless (he would not have a roommate), lobby sitting was essential to his lifestyle. "His ass was made of iron," a teammate said. Rogers would sit interminably, those cold eyes watching every movement across the lobby.

One thing and one thing only could animate him: talk about hitting. The man who once punched his manager in the nose (Branch Rickey, St. Louis, 1923), told various general managers and club owners to buzz off, and who even told Kenesaw Mountain Landis to go to hell when that particular archangel asked him to curb his gambling, had a weakness for children. One evening a couple of youngsters approached the batting master in a hotel lobby and with trepidation blurted out their question: How was Mr. Hornsby, standing so far back in the box, able to put the swat on a low outside pitch? Mr. Hornsby promptly sprang to his feet, borrowed the walking stick of a startled old gent sitting nearby and took his stance in the middle of the lobby and demonstrated just how, stepping forward and flailing that stick around so that the air whistled and the potted plants fluttered. (One wonders how Hornsby, had he been born in a prebaseball America, would have spent his energies. Did the Hornsbys and Cobbs and McGraws of 1800 go through life with a nagging, unresolved sense of deprivation?)

"Baseball is my life," he told a reporter in 1961, "the only thing I know and can talk about, my only interest." Plain enough. And if anyone, even a peer, dared to encroach? Well, in 1928 Hornsby, then with the Boston Braves, was locked in a race for the batting championship with Pittsburgh's young Paul Waner, one of the sharpest hitters of all time. The Pirates came into Boston for a series near the end of the season, and with both teams winding up lackluster years, the papers focused on the great batting-title shootout between Hornsby and Waner (who had won the year before with .380). Waner faltered in the series, while Hornsby became demonized, whipping base hits in every direction to pull comfortably ahead. At the conclusion of the series the two encountered each other under the stands. "Well, Rog," said the mild-mannered Waner, "It looks like you're going to beat me out." "You didn't think I wouldn't, did you?" answered Hornsby. Gracious indeed. When asked by a writer if there were any pitchers he feared, Hornsby, whose candor makes Honest Abe look like a rank dissembler, replied, "No, I feel sorry for them." From a man who averaged .402 over a five-year period, this comes closer to compassion than arrogance.

After the 1926 season Hornsby was as big in St. Louis as Ruth was in New York. As player-manager, he had driven the Cardinals to their first pennant and then a pulsing seven-game World Series victory over the Babe's Yankees. One can imagine how adored, worshiped, and generally fussed over Hornsby was by the people of St. Louis. There were parades, banquets, speeches, and editorials lauding his leadership and hailing his genius. Keys to the city, trophies, plaques, perfumed handkerchiefs in the mail—they were all his. Two months later he was traded to the Giants. That's how ornery he was.

It was a near-suicidal move for Cardinals owner Sam Breadon to make, but Sam had had it up to here with his star. First there had been the business of an exhibition game in New Haven the dollar-squeezing Breadon had scheduled late in the season. Hornsby asked him to have the game scrubbed, saying the players needed a day of rest. Breadon either couldn't or wouldn't. One thinks now of Burleigh Grimes on Hornsby: "You might not have liked what was on his mind, but you always damned well knew what it was." So Sam Breadon knew, and didn't like it, especially the part about where to shove his exhibition game. Well, a .400 hitter is a special breed, but so is an employer. After the season, with the confetti still in his hair, Hornsby demanded a three-year contract at $50,000 a year. Breadon, who kept his dollars as close to him as the skin on his palm, didn't think this was a very good idea. Neither man would budge. So Breadon took a deep breath and got rid of the man who had brought all the marbles to St. Louis. He traded him to John McGraw and the New York Giants, getting in return pitcher Jimmy Ring and the one man in the league capable of making the St. Louis fans forgive Breadon and forget Hornsby—Frankie Frisch.

The New York–born, Fordham-educated Frisch was a dynamically gifted second baseman with competitive fires that burned with Cobbian intensity. He was the archetypical McGraw ballplayer, and if John J. could have designed his players they all would have had the flash, the zeal, and the fire of Frisch. In addition, the intelligent, baseball-wise Fordham Flash possessed leadership qualities that early in his career marked him as potential successor to McGraw.

And why was McGraw willing to part with his hard-driving star second baseman? Because the world was changing around John McGraw, and the stubborn old man didn't like it and wasn't going to stand for it. The game that John McGraw had entered professionally in 1890 had undergone dramatic changes, most of them coming in the last few years. The area of McGraw's particular genius—the cunning of "inside" baseball—was rapidly changing under the impact of Babe Ruth, the lively ball, and power baseball. But McGraw was enough baseball man to adjust to that; where he was unable to find flexibility was in dealing with the new men coming into the game, that postwar American man bringing with him a different brand of pride and independence, men who would not cringe under the savage, public tongue-lashings of John McGraw or anybody else. A more complicated man had emerged from the brutality of a triumphant world war, from the radical ideas of the intellectual marketplace, from the contempt for Prohibition, from the whirligig pace of the decade. The will of John McGraw was losing its capacity to break the spirits of men who were playing in front of larger, noisier, more adulatory crowds, and some of those spirits were as rock-hard and unyielding as his own.

First baseman Bill Terry, greatest of all McGraw's players, was openly contemptuous of his crotchety skipper, talked back to him, and then worse, refused to talk to him at all. Fred Lindstrom, McGraw's intense, intelligent young third baseman, was another example of the new breed. "The players that were coming in had a different approach to baseball," Lindstrom said.

Times were changing and McGraw was just not able to adapt. You see, his style of dealing with someone who had made a mistake on the field was to chew them out unmercifully. He could be brutal. He thought nothing of humiliating a man in front of the whole team. For years he was able to get away with it. But Frisch wouldn't take it, and then Terry wouldn't take it, and I wouldn't take it. It ate his craw to have anyone talk back to him, to challenge not only his authority but his expertise. But it was a different caliber of man now and tactics that had been successful before were no longer applicable. John McGraw's career had begun in 1890 and been in many ways quite remarkable. It was just unfortunate that he had remained inflexible when everything else was changing around him.

It was Frisch who sent McGraw into his blackest rages, and not because Frisch, unlike the supercilious Terry and coolly logical Lindstrom, answered the fulminating anachronism word for word, with a tongue as tart and profane as his skipper's. It was because of the similarities in their personalities and not the differences that the old generation and the new went at each other with the wrath of historical antagonists. In Frisch, McGraw saw a spiritual son (one unlike the reserved, respectful Mathewson, whose lingering death throes in 1925 were for McGraw wrenchingly personal and symbolic, too), a throwback to the young John McGraw and finally a successor.

And so McGraw made it harder on Frisch, on "his own," than on any other, and the second surrogate son refused to take it, was constitutionally unable to take it. Like any familial dispute, the fires of this one erupted and never cooled, grew angrier and more intense. "McGraw had formed a dislike for Frisch and you could *feel* it whenever they came together." Whatever the specifics of a particular argument, Lindstrom said, the true underlying cause was always that personality clash, that irreconcilable father-son hostility. "The name-calling became vicious," Lindstrom said, "and I can remember McGraw finally roaring at him, 'You're through!'" And so Frisch became Ishmael, cast from the House of McGraw, cast from New York to St. Louis in an act of wrath and exasperation, and some years later a wistful McGraw, near death, would say of his lost prodigy, "I despised him. I despised him. But, God, I hated to see him go."

Not without deeply felt regrets, the embittered McGraw rid himself of Frisch. But the new man was every bit as singular and temperamental, in his own way. Rogers Hornsby, wherever he went, brought along with him his own special problems. (Frisch, it should be noted, was in the game as player and manager for another twenty-five years after leaving McGraw and had no significant problems anywhere, with anyone.) Six batting titles, a pennant, and a world championship had brought Hornsby close to deification in St. Louis. In New York, however, the deity found himself among company that looked upon him as just another mortal, and a rather trying one at that. McGraw's hard-bitten squad included future Hall of Famers Terry, Lindstrom, Travis Jackson, Burleigh Grimes, and Edd Roush, none of whom believed that batting .400 was any excuse for being a pain in the ass. They respected their new teammate but weren't about to genuflect. Lindstrom, in rejecting some of Hornsby's unsolicited wisdom, told Rogers, "When you put that bat down you're no bargain." When he was indisposed, McGraw deputized Hornsby as manager. In one situation with men on second and third, Grimes, on the mound, heard his name called and turned to find temporary manager Hornsby coming upon him with the old, ineffable advice: Don't walk him, but don't give him anything good to hit. Grimes, who had attended the same finishing school for diplomats as Hornsby, glared at Rogers and demanded, "Do you want him walked or do you want him pitched to? Tell me what the hell you want." Hornsby punched the pocket of his glove, and turned and walked back to his position.

McGraw got along tolerably well with Hornsby. But Rogers's air of implicit superiority made the old man uncomfortable, and after one year the slugger was traded to the Braves. McGraw then had to suffer through four years of indignity, watching Frisch lead the Cardinals to pennants in 1928, 1930, and 1931, and the prodigal

Hornsby help the Cubs to a flag in 1929. The Cubs were Hornsby's fourth team in four years, the Braves having been unable to resist Chicago's offer of $200,000 for him.

Like Cobb, Hornsby never changed, never mellowed. He remained contentious, frank, bigoted, and a relentless horseplayer. They knew he was troublesome, but baseball people never lost their fascination for him, and he was seldom without a job, as a manager, coach, batting instructor, or scout, holding it until he had offended too many people, or the wrong person, and then moving on again, without regrets, satisfied that he had done it his way. He was old royalty, he represented magic, a crusty nobility. Maybe that .400 batting average is as near to a coronation that a nation that overthrew its monarchy gets. It sets men apart forever. Think of Hornsby, and Cobb, and the unsociable Bill Terry and the likable but testy Ted Williams. But then again, there was the sweet-natured Joe Jackson, the amiable Harry Heilmann, and George Sisler, who twice hit .400 despite no discernible personality at all. But leaving aside Cobb, who demonstrated an unbalanced mind to the end of his life, Hornsby was the strangest of all. A most uncomfortable hero to contend with.

THIRTEEN

SOON THE CHANGES would be incisive and crushing, leading on into still more changes that in the 1920s were wildly unseeable and too colossal to have been believed anyway. The coming eras, like those of the past, would raise their own heroes cut and measured to the times. But first there had to be observed the passage of the old, the last slow, soft burning of diminishing stars, burning down to little more than an afterglow. But even the afterglow of greatness can leave its own lasting illumination, an unforgettable pageantry of color upon the filling pages of history. Often, the final judgment of a hero is pronounced by the quality of departure.

Among those who heard the tolling bell in these middle years of the 1920s, each in his own way, was the great, permanently interlocked triumvirate of pitchers. Once more the litany: Mathewson, Johnson, and Alexander. Once more inseparable as each prepared for his own, differing departure. For two, crowning glory in the twilight; for one, a pitiful death that went keening through baseball hearts everywhere. And for each, appropriately, the backdrop was baseball's grandest time, the autumnal rites known as the World Series, when after the long campaigns of spring and summer the champion is crowned once more, the signal for the leaves to break free and blow against the skies and for the snows to come tumbling.

Sentimental America was pleased and charmed when at last, in 1924, one of its longest reigning heroes, Walter Johnson, finally, in his eighteenth season of tireless and uncomplaining splendor, made it to the World Series. The thirty-seven-year-old Johnson was 23–7, leading for the sixth and last time in wins, for the seventh and last time in shutouts, for the fifth and last time in earned-run average, for the twelfth and last time in strikeouts. It was as if the veteran, with a stubbornness to match his greatness, had been determined to go on and on until he won his moment in the brilliance of the October sunshine.

So finally he was there, and naturally the country rooted for one of its most cherished heroes, and making it easier to do so was the name of the opposition: McGraw's Giants. For McGraw it was an unprecedented fourth straight, and final, pennant. To the rest of the country McGraw and his Giants represented New York arrogance, even as Ruth and his Yankees were establishing in the sensibilities of the nation New York power. So it was the repository of the old rural values against urban swagger, and the Series unfolded to a most melodramatic script.

The great Walter went down to defeat in the opener in ten innings, 4–3. He lost again in Game Five, 6–2, and the country sighed. Washington tied the Series at three games apiece and everyone prepared for that most momentous of baseball events: the seventh game of the World Series, a phrase that carried its own unique aura of drama, portent, and decision. And what a game it was; no seventh game has yet bettered it, and because of Walter Johnson, it is unlikely one ever will.

That the gods were in attendance this day there is no doubt, and that their benevolent touch was upon the proceedings is beyond dispute. In the bottom of the eighth inning, trailing 3–1, Washington tied the score, thanks to a miraculous bad-hop single with the bases loaded by the Senators' player-manager, Bucky Harris. Score tied. And who comes walking slowly from the Washington bullpen, advancing to the mound through the lengthening shadows of that October afternoon? It is Johnson, of course, being given one last chance to score a World Series victory, a victory that would mean a championship.

Working on just one day's rest, the grand veteran begins buggy-whipping those fastballs through a heavy-hitting Giant lineup (all those future Hall of Famers), through the ninth, tenth, eleventh, and twelfth innings. Finally, in the bottom of the twelfth, another divine intervention. A runner on second. A ground ball is hit to Lindstrom at third, the ball strikes a pebble again, bounds high over Lindstrom's head into left field and the winning run scores. A nation cheers for one of its beloved titans, and dare you doubt that Other Forces were at work?

A year later Walter was given an encore as Washington again won the pennant and prepared to meet the Pittsburgh Pirates for the title. But even as the teams were lining up for Game One in Pittsburgh on October 7, eastward across the Alleghenies, beyond the leaf-strewn campus of Bucknell University, and far north of New York City and the empty Polo Grounds, in the Adirondack village of Saranac Lake, amid the royal drama of another mountain autumn, Christy Mathewson was gasping away his life. America's first unalloyed baseball hero was going to his death on an *ipso facto* American holiday— the opening day of the World Series.

Matty's Saranac deathbed was the end of a trail that had begun with his resignation as manager of the Reds in 1918 and his enlistment as a captain in the Army Chemical Warfare Division. (Remember, this was the quintessential American hero, down to the very marrow.) Like Alexander, he went to France, and, like his twin as the National League's most prodigious winner, he paid heavily for it. Inspecting the trenches soon after the armistice was signed, he inhaled some poison gas (another version is that he accidentally breathed the gas during a training session), severely damaging his lungs. After being hospitalized, he returned home, apparently all right. In 1919 he rejoined McGraw and the Giants as a coach. The following year, however, his health suddenly began deteriorating. He was diagnosed as tubercular, in those years the same as being handed a death warrant. He and his wife moved to Saranac Lake; because of its pure air the Adirondack Mountain village was considered a haven for those afflicted with the "white plague." (Dr. Ernest Trudeau had established a world-famous tuberculosis sanitorium there in 1884.)

Saranac proved salubrious for Matty, who had originally been given six months to live. By 1923 he had recovered sufficiently to assume the presidency of the Boston Braves, certainly a joyless job, for the team was a chronic loiterer among the league's lower depths. (Hopelessly inept teams would, in a gild-by-association effort, sometimes bring into their front offices or coaching staffs one of the game's old Siegfrieds or Rolands as if hoping for some of the vanished magic to somehow begin secreting.) But in the spring of 1925 he suffered a relapse and returned with his wife to their home in Saranac. There he coughed blood and lay in drenching sweats, his once "godlike" physique withering away, and saw through the summer and early fall, his old familiar seasons, the seasons of eternal youth and the glory of Christy Mathewson. He spent his last months reading baseball in the daily paper, playing checkers—"taking on all comers," the obituaries noted—and motoring along the quiet mountain roads, awaiting the last stroke of the clock.

It was as if the baseball season had sustained him, for when it was done the last props of life fell away, and the forty-five-year-old master of the fadeaway knew they were going. On the morning of the day he died, he made plans for his funeral near the Bucknell campus. Reportedly, he said to his wife, "Now, Jane, I suppose you will have to go out and have a good cry. Don't make it a long one. This cannot be helped." And as the teams were gathering for the thunder and lightning of an event he had so incomparably dominated twenty years before, he died.

Walter Johnson, in a twilight of his own, "paled" when he heard the news. (Among the many printed laments was the wistful, true-blue one that "these two cunning and magnificent knights of the mound had never faced each other.") A "shocked" John McGraw, a spectator at the Series, left Pittsburgh immediately upon learning of Matty's death, but not before eulogizing Matty as "one of the greatest of all pitchers," and recalled him "as a loyal friend," this last carrying perhaps a certain bittersweet commentary. McGraw's "good son," the "loyal," devoted one, was dead. There were no more Mathewsons for him, not in stature nor in unquestioning loyalty. The new generation was upon the embattled patriarch of the New York Giants, and he could only rant and smolder about ingratitude and insubordination, and lose them.

Before the second game of the World Series the flag was lowered to half-mast and after the national anthem the crowd sang "Nearer My God to Thee."

Mathewson was the first of the twentieth century's great baseball idols, and the first to die. The tributes came in torrents. Among them was this: "He had proved you could play professional baseball and remain a gentleman."

One year later, in 1926, with the World Series once more as backdrop, the third member of that splendid triumvirate of pitchers achieved his most imperishable moment on a baseball diamond, one worthy of balladry, and although the focus was but one batter it remains more lasting in the romance of baseball than Matty's three shutouts in the 1905 Series or the miracle of intervention from somewhere that gave Walter Johnson his 1924 Series triumph.

Unlike Mathewson, part of whose appeal were his striking good looks and the subtleties of his character, and Johnson, whose humble nature combined with his superhuman speed to make him an irresistible hero, Grover Cleveland Alexander never penetrated quite as deeply into the heart of America as his triumvirate peers. His casual, easygoing ways did not bespeak nobility or grand-scale heroism. His personal tragedies, which would surely have endeared him to his sentimental countrymen, were little known at the time; a protective press was still concerned then about the public's perception of the game and its heroes, and the tale of a solitary Alexander trying to adjure his demons with forbidden whiskey was left virtually unwritten. But in it for Alex lay a rugged justice, a conspiracy of age, weariness, and luck-of-the-draw drama that cohered into his great electrifying moment that crystallized into a legend neither Mathewson nor Johnson ever attained.

Grover Cleveland Alexander's strikeout of Tony Lazzeri in the seventh inning of the seventh game of the 1926 World Series stands in baseball lore like a piece of classic sculpture, awash in the soft amber light of memory, its flawless craftsmanship a thing to be cherished over and over. Grover Cleveland Alexander, winner of 373 National League games, is best remembered for one strikeout. Thus is the intrinsic drama of a moment—a single pitch—more given to canonization than the valor and endurance of long laboring.

This was no handsome, prime-of-life Mathewson or exalted Johnson out there on the Yankee Stadium mound on that gray misty October afternoon in 1926. Long gone to time and worldly incursions was the freckle-faced young Nebraska farmboy with the friendly, guileless grin. He was a ghost in a Cardinals uniform, a visitation, a haunting remnant of that old, unsuspecting prewar America, and for much of what was gone a fitting embodiment: a shattered, broken man with the vibrations of shellbursts aquiver in his soul. He was a drunkard, an epileptic, weary and disillusioned, a harbinger of the coming decade of vagrant hopes and rock bottom, about to demonstrate for one last time what had been, what was lost. A quarter-century of heroes had now been spent: Mathewson was a year in his grave, Wagner was long retired, Cobb and Speaker were wobbling to the finish line, and Johnson had just five wins left in his buggy whip. So it was left to Alex to bid farewell for them all as he prepared to set in place the crown jewel of his career before submitting to the same recessive tides.

He had returned to the Cubs after the stentorian shocks and shudders of France, guzzling Prohibition whiskey and falling down in epileptic fits, drunk so often that people sometimes couldn't tell which was which, but still enough in possession of his raw magnificence to win 27 in 1920 and then 22 in 1923. By then he had become a multiple legend: Alexander the pitcher and Alexander the drinker. The Cubs, chronically in the second division, left him alone, even when occasionally he walked into the clubhouse listing a bit. But whatever his condition, when he went to the mound it was like Rembrandt to an easel. Some of his speed may have drifted, but he still had those snapping curves and that meticulous control, which must have been primal with him because he controlled so little else of himself.

In 1926 the Cubs hired a new manager, Joe McCarthy, the same Joe McCarthy who a decade later would establish and enforce what became known as the Yankee image, a cold, efficient, machinelike style of play that was all business. McCarthy in 1926 was a little-known career minor-leaguer determined to make the most of his long-deferred shot at the big time and felt he could ill-afford to be tolerant or sentimental, though he could be, and was both. (A few years later he ran a team of Cubs that was peppered with prodigious drinkers, tough guys, and lovable rascals to a pennant and loved them and every moment of it.)

"I liked Alec," McCarthy said. "Nice fellow. But Alec was Alec. Did he live by the rules? Sure. But they were always Alec's rules." The Cubs had finished last in 1925 and if they finished last again, McCarthy said, "I'd rather it was without him." McCarthy, who later managed and got along with five of the most magisterial of stars—Hornsby, Ruth, Gehrig, DiMaggio, and Williams—was not ready to go the distance with his alcoholic, disruptive pitcher, legend or not.

So early in the season the Cubs waived Alexander to the Cardinals and to two of the game's more notable teetotalers—general manager Branch Rickey and manager Rogers Hornsby. Rickey handed the problem to Hornsby and Rogers accepted it in his own fashion—by ignoring it. The realist Hornsby refused to attempt a reformation and let the veteran do as he pleased as long as Alex gave a true day's work on the mound. But there were some trying moments, one of them recollected by Cardinal teammate Bill Hallahan:

Alex liked to go out before a game and work in the infield, generally around third base. One day we were taking batting practice and there's

Alex standing at third, crouched over, hands on knees, staring into the plate. A ground ball went by him and he never budged, just remained there stock still, staring in at the batter. Then another grounder buzzed by and the same thing—he never moved a muscle. Then somebody ripped a line drive past his ear and still he didn't move. That's when Hornsby noticed him. Rog let out a howl and said, "Where in the hell did he get it?"—meaning the booze, of course. "Get him out of there before he gets killed."

They led Alex off the field and sat him down on the bench. Hornsby ordered a search and they soon found "it" stashed in the rafters of a lavatory in the corridor going down to the dugout. "One of those little square bottles of gin," Hallahan said.

"Alex never said much about anything," Hallahan said. "When he did talk it was seldom above a whisper. As a rule you didn't see him around after a game. He would go off by himself and do what he did, which I suppose was drink. That was his problem. But he was a good-natured fellow. You never heard him say anything against anybody." And on the mound? "An amazing fellow," said Hallahan. "Born to be a pitcher."

Born to be a pitcher, born to be slotted into the crucial situation, born to make it memorable because when it came for him he was baseball-old, physically and spiritually broken, and when it came it was against the brimming, muscular symbols of the new order, the young, fearsomely strong New York Yankees of Babe Ruth who were making baseball America look to the skies when they swung their bats, a club just one year short of coalescing into the Greatest Team of All Time. It was the most classic of confrontations, a generational one, an endless human theme replayed over and over in every walk of life but most dramatically and poignantly in the arenas where athletes compete, where almost inevitably the young seize their destiny. But not this time.

Realistically, Alex was the last man who should have been called upon. He had pitched and beaten the Yankees in the second game of the Series, and then stopped them again in Game Six, going the route. Asking him to come back the following day and hose down a Yankee team poised to strike was perhaps asking the old-timer to stretch it a bit too far. But this was not how his young Cardinal teammates saw it, because this was no ordinary old timer, because they had been baseball-hungry pups growing up in the previous decade when the name Grover Cleveland Alexander had been awesome and monumental, and even though he had only gone 9-7 for the

Cardinals that summer, he had pitched well enough (and been aloof enough) to retain his mystique.

Bill Hallahan, rookie pitcher: "I think I smiled and nodded my head when I saw it was Alex who was coming in. We all felt reassured. We just knew Alex was going to haul us out of it."

And Cardinals third baseman Les Bell: "Doggone, there wasn't another man in the world I would have rather seen out there at that moment than Grover Cleveland Alexander."

The moment was this: It was the bottom of the seventh, the Cardinals were leading 3–2, there were two out, the bases were loaded, and the Yankees' rookie slugger Tony Lazzeri was at bat. Jesse Haines, the Cardinals' starter, had raised blisters on his right hand from throwing his knuckler and could go no further. Hornsby had other pitchers in the pen, younger, stronger, fully rested. But not even Rogers Hornsby himself was immune to the mystique and able to resist one more spin of his old Merlin. And so the call went out.

Thirteen-year-old Les Bell of Harrisburg, Pennsylvania, had seen his first big league game in Philadelphia in 1915. "Alex didn't pitch that day, but I saw him throwing on the sidelines. Couldn't keep my eyes off him." Nor could he this day, waiting with Hornsby and the others on the mound.

I can see him yet, to this day, walking in from the left-field bullpen through the gray mist. The Yankee fans recognized him right off, of course, but you didn't hear a sound from anywhere in that stadium. They just sat there and watched him walk in. And he took his time. He just came straggling along, a lean old Nebraskan, wearing a Cardinal sweater, his face wrinkled, that cap sitting on top of his head and tilted to one side— that's the way he liked to wear it.

Like an old gunfighter, summoned from time past, riding slowly into town for one last rendezvous, coming to accept the challenge of the quick new hand, Alex moved slowly across the outfield grass. He always moved slowly, but this time with purpose. He was, Bell said, "a little bit of the country psychologist." The old pitcher understood very well what must be going through the mind of Lazzeri as the rookie waited at the plate, the tension, the building anxiety. As Lazzeri fidgeted, hefted his bat, took a deep breath, stepped back to have a word with the on-deck hitter, Alex loomed out of the mist, immobility in motion, materializing particle by particle in the mind of Tony Lazzeri.

The moment lives in a cloud of legend: Alex was drunk the night before, he was dozing in the bullpen, he was hnug over when he walked to the mound, Hornsby walked out to him to see if his eyes were clear.

"All a lot of bunk," Bell says. "No man could have done what Alex did if he was drunk or even a little soggy. Not the way his mind was working and not the way he pitched. And as far as Hornsby walking out to meet him, that's for the birds too. Rog met him at the mound, same as the rest of us." While conceding that Alexander might have had a drink or two the night before, Bell reminds us that Hornsby had told Alex he would be in the bullpen for the seventh game, to which the pitcher nodded and said, "But I'll tell you, I'm not going to warm up down there. I've got just so many throws left in this arm. If you need me, I'll take my warm-up pitches on the mound."

When he reached the mound, Alexander told Hornsby how it was going to be.

"I'm gonna throw the first one inside to him. Fast."

"No, no," said Hornsby. "You can't do that."

Alexander nodded his head, very patiently, and said, "Yes, I can. Because if I do, and he swings at it he'll most likely hit it on the handle, or if he does hit it good, it'll go foul. Then I'm going to come outside with my breaking pitch."

The master of masters was telling exactly how it was going to be, speaking from layers of experience so whorled by time that not even the greatest of right-handed hitters could make contradiction.

"Rog looked him over for a moment," Bell said, "then gave Alec a slow smile and said, 'Who am I to tell *you* how to pitch?' "

And so it went, just as Alexander planned it, though it included the most resounding line-drive foul in all of baseball history. Alex threw Lazzeri the surprise fastball—way inside—and Tony's eyes must have popped, for he whipped his bat at it "and hit the hell out of it," Bell said, "a hard drive down the left field line. Now, for fifty years that ball has been traveling. It has been foul from anywhere from an inch to twenty feet, depending on who you're listening to or what you're reading. But I was standing on third base and I'll tell you—it was foul all the way. All the way."

And then with two back-breaking curve balls that snapped across the low outside corner, Grover Cleveland Alexander linked his name forever with that of Tony Lazzeri, who went on to a long, hard-hitting career but who was destined to be remembered for having passed through the shadow of Grover Cleveland Alexander for one enduring moment. (The linkage has its somber side: Lazzeri, too, was epileptic, falling to his death down a flight of stairs during a seizure in 1946. Baseball can flip its ironies in uncanny ways.)

There were still two innings left to play, but destiny would allow nothing to mar this masterpiece. Anticlimactically, Alex put the Yankees away in the eighth and ninth innings. Fittingly, the final batter he faced was Ruth, who had already poled four home runs in the Series. Alex had had his fill of momentous confrontations, however. Determined not to let the big guy tie him, he worked clinically around the corners and finally walked Babe, who promptly tried to steal second and was thrown out, and all those pups of a decade ago—the pups now in Cardinal uniforms—punched their gloves and felt surges of triumph and relief, and the redemption of their faith.

Fifty-five years later the great moment was recalled in the White House, by the president of the United States. President Reagan had convened what was described as the largest assemblage of living Hall of Famers ever brought together. In addressing his guests, the president made note of what he considered one of the special achievements of his acting career—playing the role of Grover Cleveland Alexander in the film biography of the pitcher. And of course, Mr. Reagen went on, the highlight of the film was the Lazzeri strikeout. What a thrill it had been for him, the president said, to portray the splendid old warrior during this gripping and unforgettable moment of baseball history. In attendance was eighty-one-year-old Waite Hoyt, Yankee ace of the 1920s.

"When the president finished talking about the Alexander thing," Hoyt said, "everybody applauded. Well, I didn't think it was so wonderful. Nobody seemed to remember, but, hell, *I* was the losing pitcher in that game."

FOURTEEN

WHERE PRUDENCE has lost its voice and good sense become un-moored, celebrities are many, but heroes few, and in baseball there was but one. Ruth reigned with supremacy, so unapproachable in his realm that the game's other titans were made to look like mere mortals. Not even Hornsby with his .400-caliber machine gun could come close, nor could Detroit's Harry Heilmann with batting-championship averages of .394, .403, .393, and .398 in 1921, 1923, 1925, and 1927 (Harry was the odd man in); nor could the Athletics' Al Simmons, with batting averages of .384 in 1925 and .392 in 1927, figures high enough to give a statistician a nosebleed, but not good enough for a batting title. In 1927, a forty-year-old Tyrus Raymond Cobb, playing now for Connie Mack, still had enough fume and fuss in him to play a full season and bat .357, but all that earned him was fifth place in the batting race. Anyway, Ty hit only five home runs, once upon a time enough to put a man in the home-run derby, but now, like so much else, hopelessly anachronistic. It was much more exciting to see Ruth strike out than to watch Cobb drop a double into left field, because expectations were great and people wanted bigger and better and longer and louder.

One of the most remarkable of all baseball's miracle workers was Cleveland shortstop Joe Sewell, who, playing over 150 games each year, struck out four times in 1925, six times in 1926, seven times in 1927, nine times in 1928, and four times in 1929. (Years later, on the eve of Sewell's induction into the Hall of Fame in 1977, an intrepid writer asked him what was the secret of such uncanny contact of bat and ball. The secret, as imparted by Mr. Sewell, was this: "You have got to keep your eye on the ball." Ah.)

But these were cameo wonders as far as the crowd was concerned, sideshow entertainment while awaiting the main event, for they preferred the man who elevated expectations and stirred the imagination because he was always poised to destroy. There were

160

other home-run hitters in the decade—that lively ball would jump for anyone—but somehow there weren't, not as long as *he* was around anyway. Hornsby hit 42 bell-ringers in 1922 and 39 in 1925 (while still compiling .400 batting averages, which just about sizes up the complete hitter); the Browns' Ken Williams parked 39 in 1922, the Phillies' Cy Williams 41 in 1923, each an impressive number for the time. But none of these hitters evoked thunderclaps of approval from the crowd, none minced pigeon-toed around the bases as did Ruth, none thought of doffing his cap as he rounded the bases (no vanity in the gesture either; it was all part of the performance they had paid to see), and most of all, none had raised the expectation. The fans came to the ball park to see Hornsby hit; they came to see Ruth hit home runs.

If there is a pinnacle year in the decade, it is 1927, the year of Lindbergh, of Dempsey-Tunney and the "long count," of Sacco and Vanzetti, of Ruth's 60 home runs, and the Yankees, the 1927 Yankees.

No team has managed to sustain a legend as have the 1927 Yankees, symbol of unitary greatness in baseball, mightiest of them all, from core to fringe, from sole to summit. Never before or since has there been in the game such a coalescence of talent, such a fusion of lusty hitting and sharp pitching, and all of it torrentially consistent, dismembering the league with a meat cleaver, losing just 44 of their 154 games, setting records—and muscular ones, like winning percentage, home runs, slugging average, total bases—with a near-homicidal attack, squashing by 19 games Connie Mack's resurrected second-place Athletics, who had seven .300 hitters in the lineup and three more on the bench, and who were perched on the brink of their own greatness. The Yankees were in first place every day of the season. They are still there.

They exist as a phrase—"the '27 Yankees"—an evocative phrase serving as standard and admonition to all baseball teams who would proclaim themselves great. Despite the sweep of most of the rest of the century and the undeniable rise in the quality of players, no iconoclast has been able to unseat them convincingly. Now and then their hitting has been matched, their eight regulars equaled man-for-man. But never their balance. Their hitting was, in fact, a conspicuous case of overkill; they could have batted 20 points less, hit many fewer home runs, scored far fewer runs, and still won on the strength of their pitching, which led in earned-run average (3.20, second-lowest in the league in that hit-happy decade and not to be bettered in the league until 1942), and had four of the league's seven pitchers with earned-run averages of 3.00 or less. The hitters averaged 6.3 runs per game; the pitchers allowed 3.8.

It was the quality of this pitching staff that gave the club the balance of full greatness. The five starters were Waite Hoyt (22–7), Herb Pennock (19–7), Urban Shocker (18–6), Dutch Ruether (13–6), and George Pipgras (10–3), backed up by a one-year bullpen marvel named Wilcy Moore (19–7). "When we got to the ball park," George Pipgras said, "we knew we were going to win. That's all there was to it. We weren't cocky. I wouldn't call it confidence either. We just *knew*. Like when you go to sleep you know the sun is going to come up in the morning."

And what that sun came up on every summer's day in 1927 was mayhem at home plate. Set it to music and it's "The 1812 Overture." Boom! Pow! Crash! Babe Ruth, Lou Gehrig, Bob Meusel, Earle Combs, and Tony Lazzeri, abetted by lesser mortals Joe Dugan and Mark Koenig. There was no bench to speak of; this was a cast of star performers, and what makes them so special is not just a coming together of prime-cut quality talent but the fact that each had the peak or near-peak year of his career. For the fourth time in nine years Ruth set a new home-run record when he hit 60—that enchanting 60 that still retains its extraordinary aura, Roger Maris notwithstanding. (Just as, for many people, Ruth's lifetime home-run total of 714 remains a weightier, more authentic number than Henry Aaron's 755. Aside to numerologists: .714 was also the Yankees' winning percentage in 1927.) And if you think that club wasn't pure vinegar for pitchers, listen here: Ruth batted .356, drove in 164 runs, collected 192 hits—and was outdone in each department by teammate Lou Gehrig, with, respectively, .373, 175, and 218, plus 47 home runs. And so it went: Earle Combs, .356 batting average; Bob Meusel, .337 batting average, 103 runs batted in; Tony Lazzeri, .309 batting average, 102 runs batted in.

Another achievement of these thunderers was to speed the game out of one legend into another. Hitherto, the benchmark for collective greatness had belonged to the Baltimore Orioles teams of the 1890s. For three decades this had been accepted dogma—legends are too precious to be killed and too stubborn to die on their own—and though occasionally someone might have wondered if some of Connie Mack's prewar pennant winners (the 1911 edition in particular) could have been better, the decision was not that clear-cut, and so the

"Old Orioles" with their poke-in-the-eye style of play and alleged immunity to pain remained the most venerated of teams.

Until 1927. After that, the Orioles were strictly an old man's pride, a once-upon-a-time team of quaint achievements and hearty tales. The younger generation suddenly had a club that brought baseball into line with the power-and-distance orientations of the free-swinging times. What it had taken McGraw, Keeler, and Kelley three hits and a lot of wheezy chicanery to do, the Babe could duplicate with one rip. And when the Orioles' old catcher Wilbert Robinson, currently managing in Brooklyn, ruefully but honestly said, in effect, "These Yankees would have wiped the streets with us," card-carrying Orioles loyalist McGraw fulminated and saw apostasy. But it was true. The dynamite that baseball had been packing since the beginning of the decade had gone off with its biggest bang yet, and the old Orioles were laid away with honors.

All summer long the detonations went on, and as the days flowed by, one lopsided victory after another, the rest of the league began to realize that something terrifying and diabolic was taking shape. When the cannon fire quieted and a man could take a breath and raise his head and synthesize a thought or two, it became apparent that the all-powerful king, the monstrous and unstoppable monarch of the uttermost wallop, now had right behind him in the lineup a fearsome young crown prince.

It was the most fortuitous of baseball pairings: Ruth and Gehrig. Suddenly the incomparable, one-of-a-kind Ruth had, not a rival—he could never have that—but a collaborator of near-equal proportions, batting fourth to Babe's third. Double jeopardy, disallowed in courts of law, had become a daily diet for American League pitchers.

In 1927 Gehrig popped 47 home runs, more than any other man in baseball history had ever hit, with the exception of Ruth. Between them, 107 home runs, 339 runs batted in, 214 extra-base hits, 864 total bases, a composite .365 batting average. To give some idea of what mammoth hitting this was, Ruth alone outhomered every team in the league, while Gehrig outhomered four. To the rest of the American League it all must have looked like a gigantic conspiracy against them, but it really wasn't, just the product of a mischievous destiny, for it was in the spring of 1903 that the New York Yankees were birthed and joined the American League, and a few months later, on June 19, that Henry Louis Gehrig was born a few miles down the road on the city's upper East Side, a golden egg that would negotiate those few miles and hatch on first base at Yankee Stadium and stay and stay and stay until he became the game's all-time symbol of indestructibility and finally its all-time touchstone of tragedy.

He could hit like Ruth, but that was all they had in common. Ruth had Rabelaisian flamboyance and was a booming extrovert, a prodigal spender, but his younger partner was shy, insecure, and a notorious penny pincher (a frugality supposedly traced back to the old scars of childhood deprivation) whose preferred diversion was to sit in a rowboat and fish the quiet waters while puffing on his pipe. Ruth was a satyr who used women wantonly. ("Anybody who doesn't want to fuck can leave now," he once announced to the crowd in his hotel room.) Gehrig was a momma's boy, bossed and dominated by a stern Brunhilde who somewhere along the line had decided he would become an architect. He possessed a granite, muscles-within-muscles physique, was movie-star handsome with a dimpled grin, and was doomed to one of the most heartrending deaths imaginable. There are stunning human interest stories in them all—from McGraw and Mathewson and Cobb and all the way on—but none as classically trimmed as the Gehrig story, which even includes a beautiful, adored, and adoring wife, the feisty, sophisticated Eleanor Twitchell. Not without great effort, she finally weaned him away from that Teutonic dragon of a mother who did not approve of Eleanor, or of any of "Louie's" girls for that matter, or of anything her repressed boy did that did not bear the autocratic maternal imprimatur.

For simple virtues—he seemed totally without ego or temperament—he seems close to Mathewson and Johnson, though without Mathewson's aura of aristocracy or Johnson's image of frontier sturdiness. Gehrig was strictly an urban product, and although he reeked of small-town homeyness, the image he finally evoked was one of pure concrete. In time he became the epitome of the corporate player, starring on the most corporate of teams, personifying the stolid, cold-steel Yankee image, and proud of it, frowning at teammates who might be boisterous in public or who came to dinner without a jacket and tie. "And when Gehrig frowned at you," a teammate recalled, "you felt it." For Ruth there was adulation, for DiMaggio reverence, for Gehrig respect. "I was on the team for two years before he spoke to me," pitcher Spud Chandler said. Was Gehrig unfriendly? "No," said Chandler. "I wouldn't say he was. He was Gehrig, that's all."

One never hears an ill word spoken about him, not even

obliquely. The praise and admiration of his peers are abundant, but it sounds as though they are talking about a monument. With warmth and animation former teammates will talk by the hour of Ruth and DiMaggio, but Gehrig has undergone apotheosis. There is an almost party-line consensus: Great. Good. Quiet. Strong. Modest. He seems to have been close only with catcher Bill Dickey, his longtime roommate and the only teammate invited to his wedding when finally he zigzagged through his mother's interference and married his Eleanor.

He is remembered for being part of the Ruth-Gehrig combine, for his 2,130 consecutive games, for his inch-by-inch death in the prime of life, and for a heartbreaking farewell speech that is the Gettysburg Address of baseball. He was McCarthy's favorite, the old skipper finally brought himself to admit at the end of a long interview, after having loyally extolled the virtues of all his star players. "Why not?" McCarthy asked. "He always showed up, didn't cause any trouble, and he hit."

He was the perfect son, the perfect husband, the perfect ballplayer, the perfect Yankee. All of that perfection, all that unquestioning adherence to obedience, to devotion, to responsibility, to obligation, left room for little else. Certainly no room for anything that might blur the portrait. Perhaps no room to breathe, to be himself. Such unstinting perfection does not come without high personal cost. His legend is that he was simply a quiet man who stayed at his post until fatal disease removed him from it, and when he departed it was with the same unfathomable reserve that had distinguished him always. Ennobled by death, he was left securely in American folklore, one of the game's few inviolable saints.

He was docile, the crushing maternal thumb having made him forever shy of challenging authority, and his exemplary behavior saw to it that he never had to. Unlike Ruth and later DiMaggio, he never tried to wrestle the Yankees out of his just due at contract time, asking for a little more but eventually settling for a little less than that. He got $23,000 for a Triple Crown season in 1934; it earned him a $7,000 boost, $5,000 less than he asked for.

If he had no ego, then this ambiguous virtue was less a product of saintly self-effacement than of insecurity. There was something going on inside him of course. The opposition, in the arena with him day after day, knew it, or sensed it anyway, and upon them it was stamped "paid." Ruth, bigger and mightier, could be grasped because there he was, a roaring sea of tempestuous, uninhibited surfaces, about to scramble your brains because that was what nature intended him to do. Unsophisticated men could understand Ruth. Of Gehrig they were wary. Even the fierce Lefty Grove, armed with creation's most imperial fastball, who thought nothing of tucking one under Ruth's chin now and then just for luck, felt it advisable to tiptoe around the junior member of Wham & Blast. "Best let him sleep," Grove said.

If Gehrig had a passion that was stronger than his obedience to his mother, it was his love of sports, that ungovernable primal rage that drives the superior athlete, that furious propulsion of self-expression and desire and instinct that can generate an otherwise passive man. Some good and perfect momma's boys have been known to pick up an ax and express themselves on the skulls of their neighbors; Gehrig picked up a baseball bat and there went his aggressions, dealt out in line drives that left jet streams in their wake. And he flailed out in all directions, too, his shots to left-center carrying the same authority as the ones to right. "He didn't care in which direction they went," teammate Tommy Henrich said. "He just smashed them. And I mean, he *smashed* the ball." Many of Ruth's blasts were launchings, high and majestic and lordly, befitting the king. The crown prince hit them with savagery. One Gehrig home run left the ball park with such sound barrier–smashing velocity that it hit a girder in center field and rebounded all the way back to the infield.

He never seemed comfortable as a baseball celebrity, probably the most difficult hero status to deal with, given the daily exposure. In the beginning his reserve around people was considered shyness. But that, as the passing years proved, was pretty much the beginning and the end of the public Gehrig's personality. "Lou didn't like to stop and sign autographs when leaving the ball park," Bill Werber, another teammate, said. "He was a loner, never had much to say to anybody." What Gehrig had above all else, and above any other man who ever played the game, was an indomitable, remorseless devotion to duty. "He seemed to have a great deal of tolerance for pain," Werber said. "I saw him play a whole series of ball games with a broken finger on his glove hand. This was before his consecutive-game streak had reached unique proportions and there was no special reason for him to be in there, except that he was that kind of man and that kind of ballplayer." This was more than an esprit de corps, more than a Pete Rose kind of joyous fanaticism; there was a grim, self-punishing stubbornness to this, an autonomous fidelity. The streak is finally his monument, and it reflects the man faithfully, for it is a passive statistic, unlike the 56-game hitting streak of DiMaggio, which throbs with a building, one-man-against-the-world drama, excitement, and heroism.

Fourteen years of seething line drives, of showing up every day, of humility and modest smiles. No eruptions of Cobbian ferocity, no Wagnerian folksiness, no Ruthian ribaldry. No geysers of temperament, no all-night benders or shuffling through the sheets. Fourteen years of obedient son, devoted husband, manager's pet, and stolid indifference to or suppression of whatever might have been bothering him. Walled in at the beginning by Ruth, at the end by DiMaggio; and even his greatest day, when he hit four home runs in one game, was the day McGraw chose to retire and thus became the lead story. No matter how he excelled, and excel he did as few players ever have, missing was the gargantuan joy of a Ruth, the grim pride of a DiMaggio. But finally it was Gehrig, not Ruth, who became the idealized Yankee, the man who embodied the image of colorless, deadly Yankee efficiency, the image that DiMaggio picked up and honed near to transcendence.

His mother's dream, a special obsession with immigrants, was for her boy (the only surviving child of four) to get a college education and make something of himself. As a youngster he hustled odd jobs after school, but always found time for sports. The boy athlete was slow and awkward, but he was bruiser size whatever his age, and his strength atoned for lack of grace. His mother reproached him: Time in the playground meant time away from his studies. Already feeling the parting seams of twin loyalties, he reassured her. But then his Commerce High School team went off on a trip to play in Chicago's Wrigley Field, and there the powerful teenager startled everyone by hammering one out of the big-league park.

This perked the ears of that big-game hunter, John McGraw. McGraw sent for Gehrig soon after the boy graduated high school and offered him a contract. Gehrig told McGraw he had received an athletic scholarship—for baseball and football—to Columbia University and did not want to jeopardize it by turning professional. But Lou was talking to the wily old Oriole, for whom rules were made only to be circumvented. McGraw told him that playing professionally under an assumed name and still retaining college eligibility was common practice. So Gehrig signed with the Giants, and under the name Lewis in the spring of 1921 joined the Hartford club in the Eastern League.

The subterfuge lasted but a few weeks. Columbia baseball coach Andy Coakley got wind of it, hurried up to Hartford and brought the kid back with him under threat of losing his college education. Coakley talked the school's athletic board into giving young Louis another chance, explaining how the naive boy had been hoodwinked by the wicked old John McGraw. The contract with the Giants was dissolved. Neither man forgot the episode. A few years later, when he was a star, Gehrig felt a strong antipathy for John J., feeling the older man had tried to exploit him at the risk of Lou's scholarship. McGraw, on his part, no doubt feeling the wound of having lost the future crown prince for the Giants, resented Gehrig and said the young man had deceived him. Leave it to John McGraw to leave on the record the one negative thing ever spoken about Lou Gehrig. (But this boy was Yankee-born, Yankee-destined, and not even John McGraw was going to be allowed to tamper with that. And anyway, with both Terry and Gehrig on the club, McGraw would have been risking antitrust action.)

So the chastened young man played his baseball at Columbia, all the while studying to be an architect. But those other demons, operating at those primal depths beyond the reach even of a beloved and willful mother, were roaring. There were cannon-shot home runs leaving the Columbia ball field whose orbits were only slightly lower than Ruth's. He had had two years of college when Yankee scout Paul Krichell came one evening to sit at the Gehrig kitchen table (the kitchen, not the living room, was where serious talk was made in those days) to talk with Mom and Pop. (Mostly Mom, he soon found out. Pop, working as a janitor then, said little. He has been described, by people who were being charitable, as dim. Also, he had probably been squashed into pulp by his formidable wife.) Krichell had seen Gehrig hit what is today a fabled home run, a ball that left Columbia's old South Field like a rocket, traveling an astonishing distance and ending up bouncing up the library steps as if rushing straight for the history books. Krichell told Yankees general manager Ed Barrow another Babe Ruth had been discovered, which would have been the same as finding a new continent on earth. Exclaiming what has been every scout's pipe dream since 1920, Krichell was as close to being right as it was possible to be.

The Gehrig legend bathes even the signing of his Yankee minor-league contract in nobility: He did it because his parents had sacrificed so much for him and now the money he was going to make would help them. No doubt true (he did eventually buy his parents a house in New Rochelle, New York, where he lived with them until his marriage); but also, no doubt, nothing was going to stop that baby rhino from charging out of the brush onto the infield of Yankee Stadium and there remain.

Now it was 1925, and he was a Yankee and manager Miller Huggins was wondering how to get him into the lineup. The regular first baseman was the veteran Wally Pipp, a creditable performer for many years, not a man arbitrarily removed from the card. But then one day, June 2, Wally showed up at the ball park with an annoying headache and decided to take the day off. Huggins commiserated, and then said something like, "Gehrig, you're playing today." If it had been possible to foresee just how momentous this was, someone would no doubt have made note of Huggins's exact words. So the streak that was ended by fatal disease was formally launched because of a headache (it had actually begun the day before, when Gehrig got into the game as a pinch hitter). Pipp was soon playing for Cincinnati, probably having taken a pledge to keep any future ailments to himself. (Wally would have been a natural today for a jocular headache-relief commercial on TV.)

Gehrig supposedly accepted his place in the Yankee hierarchy, which in this context means second to Ruth, with neither envy nor resentment. But one can never know. Teammate Bob Shawkey, who later managed the club for one year in 1930, remembered this from that spring training: Ruth was in the cage, hoisting one monstrous shot after another into the hot blue Florida sky. Gehrig was sitting on the bench watching, motionless, his eyes rising to follow each clout until it disappeared into wherever Babe Ruth–dispatched baseballs went. "His face never changed expression," Shawkey said. "I was taken by his fascination with Ruth and couldn't help watching him, a little smile on my face. When he noticed me, he looked at me for a moment and then turned quickly away, as if he had been caught thinking something he didn't want anybody to know about."

Ruth seemed always in a state of expansion—physically as well as mythically—growing ever larger in the public perception, becoming the embodiment of miracle. Gehrig struck his own high plane at the very beginning and there remained, as if giving staunch and resolute evidence that the perfect man does not get better. For Ruth there were dramatics, theatrical displays, man's triumph over his supposed limitations. For Gehrig there were plain old heroics, lethally sustained, and dependability. Ruth was controversy, contempt for the rules of man, God, and nature; there were suspensions, fines, remorse, contrition. He was a brass band in a teacup. Gehrig was as faultless and unvarying and ongoing as a railroad track. With his roughly affectionate ways, Ruth admired the younger man, gave him batting tips, invited him to hotel room orgies (Lou refused), and called him a "kink-headed college kid." Brought up to be properly awed, Gehrig reveled in the attention until the two had a falling-out in the early 1930s, one story having it that the lip-careless Babe made a slightly critical remark about momma Gehrig, which certainly would have done it.

The Yankees won again in 1928, but this time had to perspire for it, for they were chased all the way to the finish line by a Philadelphia Athletics team that was about to break the seal on their own legend. It seemed that one of the old ghosts had refused to be laid to rest. Baseball's Rip Van Winkle was back from years and years of last-place slumber, of quiet unoffending summers of defeat and indignity. After several years of meticulous tinkering and fine-tuning, Connie Mack had finally built himself back into contention. The club that Connie fielded at the end of that Wild West frontier of a decade was the one that would put the icing on his own personal legend, for after breaking up his 1914 pennant winner the old gent had taken the elevator directly to the basement and there languished for seven consecutive years as attendance dwindled and many Philadelphians suggested in ever more vehement tones that he go elsewhere. But pride or stubbornness or whatever it is that keeps a man hacking at a stone with a feather kept Connie in place, planning and scheming and rubbing his eyes to keep the vision clear. Gradually he started aloft, climbing through the standings a notch at a time until he had them roaring in the stands again, just as they had for Waddell and Collins and Baker.

He might have won in 1928 had he not signed and insisted on playing in his outfield one Mr. Cobb. Through as player-manager in Detroit in 1926, Cobb joined the A's to play the last two of his twenty-four seasons. In 1928 the forty-one-year-old Tyrus batted a respectable .323, but those once-mercurial legs no longer flashed on the baselines, nor did they in the outfield. Catchable fly balls became base hits in Cobb's district, but his large salary, his drawing power, and the mystique he still possessed for a baseball lifer like Connie kept him in there.

In 1929, however, Cobb was gone, out of baseball forever, affluent, unreconstructed, with thirty-two years still ahead of him, much of which he spent snapping at the abilities of modern players. Connie was back up on top, completing the miracle of resurrection and doing it with a vengeance, finishing eighteen games ahead of the Yankees. The Greatest Team of All Time had been abruptly replaced by perhaps The Second-Greatest Team of All Time. "With those two monsters in the league," a rueful Roger Peckinpaugh said, "the rest of us started the season fighting for third place."

Properly reverential, the stock market would wait until ten days after the World Series before taking its notorious dive, ten days for the country to marvel over the might of Connie Mack's world champions. They had crushed a .300-hitting Chicago Cubs team in five games, including a ten-run seventh-inning rally in Game Four that rubbed away an 8–0 Cub lead, and a three-run ninth inning bolt that ended the Series and ended baseball's greatest hitting decade with a pair of spiked shoes racing across home plate.

If the Yankee teams were known for Ruth and Gehrig, then Connie's steamrollers were known for four of the game's most indelible names. They were catcher Mickey Cochrane, first baseman Jimmie Foxx, leftfielder Al Simmons, and pitcher Lefty Grove. It is doubtful that any club, anywhere, ever had four players of this caliber playing in their prime in the lineup at the same time; it is an absolute certainty that the Grove-Cochrane battery has never been equaled in all of baseball history.

Cochrane, invariably described by the game's chroniclers as fiery, was the club leader; he is also a perennial front-running candidate for the title of Greatest Catcher, his candidacy challenged only by his contemporary Bill Dickey and Johnny Bench. (It is always something of a jolt when one finally comes to contemplate the reality that a modern career may well be rearranging some of the furniture in Valhalla. For some traditionalists, reality can border on heresy. No doubt there are narrow-eyed partisans who will insist on Roy Campanella and Yogi Berra being Bench's equal. Maybe. But when it comes to a choice for greatest-ever status among catchers, only Bench among the latter-day saints seems to have that stature.) Cochrane could hit, run well for a catcher, throw, and was superb defensively.

He was also, well, fiery, and it was this incandescence that his admirers advance as his most priceless intangible. And he was tough. "Like a piece of flint," said teammate Doc Cramer. A man trying to outrun a peg home to Cochrane was, according to Cramer, heading straight for the lion's den. "Because home plate was *his*, you see. You had to take it away from him."

In those pretelevision days most fans, scattered throughout a vast country, never ever saw their heroes in action, and this fact went a long way in accounting for the unique mythic quality certain players assumed in the imaginations of their followers. In those less immediate and instructed days it took talent plus a vibrant personality and implicit charisma that was somehow transmitted through newspapers and pictures and talk for a player to burn himself in the imagination. One of Cochrane's fervent admirers was an Oklahoma lead miner named Elven (Mutt) Mantle, who was so enthralled with the Philadelphia catcher that he was moved to christen his first-born after Cochrane, hoping the name would prove a talisman. It did.

Jimmie Foxx was a smiling, good-natured young man with a physique that might have been sculpted by Rodin. Jimmie's biceps, according to Ted Lyons, looked as though they were carrying thirty-five pounds of air in them. Foxx was a twenty-one-year-old prodigy in 1929, already capable of hitting baseballs resoundingly enough to be called the right-handed Babe Ruth. Some even said he hit the apple harder than Ruth, which is one of those amorphous judgments that might not convince us but does tell us something. Of Jimmie's physical strength, it is enough to know that contemporaries said, "Thank God he was good-natured," leaving us with a portrait of a Samson who did not push down grandstand girders. Jimmie was a Maryland farm boy who played on a minor-league team that was managed by an Athletic buster of an earlier era, Frank (Home Run) Baker. Old loyalties are sometimes hard to shake, and when the Yankees showed interest in Jimmie, Baker directed the boy to Connie Mack instead. Dreamy baseball fans can entertain themselves with thoughts of what might have been: Ruth, Gehrig, and Foxx, back to back.

Jimmie, who once upon a time was second only to Ruth on the all-time home-run scroll, never quite caught the public imagination as did Ruth and Gehrig. Maybe it was because he didn't play in New York, or maybe it was that placid personality, genial where Gehrig's was inscrutable. He had his quirks, though. Teammate Wes Ferrell remembered Jimmie leaving the hotel for dinner one night resplen-

dently upholstered in a tuxedo, only to see him dining alone in a
nondescript side-street restaurant. In 1932 he busted 58 home runs;
noble, but two fewer than Hercules. Once you get up into those
heights you had better go all the way, otherwise you're only enhanc-
ing the top man even further and firming yourself up as Number
Two, and we know what that means in status-conscious America. Or
maybe Jimmie lacked the killer instinct; maybe the real Foxx was the
smile and not the muscle, for in spring training 1932 he told his teammates he was going to try and get more walks that year, and indeed
he did, drawing 116 free trips, 43 more than the previous season. "He
did that all summer long," Doc Cramer said. "If he would have been
free-swinging that year like he always did, Ruth's record would have
gone out the window."

Al Simmons was a right-handed masher almost in Hornsby's
class, meaning high-water marks of .392 and .390. He averaged .357
for his first ten big-league seasons, leading some coldblooded statistical fiends to say that if Al had been hit by a truck after his tenth year,
he would be in third place today behind Cobb and Hornsby on the
all-time batting list.

Simmons (born Aloysius Harry Szymanski) was a testy character
who was called "a swashbuckling pirate of a man" by one contemporary. King of his league's right-handed hitters for a decade, he was an
elitist who bullied rookies, manifested a chilly disdain for lesser mortals, and even on occasion questioned the wisdom of Mr. Mack himself. (Mr. Mack would patiently explain, and then quietly ask, "Is it
all right with you, Al?" Al would always mutter his approval, knowing he had just been told to lump it.) They called him Bucketfoot Al
for his peculiar stance. He stood far back in the box and hit slicing
ground balls that second baseman Charlie Gehringer said were
meaner than anything Ruth or Gehrig lashed his way.

This irascible fellow's eyes positively filled with blood at the sight
of a pitcher. It was a loathing that never left him. Years after his
retirement, when he was coaching for Mack, a playful Tommy
Henrich cajoled the old slugger into the cage during batting practice.
A man with a sense of the history of his game, Tommy wanted to see
what the great Al Simmons looked like at bat. What he saw was a
veritable transfiguration, from gray-haired coach to young, lusting
hitter, a counterpart of what you would get if you suddenly threw
your hands up at a Rocky Graziano. "It was something to see,"
Henrich said. "When Al Simmons would grab hold of a ball bat and

dig in he'd squeeze the handle of that doggone thing and throw the barrel of that bat toward the pitcher in his warm-up swings, and he would look so bloomin' *mad*. In *batting practice*, years after he'd retired!"

If even so accomplished a big-leaguer as Tommy Henrich was impressed by the sight of a spirit raging against the slack fibers and leaden reflexes that were confining its incalculable desire to compete, then Al Simmons at the plate in his prime must have been a study in pure primitive, each time at the plate for him an apocalyptic moment, the swing of the bat providing instant revelation. And yet, inexplicably, even so furiously unfettered a zeal can slide along an ever tilting past into oblivion, the unimpeachable testimony of the record books notwithstanding. Simmons and Cochrane and Foxx— there haven't been many ballplayers to equal them, ever. But the passage of time, with its insidious process of selection, has cast them in a dimming haze, at least in comparison with their contemporaries Ruth, Gehrig, and Hornsby. Because of the paucity of multitalented catchers, Cochrane retains a certain luster, but Jimmie has been out-Foxxed by a steadily accruing list of long-ballers, and his once unassailable second-place total of 534 home runs now finds him in the seventh spot; while Simmons with his old boiling hatred of pitchers and a batting average (.334) which slots him fifth among this century's right-handed smackers, is becoming a statue in a dark and unvisited basement.

Of the four mighty players who dominated Mack's three mighty pennant winners, Lefty Grove alone maintains a unique and solitary grandeur among the *crème de la crème* of baseball's hierarchy. Grove's reputation has moved forward with the years, so far forward that he has become the touchstone of left-handed pitchers. When Sandy Koufax was demoralizing National League batsmen in the early 1960s with an efficiency that made him look, as one player said, "like a professional playing against amateurs," there was but one stumbling block before the Dodger lefty could gain instant elevation as baseball's all-time premier southpaw. The obstacle was named Grove. Was Sandy better than Lefty? The mere posing of the question was compliment enough to each.

Lefty Grove comes rumbling through history on the strength of his fastball, Johnsonian in its dash to the plate, and by the strength of a personality described at times as sullen, dour, irascible, tempestuous, and peculiarly likable. That fastball? Let sharp-eyed Joe Sewell tell about it: "Sometimes when the sun was out really bright he would throw that baseball in there and it looked like a flash of white sewing thread coming up at you." And, Sewell added—and this is what separates a legend from a mere hard thrower—"Inning after inning, he never slowed up. He could stand out there for a week and barrel it in at you. I don't know where he got it all from." And what did this famous fireball do? Paul Richards: "You know, a left-hander's ball has a tendency to tail a little bit, but Grove threw it so hard it didn't tail—it didn't have time. It was on top of you before you knew it. You thought it was waist-high when you swung at it, but it was actually letter-high. The ball was four or five inches higher than you thought it was, which made the hitters think it was jumping, but it wasn't jumping. It came so fast it created an illusion." An illusion. Magic. A hocus-pocus pitch. Well, how else to account for those 1930–31 seasons of 28–5 and 31–4?

Foxx's home runs have finally come earthward, and Simmons's line drives are no longer banshee yells upon the afternoons of old summer; but Grove's fastball still burns plateward, a chimera in the minds of those who faced it, a thing of meteoric suddenness to those who have only heard. Like Johnson, who was about to move aside when Lefty came into the league in 1925, Grove was a straightforward fellow with no secrets on the mound: His number one was just about all he threw. "Sure we knew what was coming," said Joe Sewell. "So what?"

In 1974, a year before Grove died, a writer corralled the now paunchy, silver-haired old dazzler on the back porch of the Otesaga Hotel in Cooperstown, where Lefty was one of the ornaments of the annual induction ceremonies.

"That was a pretty hard-hitting league you came into in 1925," said the writer.

"Sure was," said Lefty.

"What about the first time you faced Cobb?"

"What about it?"

"Were you afraid of him?"

"I wasn't afraid of Cobb," said Lefty matter-of-factly.

"How about Ruth?"

"I wasn't afraid of Ruth."

"How about Heilmann?"

"Harry? No, I wasn't afraid of Harry," said Lefty, not boastful, merely stating a fact.

The writer then wanted to know about that time in 1931 when Lefty's sixteen-game winning streak came to an end, 1–0, on a misplayed fly ball. A touchy subject, or so Lefty's sidled glance implied.

"That was Simmons's fault," he said.

"Al misplayed the ball?"

"No. You see, Simmons had left the club to go home to Milwaukee for a few days, God knows why. His replacement in left field, Jim Moore, loused up the play. Simmons would have caught it." He sat silently for a few moments, staring into space, no doubt seeing once again that fly ball being misplayed, forty-three years ago. "It was Simmons's fault," he said moodily, then added, in a mutter, "And I told him about it." That must have been a sweet conversation.

And yet Mack would insist that his favorite pitcher had been Waddell. Maybe it was Rube's errant charm, a commodity lacking in Grove. No question that Rube and Lefty threw whistlers of near equal velocity, but otherwise the two could not have been more unalike—Rube the laughing, guileless, simpleminded extrovert; Lefty the humorless, brooding introvert. "I'm a serious man," he said. "And baseball is a serious business." But a man like Lefty really should not have had a perspective on himself, for in his case his persona was very much part of the Grove mystique. He remained consistent and unchanging all his life; a man who took the mound with the highest self-confidence, with an intensity, with a will to win that was terrifying. Otherwise, he was a simple man, uncomfortable in the big cities of stardom, shy with strangers. Much of his celebrated irritability was probably self-defensive, a carapace to ward off the unwanted. The fewer his serenities, the greater his privacy. It did not, however, always work out that way, for where there dwells a brooding Grove, almost inevitably there lurks an impish Dykes. Jimmy Dykes was an infielder on Mack's 1929–31 pennant-winners. A solid ballplayer, this little round man with the voice that seemed always to be rising from a clearing throat, was a blithe spirit who felt that mischief was a crucial part of life's ambrosia.

One evening Robert Moses (Lefty) Grove had taken his accustomed postdinner seat in the hotel lobby, there to while away the evening in contemplation of whatever it was that legendary southpaws contemplated. The proud Mr. Grove was impeccable in his three-piece suit, legs crossed, cigar in hand, face impassive. Across the lobby, watching him, sat teammates Dykes and Bing Miller.

"Look at him," Dykes said to Miller. "Sitting there like the King of England. I think I'm gonna rile him up."

"Why?" Miller, a reasonable man, asked. But there was, of course, no answer to that.

"Watch this," Dykes said, rising and crossing the marble floor toward Grove.

Approaching Lefty, Dykes said, "Hey, Mose, would you like to go to the movies?"

Grove thought it over for a moment, then said, "Sure."

Dykes then handed him a quarter, and said, "Here, go ahead. Enjoy yourself." Jimmy then turned around and started walking back across the lobby.

"It took about ten seconds for it to sink into him and then blow on out," Dykes said. "I heard that quarter hit the marble floor and he must really have whipped it. The lobby had a very high ceiling and I'll bet he bounced it all the way up to the top because I swear it was about fifteen seconds before I heard it come pinging back down. Then he started yelling at me, clear across the lobby. 'You little bastard,' he yelled. 'You think I don't have two bits to go to the movies if I want to?' "

That personality might have been hacked right out of the sides of the Georges Creek coal mines in Lonaconing, Maryland, where Lefty was born on March 6, 1900. One of seven children, Robert Moses left school in the eighth grade, and not long after was developing his long (six-foot-three-inch), sinewy physique working in the mines alongside his father. But his churlish nature could not long abide anything as recalcitrant to move as coal, especially for seven dollars a day for helping load fourteen tons of the stuff. He told his father, "Dad, I didn't put that coal in here and I see no reason why I should have to take it out." After that, he went to Cumberland and worked as a mechanic's flunky for the B & O Railroad, helping to tear down, repair, clean, and put back together steam engines. And all the while the hum was in his left arm.

He got into pro ball with the Martinsburg club in the Blue Ridge League in 1920. He didn't stay there long, however; the lightning he was turning loose soon crackled in the ears of Jack Dunn, owner of the Baltimore club in the International League (the same Dunn who had sold Ruth to the Red Sox six years earlier). Dunn came to Martinsburg, saw, believed, and for $3,500, bought.

Grove remained with Baltimore for five years. There was no question that he was ready for the bigs after a couple of years; Dunn was just waiting for the right price. Staying in Baltimore was all right with Lefty too because Dunn paid his stars bigger salaries than they would have received from most big-league teams. Over his final two years with the Orioles, Lefty was 54–16, which finally prompted Connie Mack to hand Dunn a check for $100,600 in exchange for the ace. (The $600 was added in order to establish a record for a minor league transaction.) This was after Dunn had turned down a $75,000 bid from John McGraw, which was just as well as far as Lefty was concerned. "I wouldn't have wanted to play for McGraw," he said. "We wouldn't have got along." (Again, a brief digression for some intoxicating reverie. McGraw had now missed out on Ruth, Gehrig, and Grove. The Giants had taken four straight pennants from 1921 through 1924. Grove and Gehrig both came to the big leagues in 1925—talk about golden rookies—which means John J. would probably have captured pennants for the rest of the decade. But the fun part of the reverie is watching him trying to deal with Ruth and Grove, in addition to anarchists Frisch, Terry, and Lindstrom. McGraw would have had to hire an extra body to hold all his ulcers.)

There is no doubt that it is comfortable and satisfying at the very top. The view is stunning and the soul is at rest, and graciousness comes easy. And so the fastest pitcher the fastest pitcher ever saw was, inevitably, Walter. "I used to go to watch that bugger pitch," said Grove, voice tinged with admiration and affection. "We'd take a train from Lonaconing down to Washington on Sundays to see him. We idolized that guy. Just sat there and watched him pitch. Down around the knees—whooosh! One after the other. I pitched against a lot of guys and saw a lot of guys throw, and I haven't seen one yet come close to as fast as he was."

But the common denominator, for Lefty Grove and for them all, remains the same. "I loved baseball. If they said, 'Come on, here's a steak dinner,' and I had a chance to go out and play a game of ball, I'd go out and play the game and let the steak sit there. I would."

Money? "Sure, I looked for as much as I could get. But the truth was, I would have played for nothing. Of course I never told Connie that."

But the old boy might have guessed it.

₣IFTEEN

OPTIMISM is a healthy thing, but when it detaches from reality, health erodes. It seemed as though it would never end, that spiraling economy, the lavish spending. Corporate profits kept swelling. Personal income was up, and while not everybody was able to throw it around, enough did, conspicuously and noisily enough to leave an impression of a financial Sodom and Gomorrah. Stock prices had risen dangerously and unrealistically high, soaring like Ruthian home runs. The end of the decade was a seething volcanic cone, its rumbling energies about to fire off into the sky.

But hindsight criticism of that wonderfully irresponsible decade seems churlish. There was a hell of a good time to be had and people were having it; perhaps the last mindless, unrestrained good time ever, for out of the coming despair and then the tragedy would come the flash of the atomic age with its brooding threat of eternal unforgiveness.

The dash to the end of the decade was made with increasing speed. Automobiles were ever bigger and faster, more and more people were taking deep breaths and boarding commercial flights, and those who were afraid to were being shamed by advertising that chided them by pointing out there were still some ridiculously prudent people who were apprehensive about riding in an automobile. (And in 1929, when over seventy-five big-leaguers batted over .300, there were still a few managers who played for one run, and they were considered no fun either.)

Life in the home was being made easier with electrical refrigerators and washing machines, and more enjoyable thanks to that new gadget of disembodied noises called a radio (sixty thousand of them in 1922, nearly 14 million eight years later) that brought music and entertainment, and yes, even the World Series right into the living room—you could, by God, *hear* it when the Babe cracked one, and what that and the oceanic roars that followed did to the aspirations

179

of little boys can be imagined. Those crowds were *real*, they were right there, now, this moment, and those were enthralling moments, for some boys never letting go.

If you couldn't afford a refrigerator or a radio or a washing machine, well, they had this thing called installment buying—the 1920s version of the credit card—and for ten bucks down and ten a month you could cart the latest thing home and own it, sort of. Like buying stock on margin. People were mortgaging themselves far into the future, but the future then had the shiny look of Canaan upon it. Of course there were certain spoilsports lecturing that it was not virtuous to live beyond one's means, but those admonishments seemed as realistic as bunting in the first inning did.

Nobody was carried greater distances by the spirit of things than the Caesars of the Empire of Hollywood. Indulging themselves in architectural orgies of ego, they built sumptuous movie theaters with dazzling Byzantine interiors, replete with sweeping carpeted staircases, bubbling fountains, gilded walls and ceilings, huge glittering chandeliers, deep carpeting to muffle the shuffling feet of the pilgrims, marble statues tucked into alcoves like places of private worship. Splendid places in which to sit in the dark and enjoy the adventures of Rin-Tin-Tin (the canine was voted films' most popular performer in 1926).

"People have asked me through the years if I was wiped out in the Crash," said Wes Ferrell, a rookie pitcher for Cleveland in 1929, about to win 21 games. "They think everybody who was alive in 1929 took a bath. I tell them no, I didn't lose a cent in the market, because I didn't have a cent in the market, or anywhere else for that matter. And it was a good thing I didn't have any money, because I would have made the same bad investments as so many other fellows. Not that I knew anything. I was a country boy, just up from North Carolina, but I'd go to the ball park and get stock tips from turnstile men and bootblacks and peanut butchers and newspapermen. Everybody was going to be a millionaire. It was a little confusing."

The October 1929 financial collapse came like a slap in the face, painful and sobering. Suddenly unmoored, the high-flying economy came plunging earthward, and when it struck, its brittle pieces were shattered and unmendable. A people unaccustomed to and ill-equipped for mass poverty and unemployment had it thrust upon them with frightening suddenness. The Great Depression in all its manifestations was bad enough; its stark contrast with the expired decade of unbridled exuberance made it worse, made it seem sardonic.

Those shrewdly calculating economists and those black-frocked doomsayers who had been predicting catastrophe found more vindication than they had bargained for. First there were the brutal penalties of ruinous speculation, and then the wrath of God Himself in an unhinging of nature that saw floods, droughts, and sky-blackening, face-stinging dust storms blowing away topsoil in raging winds. Factories closed, blast furnances and mines shut down, businesses large and small—banks among them—failed. Families broke apart, either from the plague of poverty or from the need for the father to leave in search of work. The homeless and the disenfranchised took to the road, pushing jalopies piled high with twine-bound possessions, or riding the freights, or wandering through inhospitable city streets, pausing now and then to allow their vacant faces, dried-out eyes, rickety children, and shapeless, stringy-haired women to sit for what became a national portrait snapped by Walker Evans and other sensitive and gifted photographers.

"People avoided eye contact," said Fred Lindstrom, holding down one of the more secure, better-paying jobs in the country—a regular in the big leagues.

That's one of the things I remember. It was like everybody had his own thoughts and was in deep concentration upon them; or maybe it was that people were so self-conscious of their problems they were ashamed to look at one another. And at the ball park the cheering sounded forced, like it was expected of them rather than spontaneous, as it had always been. Maybe it's my imagination, but it always sounded like it was a split second later than it should have been, as if their minds were out of synchronization with what they were seeing.

In 1933 Franklin Delano Roosevelt became president, replacing Herbert Hoover, a cold, humorless man with the face of a foreclosing banker, whose proclamations of imminent prosperity were no longer believed. Soon Roosevelt's patrician voice was ringing through the land out of those ubiquitous radios, leaving for decades in the minds of his listeners a sound of vibrant optimism.

Increasingly, the plays, movies, and books of this morose, shadowy decade were presenting stark indictments, bitter recriminations, absurd panaceas, stirring paeans. Values and priorities, ideas and systems, were all put under reappraisal. Apple-sellers on the corners of big cities, breadlines, the nomadic drift of broken people across a leaden landscape—none of it seemed logical or inevitable, yet it had not happened in a vacuum. A lot of things that had looked dependable and secure had been misjudged, a lot of people who had sounded confident and assured had been wrong.

Of all the major occasions of the American land, only one remained unchanged, as if its simple, wistfully evocative character was actually sturdier than many of the nobler institutions that had fissured and crumbled. The year after the stock market's toboggan ride, baseball put on its most explosive offensive display ever, with batting averages reaching near ludicrous heights. Between them, the two leagues averaged .296 for the 1930 season, with nine of the sixteen clubs batting over .300. It was almost as if the game had decided to put on an emphatic demonstration of the magic it possessed which enabled it to live outside of its environment.

Nothing, it seemed, could stop or divert the old ball game, that pampered, nonideological American institution with its millions of custodians and defenders. The most a world war had done was snip a few games from the schedule and borrow some of its players for a while. And the immediate aftermath of its worst scandal saw the game go rollicking into its gaudiest, most prosperous decade, because the Black Sox scandal had proved that the game—the thing, the idea, the dream, and the vision—was near-spiritual in this country, beyond reproach, beyond corruption; defiled in one place, it reappeared in another, as clean and fresh as sunlight. The rotten apples, as a tent-and-sawdust orator might have said, could not contaminate the barrel. Already deemed an ancient ritual (the Constitution was little more than half a century older than Alexander Cartwright's formulation of the game's rules), it went on, forthright and unstoppable, flowing right on through the Great Depression as insouciantly as the Mississippi itself rolled through the heartland. It went on, insular and unaffected, a rock of stability, fulfilling dreams and needs with endurance and fidelity. It was its own faith, its own piety, its own drama, a fixed and simple spectacle for the bright months, a wistful remembrance for the darker. Outside of the ball park was heartache and tragedy, bleakness and despair; but passage through the turnstiles and a seat in the special sunshine meant a brief, dreamy return to an old unchanged certainty, a brief respite for the jobless men in cloth caps who came and sat and watched the evocation of once-upon-a-time serenity.

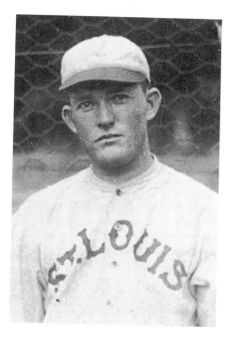

Rogers Hornsby.

Grover Cleveland Alexander.

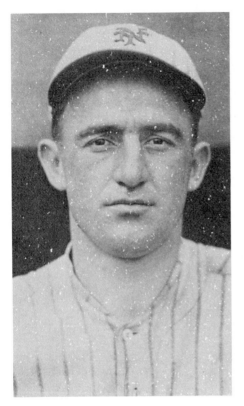

Frankie Frisch.

John McGraw.

Babe Ruth.

Lou Gehrig and his mother.

Lou Gehrig and Babe Ruth.

Joe DiMaggio.

Ted Williams.

Lefty Grove.

Mickey Cochrane.

Dizzy Dean.

Pepper Martin.

Bob Feller.

Fewer tickets were sold, of course, but no team failed to complete its schedule, no stadiums were closed down, no teams went out of business. Salaries were cut. Wes Ferrell had worked his way up to $18,000 by posting win totals through his first four years of 21, 25, 22, and 23. After that he was asked to take a cut of $7,000. "I took it without a squawk," he said. "Those were bad days. Still, I think I had more money than Mr. Bradley did—and he was the president of the ball club then. I was sure as hell driving a finer automobile than he was."

That era gave the country a brand-new hero, one who seemed right out of the folklore of the troubled land itself, as uninhibitedly cornpone an American product as could be shaped. Brash, cocky, outrageously self-confident, Dizzy Dean was a revival of the very spirit that now lay moribund across the land. Like Ruth in 1920, he was a fortuitous arrival, the perfect man for the time. He seemed to have sprung from that tumbled-about crowd of dispossessed farmers, hungry sharecroppers, migrant laborers, and the rest of the itinerant mass of bread- and shelter-seekers. He came rushing forward with a yip and a spirit as unquenchable as a revivalist homily, as if cast up from the dust, the cotton fields, and the arid pastures to deliver a message of vibrant positiveness.

There had been grass roots heroes before, of course, but they were Cobb and Joe Jackson and Walter Johnson and Rogers Hornsby, and none of them were the pure, unadulterated populist affirmer that this one seemed to be. Cobb and Hornsby had been ferocious and joyless, Johnson and Jackson modest and quiet. But now electricity was needed and Dean came fully charged, an affirmation of the allegedly disappearing rural strength and values. Humility he had left in the crib; he was good, he knew it, he felt it, and wasn't shy about letting you know about it too. "If you say you're going to do it, and you go out and do it, it ain't braggin' "—veritably his credo. Chesty loud-mouths were not generally the style in America; not even that grand-scale performer Ruth was a braggart. This one was, but with a way about him so joyously innocent and free of malice and vanity that the country loved him for it and adopted him as a kind of talisman that would help see them through to the better times that were coming. Scour the ball parks: There was nothing like him anywhere. Ruth was aging, Gehrig was monotonous, Foxx was affable, Terry was dour, Grove was temperamental. Dean, with impeccable instincts for public affection, was a showman, an entertainer, a wit, a lovable

Peck's Bad Boy in a St. Louis Cardinals uniform, with a lightning fastball that was the backbone of his confidence and his achievement. (He also threw a big, crackling curveball that he called his crooky.) He was tall and lanky, pitching with the flawless mechanics of a long stride and smooth overhand delivery. "One of those boys," said Pittsburgh outfielder Lloyd Waner, "who you knew was never coached anywhere, who was born to decorate a mound just the way you saw him do it." And he had been blessed with one of those magical nicknames that are beyond valuation. Baseball nicknames? There are three that transcend the game, trailing their surnames automatically behind: Babe, Yogi, Dizzy.

He was an overpowering combination of blazing talent, natural charm, and zany unpredictability, with a shrewd idea of himself, and an innate sense of what the public wanted to hear. Describing Dean on the mound, teammate Johnny Mize gave a summation of the man that was applicable on several levels. "His reputation was as a fastball pitcher, and he was plenty fast. But he also knew how to pitch. He could throw you off with slow curves as well as anybody. He was a very deceptive fellow." Dean learned early that big-city folk were amused by what they perceived as the crudities of so-called yokels. His given name was Jay Hanna, but at times he passed himself off as Jerome Herman. Born in Lucas, Arkansas, on January 16, 1911, he occasionally rattled off other places and other dates, for no good reason, or maybe to create a mystique, or maybe with the shrewdly self-taught bumpkin's natural disdain for facts, for the written word, a predilection he would demonstrate later in life as an ungrammatical, language-mangling, immensely popular baseball broadcaster. Always the clown, never the fool.

He had a few years of elementary schooling, and then left his Bible-preaching, Southern Baptist home ground with its blood-locked families and reddish-clay roads and hills to travel with his brothers and widowed father in the family jalopy through Arkansas, Texas, and Oklahoma. They worked the fields chopping and picking cotton, as much as four hundred pounds a day, laboring from before dawn to after dusk—"From can't see to can't see" was a migrant worker's way of putting it—for just enough payout to stay alive on, and then they boarded the jalopy and headed for the next job. Chopping and picking cotton, and building that strong rangy athlete's body and gestating that mighty fastball in his arm, shoulders, and back. Those were the 1920s for Jay Hanna Dean: no jazz or Charlestons or raccoon coats or silver hip flasks.

But even then he must have been hiding a dream, known he was special, because when he arrived it was with full trumpet, on an invincible floodtide of self-confidence, his Arkansas-twanged boasts and witticisms sure and finely honed, like an act that had been refined in the sticks for years and years. Special because nothing had ever darkened or successfully daunted the morning-dew freshness of that personality or narrowed by a centimeter the quick expansion of that wide, infectious grin. Unlike Joe Jackson, he was never intimidated by the big city; like Ruth, he was at home in all places, situations, and with all people, the pearl of every oyster; and unlike Waddell, in so many ways a spiritual ancestor, he would not let his adulators take possession of him. He came from a tradition of hard times, of independence, and of rough-sided humor and showed a depression-grim country that there was vitality in the old tradition yet. Clown and buffoon, yes; but he made sure the last laugh belonged to him.

In 1927, the full-grown sixteen-year-old boy opted for three squares a day, a suit of clothes, and a pair of shoes, and lied about his age and enlisted in the army, serving with the field artillery at Fort Sam Houston in Texas, where his mile-wide, mile-high whirlwind personality earned for him from one of his sergeants that precious tag Dizzy. But even the lax, peacetime army imposed too much discipline for this free spirit to endure, and before the boy got into too much trouble his father bought him out, a not uncommon practice in those days when the army was little more than a place that provided employment for majors named Eisenhower and Patton.

A civilian again, Dean found a job with the San Antonio Public Service Company, supposedly to read meters, but the true service he performed for the public and the company was pitching for the company team (somewhere along the line, that fastball had come out of the chute). In those years Branch Rickey was building for the St. Louis Cardinals the biggest, widest, most talent-gulping farm system ever in baseball. Cardinal scouts were fanned out across the country, sharp-eyed predators at every diamond, empty lot, or cow pasture where boys gathered to perform one more time the sunlight ritual of America. Every youngster in the land, it seemed, that could run fast or throw hard was gathered in the Cardinal net. (At one time in the mid-thirties there were some eight hundred of them under contract to the Cardinals. "Rickey's chain-gang," they were called.) Those, Rickey proclaimed, were the God-given talents, and if they were spectacular enough, you could teach a boy to hit and field. Offering contracts that paid around fifty dollars a month, the Cardinals could afford to give a shot to any gifted kid. The Cardinal minor-league camps were thundering herds of talent—"From out of quantity comes quality" was another Rickey credo—and so it was, as his system produced a plethora of gifted players like Chick Hafey, Joe Medwick, Johnny Mize, Pepper Martin, Enos Slaughter, Terry Moore, Marty Marion, Mort and Walker Cooper, Howie Pollet, Preacher Roe, Pete Reiser, Harry Brecheen, Stan Musial—and Jay Hanna Dean.

Because of the overabundance of talent they had, it was common for a player to spend five or six years in the Cardinal minor leagues before emerging from the game's most exacting winnowing process and graduating to the big club. Jay Hanna Dean made it in two and would have made it in one if he hadn't irked his manager by sleeping late, popping off, and manifesting a too-assured sense of belonging in spring training in 1931. So they sent him back to the minors, to Houston in the Texas League, and he won 26 and struck out 303. "He should have stuck in 1931," said Branch Rickey, baseball's most gigantic intellect, with a conjurer's eye and a spellbinding oratory. "But, Judas Priest, we didn't know how to handle him. He destroyed logic with a quip and admonishment with a grin. I'd never met a boy like him."

But he was back in 1932, as untamed as ever, as ever he would be. At the age of twenty-one, pitching for a seventh-place club, he logged an 18–15 record while leading the league in innings pitched, strikeouts, and shutouts, making the first carvings of the legend that would soon promulgate itself whimsically and wonderfully throughout the land but most profoundly in the South, where the youngsters on the dirt farms and in the broiling textile towns and in the brooding pine hills and backwoods suddenly had an idol to measure up to. South Carolinian Kirby Higbe, himself a top-rank fastballer in the early 1940s and, briefly, a teammate of Dean's on the 1938 Cubs, remembered a southern boy's perspective on the Great One (as Dean badgered the writers to call him). "There were other southern boys pitching well in the big leagues, like Wes Ferrell and Buck Newsom, but Dizzy was the one we followed. He was the one we wanted to be. He was the one we felt was representing us up there. One of the greatest guys that ever lived."

But the greatest upstager of them all was still on the loose in 1932, and in the World Series that year he reached the pinnacle of his personal mythology, and by definition of all baseball mythology, leaving a depression-ridden country momentarily dazzled and uplifted. At the age of thirty-seven, Babe Ruth (who had taken a five-grand salary cut to $75,000 in deference to the times) had batted .341, hit 41 home runs and driven in 137 runs, enjoying his last truly productive season. The Yankees had ended Connie Mack's three-year reign at the top and taken their first pennant since 1928. In the World Series they applied a four-game crushing to the Cubs; a forgettable Series, except for that one luminous, myth-shrouded moment in the fifth inning of Game Three at Wrigley Field on October 1.

The background and the buildup to that moment is this: When the Cubs' regular shortstop Billy Jurges suffered an incapacitating injury in August, the Chicago club reached into the minors and brought up the former Yankee shortstop Mark Koenig, who had drifted out of the big leagues. Koenig played superbly down the stretch, batting .353 and making a significant contribution to Chicago's pennant. When it came to slicing up their World Series melon, however, the Cubs voted Koenig but a half share. Though this was none of their business, some of the Yankees were offended by what they deemed the Cubs' miserly treatment of a popular ex-teammate. Consequently, when the Series opened in New York, the Yankee bench jockeys were calling the Cubs cheapskates and skinflints. Not without voice of their own, the Cubs answered back, and the colloquy quickly heated up, becoming more barbed and specific. Winning the first two games gave the Yankees fuller range for their insults, while losing made the Cubs shoot all restraints to the winds.

By the time the teams moved on to Chicago for Games Three and Four, the valves of invective had been turned up full blast. Both sides went at it, no insult was considered too profane, vulgar, or personal, and it was all loud enough for the fans in the box seats to have their ears curled. Naturally, the most conspicuous Yankee in these rancorous open-air debates was Ruth, an accomplished bench jockey, with a booming voice, crude wit, and sulphurous vocabulary. Ruth, always the magnet, soon became the focal point of the wrath of not only the Chicago players but of their fans as well. Babe and his wife were spat upon as they entered their hotel and needed a police escort to the ball park, leading one to suspect that fans were perhaps more emotionally involved back then. Today, being spat upon in public is an honor accorded only prominent elected officials and certain cabinet members.

Game Three opened with the verbal fusillades at high tide, with the Cubs concentrating on Mr. Ruth, who incensed them even more by laughing at them and then belting a three-run homer in the first inning. (Gehrig hit two home runs in this game, but, as was his fate, was overshadowed. Lou's two home runs are today best remembered for not being remembered.) Ruth was having too good a time to be offended by the diatribes flying out of the Cubs dugout; this, plus the Yankees' overpowering domination of them, was causing little serenity among the Chicagoans or their fans, some fifty thousand strong and every one, it seemed, a vocal Ruth-hater.

The innings slipped by, the clock ticking toward the purest moment in all of baseball mythology. Did Babe Ruth call his shot in the 1932 World Series? Did Washington chop down that cherry tree? Did Lincoln mourn all his life for Ann Rutledge? All are points of discussion within American folklore. But only Ruth enacted his fable before witnesses, and these witnesses are typical of any who have been sworn on a Bible. There are those who saw what they saw and heard what they heard; those who saw what they think they saw; those who saw what they wanted to see; those who saw only what they later remembered seeing. (This shows you how much havoc instant replay has wrought upon the myth-making process.)

The *New York Times*'s account of the game, written by John Drebinger, claims that Ruth called the shot, but then is incredibly reticent about the whole thing. The fact that Ruth called his home run, a startling event in any game and more so in a World Series, is not mentioned until more than halfway through the story. When Ruth came up in the fifth, Drebinger wrote, "a single lemon rolled out to the plate" (a few had been thrown at Babe earlier in the game), and

in no mistaken motions the Babe notified the crowd that the nature of his retaliation would be a wallop right out of the confines of the park. Root [Cubs pitcher Charlie Root] pitched two balls and two strikes, while Ruth signaled with his fingers after each pitch to let the spectators know exactly how the situation stood. Then the mightiest blow of all fell.

It was a tremendous smash that bore straight down the center of the field in an enormous arc, came down alongside the flagpole and disappeared behind the corner formed by the scoreboard and the end of the right-field bleachers.

So went the *Times*'s dispatch from the front lines. Drebinger says quite plainly that, like some Jehovan retribution, Ruth indicated a home run was forthcoming. But when Babe actually fulfills this prophecy, Drebinger is more mesmerized by the majesty of the clout than its forecast. After describing the home run, the rest of the story is straightforward reportage of the game. Either Drebinger did not realize the immensity of what he saw (or thought he saw), or he was astonishingly blasé about it, even for a gentleman from the *Times*. When challenged, did the Babe often make menacing or dramatic gestures at the plate that indicated what he would have *liked* to do (he was, after all, an extrovert who was here shouting back at the bench jockeys in the middle of a time at bat)? If so, perhaps this was one gesture among many he had made in his career, most of which had been forgotten, except that this one was followed by the home run. In any event, Drebinger saw Ruth indicate *something*, and thereafter did not think it particularly significant.

In his definitive biography of Ruth, *Babe: The Legend Comes to Life*, Robert W. Creamer reports that only one account of the game, that of Joe Williams of the Scripps-Howard newspapers, said that Ruth was pointing toward the outfield fence. It was not until a day or two later, after Williams's story had received wide circulation, that other writers began writing of the "called shot" as though it were irrefutable fact. Whatever the facts really were, they were already lost, swept up in the whirlwind of Ruthian mythology. Ruth, showman that he was, went along with the story, through the years embroidering, modifying, altering, and sometimes laughing at it, other times stoutly averring it.

The count was two-and-two. The Cub bench, in particular pitchers Burleigh Grimes, Guy Bush, and Pat Malone, were firing their full arsenal of insults at Ruth, the most delicate of these being "baboon," "potbelly," and "nigger" (certain people saw Negroid in that broad, wide-nostriled nose). Now, Ruth can hardly be described as deep in concentration while at bat, which makes what he did—forecast or not—even more remarkable. If any further evidence need be cited for Babe Ruth's matchless supremacy in the batter's box, this memorable time at bat will serve, for when he should have been focusing on pitch and pitcher, he was instead volleying back and forth with the Chicago bench. (Bush even came running out of the dugout with his hands cupped around his mouth to make sure his message was delivered, which tells something of the decibel count at the moment.) Ruth was shouting, he was amused, distracted, and he had two strikes on him.

He made his gesture—and we are now in a rarefied realm, miles above sea level, where clouds swirl and the air is moist, and things mundane have long since evaporated. He held up a couple of fingers, and he pointed them. Was it toward Root, the Cubs bench, or center field? And what did he mean? Root, too, had been jawing down from the mound at him, and Cubs catcher Gabby Hartnett claimed Ruth said something to the effect of, "It only takes one to hit it." Gehrig, on deck, said Babe's message conveyed to Root the idea that the next pitch was going to keep company with Charlie's Adam's apple.

The eyewitness accounts of the players break down pretty much according to party lines. Pitcher Charlie Root (who had to live with this for the rest of his life): "Ruth did not point at the fence before he swung. If he had made a gesture like that, he would have ended up on his ass." (Other players supported the contention that Ruth would never have taunted a pitcher as mean as Root was known to be.) Cubs second baseman Billy Herman: "When he held up his hand he was telling the Cub bench that he had only two strikes on him, that he still had another one coming. But he was pointing out toward Charlie Root when he did that, not toward the centerfield bleachers." Chicago pitcher Burleigh Grimes: "After the second strike, Bush yells, 'Now, you big ape, what are you going to do now?' So Babe holds up his finger as if to say, 'I've got the big one left.' He's looking right at Guy Bush. Then he hits the next one out. But he never called it. Forget it." George Pipgras, Yankee pitcher: "Yes sir, he called it. He pointed toward the bleachers and then he hit it right there. I saw him do it." Joe Sewell, Yankee third baseman: "I was there. I saw it. I don't care what anybody says. He called it." Interestingly enough, Yankee manager Joe McCarthy, who was disliked by Ruth and who returned the feeling, filed a minority report from his bench. "That's a good story, isn't it? A lot of people still believe today that he really did that. Did he? No. Tell you the truth, I didn't see him point anywhere at all, but I might have turned my head for a moment."

It was an extraordinary, emotionally fevered moment. Not only were the Chicago bench and the Chicago pitcher yelling at him, so were over fifty-thousand Chicago fans. But the eye of the hurricane was prodigiously armed, with the only weapon he needed: a baseball bat. Whatever gesture he made, we can be sure it was not one of pacification; whatever words he threw back we can be sure were utterances of defiance. The man had willfully put himself into a situation that demanded extravagant response. Failure meant thunderous catcalls and humiliation. So respond he did. With all his might, splendor, and glory. This was no mere home run. This was a clout among clouts, the longest ever struck at Wrigley Field up to that point. It was the dream shot of all dream shots, the personal circumstances surrounding it giving it a higher nobility even than that of Bobby Thomson's. Of all of Ruth's 729 homers (counting World Series play), this remains the most resounding, the consummate home run, a zenith shot that was as preposterous as the man, sending a baseball through the winds aloft to the very summit of the game's tallest peak, where it remains shrouded in regal solitude.

Is the *Iliad* true? Was there an Achilles? Did Babe Ruth call his shot? The question is securely irrelevant.

$IXTEEN

BUT NOT EVEN MR. BABE RUTH HIMSELF was immune from the scourge of the Depression. After much sulking, and a bit of bluster, he accepted a meat-cleaver cut in his salary, from $75,000 a year to $52,000. Nor was he an exception to a more eternal erosion. In 1933 he was thirty-eight years old, and suddenly it showed, as if there had been no gradations. The figures were respectable but decidedly un-Ruthian: .301 batting average, 34 home runs, 103 runs batted in. Lesser men could dine out all winter on a season like that, but for Ruth those figures were a dirge. A year later, in 1934, it was vespers at twilight for the great man as his every statistic shrank and receded, and the stone-faced unemployed took trolley cars to the ball park and sat in the bleachers and impassively watched Babe Ruth struggle on a ball field, watched his round, big-bellied, disobedient body lumber after fly balls, watched the perceptibly slower bat connect for just 22 home runs. They watched him, and for some it may have seemed it was not age that was crushing him, but that so many other cherished things were irretrievably departing and were simply taking Babe Ruth along with them.

For those susceptible to it, the lang syne mood had begun on February 25 that year, with the death of a once seemingly indestructible symbol, one that predated Ruth, Cobb, Wagner, and Mathewson. A beaten, weary, ailing John McGraw had resigned as Giants manager on June 3, 1932. Hopelessly anachronistic in a world he was by experience and temperament unable to cope with, the fifty-nine-year-old New York institution had become furious in frustration, falling into uncontrollable rages that no longer intimidated anyone. When he heard that his home-run–hitting prodigy Mel Ott had taken a young woman up to Fred Lindstrom's hotel room, McGraw tore into Lindstrom for "immoral conduct." When Lindstrom angrily denied any involvement, McGraw refused to listen, and when his informant whispered to him that it had been Ott, the old man began screaming, "It wasn't Ott! It was Lindstrom!" Ott was his pet, his discovery, and he would not believe. "There were things, and that's a good example," Lindstrom said, "that he could not handle, that he refused to handle."

Among those beginning to question McGraw's stability was Giants owner Charles Stoneham. When he finally decided that the old skipper had to go, Stoneham wondered how to accomplish it: Club owner or not, you simply did not fire John J. McGraw that easily. But it so happened that, like so many of his countrymen in 1932, McGraw was in debt, though not because of the stock market but because of what Lindstrom described as "horse racing affairs in Havana." The debt was $250,000, and it was owed to Stoneham. By agreeing to scrub the debt, Stoneham was able to get McGraw to resign.

He remained as a vice-president of the club, but he had been around too long to be taken in by that. He sat in on meetings, listening to the new manager Bill Terry and others make the decisions, and then he went back home to the twelve-room house he shared with his wife in Pelham Manor, just north of the city. Some people said he had "mellowed," but mellowing for a John McGraw meant something else. His life had been baseball, baseball had been his sustaining fire, 365 days a year, since those first zealously ambitious stirrings on the boyhood ball yards of Truxton in a time so long ago and so different it had the arrested stillness of a Currier and Ives illustration. On February 25, 1934, John McGraw heaved out his last breath of bitter and sweet and went off to join Mathewson and all the others who lay deep and undisturbed in memory.

They were the old men, the spent glories, dying, or bumbling through old age, waiting for it to end and to be transformed back, through the memories of those who had seen them in full prime and those who wished they had, back to eternal youth, to be recycled again and again through ever-ripening summers. The Depression finished off Honus Wagner's sporting goods store in Pittsburgh and in 1933, at the age of fifty-nine, the monarch of all shortstops past and of all to come was sentimentally rehired by the Pirates as a coach, continuing on in that capacity until 1951. Coach, storyteller, sideshow attraction, cherished legend in uniform. Sturdy, bow-legged, white-haired, enormously hook-nosed, a caricature of a Teutonic grandfather, he lived until 1955, and then was immediately meta-morphosed back to the swift, strong, ungainly-looking young man who did it all so well and so completely he left behind no pretenders for his spot, left behind one of baseball's few definitive and inargu-able statements: Wagner at short.

McGraw was dead. Hornsby was managing the St. Louis Browns, who in 1935 drew for the *season* an attendance of 80,922; that same year Walter Johnson was fired as manager of the Indians, his last job in baseball. Alex was somewhere, God knew where, still never more than an arm's reach from the next drink. And Ruth in 1935 was making a fool of himself trying to play the outfield for the Boston Braves, old and fat and slow, being booed and mocked, be-fore giving it up early in June, batting .181, a few days after one last defiant beyond-the-timberline display of three mammoth home runs at Forbes Field in Pittsburgh.

For years the touchstone of so many things, Ruth suddenly was the poignant manifestation of mortality itself. The nineteen-year-old Braves first baseman Elbie Fletcher watched his teammate. "He couldn't run, he could hardly bend down for a ball, and of course he couldn't hit the way he used to. It was sad watching those great skills fading away. To see it happening to Babe Ruth, to see Babe Ruth struggling on a ball field, well, then you realize we're all mortal and nothing lasts forever." With awe and fascination, they bore witness. "It was like watching a monument beginning to shake and crack," said Fred Lindstrom. "You were waiting for it to topple. You know, when I think back on it, it was an awful thing to see." The king, the father, was departing, leaving empty the place at the head of the table, and those on the field with him, some of them young enough to have grown up wanting to be Babe Ruth, felt the passage keenly.

But there was still Gehrig, going methodically on and on, game after game, year after year, inevitable and indestructible, building that streak like an iron link through the decade, giving the nation continuity from past strength through the dark times to the day of renewed vigor. And there was Dizzy Dean, in full splendor now, winning 30 games in 1934, 28 in 1935, the biggest thing in baseball and therefore one of the biggest in America, a three-ringed circus of a performer, galvanizing spirit of a Cardinal contingent known as the Gashouse Gang, one of the few bands of men in mid-thirties America to assemble without an ideology to proclaim, although there was probably an implicit one in who they were and what they did.

They were a collection of blithe spirits, entertaining the fans, driving their manager Frank Frisch to distraction with pranks and antics, but good enough to win the world championship in 1934. They were the ultimate Branch Rickey team—young, fast, spirited, and above all, hungry. The old spellbinder always preferred hungry ballplayers, and in those times he had no trouble finding them, and in his Gashousers he rounded up a band that helped lift the shades from a flogged but undefeated people.

The mainstays of the 1934 Gashouse Gang—the most famous edition—were Dean, his brother Paul (known as Daffy but actually a quiet, reserved young man who blew out his arm after two winning seasons of 19 games each), third baseman Pepper Martin, first baseman Rip Collins, shortstop Leo Durocher, and leftfielder Joe Medwick. Not every man was a bundle of joy. Durocher, who went on to carve out for himself a most distinctive niche in the tales of baseball, was a serious-minded man who bristled with an abrasive self-confidence. Dizzy and Pepper were small-town open and carefree, but Leo was big-city slick and suspicious (he was born in West Springfield, Massachusetts, but the man was pure asphalt-molded). Quick of mind and tongue, a natty dresser, he took to the bright lights like an eagle to flight, garnishing his image with a reputation as a pool shark. He had a personality that could light up a ball park, and a flair for leadership that eventually made him one of the game's most conspicuous managers. He also had a side to him that frayed welcome mats. Brilliant afield, he was light of stick (it was said of Leo that at the end of the season he often owed points on his batting average).

Medwick was the National League's premier buster for most of the decade of the 1930s, a player whose unorthodox style of hitting—he battered "bad balls"—caught the imagination of many fans with a grip that simply never let go, so that half a century after he entered the league he remained the favorite of an aging segment of fans who remembered him with passionate devotion, despite a persona that was surly, sulky, humorless, and belligerent. His nickname was Muscles, and this was not one of the game's antithetic handles, for bilious Joe was indeed muscular, hard-fisted, and quick to unload when affronted. There is no record of his having lost a fight, although teammate Johnny Mize later observed dryly, "He knew who to pick on." With a snappy Leo and a surly Joe, the *joie de vivre* of the Gashouse Gang was sometimes patchy. If Joe was quick-fisted, he was also tight-fisted, and reportedly touchy but unrelenting about the latter accusation. A teammate said, "Joe thinks tipping is a city in China." "Fuck 'em," said Joe, who had suffered the haunting curse of being born poor and never forgot or forgave.

But the soul of the Gashousers, the zaniness of lore and legend, lay in those so appropriately named Dizzy and Pepper (names that might have come out of some mid-thirties Hollywood comedy). Martin was a natural-born mischief-making rascal, out of the Oklahoma Osage country where he learned to run fast, he said, "because once you started there was nothing out there to stop you." He played the outfield and third base, playing the latter position not with finesse but with a grim determination, fighting off ground balls as if they were hydra-headed. Pepper hated to field bunts, and the opposition was loudly warned not to cloud his day thusly. If they did, the malefactors often found Pepper's pegs aimed not for the first baseman but right at their heads. "When I bunted on Pepper," said Lloyd Waner, "I always ran down the line with my hands covering my head."

Martin became a national figure in the World Series of 1931—his rookie year—when almost single-handedly he demolished Connie Mack's A's with twelve hits and five stolen bases, hitting and running like a man possessed, taking bellywhopping headfirst slides with utter disregard for his rugged, choppy profile. For a week he stirred the nation from its depression-ridden doldrums, giving sullen satisfaction to many who enjoyed watching the Oklahoma primitive discomfit Mack's lordly, big-city world champions. He came down the first-base line like no other player, snorting and chugging like a truck, and when caught in a rundown it was, said Elbie Fletcher, "like being in a cage with a tiger." He was one man surrounding three or four. Pepper was such a legend in his day that it was reported he wore no underwear and even disdained an athletic supporter: Such intimately reported details do not accrue around mere mortals. Supposedly, he found better uses for the money the Cardinals sent him for travel to spring training and made the journey by freight car, no doubt finding much congenial company along the way.

Joy for Martin was exploding matches, loaded cigars, and water-bag bombs dropped from hotel windows, with the most coveted target for the latter being the noble noggin of manager Frisch. One hotel had a mezzanine in the lobby, with a staircase leading up to it from the ground floor. At a mezzanine window Martin would lurk patiently, paper sack of water in hand, waiting for Frisch. When the skipper appeared it was bombs away, whereupon Martin would wheel around, ride the banister to the ground floor, hurl himself into a chair, cross his legs, and sit there like a portrait of innocence, just as the soaking-wet Frisch came through the front door spluttering with accusations—accusations that perished in their own froth when he saw Martin sitting peacefully. "Damn you," Frank would say, "if I wasn't seeing you sitting there, I'd swear it was you that did it!"

Summers of joy and laughter, of being paid to play baseball—for many of those dirt-poor boys the most wondrous American miracle of them all. "It did seem like a miracle," said Lloyd Waner of Harrah, Oklahoma.

We were the beneficiaries of it, and sometimes we'd forget there was a real world out there. Remember, we went from the hotel to the ball park, back to the hotel, and then onto the train for the next go-around. All of our reservations were made for us, all of our meals were paid for. Did that for six months. Then the season would be over and my brother Paul and me would go back to Oklahoma, and then we would realize how bad things were. The farms were abandoned, their owners off to Lord knew where. Stores that had been doing business in the spring were boarded up. People were glum and poor. That was the real world.

Regarding Dizzy Dean, however, it was sometimes hard to differentiate between real and unreal. His effervescence was genuine enough, but he also had a showman's shrewd awareness of the value of his personality, saving his best clowning for when writers and photographers were around. He laughed a lot for a young man who had lost his mother early and who had spent his childhood riding in a jalopy and chopping cotton under a hot sun. Those kinds of childhoods are not supposed to craft ebullient, morning-fresh personalities turbulent with joy and optimism. The laughter was too sustained, the joy too manic, not to have been at least a partial cover for something rooted in those wretched origins. There was an anxiety to get to the top in a hurry, to create distance behind. Like Ruth at home plate against the Cubs in the '32 Series, he had the comfortable arrogance derived from a talent he knew would back him up when most needed. The self-confidence oozed, but it also had to be carefully calculated and spent, consciously or subconsciously, because the spectacle of a preening Ruth or Dean stumbling in the spotlight was seldom seen. Of Dean it was said he never remembered a game he lost (of the modest, reserved Carl Hubbell the opposite was said—he never remembered games he had won). For Dizzy, failure was an aberration, an unexpected and unforgivable thing that refused admittance to memory.

In 1937 the glory of Dizzy Dean was at its zenith, held fixed and radiant in the brightness of his grin and the heat of his fastball. So precious was he to the game that he was elevated to veritable polestar by *The Sporting News*, baseball's preachy, conservative guardian of the game's good name. The paper frowned on Dizzy's "yellow cars" and his wintering in Florida, as if these were ominous indications of moral decay. Taylor Spink's officious bible urged the game's premier drawing card not to place too much emphasis on money, not to forget his origins, as if Dizzy was one day doomed to return to them. The paper referred to him as a "once-poor cotton picker," a finger-shaking warning of a phrase if ever there was one. Watch yourself, boy. Don't let it corrupt you or rattle your good sense. Would Spink's strictures have been offered to a city boy? Hardly. As far as rural America was concerned, they were all probably depraved to begin with. The soul fed on grass and creek water, not on a concrete defiled by immigrant feet.

Dizzy certainly wasn't the first bumpkin to make it to the big leagues, but he was surely the most attractive, the epitomizer, a man who worked it to so broad a caricature that none could ever follow. Joe Jackson, with his country boy's fear of the big city, was much more the bumpkin than Dean; but Dizzy was the legendary hayseed, the allegedly naive and gullible cornball who played a tune right across the backs of the city slickers. "I never tried to outsmart nobody," he told Red Smith. "It was easier to outdummy them." So it was, and so he did.

There was, and probably still is, a bit of shopworn philosophy handed out to young ballplayers along with cap and uniform: "Be nice to those you meet on the way up, because you're going to meet them again on the way down." (There were probably a few who made this silent response: "Screw those I meet on the way up; I have no intention of coming back down.") Dean had no need of this stuffy rap on the shoulder; his ascent had been so swift he hardly had time to meet anyone. Likewise, his descent. It happened with the literal suddenness of a line drive, in the 1937 All-Star Game. Cleveland's Earl Averill lashed a low line drive back at him that Dean stopped with his foot, fracturing a toe.

It proved to be the Great One's Achilles heel, this toe. The arm seemed like a steel spring, and the head had proven itself hard. In the 1934 World Series he had inserted himself as a pinch runner—to Frisch's chagrin—and rushed down to second on an ensuing grounder to try and break up a double play. He forget to slide. The shortstop's peg couldn't have traveled more than ten feet before making contact with Dean's head. Dizzy was flattened, carried off the field on a stretcher, taken to a hospital, X-rayed, and emerged with the Bartlett-sized quote: "They X-rayed my head and didn't find anything."

But the mere fractured toe sank him. He came back to the mound before the digit was fully healed, favored it by throwing out of an unnatural motion and snapped something in his arm. And that was some something he snapped: It took the fast out of his fastball and he was through. Rickey peddled him to the Cubs for $185,000 the following spring—the Cubs knew Dizzy's steamer had gone the way of a lot of chopped cotton, but maybe they didn't want to believe it. Anyway, the aura of Jay Hanna (Dizzy) Dean was still intoxicating enough for the Cubs to want to own him. He slow-balled his way to 16 wins for the Cubs over the next three seasons, scaring nobody, but still smiling. Whatever was gone, he still had to be Dizzy Dean, and that was going to prove to be plenty. Unlike Joe Wood, Dizzy's predecessor on the heartbreaking injury list, Dean did not slowly go away. No, the halls of obscurity could not hold this fellow. He resurfaced as a radio and then television announcer, popular, well-paid, spectacularly ungrammatical, handling the language like a spastic juggling raw eggs: "He slud into third." "The runners returned to their respectable bases." The batter was standing up there "very confidential."

Strangely, when baseball religionists gather for the solemn ritual of "what-if," Dean, professionally slain at the age of twenty-six, with his peak years probably still ahead of him and strong Cardinal teams around him, is not mentioned. The names most prominently intoned are those of Wood, Reiser, Score. The miracles that might have been wrought by Dean are left largely unconjured. True, he did deliver five and a half strong seasons as compared to the aborted lightning crashes of the others; nevertheless, he belongs on the scrolls of the unwritten, a splendid what-if for insomniac nights.

SEVENTEEN

IT WAS a familiar phrase, even in the 1980s, a bit of philosophical slop for some keen disappointment: "Even Joe DiMaggio struck out once in a while." Why DiMaggio? Why not Mays or Mantle or Aaron or Rose or Carew? Why, more than three decades after his retirement, DiMaggio? Well, because he was the touchstone for elegant perfection for a half-century, and because of our need not only for heroes but for ones that need never make us uncomfortable, who had been sanctioned by time, performance, and reputation. He fit the mold, this DiMaggio, through all the years of his performing and the days of his retirement, moving without blemish or misstep through the decades, solid and polished and reliable, with an impenetrable mystique made all the more intriguing by a brief marriage to America's sex goddess that ended unhappily and then tragically, and through it all he never lost a beat, never blurred for a moment, and if anything even enhanced himself.

He was Joe DiMaggio, special and symbolic, and not even Marilyn Monroe was going to intimidate the self-image. Returning from Korea, where she had entertained tens of thousands of soldiers, she told him, "You never heard such cheering, Joe." "Yes I have," he said. And he continued to, at those summertime roundups called Old Timer's Days, where he evokes the loudest and longest applause and is the only one the active players gaze at and seek autographs from and photos of. This is because he hit in 56 straight games and was married to America's sexiest woman and because he was recognizable all over again for doing television commercials; and because he has a name that won't die, and because he never compromised what he had created by becoming a glad-hander at Atlantic City casinos, and because he never complained, not about pain or injuries or hard luck or getting old. The ballplayer was riveting and perfect; the man is stoic and aloof and private. For a legend, an ideal blend.

It was as if the celestial artisan in charge of crafting baseball players had decided after a century's work and thousands of models great, good, and indifferent to produce the gem without flaw. The do-it-all Wagner looked as though he had staves and hoops holding him together. The abrasive Cobb's arm was little better than average. Speaker did not hit with power. Hornsby was near-perfect, but they said he had problems with high pop flies (surely a venial sin, but nevertheless); and anyway Rog rubbed people the wrong way; massaged them so, in fact. Ruth may have been closest, but he lacked that gazelle grace in the field. So the artisan went to work once more and this time gave unbroken concentration to every filigree of detail, this time rounded every corner and smoothed every edge, suffused the design with speed, power, grace, unerring judgment, smoldering pride, and, as a final fillip, instilled no Wagnerian folksiness, no Cobbian snarls, no Hornsbian bite, no Ruthian heartiness. The crowning touch of genius was to leave him virtually silent.

Never has there been an American hero quite like this one. He was the immediate replacement for the suddenly disarmed Dean, his taciturn dignity the intriguing opposite of Dizzy's uninhibited whirligig showmanship and garrulousness. He was the aristocrat of the diamond, playing for the right team in the right city, giving baseball a regal image in the midst of a depression. With his aloofness and businesslike efficiency on the diamond, he portended the coming urbanization of players; in a nation rapidly becoming machine-oriented, he was a marvel of blood-carrying technology; and despite the fact of there having been other Italian players of stature before him, he came to symbolize for many the triumph and success of an entire immigrant movement.

This immigrant's son was going to become a new-style all-American boy, as modest and undemonstrative as Mathewson and Johnson and Gehrig, but carrying with him the implication of greater sophistication. The big city was bigger than ever now, and this silent hero paradoxically represented it, in style, grandeur, power, and complexity. He became more big-city than his New York–born and –bred teammate Gehrig, whose dynamite was packaged in colorless devotion to duty, whose modesty and humility seemed all too genuine to generate excitement. Somehow, one got the conviction that while soft-spoken and withdrawn, this DiMaggio knew exactly how good he was and wanted you to know it too.

Gehrig was content to perform at the top of his considerable ability, but DiMaggio was driven to excel and scintillate, and every day the trigger of unrelenting compulsion was reset and cocked. Why did he so regularly hit the most unhittable of pitchers, Bob Feller? "I felt he was the best and that I was the best," said Joe, "so I bore down against him." (Acknowledging that DiMaggio gave him a lot of trouble, the pragmatic Feller had his own explanation for it: "Joe gave everybody a lot of trouble.")

He was the eighth of nine children of Giuseppe and Rosalie DiMaggio, turn-of-the-century Sicilian immigrants who had traversed the full continental span of the new land and settled in northern California because that's where relatives were and because Giuseppe had been a fisherman and there he could earn his living from the sea. Their eighth child and fourth son, Joseph Paul, was born on November 25, 1914.

He seems to have grown up generally with a sense of alienation, despite a lifelong devotion to his parents and siblings. Shy as a boy, a loner, he had few friends, few interests. He did have one interest, however, inevitable in these recitations of baseball boyhoods: He loved to play the game, and he was good at it. Like so many of them, his epitaph was written early and need never be changed. The future paragon of baseball grace and sophistication had little education, dropping out of high school in his mid-teens to work on the docks of Fisherman's Wharf, San Francisco's world-famous wharf just down the street from the crowded DiMaggio household. If the boy did not want to go to school, then all right, his father thought; he could join the old man on the boat and work the waters for the fish and crabs that were hauled landward for the city's restaurants and provided the family's livelihood. The roll of the sea, however, was not for a man crafted to dominate the green grass of America. And anyway, the young man had developed a strong dislike for the smell of fish and fishing boats: quite an assertion of independence on the part of a fisherman's son. The shy, taciturn teenager, already with the athlete's lean, strong, cord-muscled body, was potentially a man of seething frustrations, for he contained gifts of living distinction, and ironically for this introverted man they were gifts that demanded for expression the huge arena and cheering tens of thousands.

DiMaggio's father frowned upon his son's ballplaying. This was the good old immigrant attitude. They hadn't come all this way— across an ocean and then a continent too—and struggled and bum-bled through a foreign language and worked hard to see their sons go out and burn the sunshine playing a game. The boys had such a good time playing baseball there had to be something morally wrong and wasteful about it. But try and stop the ones with the raw talent. Like proponents of some vitalist philosophy, they drive on, Daniel Boones hacking through an enchanted wilderness toward the sunlit symmetries of a big-league stadium. Try and stop the antelope from galloping, the shark from swimming, the eagle from soaring. Try and stop DiMaggio from playing baseball. The old story.

In 1932 his older brother Vince, playing for the San Francisco Seals in the Triple-A Pacific Coast League, at the time probably the fastest of the minor leagues and one step below the bigs, got him a tryout as a shortstop. Joe made the team and appeared in a handful of games at the end of the season. He was seventeen years old.

Missing from the DiMaggio fairy tale is that flashing moment of discovery that clears the rheumy eyes of some trail-worn old scout. Joe DiMaggio was discovered *en masse* by the fans and players of the Pacific Coast League in 1933 when he became the most spectacular minor-league player in the country. With the Coast League playing an elongated schedule, the rookie got into 187 games, giving his statistics a mammoth aspect. Along with a .340 batting average, he drove in 169 runs and collected 259 hits, flavoring it with one of those performances that became uniquely DiMaggio—a 61-game hitting streak, going nearly a third of that endless season without taking a collar.

All summer long the news, like the winds of changing weather, flew eastward: Something big was happening in the Coast League. This was no kid merely piling up statistics, and those big-league scouts with their aviator-to-groundhog view of the baseball diamond knew it. You didn't have to be a particularly sharp bird dog to see this jewel polishing itself with every sweep of the bat and every stab of a line drive. But if you were a scout you had to gulp and tremble knowing that this gem was for sale; you had to know that in the world you worked this was a canvas by Rembrandt, a sculpture by Rodin, a score by Mozart; you knew that watching this vindicated those endless drives along broken roads into and out of small towns with their bleak hotel rooms and side-street cafés; you knew that this gave credence to all you knew and were and lived for.

But the following summer the scouts, and most especially the ownership of the Seals, gnashed their teeth when this born-to-a-pedestal work of art injured his knee stepping out of a taxi. "It sounded like pistol shots going off in there," DiMaggio said. Shots indeed, and heard around the baseball world they were. A vandal had taken a hammer to Michelangelo's *David.* Joe was suddenly damaged goods, a young prospect with, in baseball parlance, "a bum wheel." The Seals' dreams of realizing as much as $75,000 for him (about eighty-five years' income for a construction worker at Depression wages) suddenly took on chilblains. Most clubs lost interest. But Yankee scouts Joe Devine and Bill Essick remained enchanted. Like two little boys shaking hands with Santa Claus, they refused to let go because they had been infected with a grandiose Yankee dream spun out of the heads of owner Jacob Ruppert and general manager Ed Barrow, a dream so audacious it sounded almost quaint, but a dream they were serious and eager about. They were looking for a new star to replace the aging Ruth. Replace Babe Ruth? With what? A cannon? The thought bordered on the sacrilegious. But then they saw the San Francisco Seals' prodigy and the contours of the dream hardened. The Yankees would not relinquish it.

The hard-headed Barrow, who after all had found Honus Wagner throwing chunks of coal against a hopper car and so believed that dreams belonged to those who would dream them, had DiMaggio's knee checked out by a Los Angeles orthopedist, who pronounced it a knee with a future. So the Yankees bargained the Seals down to $25,000 and the dispatch of five minor-league players. The Yankees, beginning to out-Rickey Rickey in the fertilization of a minor-league system, always had players to deal away in those days, each of them coming with what was already the mystique of the Yankee imprimatur, a mystique that would cloud the judgment of general managers for decades to come.

The brains behind this farm system were Barrow and George Weiss (both of them frosty, humorless, tight-fisted, wholly unsentimental), but the godfather was Ruth, then and forever the magical name; those youngsters came storming out of the woods and down from the hills and out of the city playgrounds eager to sign a contract simply because it had "Yankee" on it, which translated as Ruth. (Tommy Henrich spurned higher signing bonuses because he wanted to play where Babe Ruth played. Other gifted boys were similarly enthralled.) Having once employed Babe Ruth was akin to owning the bar where Dylan Thomas chose to drink. Ghosts can be formidable enchantments.

There was a proviso in the deal: DiMaggio would remain with the Seals in 1935. It proved to be a long summer for the clubs that had lost interest. They had been out-slicked by the Yankees. At the age of twenty-one DiMaggio became a redwood among saplings. He played in 172 games, collected 270 hits, drove in 154 runs and batted .398, in addition to playing the outfield with grace and perfection and displaying an arm straight from the firing range. By the time he arrived for his first spring training with the Yankees in 1936 he was a star.

So twenty-one-year-old Joseph was a star, a heavenly body forever ascending, and more, was shining in America's city of cities. Could he handle this almost unprecedented success and adulation? It was hard to tell. Shyness in an ordinary man is shyness, so perceived and accepted. In an uncommon man, one regarded as public property, it can be grossly misconstrued. DiMaggio's personality gave out monotonous, ambivalent signals, and depending upon your angle of vision or your preconceptions, he was aloof, cold, a dullard, sullenly inarticulate, a snob, or just plain shy. "If he doesn't know you," a sportswriter said, "he'll ignore you. If he does know you, he'll barely talk to you. There's a difference." Surely, this was no Dizzy Dean, with a salesman's grin and a bear hug for the world.

But the young man did handle it well, for he showed up perfectly equipped to handle stardom in the most glamorous, demanding, and tempting of cities. The shell he lived in had been built a long time ago, and it was tough and many-sided enough to deflect all unwanted incursions. He was ready, all right, for he never changed, not then, not ten years later, not ever. Alertly self-protective, he could sniff out sycophants, kick over unsought canisters of incense, and chase away intruders with an élan of silence. He was never awed by the big city; in fact, he settled in with such powerful self-realization it was as though he had at last attained home and milieu. Who or what was going to impress one of the dynamos that made the city roar and glitter? The fact that he chose his friends from the city's pool of celebrities and chose not to be at ease with the multitudes only enhanced his image and began the creation of the DiMaggio aura.

The bleacher fan who worshiped DiMaggio really got his money's worth: creation's greatest baseball player and a man who spent his evenings in those pre–night-ball days sitting in The Stork Club, El Morocco, Lindy's, and the other centers of New York's cozy nocturnal celebrity world. He sat with the sportswriters, the politicos, show business ornaments, breathless columnists like Walter Winchell and Ed Sullivan, and assorted Broadway characters often described as sportsmen, a generic that covered a lot of sins. If Joe sat there with maybe your cheer still echoing in his ears, then you were a small part of it, or at least you were entitled to think so, and that moat of a personality he carried around with him couldn't stop it.

Those who were close to him said his quiet friendship was to be cherished. They tried to explain and defend him by saying he was a passionate guardian of his privacy. The doubters said if he was such a private man, then why did he so readily associate with writers and those devouring columnists? The doubters believed they detected snobbery and unfriendliness, an elitism that was odious because it emanated from what they considered an uncultured, inarticulate clod. Unlike Ruth, who would happily charge into crowds of thousands and not leave until each had been rewarded with an autograph, DiMaggio often sat for hours in the clubhouse to avoid the crowd he knew was waiting for him. The youngster who had brought with him to the big time a prepossessing pride that was white hot and a dignity that was cool would never relent, never compromise, on the field or off, and while this offended some, most accepted him for what he was, what he chose to be.

By rights his blanched personality should have left him in the category of a Lajoie, a Speaker, or a Foxx, a dynamite page in the record book but little else to talk about. This man, however, possessed in surpassing measure an intangible that is beyond simple explanation. For a successful pub it's called atmosphere; in a human being it's charisma, the word itself freighted with a conjurer's intimations. In its theological context it means a gift or power that has been divinely conferred. In a baseball context, DiMaggio comes as close to embodying the definition as anyone. Without intention, his magisterial presence on the ball club created a social stratification between himself and his teammates, who considered him so especially blessed as a player that it was understandable (perhaps even preferable) for him to be remote. It completed the image that existed in even their minds. Playing on the same team as Joe DiMaggio was for many of them the ultimate sanction of their big-league status. If there was snobbery in him it was not detected by the men he lived with for half a year. (Or at least it has never been spoken. Criticizing DiMaggio, one suspects, would be considered gauche.) They said that if he became your friend you had a friend for life (and conversely, if he crossed you off, you remained crossed off for life).

His rare quips were remembered and quoted, as if to demonstrate that this deity was the more godlike for being human. Tommy Henrich remembered a game in Detroit when Yankee relief pitcher Johnny Murphy was crossing the outfield grass on his way to pitch to Hank Greenberg with the game on the line in the bottom of the ninth. "Murphy is going to curve him," Henrich said, "that's all there is to it. He passes by DiMaggio, and for the only time in his life that I ever heard of, DiMaggio has a thought for the pitcher. 'Why don't we fastball this guy once?' says DiMaggio. So Johnny changed the pattern. And on the second pitch, Pow!, in the seats. That's the end of the ball game. We get into the clubhouse and Murphy's sitting there with his head in his hands, and DiMaggio's saying nothing. All of a sudden, after about five minutes, DiMaggio gets up and walks over to him. 'Let me tell you something,' Joe says. 'Don't you *ever* listen to anything I ever have to say again.' That was pretty funny, for Joe," Henrich concluded.

His teammates conceded that with rare exceptions—Lefty Gomez (whose extrovert personality and facile wit DiMaggio envied) was one—he was not close to them. But when they needed something—a favor, advice, encouragement—he was there. He seemed to be in their lives like some benevolent government agency, amorphous and circumscribing, a reassuring presence. They counted him as shy—"mysterious," Gomez said of the young DiMaggio. "You never knew what he was thinking." None resented his status or his privileges; once they had seen him play for a time they knew he was from somewhere else, the dream player so good he was beyond envy.

But he was not without certain stringent demands, albeit silent ones. No player ever came to represent his team with more precision than he, and it was all done by example as the Yankees began reflecting his style, his pride, his efficient authority. This most withdrawn of men became to his teammates an inspiration and a model. Like that other corporate player of unimpeachable credentials, Gehrig (ironically, it was the tenement-born and -bred New Yorker who went fishing to relax, while the fisherman's son chose smoky nightclubs), he played uncomplainingly through pain and injury, with a fixed emotional barometer. Complainers, malingerers, and image-breakers received from him—as they had from Gehrig—a frown that in the

Yankee clubhouse was like a black cloud descending from on high (and in the world of baseball this was indeed the sublime height). There is no telling what an infuriated DiMaggio might have registered on the local seismographs, but it never happened, because who would have ever dared to challenge that frown?

His lone demonstration of emotion on a ball field serves to illustrate perfectly his iron control—the control of a man who knows he is being watched and has the concentration and self-confidence to handle it. When Brooklyn's Al Gionfriddo robbed Joe of a game-tying three-run home run in the 1947 World Series with a spectacular running catch, DiMaggio, rounding second convinced the ball had gone out, gave a little kick at the dirt. Captured on film, the DiMaggio frustration is as much a highlight as the Gionfriddo grab, for commentators never tire of reporting the moment as the only time in twelve years that Joe DiMaggio ever displayed emotion on a ball field, as if to emphasize that by being capable of it he was all the more remarkable for his composure. Once, in twelve years and nearly eighteen-hundred baseball games. A brief, barely noticeable poke at the dirt with his toe. See the leaping, arm waving, high-fiving, teammate-hugging players of a later date. Imagine DiMaggio engaging in any of that and you can believe a papal rhumba in St. Mark's Square.

By his sophomore season he was the game's most popular player. Quiet and reserved he was, passive he was not—by 1938 he was holding out for more money. Based on a 1937 season during which he batted .346 and hit 46 home runs (a monstrous total for a right-handed hitter who played half his games in Yankee Stadium) and drove in 167 runs, he was asking for $45,000, an enormous salary for the time and unprecedented for a third-year man—back then hefty salaries had to be worked up to after years and years of high-caliber performance. When told by Barrow that he was asking for more than Gehrig, Joe answered that in that case Gehrig was being underpaid. With ownership holding all the cards in those days, he eventually had to settle for twenty-five grand, but not before having let the Yankees know not to take that poker face for granted.

A half-century at center stage and he remains for the most part an enigma, an anomaly in an age of probed, scrutinized, and anatomized celebrities. Considering his stature and its unique longevity, there is a paucity of anecdotes told about DiMaggio. His is a myth that has had little apocrypha take shape around it. It cannot be said of DiMaggio, nor of any human being, that he is empty. But as far as the public is concerned, he is the great unknown, the great undefined, careful and unrevealing. Is he happy? Is he lonely? He seems so far above the roar of the crowd that in the universe of baseball he has achieved a sort of transcendence, sent higher still, after all had been said and done, by yet another American myth named Marilyn Monroe whose tomb he sees is decorated by fresh roses three times a week, a gesture that tells us something about a man who tells us it is none of our business. Is he a Republican or a Democrat? Apolitical? Does he really root for the Yankees? Where does he go and what does he do? It is said he travels constantly, living out of a suitcase, and that a sister keeps home for him in San Francisco when he is there. When needed, he appears, like some responsive nobleman. Dinners, testimonials, golf tournaments, benefits. Suddenly he is there, handsome, dignified, the pride of the event, as untouchable as ever, acknowledging one more standing ovation from old-timers whose applause snaps from high-held hands and who lean to tell a younger man over the noise that this was "the greatest ballplayer ever lived," and the younger man applauding and nodding his head to this spoken bit of Scripture.

Shy he may be, but DiMaggio seems never embarrassed by the esteem, the tribute, handling it gracefully, with a controlled smile, a few nods of the head, perhaps a wave of the hand, so accustomed to being cheered, applauded, stared at, wondered about, envied. For many people he has become a symbol to hang on to and cherish, a man from the old, strong, flawless America when Franklin Roosevelt was president and Joe Louis was heavyweight champ and Clark Gable was the king of Hollywood and Ernest Hemingway was shooting lions in Africa. What each of them was in his sphere, Joe DiMaggio was in baseball, and, *mirabile dictu*, there he was still.

EIGHTEEN

AN EXTRATERRESTRIAL VISITOR, piloting his spaceship over the United States, would no doubt begin puzzling over the significance of those endlessly reappearing diagrams beneath him. Though some lay in more grandiose settings than others, each was the same diamond-shaped, grass-covered configuration lying inside of a beige-colored half circle. The geometric constancy of the design and its ubiquity surely had to possess some occult meaning, some cabalist message or transmission of hope or faith in the benevolence of noticing gods.

All over America, in every city and town and village, lie the baseball diamonds, and indeed each is a sort of fertility rite rich with hope and striving, the potential of miracle and wonder stitched into each unchanging and repetitive design. Each of these diamonds holds its fascination, for the one in the teeming city is no surer of releasing another lightning bolt of baseball history than is the one remote in a forest clearing. The one in Van Meter, Iowa, was unique above them all, crude and homespun, yes, but, befitting the lush heartland in which it lay, more fertile than almost any other. It was the lovingly built and attended work of one man for his son, a father acting out the not untypical American vision he had for his boy.

"When I was twelve," Bob Feller said, "we built a ball field on our farm." What an irresistible act of faith—not only nurture the dream but design a landscape for it. How high and wide and daring the corn and hog farmer William Feller dreamed, we cannot know, but surely his boy filled that dream to its furthest dimension and illuminated it with blazing reality. Van Meter, Iowa. A historical landmark in baseball America.

We fenced off the pasture, put up the chicken wire and the benches and even a little grandstand behind first base. The field was up on a little hill and we called it Oak View because you looked right down over the Raccoon River and saw a lot of oaks in the forest there. The crops and the trees and the river made a very pretty view. Artistically speaking, it was rather an interesting ball park.

He could always throw hard, he said, even when he was eight or nine years old. "I used to play catch with my father in the house. I'd throw from the kitchen into the living room and he'd sit there on the davenport and catch me with a pillow." Lord, but that dream must have been a furnace of relentless passion inside of William Feller, an amelioration for whatever disappointments and frustrations accrue within an Iowa farmer. In the wintertime they would throw in the barn. "In 1924 we got a Delco plant to electrify the property—this was about fifteen years before the power lines came in. We had a windcharger, and on a windy day that would charge the batteries, and we would use the lights in the barn to play night baseball—if you want to call it that—two or three nights a week to keep my arm in condition." In the wintertime, as the snows swirled through the empty grandstands and drifted across the cold grass of the great stadiums of America, young Robert William Andrew Feller was keeping his arm in condition in a barn in Van Meter, Iowa, popping the ball into his father's mitt with insidiously increasing velocity, enough velocity to cave in a couple of William Feller's ribs one night when he was expecting a curve and got instead a hopping smoker. "They had to tape him up from his waist to under his armpits, and for a farmer to have to work under those conditions was miserable."

There were sufficient years and men and enough appropriate history behind him now to call it a tradition and to place him squarely in its onward surge, from Amos Rusie on through Cy Young, Rube Waddell, Walter Johnson, Joe Wood, Lefty Grove, and Dizzy Dean— the great American fastballers who could pump for nine innings and leave the mound with speed undiminished. And now it was the hour of Bobby Feller, a boy with an Americana lilt in the very sound of his name, although his formal baseball monicker is Rapid Robert. He was the last of the mound titans who both started and relieved, three times in his prime leading American League pitchers in appearances, an astonishing statistic for an ace of aces.

He was born on November 3, 1918, a week before the armistice, a sturdy, fresh-faced, dimple-chinned postwar baby destined to become the national game's one and only prodigy, a storybook detonation upon the mounds of major-league baseball. No one, not Mathewson or Johnson or Grove had, or has, ever struck with the electrifying suddenness of this wide-shouldered, cannon-armed youngster who, with DiMaggio, appeared in tandem like spirit-raising symbols for a spiritually broken country still plodding through the morass of the Great Depression. Of the two, Feller, with his awesome unharnessed power, was the larger symbol of the America soon to erupt with blazing and dangerous energies.

This heartland-bred farmboy of supreme self-confidence and forthright utterance could have beaten the draft with his 2-C (farmer) classification, but didn't; could have spent the war "sitting in Honolulu drinking beer," but didn't; asking instead for combat duty and getting plenty of it on the battleship *Alabama* at Tarawa, Kwajlein, and Iwo Jima, figuring, "If I was in, I might as well be in all the way." Later he became the most acute and urbane of players, incorporating himself (Ro-fell), flying his own plane, and demanding, and getting, attendance-bonus clauses in his contract. If he were playing today, his would be the lodestar contract.

He grew up under two regimens—filling in the silhouette of his father's dream (a dream that some neighboring farmers thought might make the boy grow up "impractical") and performing the farmboy's chores, milking the cows, feeding the pigs, cleaning the barn, putting up fences; always serious and positive, inculcated with his father's faith. But he was a farmboy, and we know what that meant in 1930s America—the havoc of dust storms, grasshoppers, drought, starving livestock, barren land, a veritable biblical plague of trials. But they survived, Bob Feller and his father and the dream that lay embodied in the most fertile patch of land around—that hand-made, "rather interesting" little fantasy ball field that neither drought nor dust storm could dry or obliterate, because, "Whatever we didn't have, we always had baseball." That good, old, faithful and indestructible American nourishment, that unfailing reliable fifth season, reassuring in all its promises and manifestations.

Perhaps it is right that the storybook melodramatics of great discovery do not figure in the DiMaggio story, that DiMaggio, who belonged to the multitudes on the heroic scale longer than any other player should rightfully have been discovered in full sunshine by tens of thousands; and anyway, DiMaggio the player was not breathtakingly "sudden." You had to watch him hit, field, run, and throw; DiMaggio was a work of art your enthralled senses put together piece by piece. Feller was "sudden," stepping out of a lightning bolt and swirl of smoke, springing to life, as H. G. Wells said of the precocious Stephen Crane, "fully armed." For Bob Feller, in so many ways Americana virtually in transparence, a storybook tale of discovery seems absolutely correct and even necessary. The boy was a composite of so much of what so many like to believe is typical American youth. He was big and strong, of course, and refreshingly honest and candid, though never hurtfully so like Hornsby. Sturdily self-confident, but unlike Dean never a braggart. He worked hard and abided by an admirable code of principles, loyalty and dedication high among them.

Like Walter Johnson in Weiser, Idaho, Bobby Feller, laboring in obscurity in Van Meter, Iowa, had his band of true believers, and these were even more credible than Johnson's traveling salesman, for they were genuine under-the-gun eyewitnesses—the American Legion ball umpires who were watching the boy streak his BB's plate-ward in the early thirties. The umpires began writing letters to Cleveland scout Cy Slapnicka, informing him of what was loose in the jungles of Iowa. This was in 1934. Umpires are not noted for the same level of hyperbole as traveling salesmen; still, Slapnicka paid no heed to the tom-tom beats of this planet-sized opportunity. One assumes he had other missions to attend to; and anyway, 1934 was not a good year in which to believe in miracles.

In 1935, however, Slapnicka had some serious business to attend to—scouting right-handed pitcher Claude Passeau, then pitching for Des Moines, in the Western League. Slapnicka's route of travel, he realized, would swing him close to Van Meter, and the not unreasonable gentleman felt he could achieve a dual purpose on the expedition: scout Claude Passeau and humor those persistent umpires by glancing at their sixteen-year-old miracle worker.

It becomes a good news–bad news tale. The bad news was that, stopping off in Van Meter first, Slapnicka never did get to see Passeau, who was soon to launch a fine thirteen-year career with the Phillies and Cubs. The good news was that he saw Bob Feller, thereby ensuring himself one of baseball history's more glittering footnotes. What the veteran baseball man saw was a prodigious display of raw power unlike any he had ever seen. (Only a handful, like La Salle and De Soto, have made grander discoveries on the North American continent.) Cy Slapnicka had realized the dream of every baseball scout who has ever had a flat tire on a country road, the definitive dream, the one that remains the touchstone. If actors want to be Olivier and violinists Heifetz, if physicists want to be Einstein and lawyers Clarence Darrow, then baseball scouts want to be Cy Slapnicka, who, when he returned to Cleveland, told a meeting of front-office executives, "Gentlemen, I have found the greatest pitcher in history." Even if he was half-right in his estimate, Van Meter would have been worth the carfare. The fact is, he may well have been very close to 100 percent correct.

So Robert Feller signed with the Cleveland Indians. His bonus? An autographed ball and one dollar. Just one. His contract called for seventy-five dollars a month. "I'm glad I didn't get a bonus," he said years later. "I think you're supposed to get paid after you do your job." Quoted at a later date, old-fashioned scruples sometimes have the ring of heresy.

In the spring and summer of 1936 Feller traveled and worked out with the Indians as a nonroster player, the big club not wanting to risk the youngster being mishandled by a minor-league manager. On July 6, with the schedule at pause for the All-Star Game break, the St. Louis Cardinals, the Gashouse Gang themselves, came to Cleveland to play an exhibition game. With an opportunity to see Frankie Frisch, Joe Medwick, Pepper Martin, Rip Collins, Leo Durocher, and perhaps a glimpse of the great Dizzy Dean himself, a fair-sized crowd came out to take a day in the sun. What they got was a genuine, man-sized slice of baseball history, the first cannon roar of the Bob Feller legend.

Slapnicka suggested to Cleveland manager Steve O'Neill they let the kid pitch a few innings, letting him get his feet wet against big-league hitters and also saving a bit of wear and tear on the pitching staff.

"It's a pretty tough lineup," the cautious O'Neill said.

"I don't think he'll embarrass himself," Slapnicka said, perhaps dryly. ("He knew me better than anyone else did," Feller said.)

So he walked out to the mound with his ploughboy's rolling strides, seventeen years old, not yet a high school graduate, serious-minded as he always was and would be, all business and never with more intensity than when he was on that mound, one of the very, very few natural-born kings of the hill, armed with two insuperable assets—his blinding speed and his father's dream. "No, I wasn't nervous," he said. "I never had any concern about the hitters as long as I could get that ball over the plate." Not bragging; a simple truth, as simple as digging a posthole and hammering the post in. And anyway, nobody had ever hit him, and these were just another set of fellows with bats in their hands, same as the others. But this was the Gashouse Gang, wasn't it? "I knew who they were," he said.

Nor did they hit him. For his three innings of work he yielded a single and a bloop double. Very nice work, but that wasn't the news. Of the nine outs he recorded, eight were strikeouts, and *that* was the news—an unknown seventeen-year-old whiffing eight Gashousers in three innings. Cy Slapnicka, sitting in a box seat, watching with an inventor's pride, must have been saying silently to himself, "It works! It works!" For there "it" was, for the first time in action on a big-league mound, in that full-motion windup: Bob Feller bending deeply forward from the waist, swinging those arms far out behind him, and then sweeping them back and up as his right foot pivoted and his left leg rose and kicked across his body almost face-high, and then out and down in a powerful stride, the entire farm-bred muscular body following in inelegant but emphatic rhythm, releasing a baseball as hard as ever a human being could, ending with his right leg in airborne follow-through, making those photographs of a Feller release fairly vibrate with strength and excitement.

How fast? Unlike Waddell and Johnson and Grove, he worked in a more technologically sophisticated era and his speed could be measured. In 1946 Clark Griffith obtained from the army ordnance plant in Aberdeen, Maryland, a photoelectric-cell device and set it up over home plate in Griffith Stadium, announcing that Bob Feller would throw his swifty through it and have his speed clocked. A neat drawing card idea, and the customers came out for it. (Griff forgot to discuss it with the practical Mr. Feller, who told the old guy it would cost him $1,000 or no go. Griff chewed him down to $700 and it was a deal.) Feller threw the ball thirty or forty times through what he described as "that Mickey Mouse–Rube Goldberg device" and was clocked at 98.6 miles an hour, a speed that he maintained fairly consistently throughout a game, and probably exceeding 100 miles an hour when he really "opened up." And what did this lethal pellet do at full operational force? "My ball had a hop, and it would rise. When I threw it sidearm to right-hand hitters, it would run in on them." In addition, he threw a curve that was almost as fast, and he was just wild enough to cause high anxiety at home plate, especially in those prehelmet days.

What is now a well-grooved quote emerged after the exhibition game against the Cardinals. A photographer asked Dean if he would pose for a picture with Feller, and Dean reportedly laughed and said, "You'd better ask *him* if he'll pose with *me.*"

Feller's full-throttle valves had let some of the gas out of the Gashouse Gang, received appropriate newspaper coverage, and quickly added the teenager to the Cleveland pitching staff. The boy's debut had been spectacularly improbable; nevertheless, it left behind no skeptics, or if it did, they were soon blown into extinction. On August 23, 1936, to be precise. Handed the ball for his first big-league start, against the St. Louis Browns, Feller hit the headlines ("Indians Rookie," they said) with an extraordinary performance, striking out 15 of the Brownies. And lowly though the Browns may have been, this was no daisy-picker for Feller, for the team had some real hitters in the lineup—Harlond Clift (.302 that year), Beau Bell (.344), Moose Solters (.291), Lyn Lary (.289), Jim Bottomley (.298), Sammy West (.278). Feller's 15 strikeouts were one under the league record held by Rube Waddell since 1908, and two under Dizzy Dean's 1933 major-league record. Emmett (Red) Ormsby, one of the umpires in that game, and in the league since 1923, declared that the youngster had shown him more speed than any American League pitcher he had ever seen. More than Grove? "Yep." And then the great, big, touchstone question: "More than Johnson?" "Yes, sir." This was as heretical as it was possible to be in baseball. It brought forth the refuters; a generation's pride was at stake. If a seventeen-year-old was faster than Walter, then this was indeed a strange new world we were entering, and when were people ever ready to accept the demise of a comfortable fit?

Home-run hitters and fastball pitchers: power and speed, ever the lords of the game, the imagination-gripping natural forces, evokers of awe and wonder. But never anything like this. This was fairy tale stuff. Those who describe baseball as a boy's game are putting a highly misleading gloss on it. At the big-league level it is a game played by men remarkably gifted, the most multigifted athletes in America. If there is a seventeen-year-old on the premises he is there for a bit of shock treatment, to be shown how it is done before being ticketed for years of minor-league apprenticeship.

But not this seventeen-year-old. He was no glittering embryo with press-release promise, he was the second coming of Walter Johnson, not up from the minors but dropped from the clouds, a miler leaving the blocks with the unrelenting and undiminishing speed of a sprinter.

On September 13, 1936, he broke the American League one-game strikeout record and tied Dean's major-league mark when he fanned 17 Philadelphia Athletics. He must have been singularly brilliant that day, with adrenalin helping to drive the terrifying speed.

"I was pretty excited. I knew I was approaching the record. I was counting those whiffs. And the closer I got to that record, the more I wanted to break it. I just kept pouring them in." Heaven knows how fast he was throwing that day, with a boy's excitement, a man's arm, a searing desire to break a record. It hit the newspapers, Feller said, "like thunder and lightning, and I guess that's when people began to realize I was for real." The discovery of the rumored new planet had been verified.

Was he the most famous kid in America in 1936? "Come on now," the no-nonsense Mr. Feller said. "You're forgetting about Shirley Temple, aren't you? And what about those kids in the *Our Gang* comedies? Anyway, I was seventeen years old. You want to call that a kid? Okay, maybe by baseball standards." Absolutely—by baseball standards. The child Mozart improvising at the harpsichord, the youthful Keats writing his odes, Bob Feller setting a big-league strike-out record at seventeen. Everything in its context.

A dazzling new young hero in a country that had a need for them. For those of unshakable parochialism, for whom DiMaggio was an exotic and who belonged in New York anyway, this lad with the 4-H boy aura and the heroic strength of the biblical David seemed instantly at one with those other vast American originals, Mathewson, Johnson, and Dean, each possessing something grippingly unique and quintessentially American, exuding qualities that appealed to fans and gave the intimacy of kith and kin. For those who were around at the beginning, the impact of Bob Feller was truly unforgettable. In those pretelevision days, if you did not or could not attend a big-league ball game to see this intimidating phenomenon with your own eyes, then news of him was passed on to you via the newspapers, radio, or—and far more glorifying—word of mouth by those who had seen him or spoken to one who had and thereby felt compelled to describe the phenomenon to the furthest limits of credibility.

After less than half a season in the major leagues he came back to Iowa a celebrity. "People would gawk at me and point me out like I was some circus freak. Sometimes your best friends are your worst enemies, wanting to keep you out late at night so they can be seen with you." (How late was late in Van Meter?) But neither temptation nor adulation could undo this boy, not with the Iowa-rooted sense of values his parents had instilled in him. And anyway, he was so secure in the depths of his ability, so absolutely intent upon the road ahead, he had no need nor desire for fawners or sycophants. Pea-green farmboy or not, he had an innate sense of what was right and a cool disdain for what was not. Nobody was going to use him, exploit him, get him to do anything he did not want to, and one of the first to learn this bedrock fact was the glowering, commandment-giving bass drum of baseball himself, Kenesaw Mountain Landis.

At that time, there was an agreement among major-league clubs not to sign free agents below the college level. High schoolers and sandlot players were the province of the independently owned minor-league clubs, who were free to sign them, develop them, and then sell them to the majors. In order to get Feller, the Indians pulled what they thought was a slick piece of work by signing the boy to a contract with Fargo-Moorhead of the Northern League and then beginning a series of manipulations that brought him to Cleveland. When Feller exploded on the big-league scene the big bang was brilliant enough to light up all the dark corners, and Cleveland's chicanery was exposed. In the chambers where Landis dispensed his autocratic life-and-death baseball justice, a rumbling began.

In the winter of 1936 word came that the commissioner was considering voiding Cleveland's contract with Feller and declaring him a free agent. This was tantamount to tossing the Hope Diamond into the air and declaring ownership for whoever, through his mightiest efforts, caught it. So the scouts came to Des Moines, ten or so miles from Van Meter, and like field marshals waiting for a tantara, sat in the Chamberlain Hotel armed to the teeth with checkbooks, depression or no depression. The club that put this boy on the mound would enjoy instant economic recovery.

So Willaim and Bobby went to Chicago and into those August chambers and faced the judge. Farmers are legendary the world over for their singularity and independence; a man who plays give-and-take with nature is not about to be cowed by a mere federal judge—baseball commissioner—grand panjandrum.

"It's our intention," said corn and hog farmer William Feller to Kenesaw Mountain Landis, "for him to play for Cleveland, if they want him, and they want him. And if you won't permit that, then we're going to sue you in civil court, because we have a civil law contract and we want to test it to see if baseball law supersedes civil law."

If you know your baseball history, you know that Bob Feller pitched for the Cleveland Indians and for no one else for twenty-one years. Landis, like any sensible bully who meets an unfaltering gaze, gave a harrumph, slapped the Indians with a $7,500 fine, and let destiny spin out what destiny had wrought.

And how did young Robert feel about giving up what could well have been a $100,000 bonus? Those quirky values again. "I didn't care about that. I wanted to stay where I was. I was happy. I figured if I was worth that kind of money, I'd make it later, after I'd proved I was worth it. And if I wasn't worth it, then I had no business having it." (And from baseball's later-day agents and financial advisers, a chorus of, "*What? When was this?*")

A lame arm limited Feller to 149 innings of work in 1937. When he was out there, though, he was throwing hard, with 150 whiffs in his 149 innings. Johnson had never come close to a strikeout-per-inning average; neither had Grove nor Waddell, and neither did anyone else until the Age of the Strikeout decades later. The boy was wild, too, walking a major-league record 208 batters in 1938. Those unguided missiles helped the batters to concentrate at home plate, but not necessarily on hitting. When they were facing Feller, Bucky Harris would tell his men, "Go on up there and hit what you see. If you can't see it, come on back." And White Sox skipper Jimmy Dykes gave certain of his weaker right-handed hitters the take sign on three-and-two against Feller. "Since they weren't going to hit it anyway," he explained, "I didn't want to chance them swinging at ball four."

On the last day of the 1938 season, Feller broke the single-game strikeout record when he fanned 18 Detroit Tigers in the first game of a doubleheader. Ironically, he lost the game, 4–1, giving up seven walks and seven hits. Newsreel cameras had been brought in from New York to film the game, though not because of Feller—nobody could have known what the young man was going to do—but because of Detroit's Hank Greenberg, because of what Big Henry was on the brink of doing. He was going into that doubleheader with 58 home runs, and here he was, versus Bob Feller. Talk about confrontations! This wasn't Joe Wood against Walter Johnson, this was two different species of mammoth in contest. The world's quickest fastball against 1938's most thunderous power bat. Enough to make the stars pierce the blue canopy of afternoon to bear witness.

Big Henry was one of the most powerful of all right-handed sluggers, and he looked it at home plate, his classic stance sculpted in nearly six feet four inches of well-distributed muscle. He held the bat up and high, standing there with the poised confidence of the great hitter, a confidence born not just of ability and achievement, but of the eagerness and anticipation he brought with him to the plate, the raw knowledge that this job was going to be done with impact and emphasis. For these hitters, with their primitive bunchings of intuitive coordinates, the job of the pitcher was akin to that of public servant. For the Henry Greenbergs of the world, that bat was as menacing as a policeman's billy, as decisive as a judge's gavel. And for him 1938 was the pinnacle year, the year he joined the sonorous procession of Ruth, Gehrig, and Foxx, the year he followed the Ruthian trail up and up all summer long into ever-thinning air toward the most exclusive Olympian height in baseball. Five games to go in 1938, and 58 home runs in his bag, and then four games, then three, and still at 58, and finally this season-ending doubleheader, and Bobby Feller in the opener.

What a summer for this twenty-seven-year-old Bronx-born giant, and what a summer the year before—183 runs batted in, one under Gehrig's American League record. How he loved to drive in runs; they were his obsession; the RBI tasted better to him than the home run. With a man on first, he would nag Charlie Gehringer, batting ahead of him: "Get him over to third, for God's sakes. I'll drive him in." And he did: 139 runs batted in in 1934, 170 in 1935, 183 in 1937, and 146 in 1938.

The Yankees wanted this local boy, in fact offered him $10,000 to sign a contract, but young Henry was a first baseman and so was Gehrig and there was no future in that. So he signed with Detroit for less money and went off to the minors and played in some southern towns where Jews were as rare as Tibetan lamas. There was some hostility, he said, but more curiosity. The good ole boys came out to see a baseball game and a Jew, surely worth two bits on a hot afternoon. Only in melting-pot America are men ambassadors in their own land.

He was just as much an anomaly, if not as exotic, in the big leagues as he had been in the minors, for, like DiMaggio, he was the ballplaying capstone of another immigrant movement, one that preferred acclimatation to acculturation and that purposefully directed its young away from frivolities like baseball into more serious pursuits. There had been Jewish ballplayers before (many of whom had changed their giveaway names), but nothing like big Henry Greenberg. In a country that believed in stereotypes, it wasn't easy, as with an implied sense of relief *The Sporting News* reported in 1934 that there "was little suggestion of the Jewish characteristics in his appearance, the nose being straight," as if a Jew with a crooked nose would somehow have tainted the game's pure image. And from out of the stands and opposing dugouts flew the good old ethnic goads and insults that fester in joyously vacuous minds, aimed at the lone giant who stood at first base for the Detroit Tigers, who heard them all of course but accepted them with equanimity, sorting out normal bench jockeying from blatant anti-Semitism, answering both with long-distance home runs and those cherished runs batted in.

In 1938 he was swinging against Ruth (who that very summer was a sideshow attraction in Ebbets Field, coaching first base for the Dodgers but more importantly swinging lustily in advertised batting practice to help squeeze some rust from the turnstiles), enough of a burden for any man, much less one named Greenberg. All season long he was dynamite-laden, eleven times hitting two home runs in a game (a record) and piling them higher and higher until he was just footsteps from the Everest peak of single-season records. He was exciting that year, and he was needed, for Hank Greenberg was about all that American Jews had going for them in the middle thirties, and in 1938 it was only getting worse. The stories coming out of Nazi Germany were ominously darkening, and the lone thunder of Henry Greenberg's home runs were for many the sole respite from the enlarging cadences of jackbooted zombies upon the cobblestoned streets of German cities and towns. Swastika-waving German-American Bunds were holding open meetings in Madison Square Garden. The crack-brained demonic speeches of Adolf Hitler were broadcast over the radio, made the more sinister by the crackling static of shortwave transmission and swollen by the perverted death's-head roars of "*Sieg Heil!*"

Take away Henry Greenberg in 1938 and for a Jewish boy there was little but fear and dismay. And there he stood on October 2, already tied with Foxx for most home runs ever by a right-handed hitter, already among the game's nobility, the newsreel cameras ready to grind it into history. But instead they got something else, the nineteen-year-old Bobby Feller at one of his own majestic peaks, setting a strikeout record. Big Henry struck out twice, collecting just a double in four trips against "the Cleveland marvel." In the second game, called after seven innings because of failing light, he singled three times in three trips, a nice day's work but no cigar, and he went into the winter with his 58 home runs, and the darkness fell.

NINETEEN

IT WAS exactly twenty-five summers after the cannonading of the Great War had begun in 1914, as tidy a chronological cycle as history has to offer. The ministries of the great European democracies finally came to the realization that what they had been trying to prevent was the inevitable. On September 1, 1939, German armor crossed into Poland; two days later England and France declared war on Germany. The longest, costliest, most blood-drenched misadventure in the history of planet Earth had begun. It would be a six-year journey through a macabre twilight before emergence into the sudden blinding primal light of unprecedented menace and promise.

In its own private, insular universe baseball offered up its own evidence that the world was changing in that watershed year of 1939, that the old immutable verities could no longer be counted upon, for something that for a decade and a half had been as sure and dependable as God's own sunrise, suddenly ceased. It was no longer Gehrig at first base for the Yankees. On May 2, 1939, at Detroit, Gehrig, the last of the '27 Yankees, removed himself from the starting lineup for the first time since June 2, 1925. Appropriately, the end of this monotonously heroic feat of endurance struck from outside of baseball. It wasn't years—in the baseball sense—nor was it an injury or a slump or reduced efficiency. It was amyotrophic lateral sclerosis, an insidious, incurable disease that atrophies the muscles. It is more plainly and graphically known today as Lou Gehrig's disease.

It was unsuspected but evident in 1938—any statistical buff with hindsight will tell you that. His .295 batting average and 114 runs batted in—notable for your normal hitters—were his most meager showings since 1925; his 29 home runs his least since 1928. Well, they said, he was thirty-five years old. That was probably it.

Always a fanatic about physical conditioning, he worked hard over the winter to be in the best possible shape for spring training, trying to strengthen muscles that were already beginning to die. By the time he reported to St. Petersburg at the end of February, the deterioration had become obvious. He moved sluggishly. He stumbled over invisible impediments. His reflexes were turning to sere leaves. Line drives that should have been howling in right field were dropping limply into left-center. He was out stretching sure doubles by wide margins. Moving as fast as he could, he looked as though he were running through waist-high water. He was becoming so many dead batteries.

His teammates laughed and joked about it. "Hey, Lou, you're getting old." Gentle, good-natured raillery. You didn't get too familiar with Gehrig to begin with. By seniority he was the lion and the bulwark of the team, though everyone knew that the sleek Italian greyhound in center field was the star, and one wonders what Gehrig might have thought watching the twenty-four-year-old DiMaggio racing through the hot Florida sunshine with those thoroughbred's strides and that exquisite coordination. They were both quiet men, these Yankee essences, seldom speaking to anyone, almost never to each other, though as far as anyone could tell they had nothing but respect and admiration for one another. That whole team was quiet; outside of the witty Gomez and the gregarious Henrich, there seems hardly to have been a spark of personality anywhere. No Gashousers here, no boasting, no bragging, no antics, no clowning. Not with Barrow and Weiss in the front office, not with McCarthy in the dugout, and surely not with Gehrig and DiMaggio on the field. But now in the spring of '39, with the frontiers of the world's nations about to be violated, and with another baseball season looming, Gehrig was dying.

Wes Ferrell, trying to make it with the Yankees that spring, his own best years now beyond revival in the record books, recalled it. "I remember one time out on the golf course, it was during the St. Petersburg Open. A lot of us went out to watch the pros. I was following the crowd, and I noticed Lou, walking all by himself along the edge of the woods. I watched him for a while and noticed something peculiar. Instead of wearing cleats, which normally he would have worn for walking across the grass, he was wearing tennis sneakers and was *sliding* his feet as he went along, instead of picking them up and putting them down. Looking back now, I realize why. His muscles were so deteriorated that just the effort of lifting his feet a few inches to walk had already become too much. God, it was sad to see—Lou Gehrig having to slide his feet along the grass to move himself."

Forget the 2,130 consecutive games played from one era into another, through pain and injury and weather raw and sweet—the granite constitution of Gehrig was displayed most compellingly that spring, when despite an inability to move or run freely, he continued to drive that slowly deadening body to play big-league baseball, scraping every last drop of strength and determination from the sediment of a once-bottomless reservoir. A man who had performed through pain in so exemplary a fashion had in a way compromised that pain, the same as a totally fearless man compromises courage. Now, faced with something he could not ignore or understand, and by again facing it stoically, Gehrig ennobled himself, became almost spiritual. It was his death rather than his life that was to give him unique enshrinement in the national pantheon.

Eight games into the season the streak rose to a total of 2,130 games. The streak had long since become one of baseball's accepted facts, given special acclaim only when it reached an anniversary number like 2,000. There were no headlines announcing that Gehrig was playing another game. Eight games into the 1939 season, and he was batting .143, with four singles and one run batted in. Whatever anyone else thought, he knew it was no mere slump, nor was it age.

The situation became embarrassing for Gehrig and awkward for McCarthy, because Lou was hurting the team, at bat and in the field, and more and more players were becoming more and more uncomfortable about it. They may have liked and admired the great first baseman, but they were professionals, they were playing to win (remember, they were Yankees, going for the pride and the money of a fourth consecutive pennant). There were silent clubhouses, averted glances; there were the pathetic, foredoomed efforts of Gehrig to tear those muscles free of the noose of amyotrophic lateral sclerosis, and there was McCarthy's watchful silence. The streak was the problem, of course. If not for the streak a "slumping" Gehrig could have been sat down for a few days to no great notice. It was the streak and the fact that this was McCarthy's surrogate son, the player he loved above all others, and this was making it an extra-baseball decision. But a man can't play 2,130 consecutive games without stubbornness and certain understandable illusions of indestructibility. Nor can he do it without pride, and those silent clubhouses and then those no longer sotto voce mutterings rose the pride above the stubbornness and the illusions, and on the night of May 1 Gehrig and McCarthy met in the skipper's hotel room in Detroit.

"He asked me how much longer I thought he should stay in," McCarthy said. "I told him he should get out right now. He agreed with me." It was more than just Lou's hurting the team, McCarthy said. "I knew there was something wrong with him, but I didn't know what it was. His reflexes were shot. I was afraid of his getting hit with a pitched ball. He wouldn't have been able to get out of the way, that's how bad it was. That was my chief concern, to get him out of there before he got hurt."

In June, Gehrig went to the Mayo Clinic in Rochester, Minnesota, to undergo tests, although one look at his shuffling gait and lifeless eyes was diagnosis enough. Two years, the doctors said, two and a half at most, during which time this most strapping and indomitable of baseball players would be reduced to infantlike helplessness.

"Lou Gehrig Appreciation Day" was held on July 4 at Yankee Stadium. Members of the 1927 squad were rounded up, including Ruth, and the emotional Babe threw his arms around the erstwhile crown prince, who stood firm in his old hurts and did not return the embrace but only smiled. It is one of baseball's memorable photographs. And then, in a speech that the PA system bounced in ghostly echoes through the packed grandstands and bleachers, Gehrig, conceding "that I may have been given a bad break," avowed that he "considered myself the luckiest man on the face of the earth."

New York's Mayor Fiorello LaGuardia gave Gehrig a job as a parole commissioner, and the dying Yankee had to sit and listen to the hard-luck stories of others and their "bad breaks." He listened. But soon he was too weak to go to his office and became bedridden, spooning out his life one suffocating breath at a time. He died a few weeks before his thirty-eighth birthday, on June 2, 1941, sixteen years to the day he replaced Wally Pipp at first base and began his stolidly spectacular day-in, day-out climb to baseball's "unbreakable record."

The immigrant parents, the humble beginnings. The devoted son. The shy, handsome young man. A New York Yankee. Fame, success, devastating power. Husband to a loyal and feisty wife. That streak, a symbol of stouthearted fidelity and steadfastness, stretching like a cable from one era to another, and then snapping. The slow, heartrending death. It was too choice a story; it called for nothing less than apotheosis by Hollywood, a sure sign of Gehrig's elevation to secular sainthood.

Initially, producer Samuel Goldwyn was dubious about the project. Gehrig was, after all, only a baseball player. (Brought to America by his own immigrant parents as a boy, Goldwyn was still upholding some of the original old shibboleths about baseball.) But when he saw newsreels of Lou Gehrig Appreciation Day and listened to the dying man's speech, Goldwyn wept, and immediately ordered the purchase of rights to the story. It was another example of the Hollywood mogul's belief in his archetypic emotions: If Samuel Goldwyn wept, America would weep.

To portray Gehrig on the screen, Goldwyn signed one of Hollywood's .400 hitters, Gary Cooper, whose public image exuded the same solid bedrock values associated with Gehrig. It proved a splendid choice, Cooper giving one of his patented highly controlled, dryly understated performances. Ironically, the lean, athletic-looking Cooper's baseball-playing skills were not even of sandlot level. A natural right-hander, there was no hope of his taking even a passable rip as the left-handed Gehrig, and so his stiff, rusty-gate cuts had to be filmed right-handed and the film later "flopped." In order to make everything come out right, the lettering on Cooper's uniform and the number on his back were reversed. (It wasn't the first time Hollywood had done something assways and come out a winner: *Pride of the Yankees* is a first-rate film biography and was a box-office hit in 1942.)

So here we had a meshing of two of America's most fertile hero-making institutions—the great sunlight game and the surrealistic watched-in-the-dark celluloid fantasies of the dream factory. There was no way reality could get out of this alive, nor did it; the juxtaposition created its own doctrine of determinism. Charging out to Hollywood to play the role of Babe Ruth was the now forty-seven-year-old king of all hitters himself. Ruth acquitted himself well—he was a natural-born ham—but there was one problem: Babe Ruth could no longer hit like Babe Ruth. There were certain long shots wanted by director Sam Wood that called for Ruth to pop a long one, but Babe was unable to lift the ball to Wood's satisfaction. The oil and water of fact and fantasy were not mixing, and anyway Ruth himself was by now fantasy, and two fantasies surely could find no compatible blend. So Wood called in Babe Herman, himself a legend of sorts. When he had been Brooklyn's premier slugger a decade before, Herman had hit well enough to be known as Brooklyn's Babe, and despite some lusty whacking (a .393 batting average in 1930), he was best known for having been hit on the head with a fly ball and for tripling into a triple play, neither of which had ever happened, but it was by now too late to relate truth to these cherished fictions. The thirty-nine-year-old Herman was still very much active, playing for the Hollywood Stars of the Pacific Coast League.

"That's right," Herman, a highly cultured gentleman despite his ragtag image, said years later with evident wryness. "I pinch-hit for Babe Ruth. That's me you see in those long shots when it's supposed to be Babe. I also batted for Cooper in the long shots." (Herman batting for Cooper batting for Gehrig. Pure Hollywood.)

And appropriately enough, it was here, among this mélange of the real and the illusory, that one of baseball's treasured legends came in for a severe shaking. One day, during a break in the shooting, Herman and Ruth were in conversation when onto the set walked a visitor. He was none other than Charlie Root, out of the big leagues now, pitching for the Hollywood club, and then and forever toting around his Branca-like reputation as the man who threw the famous pitch. Herman introduced the two ends of the Called Shot legend and some pleasant conversation ensued. All of a sudden, Herman said, Root "kind of sternly" said to Ruth, "Hey, you never pointed out to center field before you hit that ball off of me, did you?" Ruth laughed and said, "I know I didn't, but it made a hell of a story, didn't it?"

"That's what Ruth said," Babe Herman averred. "I was standing right there."

Nevertheless.

TWENTY

WRITE IT DOWN on a piece of paper—"1941"—and show it to a baseball aficionado and the incorrigible cryptographer in him will immediately answer: "56 and .406." Nothing cryptic about it: these are two of the most hallowed numbers in all of baseball history, in a game that is a pointillist mosaic of millions of numbers, some of them glittering like a mica-studded road at midnight, and a few proclaiming themselves grandly like permanently hoisted suns. In the unique land of baseball America, at once insular and expansive, those two numbers represent grand-scale heroics and the epitome of man-against-the-world achievement. And although the game is occasionally noted for the stunning exploit of a journeyman or moderately gifted player, these wondrous digits were carved by two of nature's noblemen, baseball-style, and no coincidence about it (unless you think coincidence is Henry Hudson discovering the Hudson River).

Heroes? It seemed for a time they were dropping into the American League from the planet Krypton. In 1936 they came in blazing tandem, DiMaggio and Feller. Three years later in swaggered a twenty-year-old left-handed hitter who wasn't just a natural-born hero—Hollywood good looks and all—but one with an ambition that served as inspiration every time he came to bat, that burned with fanaticism and dedication and a concentration that was the most frightening ever seen at home plate. "I could stare down every hitter who ever came up there," said the intense, menacing Yankee right-hander Vic Raschi. "Except one. That's right—Ted Williams. Well, what do you do with a guy that's been staring at *you* from the moment he's left the dugout to go out into the on-deck circle, and keeps his eyes on your eyes when he steps into the batter's box. Ted's concentration up at the plate was so intense I don't think he even knew what I was trying to do." No, only what *he* was trying to do, which was to keep that eternal flame of ambition at white heat until the last line drive had been solidly nailed and the achievement had

228

fulfilled that vast ambition, which could then rest, sit back, and survey it all with parental pride.

Williams evoked awe and wonder among his peers. As when speaking of Ruth, it was almost a point of pride for pitchers to describe how hard or how far Williams had struck one of their deliveries, as though they had been specially chosen to make sacrificial offerings to this demigod of the bat. They knew what he was doing up there, knew how rare he was, what sublime standards he was setting for their game, and as professionals they respected him for it. Watching him at the plate, watching him uncoil with a lash of the most savagely faultless swing in all of baseball, watching the sonic intoxication of another high and mightily driven Williams home run was for many of them the most affecting experience they took out of baseball with them. Personal contact with him may have been tenuous, but for them it had meaning and they never forgot. Talk to the men who played with or against him. "Ted's a great friend. He always calls when he's in town." And you know, just know, that some of these towns are places Ted Williams never heard of, much less passed through. But it doesn't matter.

The ambition was no small one. "I wanted to be the greatest hitter who ever lived." There it is, right up front, in the second paragraph of his autobiography (*My Turn at Bat*, written with John Underwood, a fine, friskily candid book). "It was the center of my heart," he says, "hitting a baseball." A boy's dream? Hardly. In the context of the American ethos, quite a man-sized design, and very much part of the national character, wanting to be the greatest, the strongest, the fastest, to be preeminent where preeminence was measurable and possible. Hemingway said he had "beat Mr. Turgenev. Then I trained hard and I beat Mr. de Maupassant. I've fought two draws with Mr. Stendhal, and I think I had an edge in the last one. But nobody's going to get me in any ring with Mr. Tolstoy unless I'm crazy or I keep getting better." So Teddy was of the mold, only he was setting out to cross bats with Mr. Cobb and Mr. Joe Jackson and Mr. Hornsby and Mr. Gehrig, and he would train hard and get into the ring with the Tolstoy of hitters, Mr. Ruth, and give him at least a draw, if not better.

Every boy who has ever swung a bat indulges the thought of being the greatest of hitters. But this one meant it. For him this was no mere time-passing fantasy. If a whaleship was for Melville "my Yale College and my Harvard," Ted Williams's was a batter's box and a pitching mound, for there he observed and studied and performed, bringing science to primitive instinct and reflex. He came equipped, of course, with eye-hand coordination that was electrically precise, physical strength, phenomenal eyesight, unremitting desire, and that ambition. And just for luck, nature threw in a few added fillips like those outdoorsy good looks and enough tabasco in his personality to keep him from ever being dull, on the field or off. He humanized his stature by being hypersensitive—to booing fans and most especially to what the Boston sportswriters wrote about him, and this was largely, often vituperatively, negative. (This was no regal DiMaggio loftily above the fray.) He was young, conspicuously self-confident, independent, outspoken, irreverent, and this the Boston writers, who apparently preferred their .400 hitters to be mannered George Apleys, could not abide. It was an unrelenting, career-long feud. (But only in Boston; writers in other cities had only praise and admiration for Williams, the player and the man.)

After Ruth, he was the most charismatic at-bat in baseball history. It wasn't just his power; it was as if the fans knew that each time he came to the plate Williams was again giving challenge to the highest standards ever established. He was baseball's ruthlessly honest man and scholar—he would never swing at a pitch unless his near-flawless judgment told him it was a strike, even if the winning run was at third base. Critics maintained that this kind of integrity could be costly, that in team sport insistence on perfectionism equaled selfishness. His statistics, Williams responded, proved that he knew what he was doing. In the larger, cosmic scheme he was right. Integrity is not so common as to be easily compromised, nor would something forged in a foundry of enormous work and steely discipline allow compromise. What is a runner left on third now and then compared to the all-time standard he lifted high enough for all hitters to see and thrilling enough for all to feel?

The perfectionist, and the stylist, too, for supremacy wasn't enough: He wanted to look good at it. This was part of the dream—more design than dream, actually; it was like a stratagem for total conquest. There is enchantment in it. Combined with all the other urgencies needed to mash a baseball—timing, judgment, co-ordination—was the need to do it stylishly. At home or in hotel rooms, he could hardly pass a mirror without pausing and setting one fist atop the other and drawing them back and taking his stance and then rip, watching himself not with vanity but with a soberly critical eye.

He was a .400 hitter with a sharply delineated personality and a vinegary pride, which is what you want in that particular elite, and which is what you got in Cobb and Hornsby, that tough, slap-leather frontiersman's stance against the world. Without it, you have those bland titans who left behind their .400's and not so much as a shadow or scintilla to go with it. Joe Jackson hit .400, and is remembered chiefly for having kept bad company; George Sisler (twice) and Harry Heilmann hit .400, and so did Bill Terry, and perfunctorily we honor them and wonder who they were. With those other fellows, the pungent ones, you get the feeling of a fanatic's pride behind it. Cobb admired Williams and they talked hitting when they got together, until the irreverent Teddy one day twitted the humorless Tyrus by reminding him that Hornsby's best (.424) was better than Ty's best (.420). Cobb became sullen and would not speak to him. Ted probably thought it was funny, but note this exchange, reported by Ted Lyons:

I was in the service with Ted, out in Hawaii. We rode together in a jeep every day, in and out of Honolulu. All he'd want to talk about was hitting. One day we were riding back from Honolulu, and all of a sudden from out of the blue he says to me, "Ted, do you think I'm as good a hitter as Babe Ruth?"

I said, "Well, wait till you get dry behind the ears. You've only been in the league a few years." I was kidding him.

You know, he wouldn't talk to me all the way home. He just sat there brooding. I had to laugh; I knew what was eating him.

When we got back to the base, I said, "Now, let's get back to the subject. Listen, Ted, you're a little different from Ruth. Babe would hit at balls up around his cap—and those are the ones he'd hit nine miles. You wouldn't swing at one above your letters. Babe didn't mind going after a bad ball. You won't go a half inch out of the strike zone. You're two completely different hitters." And then I told him, "Of course you're as good a hitter as he was."

Then he was all right again.

Is he the greatest hitter that ever lived? Yes. And now, having bitten off that chunk, how does one chew it? How does one define something that logically is indefinable? Shouldn't it automatically be Cobb with his .367 lifetime average, or Ruth with his average plus power, or Hornsby with those averages that still look like misprints in the record book? No, because if statistics alone could solve every debate baseball wouldn't be baseball. Cobb, in fact, does not figure in the debate because Ty did not hit with power. Accept that bit of effrontery, and we can go on.

Different eras, different playing conditions, different pitchers and style of pitching, different equipment. Different everything. How can one make reasonable judgments and comparisons? Well, by weighing it all in context.

One must begin by accepting certain givens: The four greatest hitters of all time were Joe Jackson, Rogers Hornsby, Babe Ruth, and Ted Williams. Why Jackson? Because we are talking about natural hitters, men endowed by nature as no others have been to swing a bat and hit a ball. Jackson is included because of the testimony of his contemporaries, all of whom without exception said he was the purest hitter of his time (even Cobb envied, and Ruth tried to imitate, that swing). The praise is so high and so voluminous that he must be included among the handful of hitting icons. Joe, however, played only nine full seasons and just about all of them in the dead-ball era before being booted from the premises at the age of thirty-two, leaving him with an amputated career. While he may well have been the paragon, there just isn't enough in the books to carry him all the way to the top.

Ruth and Hornsby were virtually exact contemporaries, each making the 1920s his heyday decade. Thus each man was at his peak during the Golden Age of Hitting, when all averages were inflated due to the introduction of the lively ball and the banning of trick pitches. This is not to say that these two men would not have excelled anytime, anyplace. They surely would have, but probably not to the same excessive degree. Thus it is important to bear in mind that Ruth and Hornsby were contemporaries, because no one since their time has achieved the figures that they did.

Now, there is absolutely no argument from any well-informed baseball fan that since the fading of Ruth in the early 1930s, the totemic batsman is Williams. This is a half-century's worth of time and hitters we're talking about, a time during which baseball gradually became a harder game to play, especially at home plate, thanks to more cultivation in the art of pitching (relief specialists, the development of the slider, and so forth), and the introduction of night ball. (Remember, Ruth and Hornsby played all their games in Abner

Doubleday's own golden sunlight.) Furthermore, baseball has become a tougher and better game because of the filtering into it of the finest talents of some 15 percent of the population that had been kept out before 1947. We're also talking about a time during which all athletes, no matter the sport, have improved, have become bigger, stronger, faster, and better trained and coached. In all sports, only one man has been acclaimed without dispute as the unapproachable best at his job for more than a half-century of steadily improving athletes. The best heavyweight? The best quarterback? The best basketball player? The best pitcher? All open for debate. But the best hitter? There is only one, and he is unchallenged. He towers. So, if inarguably he spans the field for a half-century, is it not reasonable to assume that if he had played with the grand sluggers of the 1920s, when hits came like hailstones, Ted Williams would not have outdone them all then too? After all, that was his ambition, wasn't it?

That surge of ambition began in San Diego, a continent away from the proving grounds of Fenway, where he was a summer baby, born on August 30, 1918, to what seems to have been a pair of mismatched parents. His mother was a devoted servant of the Salvation Army, working the streets of San Diego with the tireless faith and zest and fidelity of the true believer, sometimes having her tall, lanky older son march with the army band, which naturally he hated to do. Some aspects of her hard-core religiosity made him "cringe," and she worked full days and into the nights, often not coming home until nine or ten o'clock at night, leaving young Theodore and younger brother Danny to fend for themselves. Nevertheless, Ted, zealous disciple of his own peculiar ambition-faith, loved and respected his mother for what she was trying to do. His father was a remote, uninterested man whom Ted was never close to but was able to empathize with. Sam Williams might have had a dream of his own—at sixteen he had run off and joined the army and later saw action in the Philippines in the Spanish-American War. In San Diego he ran a small photographic shop, never made much money, never seems to have cast much of a shadow anywhere, and finally packed up and left.

Williams could have become a problem child, but he didn't, because he had baseball, the surrogate parent, the fantasy he probed so deeply into that there was no way out for him and it became the reality. Like a grimly determined Gehrig trying to smash his way out of oedipal transgressions with those murderous line drives, here was the youngster Williams with the same obsessed power swing, calculating his escape from the ministering angel and the somberly remote ex-soldier. The season was endless in the southern California sunshine, and there he was, at every opportunity, a tall, skinny kid with a bat in his hands, always with a bat in his hands, as it would later be in the big-league dugouts and clubhouses and even in hotel rooms, where he once dismantled some furniture taking practice rips in front of the mirror. This was not a boy to monkey with his own destiny: Born to swing a bat, he swung a bat.

He may have broken out of his origins, but that doesn't mean he didn't take them with him. He was always the simple democrat who preferred the company of "the little man"—bellhops and cops and firemen and fishermen—to that of the celebrated and socially high-powered whom he could have flicked into his orbit any time he chose, but never did. He shunned the formal and the ceremonial and all that went with the occasion, especially neckties, which he said had been designed solely to fall into your soup. Simple, direct, uncomplicated. That's how he tried to live, how he wanted to be perceived. The hero's hero was movie actor John Wayne, which is certainly in the mainstream, but ironic, because here was a man who out-Wayned Wayne, a real-life character who went to war twice (bitching loudly about it the second time, as most true-blooded Americans would have), and batting .400 and hitting all those home runs, doing it for real, without benefit of retakes or stunt men. There were surely no retakes for a Navy pilot in two wars, nor were there when you had Bobby Feller staring down your throat, and if one got away from that kid there was no tomorrow either. With all he did, and add that face and smile and that curly hair, this was a prince among American heroes, cut from the cantankerous Andy Jackson mold, stubborn and tempestuous, refusing to tip his cap yet revered by millions, and from all the yesterdays unto the last sunset.

All he ever wanted was to be left alone and to hit, but when you can hit like that you're not going to be left alone. The lair was peaceful until you rustled the grass in front of it, and then the lion leaped out, a genuine, full-maned, .400-hitting American lion. He could growl and snarl with the best of them and make it seem even worse than it was because he was Ted Williams, for when a monarch is out of temper eagles shield their eyes. (Exasperated by his antagonists in the press box, he once spat at them from the field, a display that saddled him with a $5,000 fine.) His sulks, his sometimes childish tempests, they all made his considerable charm the more considerable when he chose to turn it on. The beneficiaries of this charm were generally so beguiled by it that in the Williams catalogue of virtuoso powers, charm ranks right behind hitting. Relaxed and unbothered, in the company of those not looking for favors or reflective glory, he was the boonest of companions. A man's man. A regular guy. And an extremely tenderhearted and compassionate man when it came to sick children, an area in which athletes realize they are able to make their greatest personal impact, in which their brawny health and stellar glitter are almost enough to make the sick believe in miracles and the dying in heaven. The time and energy Williams has devoted since the late 1940s to the Jimmy Fund—the fundraising wing of the Children's Cancer Hospital of Boston—has been enormous, the commitment deep and sincere. He has chartered private planes to visit dying children, sat at countless bedsides, wept with countless heartbroken parents, and always in private, not for publication, no writers or cameramen allowed.

In some players, the desire helps shape the ability; with Williams, the ability and the desire probably electrified one another right from the start. It was the same old story again—baseball, baseball, baseball, transcending everything, including school, the future, and all that went with it. Pity those so driven that lack the talent to appease the dream—those lives of quiet desperation, or worse. But this youngster had it, and by the time he reached his mid-teens and his tall frame had begun filling out, it was evident to all who saw him swing a bat.

In the spring of 1936 Yankee scout Bill Essick came to see Ted's mother with an offer: $200 a month and a $500 signing bonus. Mrs. Williams asked for $1,000 in bonus money. (The Salvation Army angel ministered to down-and-outers, not to the New York Yankees.) Essick would not, or could not, go that high. So he went away, leaving behind Ted Williams. A Yankee fan can only close his eyes, sigh, and dream extravagantly of what might have been. Williams and DiMaggio in the same outfield, backed up in the same lineup. And then Williams and Mantle. Perhaps if young Teddy had been one of those millions of American boys whose passion it was to play for the Yankees he might have nagged his mother into accepting Essick's offer; but even back then he was singular. The future epitome of American idols did not himself indulge in idolatry, and perhaps this should not surprise: If you're as good as Babe Ruth, then part of it is not being impressed by the fact. Appropriately, his heroes were playground and high school coaches and neighborhood nice guys and others who had taken a personal interest. So the Yankee scout went away, walked out of the little frame house on Utah Street in San Diego, California, and for want of a few hundred dollars left sitting there the greatest hitter in baseball history, and the Williams-DiMaggio tandem occurred only in the celestial archives along with the Dempsey-Louis fight.

Soon after this historical missed opportunity, in June 1936, Ted worked out with the San Diego club in the Pacific Coast League and was signed to a contract. He was a few months short of his eighteenth birthday. Like his fellow Californian from up north, he started at a tender age in fast company, but whereas DiMaggio's career was rocket-launched, Ted began modestly, getting in 42 games and batting .271, with no home runs. But never mind; he had that swing, and it was like a mysterious glitter on a mountainside, waiting for a prospector with a shrewd eye and bottomless faith.

The prospector's name was Eddie Collins, Connie Mack's old second baseman and now general manager of the Boston Red Sox. Eddie went out to San Diego to check on their second baseman Bobby Doerr, on whom the Sox held an option. Going out to see Doerr, Eddie was about to stumble upon the grandest discovery in California since James Marshall's at Sutter's Mill in 1848. Eddie liked what he saw of Doerr and told San Diego owner Bill Lane the Red Sox would exercise their option, a salutary bit of decision making, as Doerr went on to become the greatest second baseman in Red Sox history and for nearly a decade the best in the American League. But for all that, Bobby turned out to be the trip's dividend, for into Collins's lap fell Theodore Williams.

Eddie was watching the San Diego club taking batting practice, and suddenly the old second baseman realized that bells and alarms were going off inside of him. It was magical because he did not even know who the boy was in the batting cage. But he didn't have to. Eddie had played with Jackson and Ruth; he knew the swing, knew what it meant. "He got to talking about it one time in Boston," Lefty Grove recalled. Now, a Lefty Grove does not ask an Eddie Collins what he thought the first time he saw a Ted Williams, nor does an Eddie Collins volunteer breathless superlatives to a Lefty Grove. After all. But from Grove's years-later recollection of the conversation, we do know what Eddie Collins thought when the significance of that swing began delineating itself upon his mind. He told Grove: "I said to myself, 'Oh-oh.' "

Collins took an option on the young man and returned east to Boston. When Red Sox owner Tom Yawkey, who had been spending big bucks for players like Grove, Jimmie Foxx, Doc Cramer, Wes Ferrell, and others, balked at giving Williams the $1,000 bonus the boy's mother was still holding out for, Collins talked him into it. One assumes that an Eddie Collins could be quite persuasive when it came to describing a Ted Williams to the man who signed the checks. In December 1937, after Williams had batted .291 with 23 home runs for San Diego, the Red Sox bought his contract from the San Diego club for $35,000.

He went to spring training with the Red Sox in Sarasota, Florida, in 1938, all of nineteen years old. By all accounts, he seems to have made an impression. Using irreverence and braggadocio to camouflage his insecurities, he called manager Joe Cronin "Sport," alienated some of the team's veterans, and lofted some eye-catching long-distance shots. And it wasn't easy to impress with your power in that camp, not with Jimmie Foxx on the premises. A now-ingrained part of the William's legend is the quote attributed to him that spring. When Bobby Doerr said to him, "Wait'll you see Foxx hit," Ted is alleged to have replied, "Wait'll Foxx sees *me* hit." Ted claims he never said it, but concedes, "I suppose it wouldn't have been unlike me." Another oft-quoted Williams line came out of that camp, this one acknowledged, and prophetic. When he was assigned to the Minneapolis club in the American Association, the brash kid received some farewell badinage from the Red Sox outfield regulars, Doc Cramer, Joe Vosmik, and Ben Chapman. "Tell them I'll be back," Ted said (not as grand as Douglas MacArthur's "I shall return," but the same idea), "and tell them I'm going to wind up making more money in this game than the three of them put together." That's a rather gaudy gauntlet for a nineteen-year-old kid who had never batted .300 anywhere to have thrown down to a trio of .300 career big-leaguers, but it's a marvelous quote for an incipient legend. It puts young Teddy, with his pride ingenuously radiant and adolescently sulky by turns, in sharp perspective. We shall know them by what they did; we shall know them ever better for saying they were going to do it.

If American League pitchers were paying attention to what was happening in the American Association that summer, they got a pretty good idea of what was in store for them. While the guns of Europe were being primed that summer of 1938, so was the big cannon in Minneapolis. He batted .366, hit 43 home runs, and drove in

142 runs. In years to come, he would equal or better all of those statistics in the American League, one of the very, very few minor-league sensations to do that in the majors.

After that '38 slugfest he put on in Minneapolis, the Red Sox knew what they had. They couldn't have been more confident of it—that winter they traded their .340-hitting rightfielder Ben Chapman to make room for the new man. Quite a resounding vote of confidence. But the new man began justifying it in the spring of '39 with long, high, booming shots into the blue skies of Florida. Nobody hit them like Williams, it was said. Watch those long, towering clouts. They rose with stunning suddenness, and once up there they really began to move, like something with a second-stage rocket in it, like something in soaring return to the galaxy of its birth. His grounders were the same way—every hop was faster than the previous one. He was a significant force in every game, teammate Billy Goodman said. When you were on first base and he was at bat, you were reluctant to steal; that open base would be too much of a temptation to a pitcher who didn't want to pitch to him in the first place. And if you were on first base, Goodman said, you had something else to think about, because Ted "could take your head off with a line drive if you weren't careful." He could unnerve a pitcher like no other hitter. Gene Conley, who pitched against him in an exhibition game in 1952, said, "You talk about a guy putting you back on your heels on the mound. He dug in, and he looked so *big* up there"—this is to pro basketballer Conley, who stood six feet eight—"and the bat looked so light in his hands, and he didn't swish it around, he *snapped* it back and forth, and he looked so darned anxious, as if he was saying, 'Okay, kid, let's see what you've got.' Confidence just oozed out of him. He took something away from you even before you threw a pitch."

No, there was no question about his hitting. But in the spring of 1939, when the accolade of American League's most powerful left-handed hitter was about to pass from the dying Gehrig to the rookie Williams with hardly a beat, Cronin felt the young man's fielding needed a bit of polish. Well, a lot of polish. It wasn't that Ted couldn't hawk a fly ball or didn't have a decent arm, it was that he left an impression of indifference as far as the defensive side of the game was concerned. When Williams was working on a ball field, or thinking baseball, it was always from the batter's box to the pitching mound. Cronin prodded and nagged him. Ted nodded, said okay, and went right on thinking about Bob Feller's smoker and Tommy Bridges's curve. It came to a head one day in Atlanta when the club was barn-storming its way north after breaking camp in Sarasota. Williams muffed a ground ball in right field and after the easily frustrated young man had chased it down, instead of returning it to the infield he wound up and threw the offending ball over the fence. Now, when an exasperated Ted Williams, already with the peach fuzz of legend on him, throws a ball over a fence, it doesn't simply bounce into the street. No. It bounces into the street, yes, and then right through the plate glass window of the local Sears, Roebuck store. "You could hear the window go," Doc Cramer said. "It was like an explosion."

So Cronin said to Cramer, a most accomplished veteran out-fielder, "I want you to take Ted out and teach him how to field."

"So I had him out there with somebody hitting them to him," Doc said. "He'd miss one, catch one, then miss a couple more. Finally he said, 'Ah, Doc, the hell with this. They don't pay off on me catching these balls. They're gonna pay me to hit. That's what they're gonna do.'

"And I said, 'Well, I can see that, Ted. They're gonna pay you to hit.' There was no trouble seeing that. He had that swing."

Ah, yes, that swing. It mesmerized them all. It was too rare and beautiful to envy; it could only be admired and appreciated. Like a command from the heavens, it could make everything on a ball field suddenly hold still: In batting practice they all paused to watch it, teammates and opponents alike. In their tough, manly world, this was the poetry.

In his freshman year he batted .327, hit 31 home runs, drove in a league-leading, still-standing rookie record 145 runs. A year later he batted .344. In each of those years DiMaggio outhit him and won batting titles with .381 and .352. Never again would Joe D., on a full-season basis, outhit him. Soon Williams could say, after conced-ing DiMaggio's all-around supremacy, what no other man from sea to shining sea could say: "I'm a better hitter than Joe," and say it with-out ego or vanity or even pride, but simply be a man stating a cold, hard, indisputable fact.

In 1941 these two towering midcentury American heroes wrote it in flames that have left a permanent glow on the baseball horizon, a shining mirage of a lake that all of their successors have thus far failed to attain. For DiMaggio it went on for more than a third of a season, for Williams it was season-long but culminating in the most challenging last-day-of-the-season any hitter has ever faced, facing it with a nerveless bravado that even the illusory John Wayne would have cheered.

For DiMaggio it was a pounding 56-game hitting streak that began on May 15 with a single against Chicago's Edgar Smith—talk about the source of a rolling river being a modest trickle—and went on and on, riveting the nation's attention day after day, game after game, breaking all relevant records like a child playing with crystal, records owned by hallowed names Sisler (41 in a row) and Keeler (44), until like some mythic Olympian he had hurled his javelin beyond all reach, crashing it into the earth, where it was marked "56."

It was all so typically DiMaggio. The pressure must have been suffocating—one blanches at the thought of what it would have been like forty years later under television's brutally unblinking eye. But he never showed it. If it was possible for something to show under that icy exterior, this would have been the time. But he remained the quintessential DiMaggio through it all, outwardly calm, stoic, even contemptuous in the way he attacked during the last ten games, getting 23 hits in 40 times at bat—that's a man batting .575 under blood-draining circumstances.

That was our last prewar summer. With German panzers bloodying the European earth and the German Luftwaffe darkening European skies, America had its diversion, a two-month, one-man-against-the-world display of nerve and skill and power against the strong-armed onslaughts of the pitching staffs of the American League, and each one of those pitchers was out for the blood coup, each one was the young gunslinger out to slay the frontier legend and make a reputation. Well, they got Wild Bill in Deadwood and Jesse in St. Joe, and they finally got Joe D. in Cleveland, but it took until July 16, and even at that it required two pitchers and a third baseman. The pitchers, Al Smith and Jim Bagby, weren't shooting too straight; it needed Ken Keltner to pick off Joe from third base with two memorable sweep-ups of hard-struck ground balls, making Keltner a permanent adjunct to the legend.

Over sixty-seven thousand people had crowded the Cleveland ball park that night, come to see the great DiMaggio hit. With a wry observation, Joe McCarthy recalled it. "After the game I saw the president of the Cleveland ball club, and he was so happy and excited that his pitchers had stopped Joe. He was congratulating everybody in sight. But the next day, you know what happened, don't you? The

park wasn't half-filled and he was wondering where everybody was."
That's how good the Yankees were in those days—do them some
damage and it still cost you.

And so on the fifty-seventh day DiMaggio rested.

After July 16, DiMaggio could breathe easier and play his game
with just the normal pressures, which were no small burden either,
since the man felt it incumbent upon himself to be as good as Joe
DiMaggio could be every day. But for Ted Williams it was a season-
long effort, and while there was not the coercive need to rap a base
hit at least once a game, there was something equally extortionate
and imperative to face: two hits for every five times at bat, or else.
DiMaggio's flight to glory had been shorter, more concentrated, more
intense; Williams's was broader, more majestic, and for him to remain aloft for the full schedule meant fighting the fierce gravitational
pull of those one-for-fives and oh-for-fours.

In June he was as high as .436, establishing his credentials as one
of baseball's all-time natural forces—a Ruth, a Johnson, a Grove, a
Feller. By late August he was at .402, still cracking away in the dead,
unforgiving summer heat. By mid-September he was up to .413, but
then began slipping, almost a point a day. He became the grim mara-
thon runner trying to breathe through those final laps, trying to keep
enough kick in his heels to finish. The Yankees had cleared the track
of all distractions for him by achieving the earliest pennant-clinching
in history, September 4. He was the whole show now. Fascinating
supporters and doubters alike, he kept to the pace. Harry Heilmann,
broadcasting games in Detroit then and secure in his own .403 average, offered advice and encouragement. The advice? As profound as
Melba toast: "Hit your pitch." Well, what would Schopenhauer have
said? Al Simmons, coaching for Connie Mack, was of a different cut.
Al, who once got as high as .392, wanted to bet Ted the youngster
wouldn't do it. Tacky, but at least we know Al never mellowed,
which is good, and Ted told him to buzz off.

The boy with the Hollywood good looks played it like a Hollywood script. On the morning of the last day of the season, with a
doubleheader scheduled against the Athletics in Philadelphia, he was
batting .39955, which rounds out to .400 on the nose. Cronin offered
to bench him. Ted refused, saying later, "If I couldn't hit .400 all the
way I didn't deserve it." Here he was, fooling with what would become the very foundation of his legend. Suppose he had flunked that
last, demanding test? Suppose he had gone home with .399? How

does the Williams tiara look without that .400 jewel setting? Melville without *Moby Dick*? Well, not quite. But that line, "The last man to hit .400," is a mighty compelling and ennobling tag; an epitaph by itself. Lefty O'Doul once batted .398 (in 1929). He collected 254 hits that year—a National League record he shares with Bill Terry—but they weren't enough. One more would have done it. Somewhere in April or June or September a blooper didn't drop or a line drive fell an inch foul or an umpire made one of those millimeter calls against him at first base, and Lefty fell tantalizingly short and thus will never be more than a servant in Valhalla.

There have been hitters, good hitters—Cobb among them—who have chosen to sit it out on the last day in order to ensure a batting title. How many would have chosen the same discretion to ensure a .400 batting average? And who would have faulted them? But this is a tale of heroes, and the possibility of failure does not enter into the equation. It was inevitable that Williams accept the challenge. In so doing he set for baseball an insuperable standard, both as man and hitter. The motivation behind his decision to play that day is not to be found in courage or youthful bravado. It is all quite simple and understandable when you remember the ambition: to be the greatest hitter that ever lived. For Williams, this last day of the 1941 season was not a gamble but an opportunity.

So young Teddy had it in his possession and put it on the line simply because it was a thing that had to be done. If he didn't go "all the way," then he didn't deserve it. A man abiding by the path of his own rugged ethic. There is a becomingness in this, for the prudent and audacious both.

He walked the streets of Philadelphia the night before (what is a great occasion without a night before, with its brooding, with its chimeras?), stopping for ice cream a few times and then going on, covering ten miles he later guessed, walking off that fidgety energy he always had anyway but that night more than ever.

It was a cold, nasty Sunday in Philadelphia, that September 28, 1941. Some ten thousand Philadelphians came out to Shibe Park to see history made, or unmade, as the case might be. The Philadelphia players wished him luck but told him they were giving away nothing, which is what a volunteer expects anyway. Whatever he may have felt when he stepped into the batter's box—nervousness, anxiety—quickly came under the iron control of the most disciplined batsman that ever lived. A single the first time up. Then a home run. Two more singles. Four-for-five in the first game. The prize was his. And then two-for-three in the second game, adding the final high sheen to that lustrous .406, achieving it in a game that saw the final big-league appearance of a proud old myth named Robert Moses Grove, who had labored to his 300th win in July and none thereafter, and who was shelled in the first inning of the game in which young Ted Williams notched his .406. The high, rough seas of the big leagues are always filled with vessels, each in its own unique passage.

So the American League season of 1941 belonged to DiMaggio and Williams, to "56" and ".406," and hardly anyone noticed what Washington shortstop Cecil Travis had done. Completing his eighth full year in the big leagues, Travis for the seventh time finished over .300. In his first three years with Washington, Travis had batted .319, .318, and .317. "That enabled Griff to withhold an increase each time and even threaten a cut," Travis said years later with a laugh, maybe joking, maybe not. But there was no doubt he was working for the most parsimonious man in baseball, Clark Griffith—ex-pitcher, ex-manager, owner, patriarch, and skinflint. Travis, however, was an understanding man. "Mr. Griffith never had as much money as some of the other owners," he said, "and it was like pulling teeth to get it out of him." In 1937 and 1938 he batted .344 and .335 and Griff "edged me up a thousand or two. But he kept telling me, 'You have that really big year and then you can come in here and put the squeeze on me.' "

Well, it finally happened for the twenty-eight-year-old Travis in 1941. While the rest of the world and the other eight planets were transfixed by the adventures of Joseph DiMaggio and Theodore Williams, Travis quietly and methodically went about his business, collecting a league-leading 218 hits and batting .359, second best to Williams. The Golden Year he'd been waiting for. He went home after the season and spent that autumn looking forward with gleeful anticipation to his contractual meeting with Griff. Like it or not, the old boy was going to have to cough up now.

Early in December, still thinking about that contract, Travis went up from his Georgia home to Hilton Head, South Carolina, for a bit of deer hunting. After a relaxing few days, he prepared to leave for home. It was a Sunday morning. He got into his car, started up the engine and turned on the radio. "They were announcing it," he said. "Pearl Harbor. There went my big fat contract, and a lot of other things."

TWENTY-ONE

EVEN IF YOU were not an attentive student of current events, you would have known something ominous was brewing across the western waters in the summer of 1941. In August, the Japanese banned the playing of one of the country's most popular sports, baseball. This archetypical American institution had been introduced to Japan by missionaries in the nineteenth century and had become a growing goodwill link between the two countries, the imitative Japanese taking to the game with zest and increasing skill. When Connie Mack led an all-star team to Japan after the 1934 season, the players were given a riotous welcome when they docked, and then a hero's parade through the streets of Tokyo. Detroit's Charlie Gehringer, one of the members of the squad, said, "They knew who we were and that surprised me. But they'd been following the big leagues for years and they knew all of us." The team included Lou Gehrig, Jimmie Foxx, Bing Miller, Earl Averill, Lefty Grove, and the man the Japanese had been most avidly looking forward to seeing, Babe Ruth. When Ruth, Gehrig, and Foxx took batting practice, Gehringer said, the Japanese fans were awestruck. "They just couldn't believe anybody could hit a ball so far." That should have told them something, but they went to war with the land of Ruth, Gehrig, and Foxx anyway.

Pearl Harbor may have been a surprise to everyone, but the advent of war probably was not. More than a year before the attack on Hawaii, the government had instituted a draft and begun building up its armed services. The first of the big stars to "swap his bat for a rifle," as countless sportswriters were to write it countless times, was Hank Greenberg. Big Henry was drafted soon after the 1940 season and then discharged two days before Pearl Harbor by dint of a regulation that released draftees over the age of twenty-eight. Two days later America was in it and Greenberg quickly rejoined. "We are in trouble," he said, "and there's only one thing for me to do—return to the service." Big Henry, wrote the apoplectically patriotic Taylor

244

Spink in *The Sporting News*, "gave the game and the nation a special thrill." While segments of a later generation might find those sentiments ingenuous, that was how people spoke and wrote and felt in those days. Forty years later in an interview, Greenberg would say that his military service remained one of the things in his life he was proudest of.

The major-league club owners were at their winter meetings when the bombs began falling on Pearl Harbor. The outbreak of war caused the tabling of an interesting proposal that was about to be put forward by Donald Barnes. He was the owner of the St. Louis Browns, which is as close to masochism as a big-league executive has ever come. Since 1930, the Browns had been drawing an average of fewer than two thousand fans per game (in 1935, the Browns' season attendance was eighty-one thousand, three thousand less than Cleveland's all-time high for one *game*). Tired of watching his heroes performing in privacy, Barnes had asked for, and was about to receive, permission to move his club to Los Angeles in 1942. Only the outbreak of war prevented it. So, relieved of the threat of invasion by the St. Louis Browns from the East, southern Californians were able to concentrate on the almost equally demoralizing idea of Japanese soldiers dashing across the sands of Malibu.

In the spirit of the Americanism it always professed to embody, organized baseball immediately enlisted in the war effort, National League President Ford Frick sending President Roosevelt a telegram asserting that "we are yours to command." On January 15, 1942, Judge Landis received a letter from Roosevelt that said, in part, "I honestly feel that it would be best for the country to keep baseball going. There will be fewer people unemployed and everybody will work longer hours and harder than ever before. And that means they ought to have a chance for recreation and for taking their minds off their work even more than before."

This was the famous "Green Light" letter, giving the game official sanction to continue as best it could, and so it did, under steadily worsening conditions, most notably the methodic depletion of rosters by enlistment and by the draft. Soon only Stan Musial, of all the neon-light names, was still playing, the Cardinals' numbingly amiable belter missing only the 1945 season. Musial was more fortunate than Williams and DiMaggio, who missed three full seasons each, than Feller, who was away for the better part of four seasons, and Greenberg, who missed four and a half.

By 1944 the quality of play was at its nadir, but by proclamation it was still major-league. It was played in major-league ball parks, by men young, old, worn, and slow wearing major-league uniforms, some of whom, like Paul Waner, were stretching out the flaccid elastic of exhausted careers almost as a patriotic service. The nadir received permanent certification that year when the St. Louis Browns, for years a faithful reference point for ineptitude, won the American League pennant (their first and last). That pennant continues to wave as a flag of caution to future baseball historians whose concentration on the game may cause them to overlook a world war.

To make the game's agonies ever more vivid, a year later there appeared on the playing fields of the American League—employed by these same St. Louis Browns—the man who remains the symbol of wartime baseball. He was an outfielder named Pete Gray and he had only one arm (Pete and Three Finger Brown hold what are probably two of baseball's unbreakable records), having lost the other in a childhood accident. Despite his handicap, Pete managed to bat .218 and strike out only 11 times in 234 at bats.

The National League in 1944 created its own symbol of wartime baseball when the Cincinnati Reds sent to the mound the youngest player in big-league history. He was a fifteen-year-old left-hander named Joe Nuxhall. The youngster worked two-thirds of an inning against the Cardinals and ran up a national-debt earned-run average. Joe, however, redeemed himself when he came back a decade later and began a long, respectable career as a winning pitcher, though he was never able to expunge fully his image as a wartime oddity.

The pregame playing of "The Star-Spangled Banner" had a sobering quality in it in those days, like a secular prayer rising up and beyond the grandstands and outfield walls. The flag that beat against the blue sky was watched thoughtfully. There were servicemen among the crowd, admitted free, of course—"Your uniform is your ticket"—and soon wounded servicemen, with empty sleeves, or in wheelchairs, come from the roar of Pacific dreadnoughts and the hellfire invasion beaches of Europe to see in action part of the great democratic mosaic they had been fighting for, watching it in an American Parthenon replete with infield, outfield, and bullpen.

Ted Williams was an instructor in Pensacola, Florida, flying Navy SNJ's, finally being shipped to Honolulu just as the war ended. (He would go back in again in 1952, this time to combat in Korea, where he would have one hellish experience when his jet was struck by ground fire and he had to bring it in streaking thirty feet of flames.) Feller was in the Pacific, under bombardment aboard the battleship *Alabama*. DiMaggio was also in the Pacific, though in a noncombat situation,while Greenberg served in Burma. Cecil Travis found himself caught in the icy horrors of the Battle of the Bulge in December 1944, suffered frozen feet, and never did get that big contract when he came back.

They were all over the world, the big-leaguers, mostly doing what they did best, playing America's game to divert and entertain their countrymen. The slow, sweet game of old rural America ran through its rituals in Europe and Africa and Asia, and on Saipan in the Mariana Islands, which, as country boy Enos Slaughter said, "was a long way from Roxboro, North Carolina."

"I was assigned to the B-29's of the Fifty-eighth Bomb Wing on Tinian," the Cardinal outfielder said. "We had two teams there and one over at Saipan, in the Mariana Islands, and we played back and forth. The bleachers were built out of empty bomb crates and sometimes we had as many as fifteen thousand troops at a game. We were drawing better crowds on Saipan than they were in Philadelphia.

"You've heard what great baseball fans the Japanese are. Well, when we got to Saipan there were still quite a few of them holed up in the hills. I'll be damned if they didn't sneak out and watch us play ball. We could see them sitting up there, watching the game. When it was over they'd fade back into their caves. But they could have got themselves killed for watching a ball game. Talk about real fans!"

As ever, there was time to kill between ball games, and in the Marianas there weren't hotel lobbies, the familiar bars or restaurants where the sporting crowd hung out, or the variegated allures of a big city. "A lot of times," said Slaughter, "we'd go out and sit on the edge of the runway and watch those B-29's taking off, one after the other." He was on Tinian on August 6, 1945, when the B-29 called *Enola Gay* flew off into the darkness at 2:45 in the morning. At 8:15 A.M. the plane was over the Japanese city of Hiroshima.

Eight days later the war was over.

"Later on we met the crew that had dropped the bomb," Slaughter said. "They were a pretty quiet bunch of guys."

TWENTY-TWO

THEY ARE in a way like ghosts, tantalizing figures moving soundlessly and endlessly across an old ruined and shrouded landscape. They traveled in buses, always those buses, and always described as broken-down and rickety; and they traveled at night, always late at night, through the darkness to the waiting dawn, along the white-lined highways and inhospitable back roads; always traveling, always in those buses, always in the night, moving spectrally like the very secrets they are. And as the buses ran the lonely highway nights of America, the men slept in them because it was cheaper than a hotel, and anyway no hotels, not even the dismal ones with a single bulb over the entrance, were open to them; nor were the roadside restaurants open to them, except maybe the ones that would sell them sandwiches and coffee out the back door. So they traveled, following the baseball sun all around the United States, and when that sun grew chill, into Mexico and Cuba and Puerto Rico and the Dominican Republic. "I played from 1922 through 1950," said James (Cool Papa) Bell, an outfielder and one of the greatest of the black ballplayers. "That's twenty-nine seasons. Plus twenty-one winter seasons. That makes a total of fifty seasons." Didn't he ever get tired of it? "No," he said. "I only got old."

Was the fastest pitcher that ever lived not named Walter Johnson but Satchel Paige? Was the greatest right-handed power hitter named Josh Gibson and not Jimmie Foxx? How good were those shadows that continue to prowl the haunted landscape?—Oscar Charleston, Buck Leonard, John Henry Lloyd, Smoky Joe Williams, Martin Dihigo, and Paige, Gibson, and Bell? Quite good, we can assume, because we do know about Robinson, Mays, Campanella, Bob Gibson, Aaron, Banks, and Clemente.

If you want to preserve the sanctity of your beliefs, take the unwritten law over the written, for the latter can be broken, circumvented, and turned into obfuscating ambiguities by a clever lawyer.

It was by no written decree that blacks were excluded from organized baseball, so that the old hypocrite Landis could in 1942 say with a straight face, "There is no rule, formal or informal, or any under-standing—unwritten, subterranean, or sub-anything—against the hiring of Negro players by the teams of organized baseball." The judge obviously had become transported by two decades of unchal-lenged I-am-the-law supremacy to the extent that he believed, or at least was not ashamed of, any nonsense he uttered.

But baseball's "savior" knew he was occupying high ground when he made his statement, for organized baseball was only reflecting the racism and benighted attitudes that were generally abroad in the land. Baseball was no more interested in establishing total equality than were other entrenched interests like Hollywood, the world of commerce, and even such supposedly enlightened places as certain colleges and universities. That the lords of baseball should have dwelled in the same prejudices as other executives should not sur-prise. The difference was that for decade after decade baseball and its indoctrinated trumpeters in the press had been proclaiming its realm as a showpiece of democracy, of egalitarianism, of American-ism in action. Only the last of these bore some semblance of truth, for Americanism in action had long been laced with bigotry, discrimina-tion, and closed doors, and not for blacks alone. The game that had recoiled with horror at the treachery of the Black Sox and then later prided itself upon its integrity and image of purity and fair play, was actually run, in the main, by a cartel of bigots and sanctimonious hypocrites who saw nothing wrong in refusing opportunity to fellow countrymen because of their skin color.

Baseball later tried to make amends of a sort by enacting special niches in the Hall of Fame for Paige, Gibson, Leonard, Bell, and a handful of others who had ridden those buses through those long, empty nights and who, unlike minor-league ballplayers, sandlot ball-players, and so many little boys who went to bed at night wearing their baseball caps, weren't even allowed to dream. If those plaques on the Hall of Fame walls could speak, what would some of those late-night conversations sound like? For there Paige and Gibson and the others are sharing space with many of the very pharisees who sternly oversaw and enforced baseball's law of exclusion: Landis, Comiskey, Griffith, Mack, MacPhail, Weiss, and Yawkey. To say that these executives were victims of the prejudices of their time and place is true, but this mitigates only so far, for when their colleague Branch

Rickey, in an aroused postwar atmosphere, finally took them off the hook with a courageous act, they remained adamantly fixed in their attitudes, not only fixed but resentfully in opposition. It took the grimly narrowminded Weiss, running the Yankees in liberal New York, eight years after Jackie Robinson to integrate the Yankee roster. Boston's Tom Yawkey, one of the game's truly sentimental and benevolent owners, was the worst offender, his Red Sox not bringing a black player to the team until 1959.

The blacks had organized their own leagues in 1920, playing some of their games in rented major- and minor-league ball parks. So it wasn't as if anyone could say that the blacks were being denied the right to play baseball—that was every American's birthright, wasn't it? To hire black players, organized ball said with self-righteous rationale, would destroy black baseball.

"You'd be surprised at the conditions we played under," Cool Papa Bell said.

We would frequently play two and three games a day. We'd play a twilight game, ride forty miles, and play another game, under the lights. This was in the nineteen-forties. On Sundays you'd play three games—a doubleheader in one town and a single night game in another. Or three single games in three different towns. One game would start about one o'clock, a second about four, and a third at about eight. Three different towns, mind you. Same uniform all day, too. We'd change socks and sweat shirts, but that's about all. When you got to the town, they'd be waiting for you, and all you'd have time to do would be to warm your pitcher up. Many a time I put on my uniform at eight o'clock in the morning and wouldn't take it off till three or four the next morning.

Yes, they had their leagues, and they had their Paiges and their Gibsons. They also had owners who did not honor contracts, teams that went bankrupt, wretched living conditions, no recognition from the majority world around them nor indication that something was wrong, and those buses, those highways, and those nights, and not even a dream to hang any of it on.

Often they played postseason games against barnstorming teams of major-leaguers and more often than not held their own against the grand names of the game. Hookups between Paige and Dean were widely heralded, avidly attended matches. "We saw that our best was as good as their best," Buck Leonard said. "Then when the game was over, we'd go our way and they'd go theirs. It was frustrating."

But baseball had an incipient Lincoln in its midst, a schemer, a dreamer, a revolutionary. He kept his great proclamation in his head, because he knew there was no outcry for it, he knew anyway that it would take action and not promulgation, that the time would have to be right, and then, even when the time was right, there would be hell to pay. He knew that baseball was perceived as public property, that the public was content with the game as it existed, and that before one proclaimed the rights of man above the indifference of the public, one had better not only be ready to endure the firestorm that could rip from that indifference, one had better be pretty damned sure he had the right man to go forth into it. But Branch Rickey knew, too, that even if it had to be force-fed, the public would respond to the right medicine. A serum against bigotry? Well, one could try.

To Rickey's scripturally oriented mind, the cause of baseball integration included the gratifying elements of converting a sinner. In addition to rectifying its own omissions, baseball at the same time could help show the way toward salutary social change in other, unrelated areas.

Those who met Branch Rickey remember the bushy, expressive eyebrows, the cigar, the mesmerizing rhetoric, the sense of purpose, the intimidating intelligence. He had a reputation for being parsimonious ("He would go into the vault to make change for a nickel," said employee Enos Slaughter). He could be devious. He could make you suspicious. (Employee Johnny Mize: "I'll tell you what the talk used to be about Rickey: Stay in the pennant race until the last week of the season, and then get beat. I heard some talk to the effect that that was what he preferred. That way he drew the crowds all year, and then later on the players couldn't come in for the big raise for winning the pennant and maybe the World Series. I don't know if it's true or not, but that was the talk.") He was unashamed about respecting baseball for exactly what it was—a business. He never hesitated to peddle a star player for all the cash he could get, one of his most famous credos being, "Better a year too early than a year too late." But his moves were seldom detrimental; when he sold his superb outfielder Chick Hafey it was because he knew young Joe Medwick was ready, and when he sold slugger Mize he had the young Stan Musial waiting in the wings. He is credited with bringing the farm system to organized baseball when he was general manager of the Cardinals in the 1920s. He was an activist in a game of fixed postures and conservative temperament. He has been called pompous and self-righteous and mercenary, as well as compassionate and visionary and dynamic. In other words, if he passed your way, you knew it. This was Wesley Branch Rickey. The Abraham Lincoln of baseball, and as far as analogies go, just about the best you can do in the United States of America.

He was born in Lucasville, Ohio, on December 20, 1881, five years after the birth of the National League. His parents were strict Methodist fundamentalists who hammered piety into the boy who, years later, could recite an appropriate bit of Scripture at the drop of a pop fly. He was bright and he was athletically inclined, with enough ability to win a partial scholarship to Ohio Wesleyan. He soon became one of the campus ornaments, ringing up an excellent scholastic record—including ninety-plus averages in Latin, Greek, physics, and history. The historical image of Rickey is of an old man smoking a cigar, tight with a buck, something of an eloquent windbag. But in college he played halfback on the football team and caught for the baseball team. He was good enough at football to play briefly for a semipro team in nearby Shelby, briefly because he broke an ankle in his third game. He stayed in for several plays until the pain became too severe and he had to be carried from the field. This bit of grit, along with these activities (catching was hardly a dilettante's position), tells us this was no cloudy introspective scholar walking around the campus with vague dreams of grandeur. This was a tough, determined, brilliant, and ambitious kid working his way up from hardscrabble beginnings. The steel had been forged very early in Branch Rickey and those who tried to take him on during the many stages of his long career could never break it.

In addition to everything else while he was at Ohio Wesleyan, he accepted a request to coach the baseball team, and this led to the first of the many dramatic scenes that are so vivid a part of the story of Branch Rickey.

One of the school's first black students, Charley Thomas, was a member of the baseball team. In the spring of 1904 Rickey took the squad to South Bend, Indiana, to play Notre Dame. When the boys arrived at the Oliver Hotel in South Bend, where they had reservations, Charley Thomas was told the hotel did not register Negroes. After threatening to pull the entire team out of the hotel, Rickey won a concession: He would be allowed to bring Thomas to his own room as an unregistered guest. Later, he found a distraught Thomas sitting in the room crying, rubbing feverishly at his hands as if trying to make disappear the incriminating color. "It's my skin, Mr. Rickey," he said. "If I could just make it go away I'd be like everybody else." The scene burned itself indelibly into Rickey's mind, and when finally he was preparing Jackie Robinson's entry into organized baseball and he said he had been waiting forty years to do it, he wasn't just blowing smoke from one of those cigars.

He was good enough to get to the major leagues, catching for the St. Louis Browns and the New York Yankees, but not good enough to stay, playing just parts of the 1906 and 1907 seasons. He is in the record book, though, ingloriously. While catching for the Yankees on June 28, 1907, he saw the Washington Senators steal 13 bases against him, most ever against one catcher in a game. He later managed the Browns and the Cardinals, again without distinction, even though Rogers Hornsby called him "the smartest man in baseball." So he moved into the Cardinal front office, where his true baseball genius lay.

Tired of being outbid for minor-league stars by the monied John McGraw and others, he decided to develop his own players and began building the Cardinal farm system, an innovation that by itself would have earned him a place in baseball history. There was a seemingly endless procession of talent from the far-flung Cardinal organization into St. Louis, winning pennants in 1926, 1928, 1930, 1931, and 1934. And far-flung the Cardinal empire was: At one time it seemed every small town in America was sure of having two things— an A & P and a Cardinal farm team. At its peak, in the late 1930s, the organization had over fifty farm clubs—sometimes two in a league— and over eight-hundred young ballplayers under contract. The excess talent, and there was plenty, Rickey sold off to other clubs, most of whom would wait in line to buy a Rickey-trained player, and it was said he pocketed as a personal bonus 25 percent of the selling price. He became a rich man. He was successful, a winner. He had it all, it seemed. But that image of Charley Thomas sitting in a hotel room in South Bend, Indiana, in 1904 never stopped burning in his mind; the memory was like some sort of compact this fervent Methodist justice-seeker had made with his God. He kept looking around at his America, taking stock, testing the wind, waiting. Waiting.

In 1942 he left the Cardinals and became general manager of the Brooklyn Dodgers, replacing his one-time protégé, the army-bound Larry MacPhail, himself an innovator—night baseball, baseball broadcasting—and a man who had the toughness and the courage to shatter an unjust barrier, but who in the end came to oppose Rickey over it.

By 1945 Rickey was ready. By 1945 his genius had created disciples and enemies. He knew who would follow, who would oppose. And most importantly for any calculating man, he knew the strengths of his enemies, he knew the weaknesses of indifferent people, and he trusted the basic decency of the masses. With all the conviction and evangelical fervor of one who knows he is right, he went ahead, too old and too much of his world to be taken by surprise. The war would soon be over and he knew the world had been changed radically and forever by six years of cataclysmic upheaval. The repeated shocks of the war had shaken loose too many things that would not—could not—return to place. Hundreds of thousands of returning black servicemen were no longer going to accept the status quo; northern cities—the cities of major-league baseball—had seen the wartime migration of thousands of southern blacks come to find jobs and a better standard of living. The nation had sobered and matured in a way it had not after the first war. So Rickey chose the moment when the guns had stopped and the smoke had cleared to begin his revolution, moving to confront a triumphant but weary nation that had fought to bring liberty to people around the globe, saying, "And now our own. *Now our own.*"

He began with a deception. He was, he told people, bringing a team called the Brooklyn Brown Dodgers into the Negro League and installing them in Ebbets Field where they would play when the big-league team was on the road. Naturally, he wanted to stock this team with the best black players available. Accordingly, his top bird dogs were sent scattering around the country in that summer of 1945 to find the right talent. None of the scouts knew the true nature of their mission, but one of them was a wily customer in his own right, and, he said, he "got to thinking." His name was Clyde Sukeforth, a former catcher in the National League. A canny gentleman who spoke with the twangy precision of his native Maine, he was one of Rickey's most trusted lieutenants.

"We had been scouting the Negro leagues for more than a year," he recalled. "But you know, there was always something strange about it. Mr. Rickey told us he didn't want this idea of his getting around, about the Brooklyn Brown Dodgers, that nobody was supposed to know what we were doing. So instead of showing our credentials and walking into a ball park, as we normally would have done, we always bought a ticket and made ourselves as inconspicuous as possible."

In August 1945 Sukeforth was summoned to Rickey's office. Rickey instructed him to go to Chicago to see a game between the Kansas City Monarchs and the Lincoln Giants, both of the Negro National League. Specifically, he was to see "that fellow Robinson" on Kansas City. Sukeforth was to tell Robinson who he was and who had sent him out to see Jackie. For Sukeforth it sounded like just another routine scouting assignment. "But then," Sukeforth said, "the old man said, 'Now, Clyde, if you like this fellow, bring him in. And if his schedule won't permit it, if he can't come in, then make an appointment for me and I'll go out there.' "

This raised the antennas of the gentleman from Maine. "Mr. Rickey go out there? To see if some guy named Robinson was good enough to play shortstop for the Brooklyn Brown Dodgers? Well, I'm not the smartest guy in the world, but I said to myself, *This could be the real thing.*"

Sukeforth went to Chicago and met Robinson at Comiskey Park before the game. After hearing what Sukeforth had to say, Robinson spoke right up—"Jackie was never shy, you know," Sukeforth said dryly. Seemingly skeptical about the Brooklyn Brown Dodgers, Robinson wanted to know why Rickey was interested in him. Sukeforth could only repeat what he had been instructed to do.

It developed that Robinson (then a shortstop) had a sore shoulder and was temporarily inactive. Sukeforth's instincts, however, had been picking up signals since leaving Rickey's office. He arranged to meet with Robinson that night to talk. He soon learned that Jackie's instincts were operating just as keenly. When under Robinson's constant badgering for Sukeforth to repeat word for word what Rickey had said, Sukeforth recalled what Rickey had said about coming to Chicago to see Robinson if Jackie could not come to Brooklyn, and Robinson became quietly thoughtful for a while.

"The significance of that last part wasn't lost on him," Sukeforth said. "I could see that." Robinson asked him what he thought. "I was honest," the scout said. "I'd learned in a short time that that was the way you had to deal with Robinson. 'Jack,' I said, 'this could be the real thing.' "

It was a very quiet reaction that Sukeforth gauged. But already he was getting a sense of this proud young black man. "The idea evidently sat well with him," Sukeforth said. "It pleased him. Was he afraid of the idea?" Sukeforth laughed at an interviewer's deliberately provocative question. "He was never afraid of anything, that fellow."

The youngest of five children, grandson of a slave, Robinson was born to a poor sharecropping family in Cairo, Georgia, on January 31, 1919. When he was six months old, Jackie's father skipped out with someone else's wife and was never seen again, leaving Jack's mother Mallie to become one of those indomitable women so familiar in stories of black trial and tribulation. Like Faulkner's Dilsey, they "endure," in tragedy resolute, in despair mute, givers of strength and wellheads of inspiration. Mallie Robinson must have been all of that and with a bit of kick to spare. In the spring of 1920 she told southern hospitality, south Georgia style, to kiss off, and gathered her brood and whatever they could carry in boxes and straw suitcases, boarded a rattler with Jim Crow accommodations, and headed for California, settling in Pasadena. They encountered prejudice in this nearly all-white community, of course, and it was a variety that many blacks resent the most, implicit instead of the South's unashamed explicitness. The subtle, sensitive mind of young Jack Roosevelt Robinson picked up every nuance.

He was a multitalented athlete, in high school winning letters in baseball, football, basketball, and track, following in the footsteps of his older brother Mack, who had been good enough to make the United States Olympic track team in 1936. His exploits at Pasadena Junior College earned him dozens of scholarship offers. He chose UCLA, becoming the school's first four-letter man in sports. In 1941 he left school to take a job with the National Youth Administration, but by the fall of that year he was in Hawaii playing professional football for the Honolulu Bears. On December 7, two days after the season ended, he was sailing home when war broke out.

In 1943 Pete Reiser, Brooklyn's incomparably talented young centerfielder, was at Fort Riley, Kansas. The post had a superb baseball team made up of major-leaguers. "One day a Negro lieutenant came out for the ball team," Reiser said. "An officer told him he couldn't play. 'You have to play with the colored team,' the officer said. That was a joke. There was no colored team. The lieutenant didn't say anything. He stood there for a while, watching us work out. Then he turned and walked away. I didn't know who he was then, but that was the first time I saw Jackie Robinson. I can still remember him walking away by himself."

Lieutenant Robinson became outspoken about the army's institutionalized policies of discrimination. In July 1944 he boarded a military bus at Fort Hood, Texas, and was told by the driver to do the classic thing: "Get to the back of the bus." But military buses had recently been ordered desegregated by the army. Robinson knew this. The driver either did not know or did not care. Robinson stood his ground. A few weeks later he was court-martialed. He escaped conviction when the judges realized he had acted well within his rights. But the army had evidently compiled a dossier on this troublesome young officer and rather than put up with him any longer, handed him an honorable discharge.

It is important to remember that this was no docile foot-shuffler the Dodgers were going to put into a crucible. This was an angry, seething, highly competitive athlete with a razor-sharp resentment of ingrained, infuriating injustices—important to remember because for years he was going to have to abide by the vow he made to Rickey to remain mute and passive no matter what came his way.

The personalities of Rickey and Robinson are decisive in this story. Each had the capacity to forgive the sinner but never the sin. Each had, in his own way and from his own direction, been crusading toward the destruction of racial barriers. For Rickey it was baseball that had to be integrated and equalized; for Robinson, it was the world—the world of slights and glances as well as the world of torrential abuse and abject humiliation. Rickey turned Robinson loose on a path that never ended; even after retirement Jackie remained the crusader, volatile and outspoken. Rickey had faith in God and in his own lifelong convictions. Robinson had lifelong bitterness whirling out of the burning friction of unceasing cylinders. Rickey was cunning. Robinson was direct.

Rickey had a masterful sense of what he wanted in the man he needed, the man he had been looking for. Because the scenario called for a man who would be willing to submit to the vilest invective and ignore the most flagrant provocation without fighting back, one would have thought Rickey would have sought the docile personality. But no; instead he chose an explosive militant, because the old conjurer understood that the passionate soul, one relentlessly committed to change and betterment, would be the strongest when it came to withstanding the inevitable firestorm. A mild man, never having been broken, was unpredictable; a strong man, by dint of his commitment, may have been broken many times, but always mendably so, his great strength built from having time and again been forced to its limit. Only a man with blazing pride, only a man with the purest sense of destiny, might slip his chains in restraint.

Passive resistance? Not quite. He still had that bat and those legs and that special daring and fury, enhanced by those very restraints. Every day on the ball field the catcalls and the vituperation lit the fuse anew, sending this human missile crashing again and again into those man-made barriers until he had made dents that earned respect and admiration and the beginnings of equality. For those who cared to pay attention, Robinson's style of play should have been both threat and warning, for this was not merely an athlete expending brutal amounts of energy to win baseball games; this was a black American releasing torrents of pent-up rage and resentment against a lifetime portion of bigotry, ignorance, and neglect; this was a messenger from the brooding, restless ghettos. Only Cobb had played with the same unbuckled zeal that Robinson displayed, and Cobb was psychotic. Robinson was lashing back, and his naturally high-voltage abilities burned the more fiercely on the white-hot scars of old and unforgettable searings. Those who were sensitive to the sizzling drive and fury shown on the ball field by this symbol of black emancipation should have guessed that it was transcending baseball and not been surprised when two decades later that representational fury boiled over in flame and riot in Detroit, Los Angeles, and other cities. Warning had been given on the basepaths of the National League by Jack Roosevelt Robinson. Leo Durocher, who both admired and feuded with him, said of Robinson, "He didn't just come to play, he came to beat you. He came to stuff the goddamn bat right up your ass."

So, following his good instincts, Sukeforth decided to bring Robinson to Brooklyn to meet Rickey, even though the scout had not seen Jackie play. When Sukeforth brought Robinson into Rickey's office on August 27, 1945, he started to explain this, but Rickey paid no attention.

"The old man was so engrossed in Robinson," Sukeforth said, "he didn't hear a damn word I said. When he met somebody he was interested in, he studied them in the most profound way. He just stared and stared. And that's what he did with Robinson—stared at him as if he were trying to get inside the man. And Jack stared right back at him. Oh, they were a pair, those two! I tell you, the air in that office was electric."

That first meeting between Rickey and Robinson was historic and memorable, a scene a master dramatist would have been driven to the furthest limits of inspiration to create. It was revelation and it was confrontation. After advising Robinson what was the true purpose of Jackie's having been brought there—to integrate organized baseball via Brooklyn's top farm club at Montreal—the old spellbinder let the young man have it. Robinson would face anger and hostility from all quarters—fans, teammates, opponents, the press; he would arouse every vile and rancid instinct people were capable of; he would face it alone, armed only with his pride and dignity.

Rickey poured out a speech that had been burning in his head for decades. This man, who could be stemwinding in casual conversation, left nothing unsaid. He knew exactly what Robinson would face—there were no imponderables. There would be beanballs. There would be collisions on the field and a white player snarling, "You dirty black son of a bitch!" There would be spikings and a white player saying, "How do you like that, nigger boy?" There would be taunts from opposing dugouts: "Nigger bastard! Porter! Shoeshine! Spade! Coon! Eightball!" Hotel clerks, waiters, saying it bluntly: "No niggers."

No man had ever spoken to him like this passionate old man. Robinson finally asked, "Mr. Rickey, do you want a ballplayer who's afraid to fight back?" And the old man roared back the seemingly impossible injunction: "I want a ballplayer with guts enough *not* to fight back!" Rickey was enjoining him to cease doing what he had always done in the face of these situations. Robinson soon grasped the reasoning, the logic, the necessity.

"You will symbolize a crucial cause," Rickey said. "One incident, just *one* incident, can set it back twenty years."

Sukeforth, witness to this first, dramatic beginning, remembered Robinson sitting quietly when at last Rickey was through. "He just sat there, pondering it, thinking about it. I'd say he sat there for the better part of five minutes. He didn't give a quick answer. This impressed Mr. Rickey. Finally Jackie said, 'Mr. Rickey, if you want to take this gamble, I will promise you there will be no incident.' Well," said Sukeforth, "I thought the old man was going to kiss him."

At the conclusion of the meeting Rickey handed Robinson a copy of Giovanni Papini's *Life of Christ.* Several passages were marked. Rickey asked Robinson to read them. They included the following:

> Ye have heard that it hath been said: An eye for an eye and a tooth for a tooth. But I say unto you, that ye resist not evil; but whosoever shall smite thee on the right cheek, turn to him the other also . . . Every man has an obscure respect for courage in others, especially if it is moral courage, the rarest and most difficult sort of bravery. . . . To answer blows with blows, evil deeds with evil deeds, is to meet the attacker on his own ground, to claim oneself as low as he is. . . . Only he who has conquered himself can conquer his enemies.

For seventy years baseball had given the nation fun, excitement, and diversion, all the while congratulating itself as a self-proclaimed paragon of democracy. Now, to its sudden shocking surprise, it was being called upon to prove that it was what it had been proclaiming itself to be. Branch Rickey had, without prior discussion, enlisted it in a cause.

The announcement, on October 23, 1945, that the Dodgers had signed Robinson to a minor-league contract evoked varied reactions throughout the baseball world: dismay, incredulity, cynicism, and a few dollops of cautious optimism. Rickey received not a single word of praise or encouragement from any club owner; in fact, reportedly, he received angry phone calls from Connie Mack, Clark Griffith, Sam Breadon, and a few others. Their ire was understandable. Rickey was demonstrating highmindedness to men who were his intellectual inferiors to begin with and to end with didn't like him anyway. He was telling elderly gentlemen like Mack and Griffith, long honored as patriarchs and founding fathers, that they were in effect obstructionists and moral scoundrels. "I never liked that man," Mack confided to Jimmy Dykes in a neat phrase of self-acquittal.

Rickey was of course not acting in a total vacuum. The time had been ripening. A group of blacks, shouting, "Good enough to pay, good enough to play," had picketed Yankee Stadium in 1945. New York's Mayor Fiorello LaGuardia was openly demanding that baseball integrate. Committees, both in and out of baseball, were being formed to "study" the question.

Rickey did have an important ally in baseball, albeit a passive one. Albert Benjamin (Happy) Chandler, the Kentucky politician who had succeeded the deceased Judge Landis as commissioner, was behind Rickey, discreetly. Chandler's role in the integration of baseball remains clouded with ambiguities, despite his claims to having given Rickey unqualified support. One thing is certain, however— the new commissioner did nothing to impede Robinson's entry into organized ball, which in the context of the time was more laudable than it looks in retrospect.

Cynicism about the move was not limited to whites, many of whom accused Rickey of self-interest, claiming the old man saw Robinson as a gate attraction and little else. The lofty rhetorician was of course not immune to such imputations, for doubtless the sound of spinning turnstiles was nearly as sweet to him as the Lord's Prayer at eventide. And for blacks, suspicion always went along with the territory they had been handed. Some were dubious about Robinson's ability and suggested that Rickey had deliberately selected a man he knew could not cut it in the major leagues; thus, went this scenario, Rickey would receive credit for having made the attempt, defuse the racial issue, and leave things in place. Many blacks thought that Monte Irvin (soon to be signed by the New York Giants) was the Negro League's finest player and should have been chosen. Satchel Paige, for years acclaimed as the premier black baseball talent in the land, openly supported Robinson and lauded his ability, but Satchel later wrote in his autobiography of the bitterness he felt at not having been chosen, feeling he had earned and deserved the distinction of being first. Rickey, however, was not just looking for talent but also a man of impeccable personal credentials, and Paige had been around too long and too restlessly to have a clean sheet. There is no doubt that Irvin, Roy Campanella, Larry Doby (who integrated the American League with Cleveland in 1947), or other black players could have done the job, but it turned out that Robinson packed the special dynamite, the unique blend of daring and restraint that made it work as well as it did. (He also possessed in abundance something else that didn't hurt—that well-known but seldom-seen intangible, that mysterious devil's brew known as charisma. Said Clyde Sukeforth: "There was something about that man that just *gripped* you.") Whatever baseball fans may have felt about this unique intruder upon their game, they came out in droves, black and white, to see him.

Robinson had a spectacular season at Montreal in 1946, his .349 batting average leading the league and helping his team to the International League pennant and later victory in the Little World Series, played between the champions of the International League and the American Association. After the final out in the final game, which was played at home, the jubilant Montreal fans came pouring onto the field to thank their players and Robinson in particular for a triumphant season. Jackie was hoisted onto shoulders and carried around the field amid cheering and applause. He finally had to make a dash to the clubhouse to get away from his pursuing admirers, "probably the only day in history," a reporter noted, "that a black man ran from a white mob with love instead of lynching on its mind."

Robinson went to spring training in 1947 with the Montreal club, but now there was an air of poised inevitability. Joining the Dodgers was simply a matter of time, or timing. Rickey had thus far grandmastered every move with wily patience and caution. There was just one more move to make: the big one. Robinson had integrated organized ball all right, but only at the minor-league level, meaning that for many nay-sayers he could still be classified as an experiment. But now he was looming larger, and among certain quarters of the Brooklyn Dodger squad that spring there was the rustle of disquiet, which should have been to no one's surprise, for baseball is a game in which innovation is as welcome as a bad hop. This was, after all, the game that had resisted everything from shin guards to arc lights to batting helmets. Its innate conservatism was like something vestigial, as though the game had a genetic tie to its nineteenth-century rural heritage.

After it has played out its dramas, history affords the hindsight view, clarifying opportunities lost and unseized. The spring of 1947 was a time for the Brooklyn Dodgers squad to display clarity of vision in recognizing a changing world, or at least to show character by lending support to a man who was being subjected to unfair abuse and unreasonable pressure. Among those Dodgers, shortstop Harold (Pee Wee) Reese of Kentucky, who for more than a decade was to exemplify the class that Brooklyn fans had always intuited in him, drew acclaim (as well as the lasting gratitude of Robinson) by showing open support for the black man. Others who treated Robinson as just another teammate—which was all Jackie was asking for— included Pete Reiser, Duke Snider, and Gil Hodges.

Most of the intrasquad opposition to Robinson was predictable, originating south of the Mason-Dixon line. It appeared in the form of a petition stating that the undersigned would not play with Robinson. The petition initiated with veteran outfielder Fred (Dixie) Walker, whose nickname speaks for itself. The Alabaman was the team's most popular player. Other signeres were pitcher Hugh Casey, a Georgian (and a not very subtle one either; displaying a good old southern superstition, he once rubbed Robinson's head for luck during a poker game); catcher Bobby Bragan, another southerner; and Carl Furillo, of Reading, Pennsylvania. Pitcher Kirby Higbe, a South Carolinian, who out of loyalty to Rickey did not sign the petition, was also feeling fractious, concerned about what playing on the same team as a black man might do to his social standing back home. (Higbe once told an interviewer that he had developed his strong right arm by "throwing rocks at niggers," and then mitigated it by adding, "and the niggers threw the rocks right back at us.")

When he heard about the petition, manager Durocher took a characteristic bold leap to action. He called a midnight meeting and told his troops to "wipe your ass" with the petition. *He* was the manager, Leo reminded them (in case any of them were so detached from reality not to have noticed), and he would decide who played, and if Robinson was good enough it did not matter if the man had zebra stripes all over him—he was going to play. End of meeting.

Rickey, whose understanding of the facts of life embraced the realities of southern cultural heritage, was not angry at any of the signees, realizing they were being asked to do something they had from childhood been told was wrong. He spoke to the rebels one by one. He convinced Furillo that Carl had been misled. Casey he placated. Walker, absent from camp at this time, later recanted. Bragan, however, would not budge. The Rickey-Bragan confrontation was heated. The young player, marginal to the team and easily expendable, demanded to be traded. The shrewd Rickey, however, saw that Bobby was standing on principle, and the old man resolved to harness this strength of character. He did not trade Bragan, instead making him a manager in the Dodger farm system a year later.

"That was the start of a great friendship between Mr. Rickey and me," Bragan said years later. "That's right. He didn't take offense at what I'd said because he knew I was born and raised in Alabama. He knew that I'd grown up surrounded by a way of thinking that had been there long before I came on the scene and that I couldn't help but have it imparted to me. He understood that for me it was going to be a tremendous adjustment to play alongside a black man. He took it all into account; he took *everything* into account. He was a great student of human nature, that man, a great psychologist.

"Being Jackie Robinson's teammate was one of the best breaks I ever got. Watching what he had to go through helped me. It helped make me a better, more enlightened man."

How many people were unwittingly snared into enlightenment by Branch Rickey and Jackie Robinson, we shall never know. Certainly many Brooklyn Dodger fans were. They couldn't help but know—it was in the sports pages now—that blacks were discriminated against, that there were hotels and restaurants that would not serve them, drinking fountains and public rest rooms they could not use. If you were a Dodger fan you could not remain totally indifferent to this; you had to think about it and resent it, because it was happening to one of your twenty-five revered heroes, and while it may not have suddenly converted you to egalitarianism, you knew something was wrong. Robinson's rights had to be defended, because he was a member of the team now and the team was family. The racial raillery you heard from Giant and Yankee fans only stiffened your resolve. (You could always, if need be, rationalize it to yourself: You were rooting for a black man because it was in a higher cause— helping the Dodgers to win. Loyalty to the team smoothed many a rocky Brooklyn landscape in 1947.) And the more you became accustomed to Robinson, the more you shared pride in his performances with the black person sitting next to you, the more you felt resentment at the treatment he had to endure. This is not to say you still wouldn't have disowned your sister if she married "one." But disown the *Dodgers?* What then? Root for the goddamned *Giants?*

On April 10, 1947, Robinson was formally promoted to the Brooklyn roster, thereby becoming, along with Charles Lindbergh, Neil Armstrong, and a handful of others, a notable American "first." On April 15 he was in the opening-day lineup against the Boston Braves at Ebbets Field. The first few days passed uneventfully. And then the Philadelphia Phillies came to town. Their manager was Ben Chapman of Alabama, a man never known for gentility of disposition or sweetness of tongue. If Chapman had been hired to put Robinson to the acid test, he could not have done better.

The venom that poured forth from Chapman toward Robinson at Ebbets Field stunned and offended all who heard it. Chapman defended it as being just the usual dugout stuff offered to make a rookie feel welcome. They called Poles "Polack" and Italians "Wop," didn't they? Ben fooled no one, however; the quality of this particular venom was much too pure; so pure, in fact, that he was reprimanded by Happy Chandler. The tirade also evoked resentment among

Robinson's Dodger teammates, notably second baseman Eddie Stanky. Even Dixie Walker, he of the infamous petition, and an old friend of Chapman's, reportedly reproached Ben. To underscore just how brutal this verbal assault was, Robinson later wrote that it was the occasion that "brought me nearer to cracking up than I have ever been." He had been on the verge of storming the Phillies' dugout and performing some dental work therein. But like a Frank Lloyd Wright building in an earthquake, he withstood the tremors and remained intact. One of the milder epithets thrown at him was "snowball"; but this was one snowball that did not melt in hell.

Admiration for Robinson's abilities and for his fortitude, plus appreciation for the fact that he was helping them win ball games, soon mitigated the hostility and eased the awkwardness among his teammates, even Walker and Casey. Slowly, tensely, and often painfully, Robinson made his revolution. Throughout the lonely crucible of 1947 he played his game and became a star, enduring taunts, insults, beanballs, attempted spikings, and every other provocation. He drove the Dodgers to a pennant, was voted Rookie of the Year, and when the season was over almost had a nervous breakdown.

Soon they were no longer riding the buses through the long nights and along the empty highways. The dream had at last been extended to all Americans, and the talent started coming down the sluices, a trickle at first, but a trickle that remained in motion, gathering force. Satchel Paige finally got to the big leagues, with Cleveland in 1948, and pitched well for a man in his forties, but Satchel was little more than a ghostly wave from the past, a sort of benediction from What Might Have Been to What Was to Be. The talent that came from the once forbidden vineyards was ripe and lush, and had to be, because if many of those still-grudging teams were going to be lassoed into the new age it was going to be with the very best. They weren't going to pay a black player white man's green money to bat .230 and sit on the bench. You didn't see a .230-hitting black player hanging on for years as a utility man as you saw with many whites.

In 1948 the Dodgers added catcher Roy Campanella to the team, while the rest of the club owners continued to watch with their arms folded, but they didn't mind unfolding those arms to count the money that Robinson and the Dodgers were earning for them with sellout crowds around the league. The reactionaries continued to dig in in the American League as well, with the Yankees' George Weiss, that taxidermist's delight, the most adamant. George was concerned about a black Yankee drawing black fans to the stadium and thus possibly offending the sensibilities of white Yankee fans. That he was slandering many of his own customers did not seem to occur to Weiss. Only Cleveland in the American League—thanks to maverick owner Bill Veeck—had an integrated roster, and just to show that justice was not unmingled with poetry, Satchel Paige and Larry Doby were instrumental in bringing the Indians a pennant in 1948.

In 1949 Brooklyn added pitcher Don Newcombe, meaning that on days when Newcombe pitched a writer could, and many did, point out that one-third of the Dodger team was black (people were still self-conscious about it). The Giants finally became believers and in 1949 brought up infielder Henry Thompson and outfielder Monte Irvin, and were about to sign a good prospect named Willie Mays.

It took a few more years for other clubs to work their way through the equation that the future was here to stay, but then the black talent began spreading out. Milwaukee had Henry Aaron, Chicago had Ernie Banks, and soon there were Roberto Clemente in Pittsburgh and Frank Robinson in Cincinnati, along with the ever-growing Brooklyn contingent. In 1955 the Yankees finally risked contamination by hiring Elston Howard, extolling him as "dignified" and a "gentleman," qualifications heretofore never deemed necessary for big-league employment. A dignified gentleman indeed, the big, powerful, slow-footed Howard was welcomed aboard by manager Casey Stengel's loose-minded quip, "They gave me the only nigger that can't run."

Because of the American League's reluctance in bringing black players to their teams, the balance of star power, so long in favor of that league, began to shift. The most resplendent talent in major-league baseball resided in the National, and much of it was black. When Jackie Robinson won the Most Valuable Player Award in 1949, it was the beginning of nine such accolades in eleven years for blacks—Robinson, Campanella (three times), Newcombe, Mays, Aaron, Banks (twice). It would take decades for the American League to redress the balance, and not solely because they did not finally go on the hunt but because National League supremacy was being perpetuated by gifted young blacks who identified with their heroes and with the teams those heroes played on. The talented rookie Bobby Bonds, who joined the Giants in 1969, summed it up when he said, "I always wanted to play on the same team as Willie Mays."

So the major leagues were integrated without serious incident in 1947 and organized baseball found itself, ironically, in the vanguard of the civil rights movement. In the 1950s, all of the minor leagues, North and South, were gradually integrated, without serious incident. It is improbable that any hard-core racists were converted or that they necessarily checked their rancid attitudes at the gate; it was just that baseball, with its special aura of fantasy and sweet unaging innocence, was able to disarm or at least lull into suspension what was otherwise implacable. In 1957 it took federal troops to integrate a high school in Little Rock, Arkansas. In 1962 there was rioting and death when student James Meredith came to integrate the University of Mississippi. In the early 1950s Henry Aaron was playing for the Jacksonville, Florida, club; Frank Robinson was playing in the Texas League; Willie McCovey was playing in the Georgia State League; and there were many other young blacks winging baseballs and churning the basepaths of the old Confederacy, each in his way extending the highway first laid out and paved by Branch Rickey and Jackie Robinson. Were ballplaying blacks simply perceived as less threatening than educated blacks? Another tribute to Rickey and Robinson is the diminishing relevance of such questions.

TWENTY-THREE

IN A SPEECH to the winter meeting of big-league club owners in 1909, Brooklyn's Charles Ebbets said, "Baseball is in its infancy." The statement drew derisive comments from the press. Well, Charlie could have said the same thing forty years later and still been marked a prophet.

With the breaking of the color barrier, baseball found itself drifting out of its own realm of fantasy and into the wider world of the real. Ahead lay total integration, expansion, continent-hopping franchises, broadening television coverage, multimillion-dollar player contracts, lawsuits, free agency, lawyers, agents, player strikes, artificial playing surfaces (the ultimate in the new reality), domed stadiums, and even a billion-dollar television deal.

But before all these things bright, good, and dubious occurred, history had some tidying up to do, some chapters to close and endings to write. Even as Robinson and the other black players were bringing a new era to baseball, the most prominent symbol of the old was making a slow and painful exit. Diagnosed in 1946 as having cancer, Babe Ruth, aged fifty-one, began losing weight and stamina, and then even his voice too, as the disease affected his larynx.

In the decade since his retirement as a player, he had been often honored but never hired, outside of a brief stint as coach and batting-practice attraction for the Dodgers in 1938. The game's greatest player, drawing card, and personality, its highest-paid and most adored star, had left baseball unfulfilled because no one would give him a job managing in the big leagues. Ed Barrow's phrase about Ruth was like a leper's bell around the Babe: "How can he manage other men when he can't even manage himself?" Those who were otherwise embarrassed at saying no to Ruth always felt justified by that unquestioned truism when managerial jobs came along.

So Ruth remained unemployed through the closing years of his life, but hardly unnoticed, for his magic never abated. During the war he appeared at benefits to spur the sale of war bonds, and as always was the center of attraction, the known quantity. And then this most unique of American athletes began fading away, the once-expansive smile now thin and weak, the once-powerful body shrinking as if yielding to some resistless internal suction, the once-resonant voice reduced to a harsh, barely intelligible rasp. On June 13, 1948, he appeared at the twenty-fifth anniversary celebration of Yankee Stadium, hanging to life now like a loose button, listening to one more ovation, a sound as familiar to him as the roar of the sea was to a mariner, but this time it was filled with langsyne echoes; this ovation did not have the sudden uproarious spontaneity of all those old ones, the ones he had acknowledged with a tip of the hat as he rounded the bases. This one he accepted at home plate leaning on a bat that was more like a cane. The robust life that had poured out of him in cataracts was down to the sediment now. A week later he was in the hospital. When Connie Mack, eighty-five years old and still managing the Athletics, came to see him, Ruth said to this seemingly indestructible shaft of history, "Mr. Mack, the termites have got me." The termites kept at him until the evening of August 16, when he died.

Twenty months earlier, on December 10, 1946, one of Maryland's gentleman farmers, Walter Perry Johnson, died at the age of fifty-nine of the brain tumor that had paralyzed him for ten months. In less than two years, baseball's two greatest natural forces, the paragons of speed and power, were gone.

Those were the years when a World Series at Yankee Stadium seemed almost preordained. In 1950 it was the Yankees versus the Philadelphia Phillies, winners of their first pennant since 1915, now two wars ago (and now the flames of a third were rising higher in Korea). Some sentimentalist with a thoughtful sense of the game's historical continuity had decided it would be a nice gesture to invite to the Series the man most responsible for that 1915 pennant, Grover Cleveland Alexander. So the sixty-three-year-old pitcher, last survivor now of the sonorous old triumvirate—Mathewson, Johnson, and Alexander—showed up, took a seat in the press box at Yankee Stadium and was virtually ignored, a relic not so much of time gone as of things changed, still alcoholic, still epileptic, and having lost an ear to cancer. He sat quietly, staring down at the mound where he had stood twenty-four years earlier and sculpted one of the game's imperishable moments. He watched the aging DiMaggio, one year away from retirement now, in center field for the Yankees, but his thoughts were elsewhere, probing softly the corridors of memory, because when an old-time sportswriter noticed him and sat down next to him, Alexander spoke of Hornsby and Ruth and Wagner and Mathewson, feeling again for his own tides of youth and vitality.

It had been a long, hard grind for the Nebraska farmboy since leaving the big leagues in 1930 tied with Mathewson at 373-all. He had taken his fame and his demons and kept at the one thing that had given him sustenance, material and spiritual both, all his life, pitching in the minor leagues and then for a band of traveling semipros known as the House of David, whose gimmick was bearded players (this was in the 1930s, before beards became almost *de rigueur* for athletes). He kept drinking, of course, in Main Street bars and alone in his room in fleabag hotels, sipping his whiskey through his House of David beard, burned out and alone with nowhere to go. When the semipros on the irregular diamonds of America began hitting whistlers off of him he ceased being an attraction, and then even baseball was gone.

He had a job selling pari-mutuel tickets at a midwestern race track, worked in a Cincinnati airplane factory for a while, and then sank into a job that is probably second in the Alexander legend only to the Lazzeri strikeout—as a side attraction in a flea circus on New York's Forty-second Street, amid a Times Square blacked out by wartime regulations, a ghost for old men to come in and worship and young ones to gaze curiously upon. He sat on a wooden chair, still lean and lanky, legs crossed, arms folded, a certain poignant stillness about him, staring and stared at, watching fathers lean over and whisper something to their little boys whose eyes were fixed upon him, waiting to answer in a soft voice questions about Matty and McGraw and Wagner, and of course to re-create again and again the mysteriously undiminishing splendor of the Lazzeri strikeout. He was paid thirty or forty dollars a week for this, plus whatever some well-wisher, risking the old man's pride, might press into his palm along with the handshake.

Eventually he drifted back to his origins, the tiny town of St. Paul, Nebraska, where he had been born, where it had begun, where he had stood in the autumn of 1909 maniacally trying to pitch away the headaches and the double vision. No longer was he the honored native son; he was an unsteady, drink-cadging old man who was ignored and even avoided by his neighbors. Subsisting on a $100-per-month pension from the Cardinals, he took a room in a private house and quietly came and went, a gaunt old shadow fading wordlessly in and out of the local saloons.

On the chill night of November 4, 1950, he left one of those saloons and began making his way home along the empty streets, the cold prairie winds sweeping the dead leaves of autumn about him. He went up to his room, lay down on the bed, and sometime during the night died.

He was buried with military honors in the soil of his birth in the small rural cemetery outside of St. Paul, to the sound of tolling bells from the nearby Presbyterian church. Next to the casket was a large wreath in the shape of a baseball diamond, sent by the St. Louis Cardinals.

TWENTY-FOUR

"WHEN NATURE removes a great man," wrote Emerson, "people explore the horizon for a successor; but none comes, and none will. His class is extinguished with him. In some other and quite different field, the next man will appear."

Well, Emerson obviously was being broad and general about fields, but if he had been thinking of center field in Yankee Stadium in 1951, he would have been dead wrong. That was the year the Yankees, who had been doing it for years, gave baseball yet another emphatic demonstration of how to perpetuate a dynasty. It was the year the thirty-six-year-old Joe DiMaggio, freighted with time and flawed by injury, turned mortal and retired. He had batted .263, hit 12 home runs, driven in 71 runs. For a rookie, those figures would have excited promise for the future; for DiMaggio, they were falling leaves. "I no longer have it," he told a press conference at the Yankee offices on December 12. He did not want to be remembered "struggling" on a ball field. (Note that pride.) His once gunshot throwing arm was gone, he had pain in his heels, his legs, and his shoulder. All this he had played through for years, but there was one injury he could not and would not endure—that to his pride.

If nothing else, it would have been polite to DiMaggio and respectful of the laws of probability had the Yankee center field been patrolled by mediocrities for a while. But there was pause for neither twilight nor nostalgia in Yankee Stadium in those days, for the club had already launched in 1949 what was to become a craft of near-invincibility, destined to win fourteen pennants in sixteen years. Throughout much of this time the skipper was Charles Dillon (Casey) Stengel, former National League outfielder and manager, with honorable but undistinguished service in both areas. But this old boy with the fanned-out ears and craggy landscape of a face was about to ring up more success than any manager in the game's history. He managed the Yankees for twelve years and won ten pennants. His admirers called him a genius; his detractors—and he had plenty—claimed that a cocker spaniel could have skippered those talent-loaded clubs and won.

Stengel possessed a kind of gnarled intelligence that sounded as though it had scraped along a few back roads and maybe even a few back alleys too, taking a close reading of all experience and learning where to place mistrust and skepticism. He gave long, seemingly pointless monologues that sometimes sounded like first-draft Mark Twain, speaking in a double-talk and with a syntactical adventurism that when transcribed verbatim made him sound as though he were ready to be certified. Some of his players said this was calculated, that he liked to talk in circles to confuse people; others said no, that it was simply impossible for him to talk in a straight line. He was an oracle or a clown, depending on your witness. He had a caustic wit. He could be cold. He was an egomaniac. His favorite player was Billy Martin, which for some people is the definitive summary of Stengel.

But even with Stengel, and his wit, buffoonery, and public relations genius, those Yankee teams of the 1950s, despite the prodigality of their winning ways, would have been neither interesting nor memorable without the young man who replaced DiMaggio and soon became one of the most stunning of all baseball heroes.

As befits one who gradually takes hold of the national imagination, Mickey Mantle was unlike any of the baseball colossi that had gone before. If anything, he might have been a bit overdone by those celestial artisans who craft the special cases. If he had played in another era he might well have become—and he still might—a grandfather's fireside tale. "I tell you, right-handed he could drive the ball as far as Foxx, and left-handed as far as Ruth. And he had running speed like you never saw. And an arm like a cannon. And he had that—what do you call it?—charisma. He had that too." Stories like that have prompted indulgent winks around the room for generations. But any old shank of memories who tells such tales of Mantle had better be believed, and if the record book does not entirely support them—in spite of the 536 home runs—it's because of a dossier of injuries, of breaks, sprains, strains, fractures, muscle pulls, and just about everything short of death itself, about which he was fatalistic too, his father and two uncles having died in their early forties. (In his mid-forties he said, half-jokingly, "If I'd known I was going to live this long I would have taken better care of myself.")

Not only did he have that sumptuous raw talent, he also had the trigger for it—a searing competitive drive that made him take vora-cious cuts at the plate and exploded him along base paths and across outfield grass as though in a furious effort to deplete himself all at once. Not only did Mantle replace DiMaggio in center field, he also soon replaced him as the team's inspirational force, the man they strove to measure up to. He awed his teammates with his power, his speed, and most of all with his grit. Injury-prone throughout his ca-reer, he played on wobbly knees, with bandaged legs, with aching muscles. Playing through pain, and excelling, is one of the hallmarks of the great athlete, and some of them appear to take a primal satis-faction from it. It seems madness for them to do it, but at the same time it makes them seem dramatically summoned, elevating them to a yet higher dimension of fantasy, driving them even farther from the imaginative grasp of those who—sensibly—take to bed with a head cold. This particular quality of heroism is closely associated with the careers of three Yankee icons—Gehrig, DiMaggio, and Mantle. Teammates already impressed with their special talents were moti-vated and in some cases probably intimidated by what they saw; it gave a more sanctified glow to the aura of Big League. An injured god is a sobering sight; one who contends against the pain can be frightening.

Not only was he as pure a creature of nature as ever appeared on a ball field, he had the *beau idéal* good looks of America's boy next door (depending on your neighborhood), a winning smile, and, when he first hit the big city in 1951, a warm, shy personality and a bump-kin's classic naivety. These last two qualities gradually dissolved un-der ascending stardom and growing self-confidence, leaving him at the end with a reputation as rollicking clubhouse wit, practical joker, carouser, and man-sized drinker with the capacity to hold it. Yankee fans were sometimes rough on him in his early years—he was, after all, replacing the sleekest ship of state ever to play ball—but the ur-ban slickers soon took to the Oklahoma hayseed and rewarded him with the same vocal thunder they had roared for DiMaggio, because he was theater at home plate as no player of his time was (with the exception of Williams), suddenly cracking a ball and putting it in a far place in an unholy hurry. Switch-hitting with equal power made him unique. Right-handed, he put one out of old Griffith Stadium in Washington that was alleged to have been airborne some 565 feet. Left-handed, he sky-scraped one that came within a few feet of being the first fair ball to leave Yankee Stadium.

When power so prodigious is packed into a hero of Mantle's stature, its manifestations can evoke near-epiphanic responses. One afternoon a writer pulled some strings and got his Mantle-worshiping eleven-year-old son into Yankee Stadium to watch batting practice from behind the cage. Batting right-handed, Mickey hammered massive clouts into the left-field bleachers, one blast after another hurtling into the stadium's long, long distances. Turning around to swing left-handed, Mantle began hoisting clouts into the far precincts of right field. Each *whack!* seemed louder and more violent than the previous, as if more and more strength were pouring into the thickly muscled back and shoulders. When the writer, smiling appreciatively, turned to get his son's reaction, he saw the boy standing as if paralyzed, tears running from his wide, astonished eyes.

You can never tell where it's going to come from, from out of what mix of blood and soil, heritage and environment, fantasy and desire. With Gehrig and DiMaggio it had been New York and San Francisco, cities of multitudes where the sky-rush of talent, though always exciting, is not unique. But it had also happened in St. Paul, Nebraska, and Van Meter, Iowa. This time it was Spavinaw, Oklahoma, on October 20, 1931, and he was born to a father who was like a child wishing for that special Christmas present, the kind that is beribboned and delivered only in fairy tales and inspirational texts; for the father not only wanted the standard healthy baby with all extremities in place, he wanted one who would thunder his way to the big leagues. The father was a former semipro ballplayer himself, but now Elven (Mutt) Mantle was a lead miner down below the Oklahoma earth dreaming of sunshine and green grass and baseball glory for his first-born, whom he had named after his favorite player, Mickey Cochrane.

When Mickey Mantle was four years old the family moved to Commerce, and here the boy grew up, coached and taught to switch-hit by his father. The boy learned his game on the playing fields of the "Alkali," a stretch of Oklahoma flatland in the state's northeast corner bordering on Kansas and Missouri, as remote from big-league glory as Weiser, Idaho, or Ouray, Colorado, but with the same pulsations of baseball blood as New York, San Francisco, and Anywhere.

With a big boost from nature, young Mickey took to his father's tutelage and began filling out the contours of the older man's dream. When he was sixteen he was playing for a teenage team in the Ban Johnson League at Baxter Springs, Kansas—pitching and playing shortstop then—and reputedly stroked one 500 feet. Eventually the long shadow of one of those ubiquitous Yankee scouts, this one named Tom Greenwade, cast itself upon the ground of Kansas, where Mickey was doing most of his playing. Greenwade scouted the youngster several times—"Feeling the way Paul Krichell must have felt when he saw Gehrig," he said—before coming to Baxter Springs to sign him. The game was rained out that day, so Greenwade and Mutt and Mickey sat in the scout's Oldsmobile with the rain hammering on the roof and streaming down the windshield and talked business. They agreed on a Class D contract at $140 a month and a bonus of $1,150. The first pebble of the landslide had been launched. Later, Mickey's twin tablets of talent and charisma would earn him $100,000 a year, then a commanding sum for a ballplayer; but if his prime had come in a later decade he would have been earning at least $2 million per summer. Destiny pours largesse upon its favorites all right, but can occasionally be indifferent about timing.

Mantle reported to the Independence, Kansas, club in the K-O-M League, played shortstop, batted .313 and made 47 errors. A year later he was playing short for the Joplin, Missouri, club in the Western Association. This time he made 55 errors, but these were diminished by a .383 batting average (.383 covers a myriad of sins, on the field and off), an average potent with 136 runs batted in and 26 home runs crashed from both sides of the plate, with the awesome power of a new young continent surging from nurturing seas to the surface.

Joplin was only Class C ball, but the sound of those home runs had reached New York, and the Yankees decided to bring the young shortstop to spring training in 1951 to have a look. He came; they looked and were conquered. Especially bewitched was the old cynic Stengel, who, although he had seen such power before, had never seen it from the same man from both sides of the plate. Never mind that the boy wasn't a shortstop (they had a freshly minted MVP named Rizzuto patrolling there anyway); it was enough that he was an answered prayer. The Yankees never prayed small. Since 1920 they had not been without a Jovian thunderbolt or two in the lineup: Ruth, Ruth-Gehrig, Gehrig-DiMaggio, DiMaggio. That resonant drum-roll of noble busters was on the brink of terminating with the aging DiMaggio when the team sent up the chute a desperate plea for replacement, and some audacity-admiring god obliged by sending them Mickey, who had arrived with "a straw suitcase, two pairs of slacks, and one blue sports jacket that probably cost about eight dollars." Stengel moved the shy, soft-spoken (when he spoke at all) country boy to right field, and there he opened the season playing alongside DiMaggio. In midseason he was shipped to the Yankees' farm club at Kansas City to iron out some wrinkles but was back in a month.

His statistics approximated DiMaggio's in 1951—13 home runs, 65 runs batted in, .267 batting average (Joe was 12, 71, .263, in the same departments)—and ironically the same numbers that spelled the end for Joe were for Mickey an encouraging beginning, thus reinforcing the old truism about the ambiguity of statistics.

Despite having a couple of .260 hitters in their outfield—uncharacteristic for the club—the Yankees won the pennant, by force of habit as much as anything else now, and sealed Mantle's first date with his darker destinies. It occurred in the second game of the World Series versus the Giants. Mickey, playing right field, had been told before the game by Stengel to try and take everything he could in right-center because DiMaggio's heel was hurting. In the fifth inning a ball went into the air in right-center, and young Mantle, running as hard as he could ("at that time I could outrun anybody"), was getting ready to snare it when he heard DiMaggio call out, "I got it." Hayseed or no hayseed, Mickey was thoroughly aware of certain on-the-field precepts and canons, he later recalled, one of which was, "You *don't* run into Joe DiMaggio. So I slammed on my brakes, caught my back spike on a rubber sprinkler head and my knee just went out." He fell heavily and lay crumpled on the grass in deadly stillness, white-faced with the pain of what would be the beginning of a career-long series of injuries that read like a Sunday afternoon in the NFL: 1951, an operation on that right knee; 1952, same thing; 1954, a knee cyst removed; 1955, pulled groin muscle; 1956, sprained left knee; 1957, injured right shoulder; 1959, broken finger; 1961, abscessed hip, which often bled right through his uniform (he wouldn't sit down); 1962, injured left knee; 1963, broken bone in his left foot; 1965, surgery on his right shoulder, plus knee and elbow injuries.

He played through much of this pain because that was his instinct, and his managers let him because they were mesmerized by his strength and his ability, and because baseball is not the boy's game it is punched up to be but a hard-headed business. For the manager who pencils such a player into the lineup there must be some vicarious arousal, the presumption that the wounded lion is more danger-

ous than the unstruck. Pete Reiser, the Brooklyn centerfielder of the
early 1940s, a player with Mantle-like talent and Mantle-like injuries
who similarly believed in not serving by standing and waiting,
summed it up when he said, "They never asked me if I could, they
always asked if I would."

There was a diabolic convergence of New York center-field titans
on the play that ruined Mantle's right knee in the 1951 World Series.
Mickey, apprenticing in right field, chased it. DiMaggio, his career
just a few games from completion now, caught it. The man who hit it
was Mickey's National League counterpart, the New York Giants'
effervescent Rookie-of-the-Year centerfielder, Willie Howard Mays,
Jr., Alabama-born and from day one New York–bound by virtue of
the same undeniable dictums that had directed the fortunes of Ruth,
DiMaggio, Robinson, and Mantle.

The two Golden Rookies of 1951 were born in the same year,
Mays on May 6, 1931, in Westfield, Alabama, a long fly ball outside
of Birmingham, a city not known for glad-handing its black citizens.
If he felt the sneers and slights of racial animus, and no doubt he did,
Mays, unlike Robinson, never showed it. Although his style of play
was as breathtaking as Jackie's, it lacked the crusading frenzy and
smoldering resentments so evident in baseball's black pioneer.
Robinson had made a kind of Faustian agreement with his benign
messenger from the Other World, Branch Rickey, storing his soul for
several years in the name of progress, and therefore could only play
with viselike intensity. Mays, benefiting from Robinson's trailblazing,
could play freely, without the pressure or sense of personal repression
that Jackie felt. And play he did, performing with as complete a set of
talents as had been endowed a player since DiMaggio, and, if anything, with more speed afoot. He was, however, a different brand of
perfect player than DiMaggio. In place of Joe's seamless perfection
and radiant grace, Willie had a pell-mell buoyancy, a constantly
surging elation, a sense of a youngster turned loose upon the meadows of his personal heaven: center field at the Polo Grounds, where a
man could run and run and run in pursuit of a fly ball. Among all the
game's immortals, baseball's innocence seemed freshest and longest-
lasting in this player, who seemed to run out to center field each
inning with the boy's dream still aglow within him, resembling a kid
who was determined that this would be the day he would do something notable and make the team. Guileless youth one moment, dynamic heir to Speaker and DiMaggio the next, and for years head-to-

Cool Papa Bell.

Satchel Paige.

Josh Gibson.

Jackie Robinson.

Branch Rickey.

Bobby Thomson crosses home plate to complete the Miracle of Coogan's Bluff.

Willie Mays.

Frank Robinson.

Hank Aaron.

Roberto Clemente.

Mickey Mantle.

Roger Maris.

Sandy Koufax.

Tom Seaver.

Steve Carlton.

Pete Rose.

Reggie Jackson.

head competitor with Mantle and Brooklyn's Duke Snider for center-field laurels of the world.

Robinson accomplished many things for the black players who followed him, thanks to his adherence to the restraints that had been placed upon him. But once those restraints were lifted, Robinson made still another contribution, of a different nature but of no less impact. His personality had never been bland, to say the least. A natural militant, born to be the heat under every caldron, Jackie did not sweeten up as time passed and he gained increasing acceptance; if anything, he became more and more outspoken, sometimes abrasively so, antagonizing a lot of people, among them many who felt Jackie should accept his privileges and advantages and keep still. He was the uncompromising black, the "uppity nigger," that many whites could not tolerate, and thus he remained the lightning rod for prejudice and made it easier for the less noisesome Roy Campanella, Willie Mays, and other blacks who found their welcome mats slightly larger than might have been expected, not because they were in any way obsequious, but because they weren't troublesome like Robinson.

Willie was a third-generation ballplayer, his grandfather having earned a modest reputation pitching for black teams around Tuscaloosa, while his father played for a semipro team in Birmingham, occasionally having as teammate his muscular young son Willie, Jr. In the spring of 1950 Willie was playing for the Birmingham Black Barons, a strong club in the Negro League. The New York Giants, at the time one of the few big-league teams making a serious effort to sign black players, sent scout Eddie Montague down to Birmingham to check out the Barons' first baseman, Alonzo Perry. It was the old story: the scout coming to see one player and suddenly finding himself bedazzled by another, for Willie Mays on a ball field was like a flashlight burning in a dark room—that was all you saw. What Montague saw was what Giants manager Leo Durocher would soon describe as "Joe Louis, Jascha Heifetz, Sammy Davis, and Nashua rolled into one." The Giants paid the Black Barons $14,000, and another legend crouched at the starting block.

Willie went to Trenton, New Jersey, an outpost of the Class B Interstate League, and batted .353 and led the league in assists, nipping baserunners as yet unaware that there was a cannon in the outfield. In 1951 he began the season at Minneapolis in the American Association. After 35 games he was batting .477, a highly noticeable

figure in any league, but in Triple A one that is garlanded with Roman candles. Giving .477 an even lovelier ring was the fact that the
parent club in New York had gotten off poorly and needed a bit of
shoring up in the outfield. By this time everyone in the Giants organization suspected that the stork that brought Willie to Alabama had
cast a shadow over Cooperstown on its way south. What made the
twenty-year-old kid with the wall-to-wall personality ("His secret
weapon," said Branch Rickey, "is the frivolity in his bloodstream.
Willie Mays has doubled his strength with laughter") even more endearing was his expression of doubt about being able to cut it in the
major leagues. When Durocher telephoned him to announce Willie's
promotion, Willie voiced his doubts. "What are you hitting?" Leo
asked. "Four-seventy-seven," said Mays. "Well," said Leo, the master
logician, "do you think you can hit two hundred points less up here?"
Willie thought he could, and as a matter of fact did almost just that,
batting .274 that first season. The Minneapolis fans greeted Willie's
promotion with mixed emotions—anger and dismay—to the extent
that Giants owner Horace Stoneham felt it politic to placate them
with a newspaper ad of explanation and apology.

Willie joined the big team on May 25, carrying in his luggage the
hopes and expectations of the New York Giants. Trailing a bit of Old
South servility, he called his skipper Mister Leo, and by force of personality immediately dissipated much of the gloom that had settled
over the struggling ball club. That was his initial contribution, and
he needed it because his others were not yet in evidence as he went
0-for-12 in his first three games. The Giants won those games and
Durocher attributed it to Willie's alchemy, though reporters were beginning to murmur about the holes in the new man's bat. Willie's
first hit came in the first inning of his fourth game, at the Polo
Grounds, and he picked on a jewel of a pitcher, the Braves' Warren
Spahn. It was a home run, broad and loud, and no one will ever
know how far it traveled because this christening blast disappeared
over the left-field roof, by all accounts the first meteorite ever to leave
the planet Earth, returning in reverse trajectory to its place in the
firmament. Leo Durocher had his own lyrical description of the shot:
"I never saw a fucking ball go out of a fucking park so fucking fast in
my fucking life."

Most of the memorable defensive plays in baseball history have
been made by outfielders, who have a natural advantage in perform-

ing the spectacular. The most an infielder can do is brilliantly ambush a hard-hit ball, which is momentarily stunning but lacking the romantic dimensions of distance, of a lone man for several seconds in quickening pursuit, perhaps with the peril of a wall looming closer. The crowd has those several seconds to come to its feet and hold its breath and watch it happen, and with Mays it happened and happened. When he went after fly balls he ran like a generator being buffeted by its own energy. He made sliding catches and diving catches and leaping catches and one-handed catches and even on one occasion, in desperation, a bare-handed catch. (His flabbergasted teammates decided to give him the silent treatment when he returned, chortling and ebullient, to the dugout. The ingenuous youngster, expecting praise, was puzzled. Finally he said to Durocher, "Leo, didn't you see what I did out there?" And Leo: "No. And I won't believe it until I see you do it again.") And he made those belt-buckle catches with nonchalant ease, almost as though disappointed at the 100 percent assurance of it. (This style caused sandlot idolators to drop fly balls all over New York City diamonds for several summers.)

It isn't just the long career of consistently high performance alone that commemorates the great ballplayer. The more fortunate have that one scintillant moment or achievement that symbolizes them always. For Mathewson it is the three shutouts in the 1905 World Series; Alexander has his Lazzeri strikeout, Ruth his "called shot," DiMaggio his hitting streak, Williams his last-day conquest of .400. These are the equivalents of masterworks in the corpus of genius. For Mays, the moment came in the first game of the 1954 World Series when he ran and ran and ran to a point some 460 feet deep in New York's Polo Grounds and made a back-to-the-plate catch of a ball hit by Cleveland's Vic Wertz. It was the top of the eighth inning, two men were on base, none were out, the score was tied. A game-saver, the catch was stunning at any time, but occurring in a World Series made it forever. (Interestingly, aside from pitchers, only a rare few of the game's Mount Rushmore types have embossed their names upon a World Series. In democratic America, the grandest of all sporting events has often been dominated or electrified by Everyman—Pepper Martin in 1931, Cookie Lavagetto and Al Gionfriddo in 1947, Sandy Amoros in 1955, Don Larsen in 1956, Bill Mazeroski in 1960, Gene Tenace in 1972. There is no "Cobb Series," or "Wagner Series," or any

identified with Hornsby or DiMaggio or Williams, despite some fine
performances by some of these men. Among the hierarchy, there is
only the Ruth "called shot" in 1932 and the Mays catch in 1954.)

Appropriately, the year he came to the major leagues was the year
of "The Miracle." Baseball, existing as it does in its own insular universe, has miracles of course, but they are not cosmological in appeal.
The one in 1951 certainly wasn't, and certainly not if you lived in
Brooklyn, which in baseball America was a nation unto itself. If
baseball left for the Promised Land in 1901 with sixteen tribes, then
this one was the one fated to suffer the most severe afflictions, including an unassisted triple play in a World Series, a game-costing
dropped third strike in a World Series, a perfect game in a World
Series, and finally the extirpation of the tribe itself from one side of
the continent to the other. But the cruelest blow of all was smote in
1951, on the afternoon of the third day of October, at the Polo
Grounds. When the Yankees ravaged and humiliated their heroes,
Dodger fans could tolerate it, for the Yankees they merely despised.
The Giants they hated, with a rich, deep, tradition-drenched emotion they had been willfully curdling decade unto decade.

In 1951 the Giants had come from 13½ games behind the
Dodgers in mid-August, putting on a stretch run that gave them 39
wins in 47 games and finally a tie at the end of the season, necessitat-
ing a two-out-of-three playoff for the pennant.

The situation was dramatic enough; the fact that it embraced the
Dodgers and Giants made it more so, for every game between the
intercity rivals was a fierce, tension-ridden bloodletting that froze the
city's heartbeat until the final score was in. (When he was asked if he
was nervous going into his first World Series, the Giants' Monte Irvin
laughed and said, "No. Remember, we played the Dodgers twenty-
two games a season, and each one had more tension than a World
Series game.")

The Giants won the first game, at Ebbets Field. The Dodgers
won the second, at the Polo Grounds. For the two teams and their
fans, who had been bathed for weeks in crucial, nerve-squiggling
games, this was finally It, the decisive, ultimate, definitive resolution
to the pang and plenty of a long, long season, the last of the no-more-
tomorrows games. All had at last climbed to the summit of summits,
half to leap off in gloom, half to remain in celebration.

What happened in that game liberated all future writers of baseball fiction to wander with impunity through the most surrealistic

thickets of their imaginations, for thereafter none could accuse them of pandering to the improbable. With the ace right-hander of each team laboring on the mound, Brooklyn's Don Newcombe and New York's Sal Maglie, with his 1930s movie-villain face, the game went into the top of the eighth inning a 1–1 tie. Then the Dodgers bunched some hits, circled some baserunners, and scored three times. A few of those hits streamed down the third-base line, and some tight-lipped Giants on the bench thought their third baseman Bobby Thomson should have stopped them. But that's baseball. What was coming up was not—that was pure folklore.

It went to the bottom of the ninth, the Dodgers still up 4–1, and the dreamy euphoria that had been waiting in abeyance over the city began drifting tentatively toward the borough of Brooklyn. But then Alvin Dark opened the Giants' ninth with a single to right. Don Mueller followed with a ground ball into right field, sending Dark to third and bringing the tying run to the plate in the person of Monte Irvin, the Giants' premier crasher that year. Monte popped to first baseman Gil Hodges in foul ground. That was the last out recorded in the National League in 1951. Next was Whitey Lockman, a left-handed hitter with Polo Grounds home-run power (actually, a palm frond swaying in the breeze could have hit one out of the Polo Grounds). Lockman, a smart hitter, went with Newcombe's pitch and dropped one into left field for a double, scoring Dark and sending Mueller to third. Mueller injured himself sliding, and while he was being helped from the field, Dodger manager Chuck Dressen began a crapshoot with destiny.

Newcombe, pitching with two days rest, was clearly tiring. The call went to the bullpen, where right-handers Carl Erskine and Ralph Branca were warming up in the shadows of the loud, rocking grandstands. There, coach Clyde Sukeforth answered the bullpen telephone and, to Dressen's request for information, responded, "Erskine is bouncing his curve, but Branca looks fast." "Give me Branca," said Dressen.

And so from the visitors' bullpen deep in left-center field, Ralph Branca began his walk toward a melancholy immortality. He was a tall, sad-faced young man who a few years before had fastballed his way to 21 victories. He wore number 13, which some unearthly demon may have thought was unduly tempting. How long the demon might have been thinking this, we do not know. We do know that he chose this day to pull the plug on Ralph (who switched uniform numbers the next year. Why risk incineration after you have been burned?).

The batter was Bobby Thomson, a right-handed hitter with power. He had come to the Giants in 1946 with talent that had aroused high expectations that had never been quite fulfilled.

Branca and Thomson. A classic among America's fated confrontations, up there with Burr and Hamilton at Weehawken, and Pat Garrett and Billy the Kid in New Mexico. Ralph Branca and Bobby Thomson at the Polo Grounds, dueling with ball and bat from sixty feet six inches.

Strike one.

Thomson later said it was a meatball, and he doesn't know how he let it pass.

Postmortem experts, also known as second-guessers, said the problem was that Roy Campanella, out with an injury, was not behind the plate for the Dodgers. The catcher was second-stringer Rube Walker, a more than competent man. If Campy had been in there, say these historians, most of whom reside in Brooklyn, he would have gone to the mound and warned Branca to pitch low, to throw a curve. That first pitch had been much too juicy.

The on-deck hitter was the rookie, Mays, by his own later admission thoroughly frightened, praying Thomson would spare him by hitting one out. It was Willie's year all right, right on up to and including answered prayers.

Branca came back with the same pitch, a high, tight fastball, but not tight enough or maybe not fast enough, or maybe it just no longer made any difference, that the miracle was already out of the bottle even before delivery of that last pitch. That's if you're a fatalist and believe it's all been predestined, that when Thomson had been a gene in his ancestors' chromosomes this miracle had already been carved upon the face of the future. If you aren't then that pitch was not tight enough or maybe not fast enough. Bobby hit it, and off it went, into whatever undying realms such monuments are hoisted. Prosaically, it was a line drive into the lower grandstands in left field, into a suddenly tempestuous, emotion-maddened sea of people. But we, with our decades of historical perspective, know better, for we know that that ball flew out of the Polo Grounds, out of New York City, beyond comprehensible grasp and into irretrievable myth, traveling yet, traveling always, crisscrossing the orbits of Ruth's "called shot" and Smoky Joe Wood's unthrown fastballs.

It is probably baseball's supreme moment, in all likelihood to remain so, at least until some future generation can concoct one of its own to equal it, but it will have to be when all the participants of this one are gone—players, spectators, viewers, listeners, and memorialists. Much of the special crystal that encased the event is already gone: Apartment buildings occupy the site of the Polo Grounds, the spot where Branca stood is perhaps now a garage or a carpeted corridor, and the spot where Thomson's home run touched down perhaps someone's bedroom, where tranquil sleepers lie abed at night unaware that the origins of an American myth were launched here.

"When we fell behind in the late innings," Monte Irvin recalled, "the clubhouse people must have lost heart, because they didn't ice the champagne. So when we finally got around to toasting our pennant, we had to do it with warm champagne. Can you imagine that?"

Well, not everyone believed in miracles. Not until then, anyway.

TWENTY-FIVE

ONE MEASURE of the dimensions of Willie Mays's talent is that he was able to maintain predominance over such gifted contemporaries as Roberto Clemente, Henry Aaron, and Frank Robinson. Part of this can be attributed to Willie's playing in New York (during the opening years of his career anyway) and part to his carbonated personality. He was always "loose," always laughing or giggling, a delight to have around and be around. "Listen," someone said, "if you could play ball like Willie Mays, you'd be laughing too." Well, Roberto Clemente could play ball as well as Willie Mays and Roberto was no rib-tickler. This was a man of raw sensibilities, looked up to and idolized by Puerto Ricans the way Jackie Robinson had been by blacks, a man whose smoldering pride was affronted by what he considered second-class superstatus, and with Clemente you know the affront was indeed to pride and not ego. Not only was he a dark-skinned Puerto Rican, his command of English was ragged, and he was hair-trigger sensitive to slights on both accounts. Clemente's lasting distinction, of course, is tragically congruous with the somber profile of his public personality—his death at sea in a plane crash while bringing food and medical supplies to earthquake-shattered Managua, Nicaragua, on New Year's Eve, 1972.

Nor were Henry Aaron or Frank Robinson apotheosized as was Mays, despite their ultimately occupying the first and fourth slots on the all-time home-run list. For Aaron, who covered the indignities of his black experience with a career-long smile and affability of disposition, unseating Ruth as the game's most prolific striker of home runs probably caused him as much travail as satisfaction. Not only was he peppered with hate mail from offended racists (including death threats, bleak prophecies, and whatever other vituperation the anxiety-ridden were able to flush from themselves for the price of a postage stamp), but even the disinterested kept pointing out that it had taken him an extra 4,000 at bats to pop 41 more homers than

Ruth, and that therefore as a home-run king he was really little more than a freak of longevity. (A remarkably consistent longevity, it should be pointed out. Not until the final two of his twenty-three seasons did he begin to struggle.) Aaron's problem was that in a country that prefers its heroes be soaked with drama, charisma, and dollops of controversy, he was a steady, unexciting performer who never lit up a footlight. Even his greatest moment, the stroking of home run number 715 to break Ruth's record, was not dramatic but inevitable, the product of high-class but methodic swinging.

Henry owns first place in home runs, but it's little more than an emeritus position. When baseball people convene to discuss the home-run masters, his name, if mentioned at all, comes as an afterthought, because Henry never muscled them as far as Ruth, Foxx, Williams, Mantle, Killebrew, or Mays. It is the long, long home run, the one that travels a hundred feet farther than is necessary, that burns in the imagination and makes a scepter of the bat. The all-time home-run champ hit 40 or better eight times in his career, but never more than 47, a single-season figure topped or equaled by 21 other players 39 times.

Frank Robinson, as tough-minded and uncompromising as his pioneering namesake, was a Triple Crown winner and also Most Valuable Player in each league, the only man ever to achieve this latter distinction. But it is as baseball's first black manager that he will be most remembered, taking over the Cleveland Indians in 1975 (twenty-eight years after Jackie Robinson's debut, blacks were still racking up "firsts"). One of the last of a once-popular breed, the playing manager, Robinson took himself off the rolls with 2,943 lifetime hits, displaying an almost lordly contempt for that magic 3,000 so dear to players who get in reach of it.

Clemente, Aaron, Frank Robinson—you could make them your all-time outfield and not be embarrassed. But yet history ranks them slightly under Mays, because of talent and because of Willie's intangibles, which included the sense that if baseball were ever to be embodied in or exemplified by one man, that man, for ability, disposition, and joyous contagion, would be Mays.

And herein perhaps lies another reason for Mays's captivating popularity, a somewhat less benign reason. Through much of his career Willie was viewed by white America as an innocent, fun-loving wizard of the great game; a perennial and, ultimately, unthreatening youngster. "You've gotta have a lot of little boy in you." That was one of the ingredients Roy Campanella saw as necessary for success in baseball. Its personification was Willie Mays, and white America chose to focus upon and emphasize the "boy." The image was shaped early in Mays's career, and it stuck, perpetuated by the zest he continued to display on the field and by sportswriters who remained fascinated by the portrait as first drawn.

But the portrait of Willie as perpetual adolescent was misleading. He grew up, he matured, and though the smile remained in place and the personality continued to bead the surface like champagne, the man behind it was not totally naive, for it would have been hard to grow up black in Birmingham, Alabama, and be naive about the blunt force of reality. There may be many different responses to racial prejudice; naivety is not one of them. In time Willie became the man his black teammates looked to for guidance and leadership, and he accepted the role responsibly. In 1964 Willie's manager in San Francisco, Alvin Dark, gave an interview to a *Newsday* reporter in which the following remarks were attributed to him: "We have trouble [winning] because we have so many Negro and Spanish-speaking ballplayers on this team. They are just not able to perform up to the white ballplayers when it comes to mental alertness." The exception, Dark said, was Willie Mays.

The exception notwithstanding, this was a humdinger of a statement. Cabinet officers have been exiled for less. It should have been a farewell address because, in addition to Mays, the Giants roster included such man-sized talents as Orlando Cepeda, Juan Marichal, and Willie McCovey, not to mention Jim Ray Hart, José Pagan, and Jesus and Matty Alou. But thanks to Mays's shrewd and forceful intervention, Dark was not fired (Willie helped talk an incensed club owner, Horace Stoneham, out of the move), nor was there a mutiny on the club. Willie convened a meeting of the offended parties and with some cold logic was able to lower the fires. As reported in Charles Einstein's *Willie's Time*, Mays's main arguing points were these: To fire Dark would make a hero of him to the "rednecks." To change managers might jeopardize the club's chance of winning the pennant. And perhaps the most placating point: Willie had it on good authority that Dark would not be back next year. (Dark was fired after the season, but went on managing in the big leagues for another nine years with four different clubs, without incident.)

Mays had understood quite clearly the pressure that would be on the team's blacks and Hispanics for the rest of the season if Dark was let go. "Ain't one of us gonna have a moment's peace," the club's elder statesman told them. This was incisive, no-nonsense reasoning from a man who knew the score, on the field and off, and it kept the plunger from going down on the explosives.

But that was the private Mays, operating behind closed doors. The public Mays remained ingenuous, noncontroversial of utterance, to the extent that in his *Baseball Has Done It*, the less compromising Jackie Robinson saw fit to write, "Big-league Negroes are aware. They are eager to help in the struggle. Many [have] volunteered to speak for publication. Rarely did anyone decline. Among those who did were two of the game's greatest stars, Willie Mays and Maury Wills. . . . No doubt they did not wish to stir things up."

So, unlike Robinson, who was part athlete, part crusader, part militant, a man whose impact was historic and reverberant, Willie remained socially one-dimensional. White fans, who could uncomfortably sense the unforgiving fury of a Jackie Robinson, could be totally at ease with Mays, a black man who executed all of baseball's pirouettes with unprecedented splendor, yet remained confined to the ball park, no threat to the social fabric.

These grudging, irreconcilable regions of the national psyche are perhaps another reason for the lament that there were "no heroes" in baseball through parts of the 1960s and 1970s, another reason why Aaron, Clemente, and Frank Robinson never quite received the coast-to-coast recognition that their talents seemed to demand. None of them projected the "boyish" image that Mays did. The public perception of them—particularly of Clemente and Robinson—was of men, very serious black men, with things other than baseball on their minds, men alert to and unforgetful of a lifetime's assaults upon their pride and dignity. Suddenly they were the stars, blacks and Hispanics (winning ten consecutive National League home-run titles from 1960 through 1969, plus seven batting championships), and people were asking where had the heroes gone. Lyndon Johnson, and then Richard Nixon, neither the most lovable of men, occupied the Oval Office. Cold-eyed Sonny Liston, a menace in black concrete, and then Cassius Clay, who soon made white America gag on the name Muhammad Ali, were back-to-back heavyweight champions. Baseball, perennially fertile loam for the harvesting of heroes, seemed to have stopped producing them.

But that of course was not true. The heroes were there, in the usual variety: the amiable, the brooding, the dynamic, the dramatic.

The difference was, they were black, and by now in a second wave, and they were more the heirs of Jackie than of Willie: confident, unawed, less inhibited about who they were and where they were, and thus just a bit more difficult for even a cheering, applauding white America to accept. They had even come so far as to have a black superstar—Richie (later Dick) Allen of the Philadelphia Phillies and, later, points west—who was openly contemptuous of his status, displaying a quirky independence that no doubt outraged far more people than it would have had he been white. While there were no critics of the effort he gave when on the field, Allen's arrivals at the ball park were sometimes less than punctual, his general attitude toward baseball as an abstraction less than reverential. Those reactionary elements within the baseball fraternity, still not fully at ease with the Rickey-Robinson revolution, finally felt justified in their mutterings about what would happen if "they" were allowed into the game. Dick Allen was, in his own perverse way, a fresh tributary of progress in the river set in motion by Jackie.

When Frank Robinson became the first black to manage in the big leagues the move was hailed as a breakthrough, which it was (the press conference was anointed by a congratulatory telegram from President Ford), and baseball's self-congratulators were quick to take note. Laudable as it was, however, Robinson's appointment was not really as dramatic as it appears. Speculation about the first black manager had been evident for years, and unlike the integration question of thirty years before, this one had a great deal of weight behind it. With so many of the game's top players being black, the club owners could not temporize indefinitely. So there had been a certain inevitability in operation when Frank Robinson was handed the reins of leadership.

What was probably more significant than Frank Robinson's being hired to lead white men was the slow, informal gravitation to a leadership role of Pittsburgh's Willie Stargell. Through the explosive power of his home-run bat, his warmth of personality, his strength of character, and his unassuming dignity, the thirty-seven-year-old seventeen-year veteran became the revered "Pops" of the Pirates, paterfamilias of a world championship club whose cry of pride and unity was "We Are Family." It was corny, but it was genuine, and it was unique, unique not just because most ball clubs do not have such cohesiveness of personnel, but because it was a black man who was the galvanizing force behind it. He led, he listened, he stabilized, he

kept things loose, performing an unsought role because he had become the man his teammates looked to.

That fall, in 1979, formal testament was made to Stargell's stature as a leader. Although Willie had enjoyed a good season at the
plate, his .281 batting average, 32 home runs, and 82 runs batted in
were hardly record-shattering statistics. Nevertheless, he shared the
National League's Most Valuable Player award honors with
St. Louis's Keith Hernandez. For Stargell, the award was as much a
tribute to his leadership and inspirational qualities as it was for his
thunder at home plate. Wilver Stargell had scaled one of the peaks
that had stood so formidably when Jackie Robinson had begun his
revolution: He had induced color-blindness.

TWENTY-SIX

ON AUGUST 26, 1939, at Ebbets Field in Brooklyn, the Dodgers and the Cincinnati Reds had played, the *New York Times* reported, "before two prying electrical eyes." Major-league baseball, the *Times* said, had "made its television debut." Television set owners "as far away as fifty miles viewed the action and heard the roar of the crowd."

The coaxial cable began growing in the immediate postwar years. It was almost like something that possessed its own organic life, with each miracle of transmission soon made obsolete by the next. Once upon a time, around the World War I era, neighborhood saloons had, as a service to their customers, paid a local newspaper to deliver the day's line scores on cards, which were hung on the wall. The idea after the Second World War was the same, except this time the lure was television sets raised on platforms over the bar. The intimacies of the game were suddenly available to lines of drinkers with upturned faces. To show off the wonders of the coming age, appliance stores left television sets running in their display windows at night, attracting small knots of viewers on the sidewalk. Soon these illuminated boxes—"the ultimate in home entertainment"—were being gazed upon by passive, placid faces in more and more living rooms around the country. Mass worship of the cathode tube had begun.

Television has had a significant impact on baseball in two ways. Once the new medium established that it had interesting sums of money to shell out for the rights to televising the games (the first games to be televised coast-to-coast were the Dodgers-Giants 1951 playoffs), the die was cast. One impact was the gradual escalation of player salaries into the economic stratosphere (this was in conjunction, of course, with the advent of free agency in the middle 1970s). In 1983, NBC agreed to divest itself of over $1 billion dollars for TV rights to big-league games for six years. This assured each of the twenty-six big-league teams approximately $6 million apiece each year before a single ticket was sold.

Now, if you can be amused by the idea of a .260 hitter or .500 pitcher earning $700,000 a year, it's all very positive. But television's other heavy impact on baseball was decidedly negative. The increased piping of big-league games into various parts of the country meant the gradual demise of the minor leagues. From a peak of over fifty minor leagues in the late 1940s, baseball's imperial commonwealth shrank to seventeen in 1982. All over the country, the arc lights came down, the grandstands were dismantled along with the one-shower clubhouses, and the fields were bulldozed and paved over for housing developments or shopping centers.

Was there another impact? Perhaps. Robin Roberts, the Phillies' great right-hander of the 1950s, thought there might be:

I always thought about playing sports, but never particularly about a career in professional baseball. In those days we didn't have television; we listened to the games over the radio and baseball seemed out of reach for most kids at that time. It was all a dream. We just couldn't imagine ourselves as major-league ballplayers, whereas today you can see it on television and it has greater reality to kids. I think, too, that in a curious way it was a little easier to be a ballplayer in those days because it *was* all a dream, and so you stayed natural and enjoyed yourself. Today kids of twelve and thirteen start trying to make it and I think they run the danger of becoming too self-conscious and lose some of their naturalness.

The 1950s are beginning to assume a sort of Edwardian twilight aura for Americans today. It was the decade before political assassinations, the Vietnam War, racial fury, Watergate, and economic instability. America was still bathed in the afterglow of victory, the admired, respected, and trusted world leader, with a revered war hero in the White House. The Eisenhower years have become sufficiently removed by time and isolated by prior and subsequent history to evoke nostalgia. It seems to have been, in retrospect at least, a time when there were things you could depend on.

Eisenhower's corporate-run government—it seemed like that, anyway, with all of those many-feathered chieftains of industry serving in the cabinet and out on the links with Ike—had its counterpart in baseball's leading corporation, the New York Yankees. No team

ever dominated a decade the way the Yankees did the 1950s. All of
the national nightmares about New York power and arrogance that
had begun with McGraw a half-century before, raised to dismaying
heights by Ruth and Gehrig and perpetuated by DiMaggio, were
now coming true with Yankee invincibility. Between 1949 and 1958,
the Yankees took every American League pennant with the exception
of the one in 1954, and even then, Al Lopez's Indians had to win a
record 111 games to make sure.

Hating the Yankees was as close to defying authority as most
Americans came in the 1950s. It served as emotional spring training
for feelings and attitudes that were going to be incited and inflamed
in a broader and more meaningful scale in the next decade.

Nevertheless, the Yankees' long-projected image of baseball-as-
big-business soon proved to have been the correct one all along. After
a half-century of stability, baseball franchises began coming un-
moored. For its inhabitants, the universe of baseball had always been
a place of orderly and systematic recurrences, with the same sixteen
teams going through their cadences from spring to fall in the same
familiar places. The arrangement had been sanctified by time, tradition, and a yearly schedule. Through all the vagaries of baseball ca-
price, the teams had remained rooted in the concrete of their cities,
part of the urban landscape, privately owned perhaps, but publicly
possessed.

The first severing of ties occurred when the Boston Braves moved
to Milwaukee in 1953. Since the Braves had drawn fewer than three
hundred thousand customers in 1952, and since they had always
seemed like strangers in what was essentially a Red Sox town, the
move made sense, and especially so when the Braves nearly septupled
their attendance in their first year in Milwaukee.

The next franchise to repudiate its heritage was the St. Louis
Browns, for over fifty years a chronic loser on the field and at the box
office. Only twice in their history had they ever drawn better than six
hundred thousand, and only seven times in fifty-three years had they
finished better than fourth. More than any other team, they had become the symbol of major-league futility. Their leaving St. Louis was
virtually an act of civic responsibility. And so one midnight they dissolved and reappeared the next spring as the Baltimore Orioles. Their
first year in Baltimore showed almost a quadrupling of attendance
from what it had been in St. Louis. These gaudy new attendance

figures did not go unnoticed by the other big-league club owners, some of whom began consulting their atlases.

America west of St. Louis had at one time been largely uncharted and unpopulated, and as far as big-league baseball was concerned, it still was. Baseball's provincial mentality had remained frozen; the men who ran the game were still of the generation that thought of St. Louis as a tedious twenty-four-hour train ride from the East. One of those gentlemen, however, was aware of other things: that America west of St. Louis was no longer Indian territory, that the jet engine had turned the West Coast into a short hike, that the people out there—millions of them—were clamoring for big-league ball, that unconscionable riches were to be made, and that if he didn't get out there first somebody else would. This gentleman was named Walter O'Malley, since 1950 president and principal owner of the Brooklyn Dodgers.

Walter O'Malley will always be a part of baseball history, a respected if not beloved figure. He was sharp, manipulative, devious, suavely persuasive and, some said, ruthless. He was a lawyer. Among his alleged sins is the undeniable fact that he was far brighter than most, if not all, of his colleagues in big-league ownership, which may sound like faint praise, but the truth is O'Malley would have been an impressive figure in any gathering.

O'Malley's image to many people is that of the smoke-filled room wheeler-dealer, and his physical appearance did much to support it—he was generously overweight and was never without a large cigar. But he did have a genuinely convivial side, liked his whiskey, could be an attentive host, and was a first-rate raconteur—all of which made his innate craftiness the more lethal.

While the name of Walter O'Malley will never be set to joyous lyrics in the borough of Brooklyn, there is no doubt that from a cold-blooded business standpoint, moving the Dodgers three thousand miles west was a masterful maneuver, for in Los Angeles Walter found gold-rush riches that probably astounded even his own embroidered imagination. That taking the Dodgers out of Brooklyn shattered a lot of illusions, not just in that borough but all around the baseball world, hardly mattered, and in comparison to the illusions that would be shattered in the upcoming decades, mattered not at all. If anything, O'Malley reinforced an icy cold truth that people should have known all along—baseball was strictly a commercial venture. This was not news to the ballplayers of course. Since the game's inception, they had been hired for one thing, their usefulness in winning games, pleasing fans, and earning money for ownership, and when this usefulness became frayed it did not matter who or what they were, star or also-ran—they were disposed of without ceremony. As has been written, sentiment in baseball comes in through the turnstile and nowhere else.

How serious a business baseball really was, was probably never meditated by the average fan, who was as comfortable with his team as he was with his morning newspaper (and soon a lot of those would vanish too). The fan was suddenly betrayed by what had always been one of the sustaining props of baseball—its aura of fantasy, its unique quality of being able to exist outside of reality, in a realm immune to the deceits and incursions of the everyday world. The fantasy and the reality would hereafter have to coexist, uneasily and tentatively, for the reality had proven itself distinctly untrustworthy.

When the Braves and the Browns left their respective cities, there had been fans eager to help them pack. O'Malley, however, was dealing with a different situation. Despite operating in an old ball park with inadequate seating, situated in a deteriorating neighborhood, his team was consistently among the leaders in attendance. The Dodgers were making money. O'Malley, businessman that he was, wanted to make more—this was as ingrained a part of the American ethos as the home run—and he knew not only where he could make it, but where there were people who were eager to help him do it. These included the mayor and other top officials in Los Angeles, anxious to make their city "big-league"—the ultimate in American accolades.

In order to make West Coast travel feasible for the other National League clubs, whose permission was required to make the move, O'Malley needed a co-pioneer to go westward with him. The perfect man was Horace Stoneham, owner of the New York Giants, a team even more tradition-soaked than the Dodgers, the team of McGraw, Mathewson, Ott, Terry, Hubbell, and currently of Willie Mays. Stoneham's Giants were suffering many of the same ills as O'Malley's Dodgers—an antiquated ball park, inadequate parking facilities, and a surrounding neighborhood turning grim with poverty and blight. In addition, the Giants' attendance was sinking. For Stoneham, a second-generation owner of the club and a genuine baseball man, the idea of a move was wrenching, but he had in fact been contemplating one even before being approached by O'Malley. "I wasn't the one who convinced Stoneham to leave New York," Walter said. "He had already made that decision." What Walter did was talk him out of a move to Minneapolis and convince him that San Francisco was better.

So the unbelievable took place—the Dodgers and the Giants left New York, and the city became like a smile without its two front teeth. While the cynics smirked and the others sifted through the dust of spurned loyalties, in California it was different. "Los Angeles," said Mayor Norris Poulson, was "now major league in every sense of the word." And so was the deal O'Malley had engineered with the city. As the wooed party, Walter had been able to make a few modest requests. Los Angeles donated to him over three-hundred acres of conveniently located rough ground called Chavez Ravine, agreeing to spend millions of dollars grading the site and several million more to build connecting roads and freeways to accommodate the city's automobile culture. Upon the site Walter proposed to raise the dream palace called Dodger Stadium.

For Stoneham, San Francisco built a ball park on an elbow of land that jutted out into the Bay called Candlestick Point. Imaginatively, it was named Candlestick Park, though fans and players and writers have been calling it many other things since. The ball park seemed to have been built in the very lungs of Aeolus, ruler of the winds in old mythology, for late every afternoon in off the Bay ride the air currents, swift and snappy, swirling and whirling, chill and damp, giving the shakes to popups and fly balls, and once even blowing a pitcher (the slightly built Stu Miller) from the mound during an All-Star game. The winds of Candlestick may be the will of old Aeolus, or they may be the avenging ghosts of McGraw and Matty and all the other bygone Giants deprived of their ancestral home. But farther south no such mischief prevails. Here there is sunshine and balmy Pacific breezes, caressing winning ball clubs and record-setting crowds. Sweet benedictions for the rotund New York Irishman who heeded the ancient siren call of America and went west.

It is likely that had not big-league baseball finally taken recognition of the rest of the country, a third major league would have come into existence. As it was, one almost did, a confederation known as the Continental League. The departure of the Dodgers and Giants had left quite a vacuum in New York, and into this and other cities

moved some very determined and well-heeled men. Their chief
spokesman was the old sorcerer himself, Branch Rickey. At first this
consortium was talking about bringing the National League back to
New York, but then the proposals began expanding to embrace other
cities and finally an entirely new league. The cities were New York,
Toronto, Houston, Buffalo, Denver, Minneapolis, Dallas–Fort
Worth, and Atlanta. Baseball people who knew their history knew
that these "outlaw" league ideas weren't always just wind blowing
around between someone's ears. While the Federal League might
have turned to jelly in two years, the once-upon-a-time "outlaw"
American League had not. So rather than go back to bidding wars,
litigation, and fist-shaking, the vested interests decided to forgo one
more tradition, the eight-team league, and expand. In 1961 the
American League swore in a new team in Los Angeles and another
one in Washington, with the former Washington club now operating
in Minneapolis–St. Paul. A year later the National League allowed
into its fraternity a new team in New York and another in Houston.
The age of expansion was now upon baseball, and before long it began assuming the proportions of that good old American doctrine
known as Manifest Destiny, only in reverse, as people from cities all
over the country, and a few from Canada, too, came rushing to the
Empire of Baseball asking to have their lands occupied. Some who
were invaded and then abandoned, like Kansas City, Seattle, and
Milwaukee, begged to be reoccupied, and so they were. And so the
sixteen teams, once so fixed in their firmament like the nine planets in
theirs, had grown to twenty, and then later to twenty-six, with even
that cumbersome number being assaulted by supplicants from the
four points of the compass bearing domed stadiums, favorable taxa-
tion, and parking lots as big as Kansas. Sixteen teams. Forty-eight
states. All those who were raised upon those verities were simply going to have to adjust.

Like his idol John Wayne, the last of the old prewar heroes said
good-bye to the old and new alike with a final triumphant shootout.
DiMaggio was already mothballed for a decade, Feller had faded out
on an 0–4 record in 1956, but Theodore Samuel Williams, all forty-
two years of him, still had That Swing. The man who had played
against men who had played against Cobb and Walter Johnson came
back from Korea and batted .345, .356, and .345 in 1954, 1955, and

1956. In 1957 the young lion Mantle had batted .365 but not even been close as the thirty-nine-year-old Williams swung with uncompromising grandeur all summer and ended with an ethereal .388 batting average, embossed with a hammer of 38 home runs. A year later he was a forty-year-old batting champion, dropping sixty points to .328 but still good enough. In 1959 he slipped to .254 and it looked as though he had stayed at the fair a year too long. But he came back in 1960 for his nineteenth and final season, and a .316 average. He announced that Boston's last home game, against Baltimore, would also be his last (the team wrapped up with a weekend series in New York, but he would not be accompanying them).

The day of Ted Williams's last major-league game was reminiscent of the day two decades before when he had smashed the hits to give him his .406 average—gray and chilly, holding the crowd down to around ten-thousand. This modest assemblage was treated to the most appropriate finale any great hitter has ever carved for himself.

Edgy and nervous going into the game—he hated anything ceremonial, and Ted Williams's last game naturally had brought out the photographers, the writers, the speeches, the presentations, and probably whatever private sentimentality this greatest of all batsmen kept bottled up—he wanted to ride out on a home run. Stepping in for his last at bat in the eighth inning, he had hit a few balls well but been unable to get them through the wind. On the mound for Baltimore was Jack Fisher, a fastballing right-hander, the raw meat Williams had been feeding on since 1939. Fisher, born the year Williams had come to the big leagues, fired one through for a strike. Ted felt he should have hit it; also, he knew the youngster was going to come back with another one. He would have to be just a bit quicker with the bat this time, he told himself. Fisher, with the pride of the strong young hardballer, tried to smoke another one past the tall man at home plate, but this time there was a bullwhip lash of the bat and with this last swing of his last at bat in his last game, off into the chill, resisting winds of Fenway Park went Ted Williams's 521st and last home run; not a pennant-winner, not even a game-winner; a blast whole unto itself, a unique missile, perfect, and maybe even inevitable.

TWENTY-SEVEN

GENERATIONAL PRIDE is a breeding ground for skepticism. Never-theless, each generation is entitled to believe in heroes that have no equal in the next. These are the sanctions of one's existence. The smoke of Grove rekindled the fire of Waddell, and those who insisted that Rube was quicker than Lefty were looked upon as harmless tale-tellers who had sat too long in the bleacher sun. Old men give de-scriptions of Walter Johnson's fastball with perhaps a bit too much vehemence, making one feel it would be ingenuous to believe. The next generation grew up in the heat of Bobby Feller's burner, and already that big pitch sounds as though it is receiving some retro-spective acceleration as it bolts from that emphatic windup in hazy recollection. They are the Halley's Comets of baseball, these incom-parable fastballs, reappearing in ghostly pride and reassertion when-ever another of equal velocity hits the big-league mounds, pitches measured by the imperfect radar of old memory. In all likelihood there is only fast, and no fastest of the fast. But what each new Lord of the Smoke does is represent a kind of reincarnation. Each gives credence to the tales of the past, for when suddenly a new man is out there occupying baseball's modest summit known as the mound and for nine innings throws a baseball as fast as a human being possibly can, then we know we are being revisited by Waddell, Johnson, Joe Wood, Grove, Feller, and the handful of others of that rare breed, and we can believe all the old tales, for one day in the future we of a certain age will be telling the young skeptics the same blunt narra-tive, insisting there is nobody around who throws as hard as— Koufax.

On December 22, 1954, the Brooklyn Dodgers announced they had signed a nineteen-year-old left-handed pitcher named Sanford (Sandy) Koufax. According to newspaper accounts of the event, the young man received a signing bonus of around $20,000, a serious amount of money in those days when the average Brooklyn Dodger (and this included Robinson, Campanella, Hodges, Reese, Snider) was earning about $17,000 for a run through the schedule. There was a string or two attached to it though, for under rules then prevailing in baseball, anyone receiving a bonus in excess of $6,000 was required to spend two years on the big-league roster. This rule retarded the progress of the Brooklyn-born Koufax, who was denied the opportunity to go to the minor leagues. Playing with a contending team restricted his appearances, and when he did venture out to the mound he showed a talent that was raw, wild, and occasionally impressive. In the beginning the emphasis was on wild; he was so wild, in fact, that he attracted attention. Dodger Manager Walter Alston first took notice of the new, unharnessed natural force on his pitching staff in spring training 1955. Speaking of Koufax, Alston recalled, "He was in a little warm-up area behind the barracks playing catch with somebody. They were about sixty feet apart, and I would say that about half of his return throws were going over the other guy's head. I looked at that and said to myself, 'What the hell have we got here?' "

His original ambition had been to be an architect, and his first sport had been basketball, but when your left arm has been cast by the craftsmen who did the pay wings of Waddell and Grove, your destiny has been preordained. However, the transition from wretchedly wild left-hander to greatest pitcher of the postwar era involved a long, grueling, frustrating, resolutely determined apprenticeship. In the record book, Koufax's career is dichotomized by six years of mediocrity and six years of peerless work that kept getting better and better until his career was aborted in 1966 by a chronically arthritic left elbow. He was just thirty years old, and was left with a career that approximates that of Dizzy Dean's in glamor years.

The record book's dichotomy reflected the personality of the young man who became, after Hank Greenberg, baseball's second preeminent Jewish player. Away from the mound, the darkly handsome Koufax was reserved, polite, courteous, self-effacing, and something of a loner. On the mound he was a figure of frightening intensity, unleashing each blazing fastball and lethal curve as though his brooding pride had been freshly insulted. The first truly super pitcher of the television age, Koufax treated viewers to closeups of the metamorphosed man at work, the adrenalin-driven killer-athlete leaning forward to pick up the catcher's sign, face scowling with centripetal concentration, and then the teeth-gritting delivery of the next pitch that arrived with ferocious suddenness. Unlike most people in their endeavors, pitchers strive to be misunderstood, deceiving; but not pitchers like Koufax. You understand them perfectly, and that is their challenge, the measure of their self-assurance.

How could a man pitch this way for nine innings, without diminishment of speed, and when necessity demanded, faster in the ninth inning than in the first? For explanation, we turn to a conversation between pitcher Gene Conley, then with the Phillies, and his teammate, the great right-hander Robin Roberts, universally admired for the dynamic power he displayed under pressure. Roberts's simple, unselfconscious response to Conley's question stands not only for himself, not only for Koufax, but for any superior athlete girding under the pressure of challenge.

"I asked Roberts one time," Conley said, " 'Robby, when you're in a tight spot in the last inning and you need some extra on the ball, do you find yourself pushing off that mound a little harder?'

" 'No,' he said. 'I pitch the same all the time. The first pitch goes in the same way as the last one.'

" 'That can't be true,' Conley said, 'because I notice when there's a man on third and less than two out, that ball pops a little better.'

" 'Well,' he said, 'you can't see what I'm doing. That comes from within.' "

From "within." From how deep within? And what generated that psychic desire and need to keep going as deep within as the situation and the stakes deemed necessary? Conley went on to cite Jackie Robinson as another baseball example of a man coming from "within" to surmount an on-the-field crisis. "How the devil did they do that?" Conley asked. "You couldn't answer it. I don't think they knew themselves. They just did it." If Conley, a big-league pitcher and pro basketballer with the Boston Celtics, was mystified by the mainsprings of this inspiration, how is a nonathlete to understand it? The answer lies beyond sheer physical ability and is probably to be found in some psychoanalytical explanation. The motivation of a Jackie Robinson seems fairly apparent; but what about a naturally placid-dispositioned Robin Roberts or Sandy Koufax? Their transformation under pressure is akin to the blood lust of the hunt. And nowhere was this personified more graphically than in the reticent, modest, undemonstrative Koufax who walked to the mound and became Mr. Hyde.

After his first six years in the major leagues, Koufax's won-lost record stood at 36–40, the kind of record that guarantees a pitcher a

certain anonymity while he is active and swift obscurity the moment
he retires. The mediocrity grated at Sandy; he knew he was better
than that, and the Dodgers knew it too, or at least knew that he *could*
be better if he ever overcame the lion in his path—wildness. He
wasn't a .500 pitcher because he was being hit, but because he was
free-riding too many batters to first base. When he was getting the
ball over they surely weren't hitting it—he averaged around a strikeout per inning during those six years in the wilderness. There were
times when the Dodgers despaired of his ever squaring himself away,
but whenever there was talk of trading him they noticed that every
club in the big leagues was interested, which is the most convincing
scouting report a team can get.

No great pitcher ever took as long as Koufax did to begin making
his miracles. But once he did, they were indeed miracles, baseball-
style. They included four no-hitters, one of them a perfect game, and
a record-setting five consecutive earned-run average titles. Batters
began falling in droves to those fastballs and curves, like infantry to
machine-gun fire. Over his last five years he was as near unbeatable
as it is possible to be, posting a 111–34 won-lost record.

What brought about the transformation? Well, it was a contradiction of the old work ethic that mandates that the harder you try
the more you will succeed. It did not apply to Koufax. He was too
abundantly gifted. In reaching back and trying to put everything he
had on every pitch he was creating too much muscular tension. "He
needed a loose wrist," said Dodger pitching coach Joe Becker, "to get
snap in the ball at the position of release." By working with the patient, insightful Becker, Koufax soon realized that less was more, that
by throwing more easily the ball would not only travel as fast but
would go where he wanted it to. This was baseball's equivalent of the
splitting of the atom, the harnessing of the most blinding force seen
on a big-league pitching mound since the incarnation of Bob Feller.

"All at once Sandy got control," Alston said. "And I don't mean
control in the sense of just throwing the ball over the plate. He could
throw the fastball where he wanted to—to spots. When you have
that kind of stuff and that kind of control, well, they just stopped
hitting him. And it all happened in one year." Alston added wryly, "It
made me a much smarter manager."

He was a superstar in a city of celebrities. Standard-brand names
like Frank Sinatra, Cary Grant, Danny Kaye, and Doris Day were
out at the ball park. Hollywood stars donned uniforms for an annual

game at Dodger Stadium. Gradually, baseball itself became "California-ized," a glamorized adjunct to the entertainment world, with exploding scoreboards and fireworks displays and World Series games launched like Hollywood openings. How a Waddell or a Dean would have reacted to being the ace of aces in southern California leaves the imagination in a state of extremity. But through it all, Koufax retained his dignity. He was a private man, evidently without ego or temperament, managing to protect his privacy despite residence in a city whose celebrities seem to live within glass walls.

Fate would have its way, however, just as it had with Joe Wood's broken thumb and those career-shattering line drives that were whistled against Dizzy Dean's toe and into Herb Score's eye. By the time he reached his peak in 1965 and 1966, with records of 26–8 and 27–9, the game's dominant player and premier drawing card was pitching with unbearable pain in his left elbow due to a traumatic arthritic condition. After each game there was a ritual of obeisance to the agony in the form of pain-killing pills, a burning salve, and an ice-cold elbow bath for as long as forty minutes. He never complained. He was as tough as oak, this modest hero. Doctors said they had never seen such back muscles on a man, the apparent source of that searing fastball. But he began wondering. He knew that arthritis was a degenerative condition, worsening and incurable. He was warned by doctors that the strain of further pitching could cause permanent crippling.

He had been so stoic under pain in 1966 that it came as a shock to many when he announced his retirement after the 1966 season, a few months before his thirty-first birthday. No great player had ever left the game while at the peak of his powers. The injured, like Dean and Score, had always fought against what disabled them and left the game in slow, painful, sometimes humiliating departure. Koufax alone left at high noon, a Hamlet leaving in mid-soliloquy.

TWENTY-EIGHT

FOR THE BASEBALL PURIST the changes had come fast and become many. The St. Louis Browns had been transmuted into the Baltimore Orioles. The Boston Braves were in Milwaukee. Even Connie Mack's Athletics were no longer in Philadelphia but had gone west to Kansas City a year before the old gentleman had died in 1956 at the age of ninety-three. And more: The Brooklyn Dodgers and the New York Giants were playing in California, there was a new team in New York called the Mets, there were major-league teams in Houston and Minneapolis, and the American League was playing a schedule of 162 games. No wonder then, that into this confounding, barely recognizable temple of tumbling certainties a transgressor should be turned loose to vandalize one of the game's most honored monuments. The monument had been erected thirty-four years before, in 1927, and was known as Babe Ruth's 60 Home Runs. Like "56" and ".406," that "60" was one of baseball's touchstone numbers, and suddenly it was under assault.

"Check the history books," one disgruntled and unreconstructed old purist would say years later. "You'll see that that was when the world began to go to hell, right after a .260 hitter broke Ruth's record."

If it had been Mantle, by now winner of a Triple Crown that included a 52-home-run season, it would have been more seemly. But it wasn't Mickey, it was his teammate Roger Maris, who had belted 39 one-way bangers the year before, which was impressive but not startling. If anybody was going to break Ruth's record, the general consensus had Mantle doing it. He was also the preferred man. He had the stature, the credentials. This was, after all, no popgun record we're talking about; this was baseball's equivalent of the heavyweight championship. And Mickey did make quite an effort in 1961, coming reasonably close with 54 irretrievables; but it was the .260 hitter (.269 actually), Maris, who went ahead and did it, giving base-

305

ball in general and New York in particular the game's most thrilling one-man crusade since DiMaggio's hitting streak ("It's always a fuckin' Yankee, isn't it?" one still embittered old Brooklyn Dodger fan muttered that summer).

Maris, a pull-hitting lefty powerhouse with a stroke designed for Yankee Stadium, had two significant advantages going for him— Mantle batting behind him all season (the slugging Maris received not one intentional base on balls that year), and the added eight-game grace of the newly installed 162-game schedule.

Young people all over the country, in towns and cities alike, dream of it, of coming to New York and electrifying the big city, holding it in thrall, gripping its imagination, becoming courted by press and public, existing in a special cloud of glory and acclaim. This is what happened to twenty-six-year-old Roger Eugene Maris in his second year with the Yankees after having been acquired in a trade with the Kansas City club. He was a small-town boy, good-looking, with a brush haircut, affable and unassuming. He was the lucky one; the golden dream with all its blatant jackpots happened to him. And he loathed every moment of it. "All it brought me was headaches," he said. Roger Maris, playing the Ruthian right field for the right team in the right city, became sports' biggest story of the year, which meant, like the hole in the doughnut, he was surrounded on all sides.

Ruth would have thrived on it. DiMaggio would have tolerated what he was unable to ignore. Mantle would have deflected some of it with his sly Oklahoma wit. Maris, however, had no defenses for it. In some quarters, the hapless young slugger became an antihero. Even old Rogers Hornsby, still bristling with a quiver of sought and unsought opinions, called him a "bush leaguer" and said it was a disgrace that a .260 hitter should be challenging Ruth.

As July baked into August and his home-run total kept mounting (he had 40 at the end of July), Maris became like a presidential candidate, holding daily press conferences in front of his locker, answering a barrage of repetitive questions that ran a thematic gamut from A to B: "Do you think you'll break Ruth's record?" "What kind of pitch did you hit?" "Is there a lot of pressure?" From city to city it was the same merry-go-round, and it began moving faster as the home runs, those magical bolts, continued to mount, and August flipped over into September with Roger standing at 51 full crackers, eight more than Ruth had taken into September 1927. Adding to the pressure and heightening the drama was teammate Mantle, who kept pace with him most of the summer until falling back in early September, beset by his usual assortment of ailments and injuries.

The relentless inane questions, the incredible booing from a claque of New York patrons who regarded him as a usurper, the suggestions in the press that he was "jealous" of the popular Mantle (who was actually a close and sympathetic friend), the shredding of his privacy, all began to sour Maris, make him irritable and defensive. When he wasn't snapping at his postgame interrogators ("How the fuck do I know?" he began responding, not unreasonably, when asked yet again if he was going to break the record), he was trying to hide from them, which was like a tree trying to hide from the wind. Maris was the story, and the press would have him, and it didn't matter to them whether they painted him as amiable—which basically he was—or as a surly, ill-tempered son of a bitch—which they were accusing him of turning into, and the more they accused, the more he became. And although the cheering continued to far outweigh the booing, the latter remained to him disturbing and incomprehensible.

Most vexing to Maris was America's most frequently asked and unsatisfactorily answered question of 1961: What constitutes a season? There was no doubt that Roger had an unfair advantage because of those extra eight games. But eight did not seem like so many; if the season had been lengthened to, say, 175 games, there would have been no debate. But debate there was, as intense as any ever in baseball. Ford Frick, then commissioner (and an old friend of Ruth's, which made him suspect in the matter), said that if Roger broke the record in those additional games it should be so noted in the record books. Many people supported Frick, while others contended that "a season is a season," which sounds reasonable but really isn't, for if the season had indeed been extended to 175 games they would have been singing not just a different tune but different lyrics.

So as the days and nights of September passed, Maris continued walking up to home plate against increasingly determined pitchers, swinging against the ghost of Ruth, against the edicts of Ford Frick, and into those dust storms of boos coming from fans who for their own assortment of reasons were opposed to him. The perception of Maris as a usurping fluke with dubious credentials and the unresolved dispute whether he was a man for all season or just the first 154 games drained some of the excitement from one of the most heroic quests in baseball history. Roger ended the 154-game span (actually 155, as the Yankees played one tie) with 59 home runs. But in game number 159 he popped number 60 off of Baltimore's Jack Fisher, the young man who just a year before had dished up Ted Williams's valedictory blast. And then, on the last day of the season, Roger put Boston's Tracy Stallard on the trivia lists as "the man who . . ." when Maris drove a healthy shot into the right-field seats for number 61.

His 1961 experience with the press, that segment of unaccepting fans, and the baseball establishment left Maris a disillusioned young man. A superb all-around player, popular with his teammates, good-looking, and likable, Roger Maris should have cut it big, wide, and handsome in New York. But he never did. Nor did he ever come close to approximating his 1961 season. His remaining years with the Yankees were marked by gradually reduced productivity, due primarily to injuries. After the 1966 season, in which he batted .233 with just 13 home runs, he was traded to the Cardinals. A hand injury curtailed his ability to pull a ball, and the man who had—or had not—broken Babe Ruth's record lined most of his hits to left field. He played two years for the Cardinals, helped them to two pennants, and hit a meager 14 home runs over those two seasons—he had hit half that many in six consecutive games in glorious August 1961. Nevertheless, "Those were the two happiest years I spent in baseball," said Maris. (No doubt he would have been just as happy in Samarkand or anywhere else, as long as it wasn't New York with its klieg lights and laser-beam focus for whatever takes its interest.) He retired to the more placid groves of Gainesville, Florida, where he built a highly lucrative beer distributorship.

How good was Roger Maris? It would be presumptuous, wouldn't it, to watch a man hit 61 home runs in a season and call it a fluke? Baseball history remains ambiguous about him. One thing should be noted, however: Decades have passed, and 162 games or no 162 games, no one has yet come close to him. Ruth may be legend and Maris only history, but 61 is still 61.

TWENTY-NINE

THE TRANSPLANTATION of the Dodgers and Giants from New York to the West Coast proved symptomatic of many things both within and without baseball. The jet engine and a network of superhighways made an always highly mobile people more so; great distances were being measured by a handful of hours. The increase in cities boasting major-league franchises was a clear indication of the continuing urbanization of America. In 1933 one out of every four Americans worked on a farm, but a half-century later it was one out of thirty.

The New York Yankees, who for long had symbolized so much in baseball, soon became the unwilling symbol of the decline of the eastern seaboard and of power shifts to the West and to the "Sun Belt." After a forty-four-year reign from 1921 through 1964, during which they won 29 pennants and 20 world championships, the Yankees began a plunge in 1965 with five consecutive second-division finishes and eleven pennantless years overall. Baseball's authority symbol had weakened and crumbled. The dissolution of Yankee power ironically coincided with the rending of the national fabric under the strains and pressures of the Vietnam War, massive antiwar demonstrations, a corrosive cynicism, and the skeptical mistrust of authority, which became vindicated by the varied offenses and malfeasance known collectively as Watergate. Bracketed on one side by assassination and on the other by impeachment, the nation endured a decade as tumultuous as any in its history.

While baseball maintained the smooth-working gears of its old apolitical posture throughout the changes, protests, and upheavals, it was not immune from the effects of the social tantrums going on around it, not even when these were expressions of jubilation. Listen to the contrasts in fan reaction from these two accounts of two different world championships won at home: "Our fans let go a really good shout for us when it was over. We got a standing ovation." That's Ernie Shore, Red Sox pitcher, describing the hometown fans after the

Red Sox won the 1916 World Series. And here is Tom Seaver, describing what happened after the last out of the 1969 World Series had given the New York Mets the title: "The guys on the field had to run for their lives. There were fifty-seven-thousand people pouring out to offer congratulations." The players escaped intact, but the Mets' Shea Stadium did not. In the vernacular of the day, they "trashed" it, tearing loose bases, digging out home plate, ripping up grass sod, committing wholesale vandalism. And this was a demonstration of joy. The same thing happened at Yankee Stadium after Chris Chambliss's rousing bottom-of-the-ninth home run gave the Yankees the 1976 pennant in the championship series against the Kansas City Royals. This demonstration of mass "joy" was even more frightening and destructive than the one at Shea, causing over $100,000 worth of damage. The primitive display bordered, in fact, on anarchy. Chambliss never completed his circle of the bases. By the time he reached first base he was mobbed, by the time he fought his way to second the bag was already gone, and reportedly he reached out and touched it, whereupon he gave up and broke for the safety of the dugout. Later, he came back to the cleared field and put his feet in the vicinity of where home plate had been, making sure his home run was official.

The kind of player independence that had exasperated McGraw in the 1920s and 1930s was even more spirited in the 1970s, again in reflection of changing social attitudes. The changes were recognized by some old-time managers, now in retirement, who had spent lifetimes in a game they no longer felt comfortable with. Veteran skippers like Jimmy Dykes, Bucky Harris, and Joe McCarthy conceded they would have been both unable and unwilling to try and direct these new players, who had a union behind them and grievance committees and salaries that made them indifferent to fines. The days of unquestioned managerial authority were over. One of the last surviving links to the Old School of managerial Caesarism, Leo Durocher, found he could no longer command the obedience he once had. In his final year as a big-league manager, with the Houston Astros in 1973, Leo found himself being ignored, cursed, mocked, and contradicted. Unable to break down this new stone wall of independence and self-interest, suddenly finding himself an anachronism, Durocher retired, kissing it off with this line from the end of his autobiography, *Nice Guys Finish Last* (written with the talented Ed Linn): "It's a different breed, boy, and they're going to keep right on doing it their way."

In the midst of the turmoil and the institutionalized irreverence, an image-shattering book called *Ball Four* was published. The book remains a landmark event in baseball literature, a literature generally known for deadening humility, discretion, and narrative torpor. The author was Jim Bouton, former twenty-game-winning Yankee pitcher (in 1963) whose arm had gone bad, an event that seemed to sharpen his already acute sensibilities and hone his attitude toward hypocrisy. (Collaborating with Bouton on this best-seller-cum-television series was New York sportswriter Leonard Shecter, himself a most acidulous and cynical appraiser of the sports establishment.)

Cast as a diary of the 1969 season, when Bouton was trying to hang on to his big-league career as a knuckleballing relief pitcher, *Ball Four* became one of the most avidly read and furiously reviled baseball books ever published (as a matter of fact, it is probably the *only* reviled baseball book ever published). A bright, witty, unabashed iconoclast—he was one of the few major-leaguers to take an outspoken position against the Vietnam War—Bouton had written a book that in tone and attitude was in perfect harmony with the dividing and subdividing counterculture society around it. Bringing his notebook into the locker room, Bouton recorded the dialogue around him and published what he heard, the way he heard it, and for many people who had never thought about the way major-leaguers talked, it was not edifying. It was an unvarnished, uncensored view of life in the big leagues, on and off the field. It was all there—the hijinks, the jokes, the pep pills, the booze, the Peeping Toms on hotel rooftops, the sometimes less-than-reverential approach to the national game. The book was candid, hilarious, ribald, bawdy, profane, unsparing, and sometimes downright nasty. Christy Mathewson would never have written it. Bouton was rebuked, criticized, damned, and vilified. But never impugned. He had, apparently, contrived or exaggerated nothing, and this was the unforgivable sin.

Within the universe of baseball Bouton became as infamous as the miscreants of the 1919 White Sox. He was called a traitor, a betrayer. But what he had done, in truth, was humanize big-league ballplayers in very elemental ways, and this was unacceptable. He became an anathema.

Perhaps the most resentment generated by *Ball Four* lay in Bouton's reminiscences of former Yankee teammate Mickey Mantle. Actually, Bouton's depiction of Mantle was quite evenhanded. He recalled Mickey's humor, boyish charm, generosity, talent, courage. But he also wrote of Mantle's surliness, his occasional refusal to sign autographs, his excessive drinking, his sophomoric peccadilloes. Mantle, retired for two years when the book came out, had long since been enshrined as one of America's special heroes, an untouchable. Those who preferred their heroes to remain crisp and unsullied were outraged by what they considered Bouton's indiscretions. "I don't care what they say about me," one old Yankee teammate said, "but they shouldn't say anything about Mickey." Others expressed a similar willingness to fall on the sword for Mantle, who evidently had left behind a hypnotic grip. Since Mantle's eminence as an American hero had been predicated not upon any moral or ethical distinction but upon his ability to swat baseballs halfway to infinity, the keyholing of *Ball Four* did nothing to diminish Mickey's stature; if anything, it probably deepened the man's dimensions and made him even more vivid.

As Leo Durocher said, it was a different breed of ballplayer, and like the new men who had come along in the 1920s and infuriated and exasperated John J. McGraw, they hadn't evolved in a vacuum. Born and raised in a postwar America proud and optimistic with triumph and worldwide preeminence, an America powerful and affluent and morally untainted, and then an America ripped with the tragedy, self-doubt, and turmoil of Vietnam, they absorbed the contradictions and the ambiguities and grew up in a society more complex, permissive, and awry than any the nation had ever known. If the Oval Office could be bugged by its occupant and the tapes of private conversations in the highest echelons of government subpoenaed into court and later published, where did that leave the sanctity of a baseball clubhouse, especially when investigative reporting was taking credit for helping to unseat a U.S. president? The preening began to permeate every department of a newspaper, including sports.

Sportswriters, who once upon a time had gone out of their way to cover up the peccadilloes of ballplayers and shield the image of the game, were now asking provocative questions and receiving blunt answers, creating headlines that sometimes dwarfed accounts of the game. And it fed upon itself: The more candid the players became, the greater became the power of the press; and the greater the power of the press, the more disposed the players were to cooperate with it, as though thereby becoming shareholders in this giant machine of voracious consumption and unbolted dissemination.

Confident and secure with his high-salaried, multiyear contract, his agent, his lawyer, and his union, the new ballplayer was unafraid to speak out. Gone were the days when a "gentleman's agreement" among club owners could banish a fractious or unduly independent player. "In those days," said White Sox Manager Jimmy Dykes, speaking of the 1930s, "if you had a disgruntled ballplayer, you'd ask waivers on him. If somebody claimed him, you'd call them up and say, 'Waive on this guy. We want to send him to Shreveport. We'll do you a favor someday.' So that's what would happen. He'd end up in Shreveport. It was different in those days." The owners in their absolute power were callous, high-handed, arbitrary—which is precisely why those days are gone. Gone with them were writers willing to overlook a Connie Mack saying he would not put his team on the same field with the "nigger" Robinson.

It is improbable that Yankee skipper Billy Martin's celebrated remark about his outfielder Reggie Jackson and employer George Steinbrenner—"One's a born liar, the other's convicted"—would in an earlier time have made the papers. But this was 1977 and a newspaperman's primary loyalty no longer was to the ball club (which in bygone days picked up the tab for the writers who traveled with the team) but rather to his paper. The writers who overheard Martin's wisecrack probably realized the consequences of reporting it, but in the prevailing climate they had no choice but to do so, and Billy was gone.

The spirits of Watergate sleuths Bob Woodward and Carl Bernstein were now the models in city rooms and sports departments. No longer was the glamorous newspaperman represented in the public imagination by the trenchcoated cigarette-dangling foreign correspondent by-lining from exotic hot spots, but rather that of the investigative reporter panning the stream for quotes, controversy, and revelation. It sounded like Washington, D. C., at its most exasperated and paranoid: The contents of clubhouse meetings were leaked; "unnamed sources" among the players or from the front office confided information; club executives were sometimes reduced to a "no comment."

Two-time National League MVP Dale Murphy of Atlanta was considered "dull" and "poor copy" because his clean-cut, family-man image gave off no sparks and left behind no shadow. (A few decades before, an equally colorless Stan Musial had been revered as a paragon for American youth for displaying the same qualities as Murphy.) The similarly faultless Steve Garvey, unfailingly polite and courteous to fans and writers alike, finally began to grate on the nerves of some of his teammates and on certain writers, too, who publicly dissected his motives and found sanctimony and calculated image-polishing. Late in the 1978 season, when a dramatic, highly charged Yankee stretch run that won them a pennant coincided with a prolonged New York newspaper strike, some Yankee players attributed their success—in part anyway—to the absence of turmoil that had been created in the clubhouse by reporters asking provocative questions and printing controversial answers in the highly competitive New York press.

The power of the press became so pervasive that when a player obdurately refused to talk to journalists a special mystique quickly enveloped him. The first was Steve Carlton, the most notorious of baseball's sphinxes (there were a handful of others). A left-hander of high distinction, Carlton became noted in equal parts for his unhittable slider and his refusal to communicate with representatives of either the written or spoken word (no one thought to try semaphore with him). The Philadelphia pitcher presented an interesting paradox, for if the press is often cultivated because of its power to enhance or damage an image, and hence a career and a salary, what happens to the man who goes out of his way to avoid the press? (Yes, just that: Carlton hid in the trainer's room during the Phillies' 1980 World Series victory celebration rather than be caught saying "whoopee" by a reporter.) Well, nothing disagreeable happens. It helps, of course, if you are regarded as the game's premier southpaw, a 300-game winner. As far as anyone could tell, Carlton's resolute muteness did nothing to harm his image with the fans; if anything, it made him special, an intriguing enigma.

Taciturn players were not an entirely unique phenomenon. New York Giants player-manager Bill Terry was noted for his circumspect attitude toward the press in the 1930s, but this was considered part of the total Terry personality rather than the manifestation of some doctrinaire posture. And, in Terry's case, this was probably just as well, for his lone memorable quote, an attempt at jocularity in responding to a question about the Dodgers in the spring of 1934, "Is Brooklyn still in the league?" came back to haunt him at the end of the season when the Dodgers helped beat the Giants out of the pennant.

Carlton's silence, however, was profoundly motivated. For years the talented left-hander had followed established procedure and given interviews. That came to an abrupt halt sometime in the mid-1970s after some Philadelphia writers printed what he felt were derisive accounts of a dialogue he had with them. The serious-minded Carlton had confided to the writers some new-found mental and physical disciplines he was adhering to. According to some reports, Carlton felt that printed accounts of the discussion made him appear pretentious and woolly-headed, and the pitcher soon sealed himself off from all writers, all interviews. Posterity, however, would be none the poorer for it, for Carlton had been giving interviews for years and nothing he had said had yet crashed the pages of Bartlett's. The only damage was limited to journalistic ego.

The press became fascinated by the man who would not talk. Carlton could ignore them, but they could not ignore Carlton, not a man with four Cy Young Awards, chasing an all-time strikeout record, and a slider that snapped the air like an adder's tongue. Information about him filtered through the mesh and into the newspapers, and the more exotic, the more eccentric-sounding, the better, for how else to characterize a man who would not converse with reporters? Thus the public learned: Steve Carlton helped discipline his mind and strengthen his body by engaging in rituals of excruciatingly demanding exercises, including pushing and twisting his arms in a deep tub of rice. Steve Carlton was an exponent of the martial arts. Steve Carlton was a connoisseur of fine wines, was said to have a fine cellar and to have toured the vineyards of Europe. Steve Carlton was once spotted emerging from a New York bookstore with volumes on yoga and Buddhism. Steve Carlton was alleged to pitch with cotton stuffed in his ears to shut him off further from the distractions of the world. (This brings one near to sympathizing with Carlton that perhaps an ultimate wish—invisibility while working—was not available to him.)

So the press was up against one they couldn't harness, harass, or intimidate. The impervious Steve Carlton was probably the only man in America to defy the almighty communications media and survive unscathed, stature undiminished. One can guess how many of his fellow citizens, particularly those occupying positions of public trust, must have muttered in envy. Again, baseball the open and virtuous society: A ballplayer who did not want to talk to the press was a ballplayer who did not want to talk to the press and not a dubious character trying to keep the lid on some festering ethic.

But if it chose to, the press could, in a converse way, claim that Carlton's silence only further emphasized its importance, for by ignoring democracy's noisiest institution, the left-hander had merely added further dimensions to his fame. Thus there was the story of a writer who received a magazine assignment to do an article on players who refused to speak to the press. Carlton would, of course, be the centerpiece of the story. The writer entered the Philadelphia clubhouse and eyed his prey. With both apprehension and trepidation, he approached Carlton—apprehension because it is not the most serene of feelings to question a man whose creed of silence is sternly based, and trepidation because if Carlton chose to speak there would be no story.

"Steve," the writer said, "would you answer a few questions?"

"No," said Carlton.

"Thanks," said the writer.

Koufax had retired, Mantle had stumbled to the end of his career, Mays had begun to decline. At the beginning of the 1970s the game was bereft of the sort of heroes whose might and whose magnetism are an alchemy that seem almost daily to blur history into legend. Sportswriters lamented the lack of men like the seemingly flawless Gehrig, that model of devotion to everything that came his way; and the eternal DiMaggio, forever unmelted in his casement of ice; or even the lovable Dean, so broadly American, so ebullient, and so flagrantly obvious you indulged the con man behind the smile.

There were stars of impeccable credentials, of course, but most of them seemed as though they might be susceptible to the same winnowing process that had withered memories of Nap Lajoie, Tris Speaker, George Sisler, Harry Heilmann, Al Simmons, Paul Waner, and other "glories of their time," washing them out of legend and leaving them to the record books alone, and beyond resurrection— for baseball, immune to so many externals, is also a story that flows untrammeled by revisionist historians.

Henry Aaron, Roberto Clemente, Carl Yastrzemski, Al Kaline, and Brooks Robinson were flawless ballplayers, but none had achieved the stature of a Mays or a Mantle. Juan Marichal was one of the greatest pitchers in National League history, but he had been an exact contemporary of Koufax's, which is something like booking your flight with Icarus. The legacy of Jackie Robinson was bearing its most tangible fruit in the career of Cardinal right-hander Bob Gibson, a scowling, murderously competitive fastballer who decked batters without regard to color, and without incident; and in the career of Frank Robinson, hard-playing and tough-talking, free to play with none of the restraints of Jackie as he slid color-blind into second base to break up double plays, without incident. And they all said, all the black players from Mays on down: "Whenever I look at my house or at my bank account, I think of Jackie Robinson."

But the zealous, fearless pioneer was no longer around to watch it all happen. He had died in October 1972, at the age of fifty-three, white-haired, diabetic, partially blind, old far beyond his years, leaving behind a legend that will finally be as imperishable as only Ruth's and ultimately more significant, for his was the career that embraced the world of reality and that of fantasy, made the blend work and from it produced an even richer fantasy. "I remember once," said Clyde Sukeforth, the scout who had first brought Robinson to Rickey in 1945 and who served as a Dodger coach during that nightmarish 1947 season, during that season he was sitting in the clubhouse after a game, after a particularly bad time—and there were mostly bad times for him that season—and he was just seething. He wasn't saying anything, but you could see the anger in him. It was red hot. I went over to him to offer some comfort, but didn't know what to say. He looked up at me and I think he understood my intentions, because he said, very softly, with the fire still in his eyes, 'It's all right.' That was Jackie," Sukeforth said. "The madder you made him, the tougher he got. It took a long time for the damn fools to figure it out."

An accelerated, more activist society was beginning to make baseball appear, to some people, slow and stodgy. Certainly the 1968 season—the "Year of the Pitcher"—did nothing to diminish this opinion. This was the season when batting averages fell low enough to have roots. The National League batted a collective .243, wretched enough, but positively resounding compared to the American League's .230, lowest in that league's history (Carl Yastrzemski's .301 average brought him the batting championship). The paucity of base hits that season did indeed make the game seem a bit sluggish, especially in comparison with professional football, which was enjoying impressive growth among fans, television ratings, and in the size of its guards and tackles.

But just one year after the wretchedly dull "Year of the Pitcher," baseball once again demonstrated its capacity to deftly surprise and purely amaze. Joining the "Miracle" Braves of 1914 and the "Miracle" Giants of 1951, were the "Miracle" Mets of 1969. Those Braves and Giants teams had distinguished themselves by coming from far out to take pennants, but they were nothing like the 1969 New York Mets, who practically needed a visa just to get into the first division. This expansion club, which had spent its seven-year history losing prodigiously, often hilariously, stunned and captivated an incredulous baseball world by scoring just enough runs all summer to give a remarkably strong-armed young pitching staff the margin they needed to rack up win after win.

They were a rare and wondrous blend of talent, spirit, and oneness,, playing gutty and hard-nosed baseball and at the same time projecting an image of artless and unspoiled enthusiasm, day by day creating their own myth, shaping it with heroics that seemed the more astonishing for being totally unexpected, capturing the interest of fan and nonfan alike, temporarily diverting and lightening an otherwise confused nation grimly embroiled in a bitter Asian war. What helped make the 1969 New York Mets a less-than-believable entity was not just the surprise of their trumph and the efficiency with which they executed it, but the fact that this team had behind it no history of winning, almost winning, or even of respectability. They had not, in fact, ever so much as achieved mediocrity. They were the epitome of that old American favorite, the underdog, without enemies, without ill-wishers—one indication of how unoffending they had been throughout their comically inept and bumbling history, during which they had set records, and standards, for futility.

Initially, the Mets had been managed by all-time Yankee pennant-winner Casey Stengel, who quickly proved that managerial genius without playing talent is meaningless. The early Mets lost and lost and lost, but never their charm, most exemplified by a noble athlete named Marvelous Marv Throneberry, a bulky first baseman who hustled gallantly and clumsily and who became the symbol of those early years of unavailing struggle. He was an apt symbol, because Marv played with more pride than skill, more effort than accomplishment, and the fans appreciated what he was trying to do and sympathized with his inability to do it. (Twice he tripled in one game and twice was called out for neglecting to touch first base. When Stengel rushed out to argue the second call he was intercepted by coach Cookie Lavagetto, who told him, "Forget it, Case. He didn't touch second either.")

New York fans, deprived of their Dodgers and Giants, united in support of the new club and bore witness in astonishing numbers, giving lie to the adage that losers were not welcome in the Big City. And losers the Mets surely were, averaging 105 losses a season for their first seven outings from 1962 through 1968, yet averaging better than 1.5 million customers a year, outdrawing most of the other National League teams. "If they ever become a .500 club," said one cynic, "they're doomed."

And they did not become a .500 club—they became a pennant-winner, a world champion. It seemed like an overnight turnaround, and that's what it was, for the year before they had finished in ninth place—as high as they had ever gone—and now the chronic 100-game losers were 100-game winners, and baseball had a team spun out of pure make-believe, visitors from a fantasy land that only sports can bring to reality.

But of course there was nothing make-believe about it. The origins of old mythology are irretrievably vanished in historic winds; but this particular myth was cooked and served before the eyes of recording angels, and it was done with superb pitching, solid defense, a steady patter of timely hitting, and one of those intangibles without which goals are seldom realized in sports, an esprit de corps that was genuine, refreshing, and contagious; a blend of tough professionalism and we-can-do-it fervor that would have looked corny in Hollywood. All of it was overseen by the steady, skillful, and unflappable managing of the old Brooklyn Dodger hero Gil Hodges (along with coach Yogi Berra the only "names" on this roster of "nobodies"), a quiet, patient man with frightening physical strength. "He sometimes managed by intimidation," said one of his players.

And it seemed that timely hitting was just about the only kind the Mets got in 1969—see what is perhaps their archetypical game that year, against Steve Carlton and the Cardinals on September 15, when Carlton set a record with 19 strikeouts yet lost 4–3 to a pair of two-run home runs by Ron Swoboda. Their .242 team batting average was bettered by seven other National League teams, their 632 runs bettered by eight other clubs, their 109 home runs bettered by seven other clubs. Their top RBI man was Tommie Agee, who drove in 76, a total topped by twenty-three other National League batters.

Logic and reason say it couldn't happen. Statistics virtually say it didn't. "We were pegged as a hundred-to-one shot in spring training, and some people thought even that was being charitable." That was· Tom Seaver, 25-game winner and club leader, remembering 1969. "But that never bothered us. We didn't pay any attention to it. We knew we were a good ball club and we sensed what was going to happen a lot earlier than anybody else. They called us 'The Miracle Mets.' Miracle, my eye. What happened was that a lot of good young players suddenly jelled and matured all at once." The chemistry on the '69 Mets, Seaver said "was a beautiful thing to feel and to see in action."

And so was Tom Seaver beautiful to see in action. Prince of a strong pitching staff that included Jerry Koosman, Nolan Ryan, Gary Gentry, and Tug McGraw, Seaver won 25 games and lost 7. He was a twenty-four-year-old whose boyish good looks, clean-cut collegiate demeanor (he had attended USC), keen intelligence, infectious laughter, live fastball, and nasty slider would have made him notable in any era. He was also an ex-Marine and had a sparklingly beautiful young blonde wife. The articulate, unpretentious right-hander was cherished by sportswriters, adored by fans, admired by teammates, respected by opponents. An interest in baseball history made him almost unique in a profession whose highest practitioners tradition-ally display neither knowledge of nor interest in their game's past. (Ask almost any active player to name players of sixty years ago and you won't get very far past Ruth, Cobb, Gehrig, or Walter Johnson. To certain parochial minds this is further evidence of the decline of education in America.)

Seaver evinced particular fascination with Mathewson, which was interesting, for he was in many ways a Mathewson clone, in looks, intellect, sophistication, and the broad range of his appeal. He was also the greatest right-handed pitcher to draw wages from a New York ball club since Matty. To push the analogy further, Seaver, like Mathewson, was dealt from New York to Cincinnati, albeit under different circumstances—the fading Matty was being given an op-portunity to manage, while Seaver, still in his prime, was dealt off because of a contract dispute with a dismally inept and petty management—but unlike Matty, Seaver, contrary to Thomas Wolfe's overworked dictum, did come home again (only to be lost once more, to the Chicago White Sox this time, in a free-agent compensation scramble, by a management that was not petty, merely inept).

The Mets' "Miracle" of 1969 seemed to touch all parts of a troubled country. For a brief moment a giddy and nostalgic dose of baseball's oft-proclaimed "team spirit" had diverted the quarrels and the recriminations (and prompted the compounding question, "If the Mets can win the pennant, why can't we get out of Vietnam?"). The team's ardent unity seemed both anomalous and ingenuous in the heated America of 1969, for no matter how the Mets players saw themselves, they were perceived as innocents risen triumphantly above the fray, twenty-five unstained Davids risen to vanquish the Goliaths of their world, weaving a rags-to-riches banner, enacting a Horatio Alger story that seemed a reaffirmation of the old, now besieged, virtues. (Seaver's very nickname, Tom Terrific, seemed like an Alger parody.)

The Mets' aura of unreality retained its enchantment through the World Series against a vastly superior Baltimore Orioles team that had won 109 regular-season games. For a balance of power, speed, defense, and pitching, few teams in the game's history can match the 1969 Orioles, a fact that makes the 1969 Mets all the more delectable.

The Mets even made it more interesting by losing the Series opener. But then they came back to win the second game, and then won the third on a pair of startling under-the-gun catches by centerfielder Agee, each of which ranks with Mays's celebrated grab in the 1954 Series. In Game Four there was another daredevil snare of a ball by rightfielder Ron Swoboda with the lead runs on base in the ninth inning. This catch was so improbable that when Tom Seaver, on the mound, saw Swoboda going for the line drive he was incredulous. "I couldn't believe he was trying for a catch of that ball in that situation," Seaver said. "There was no way he could get it." But get it Swoboda did, playing in the tailwind of a miracle now, and the game went into the tenth inning when the Mets won it because a pitcher's peg hit baserunner J. C. Martin on the wrist and caromed into right field, allowing the winning run to score from second base. (Photographs later established that Martin should have been called out for running in fair territory, but by that time the event was as unchangeable as yesterday's weather; destiny had ruled unappealably against truth and justice.)

They won it all in Game Five, and then poured into their clubhouse as their jubilant fans were tearing up the grounds of Shea Stadium in search of palpable evidence of the miracle. But even as the Mets players were trying to transport themselves on the elixir of their wondrous moment, they were falling captive to the unrelenting hordes from without, who were around them with cables, wires, cameras, microphones, tape recorders, pens, pencils, and notepads. "What I wanted to do after winning that World Series," said Tom Seaver, "was get into the clubhouse and share the joy and the excitement and the satisfaction with the guys I had played with. . . . I wanted more than anything else to enjoy that spontaneous sharing with my teammates while the victory was still warm and fresh and still tingling, while the emotional high was still climbing. But I never had that opportunity, because we had in effect been invaded. One group of reporters had one guy cornered here, another group had another guy cornered there, the TV people were grabbing us for interviews. It was absolute bedlam. We just couldn't get near one another, and that aspect of it was a great disappointment." All of the planet's previous miracles had escaped documentation. The one of 1969 would not.

The triumph of the moment notwithstanding, there was a certain sadness about it, because all who had participated and all who had watched it evolve knew that this was one of baseball's rare and unrepeatable treats, that it could not happen again with quite this wonder and intoxication. The hits and strikeouts achieved by the 1969 Mets were incantations that could know no reprise; the mold had broken forever, the shards gone skyward, leaving behind an enchantment unique in its winsome exhilaration. Shortly thereafter, the storybook triumph of the 1969 Mets began to look like the event that signaled baseball's final loss of innocence.

In 1972 the first general players' strike in baseball history delayed the opening of the season for ten days. The dispute centered on how much money the owners should contribute to the players' retirement fund and on the players' request that the owners absorb a $400,000 increase in annual medical and health care premiums. The strike began officially on April 1, and it took two weeks for John Gaherin, representing the owners, and Marvin Miller, the formidable leader of the Major League Baseball Players Association, to hammer out the agreement. The players won. Eighty-six games were lost to history during the strike, which proved to be a warmup for the big one in 1981 that saw the big leagues closed down for two months.

The owners won one shortly after when outfielder Curt Flood's challenge to the reserve clause was rejected by the United States Supreme Court. Flood had objected to a 1969 trade that sent him from the Cardinals to the Phillies. In his petition to the courts, he claimed that the reserve clause, which bound him unequivocally to the team that owned his contract, constituted involuntary servitude and was therefore unconstitutional. Privately, many baseball people knew this was true, but they felt that the removal of the clause would be like taking the top off the pigeon coop. Free-agent players, they maintained, would bring chaos and destroy baseball's structure. The Supreme Court's rejection of Flood's suit, however, was little more than a temporary reprieve for the owners.

The business structure of baseball presented a very strange partnership among the owners. Partners they were, competitive, yes, sometimes devious and cutthroat, but by the nature of things locked together. Their books were closed to each other, to the players, and to the public. Salaries, they claimed, were getting out of hand and would soon become ruinous—Henry Aaron's $200,000 was the top paycheck in 1972. That the owners were only kidding soon became evident, and for this they had to thank themselves, and in particular Charles O. Finley, maverick owner of the three-time world champion Oakland Athletics.

These Athletics, twice removed from Connie Mack's Philadelphia crew, were a colorful, brawling, talented gang of athletes, most of whose swing-outs were with each other, but who were united in one thing above all—their uncomplicated dislike of their autocratic, often insensitive owner. Finley, an insurance man by trade, possessed an uncanny baseball sense that enabled him to put together clubs that took it all in 1972, 1973, and 1974, thanks primarily to a strong pitching staff that featured Jim (Catfish) Hunter, Vida Blue, Ken Holtzman, and relief ace Rollie Fingers. Hunter was top dog on the staff, with four consecutive twenty-plus winning seasons, cresting with a 25–12 season in 1974.

It was a contractual dispute between Finley and Hunter after the 1974 season that finally made the players realize that the thrones their employers were sitting on were made of gold and not wicker. According to Hunter, his contract specified certain payments be made to him. Finley, either through refusal or oversight, did not make the payments. Accordingly, Hunter claimed the contract had therefore been abrogated and he was entitled to declare himself a free agent and sell his services to the highest bidder. An arbitration hearing upheld Hunter, and suddenly vaults all around baseball swung open. With almost every team courting the pitcher at his home in North Carolina, the offers began mounting into the millions of dollars. The New York Yankees, under new owner George Steinbrenner, came in with a five-year package worth anywhere from $2.8 to $3.7 million and walked off with Hunter. It was the most lucrative contract in the history of baseball, and players everywhere began forming different ideas about what they were worth and what their employers could afford to pay.

Baseball's economic structure dissolved once and for all with another arbitration decision on December 23, 1975. Pitchers Andy Messersmith of the Los Angeles Dodgers and Dave McNally, a longtime Baltimore Orioles star then with Montreal, had played the 1975 season without signing their contracts. (McNally was planning retirement from baseball and was simply lending his name to the test case.) At the end of the season each declared themselves free agents. Their employers invoked the reserve clause, claiming that their right to renew a player's contract for another twelve months meant *ad infinitum*. The players insisted that twelve months meant twelve months and that they had therefore "played out" their option and were now free to sign with anyone they chose.

On December 23, 1975, arbitrator Peter Seitz announced his decision, and a historic one it was: A player who "plays out" his contract by not signing for a year has discharged his contractual obligations. The owners responded with the grace of scalded bulls—they fired Seitz and claimed the decision applied only to Messersmith and McNally, not generally. But it was too late; the chains of the reserve clause had turned to wet bread.

The owners fought a hopeless rearguard action that included locking the players out of their spring training camps (a neat symbol this—locking the barn door after the horses, and so forth). Citing progress in the bargaining sessions that were going on, Commissioner Bowie Kuhn ordered the camps opened in the middle of March. By the middle of 1976 the Players Association and the owners had agreed on a modified version of the reserve clause that entitled a player to declare free agency after six years in the major leagues. Under the terms of the agreement, a player so declaring would go through a reentry draft, able to negotiate with a maximum of thirteen clubs (including his own) that had acquired the right to deal with him.

After seeing what the clubs had been offering Hunter, the players knew that they were now standing at the bottom of a landslide of money.

Multimillion-dollar contracts became routine. In less than a decade, after the 1983 season, the average major-league salary was estimated as being close to $300,000, and from the other world the voices of Charles Comiskey and Clark Griffith could be heard whispering, *"We're glad we're dead."*

The Frank Merriwells had short-cut the Horatio Algers. Never mind pluck and luck, hawking newspapers in blizzards, and then marrying the boss's daughter. More millionaires were getting their start in big-league farm systems than with Standard Oil or U.S. Steel, and they were changing the traditional image of the American millionaire—that paunchy, white-haired, wintry-faced plutocrat of the culminant success story. And they kept getting younger, signing their seven-figure contracts in their low twenties, getting all that money to play the game that was once considered an activity for rascals and drunkards. (Rascals and drunkards there still were, but they were much more socially acceptable now, along with the drugs that some of them were using, and the stories of disclosure and rehabilitation were considered inspirational.)

Rock stars and Hollywood luminaries had been cashing paychecks of this magnitude for a long while and no one seemed to mind; but because baseball had always been deemed public property, a certain element among the public seemed to feel they were being personally taxed to pay the ballplayers, seemed to feel that it was within their province to regard some of these salaries as indecent, scandalous, and an offense against good taste. (That the money was in most cases literally thrust upon the players was not considered relevant.) When Pittsburgh's Dave Parker, one of the first to sign one of these mammoth contracts, went out to right field to earn it he found himself upon a few occasions the target of flashlight batteries hurled at his head. It's possible the hurlers were telling him he needed more power, but more likely they were showing their resentment for the size of his income. Letters to the editor were filled with disapproving meditations about player contracts, as were callers to those disseminators of raw opinion called radio talk shows.

Assuming that much of this hostility toward the players' sudden affluence was originating among the working class, it presents a rather curious attitude. No one, of course, felt sorry for New York's

George Steinbrenner, California's Gene Autry, or any of the other multimillionaires who were signing the checks. Perhaps it was a suddenly distorted value system in an area in which many people considered themselves expert and whose sense of expertise was offended by the idea of a .260 hitter receiving millions of dollars. In addition, many of these contracts included incentive clauses promising large cash bonuses if the player did something to actually earn the millions, like making the All-Star team or winning some postseason award. Other contracts included weight clauses, promising the player extra cash if he was able to go from first to third on a single without making a pit stop. The owners found themselves caught in a morass, with their only guides out being lawyers and agents. A man swimming in a shark-infested pool had a better chance.

Nevertheless, whatever was provoking the public's negative reaction to the largesse in these contracts, it carried the odor of double standard, for how many people had ever been offended when their idols had been woefully underpaid? The big money permeating the game blurred the boundaries of baseball's world, pulling it away from the fans. No one heard these spiked-shoe capitalists say they would have played the game for nothing; no one would have believed them if they had said it.

The higher salaries and the establishment of the pension fund virtually assured that there would be no more Grover Cleveland Alexanders sitting forlornly as sideshow attractions in flea circuses. There were, however, contemporary parallels. Caught on the wrong side of the sharp demarcation of salary changes were stars like Mays and Mantle, deprived by a decade or so of becoming spectacular millionaires. Mantle, whose peak Yankee salary of $100,000 was approximately one-third of the big-league average fifteen years after his retirement, found himself hiring on (for that same wage) as "director of sports promotions" at Atlantic City's Claridge Hotel and Casino, a job that caused Commissioner Kuhn to sever Mickey's official links with baseball because casino employment was "inconsistent" with the good name of the game. This was no serious blow for Mantle—beyond the symbolic—since his recent official contact with baseball had been to serve as a batting instructor in the Yankee spring training camps, and even at that one suspected the only reason Mickey was there was because he embodied living history.

So rare are they, these enduring heroes of ours, that they demand recycling. They are unique celebrities, famous not for what they are but for what they were, what they did, and most of all for what they evoke. Atlantic City drew the jetted and the limousined, the catered to and the fawned upon, and few were more celebrated than the once-upon-a-time grass-green kid from Oklahoma who had replaced Joe DiMaggio in center field. If he wasn't Alexander sitting on a chair in a booth on Forty-second Street giving desultory recitations about the long-ago summers of his youth and strength, he was doing something equally pungent to old sweet memories. Mickey's job was designed as a shark to lure the casino's big rollers, men who came to lose in a single night or two as much money as Mickey earned in one of his heyday years; working, one might say, in a fleece circus. The glittering line-of-credit men got the privilege, if so desired, of playing eighteen holes of golf with a bona fide American legend and later on having dinner and some drinks with him and listening to the drawling voice tell tales of Casey and Roger and Yogi and Joe D. As it has always been, Mantle and Mays were still linked, for Willie had been engaged by another Atlantic City money-spiller, Bally's Park Place Hotel and Casino, as "special assistant to the president," and despite the high-flown title, Willie, too, had been requested to dissolve all official connections with baseball. What's in a name? Well, enough to make a man forever captive to the fantasies of strangers.

THIRTY

A BILLION-DOLLAR TELEVISION CONTRACT. Players—and not necessarily the best, either—earning $2 million a year. Deferred payments well into the twenty-first century. Lawyers. Agents. Financial consultants. Free agency. Arbitration. Player strikes. Artificial playing surfaces. Domed stadiums. Would John McGraw still recognize his game? The answer to that is more astonishing than any of the above: Yes, he would. Because it was, in all of its crucial basics, still the same patient, carefully paced game with which American boys had filled their summer afternoons a century before. The ball was still round, you still had to throw it and hit it and catch it; you still had to run and slide and score your runs. There were still the same unchanging energies and desires and impulses and strivings that sent youngsters dashing across meadows that had become towns and towns that had become cities.

Something else had remained intact within the swaying rhythms and measured cadences that were baseball; there were still those few, those very few, who somehow became more than just compelling performers, who brought onto the field with them some quality— charm, ego, zeal, humility, modesty, daring, excitement—that radiated as something microcosmic upon the senses and ultimately the memories of all who saw them play. Again, that elemental mystery defined as charisma, that enabling quality giving a player life above and beyond the record book.

Through much of the 1970s and into the 1980s the inexplicable mystique focused most emphatically upon two players, Reggie Jackson and Pete Rose. An American Leaguer and a National Leaguer. A black man and a white man. A slugger and a line-driver. An articulate, vainglorious man who boasted of a 160 I.Q. A perpetual motion, nose-in-the-dirt man who at one time stated his ambition was to be "the first hundred-thousand-dollar-a-year singles hitter."

One—the black man—infuriated as many fans as he captivated. The other projected an image of Everyman as star. The common ground? Both excelled under pressure, could not be ignored, roused crowds with the long and short of their specialties, and each, to be sure, drove a Rolls-Royce. Not Willie Stargell, Jim Rice, Mike Schmidt, but Reggie Jackson. Not Rod Carew or Joe Morgan, but Pete Rose. Yes, Johnny Bench and George Brett generated gales of excitement; but Jackson and Rose created passion.

Heavy gunner of the invincible Oakland teams of the early 1970s, Jackson opted for free agency and came, inevitably, to New York, to the Yankees of George Steinbrenner and Billy Martin, expecting to take his place in the Ruth-Gehrig-DiMaggio-Mantle pantheon, alienated his teammates and his manager with his corrosive ego ("I am the straw that stirs the drink"), and charged up the fans as no Yankee since Mantle had done. His every trip to the plate was pure theater. He struck out with the gusto of a Ruth and smashed long, tail-wind home runs at moments Frank Merriwell would have envied. Removed from a game in the middle innings by Martin for allegedly not hustling in the field, he came near to a dugout punch-out with his emotional skipper on network television.

Reginald Martinez Jackson. "Your first name's white," said teammate Mickey Rivers. "Your second is Hispanic, and your third belongs to a black. No wonder you don't know who you are." Not true. Reggie had always known full well who he was, and more than that—where he wanted to go, what he wanted to be. He had the talent, the looks, the brains, the wit, the ambition, and if being black made it a bit tougher, it probably also made him a bit grittier, the same way it added dimension to Jackie Robinson, Bob Gibson, Roberto Clemente, and the other blacks who had never liked having to be twice as good in order to compete equally. By the time Reggie came along, the path beaten by Robinson had been paved—partially anyway—and a black man could prepare for a fistfight with his white manager without fear of impeding the civil rights movement; and Martin, for his part, could have the latitude to refer to his star slugger as "a piece of shit" without fear of being called a racist. Progress has many contortions. So with much of the pioneering work having been accomplished, Jackson could concentrate on solidifying the gains, which to a large extent meant satisfying his cavernous ego.

A black egotist, by all historical and social precedent, should have been an unpopular figure. But despite having his detractors, Reggie was not. His teammates in Oakland, Baltimore, New York, and Anaheim soon learned he was a piece of work and that you had better give him the room he needed, because if you got too close those bright rays of personality would blot you out anyway. Citing Reggie's generosity, Catfish Hunter, a teammate both in Oakland and New York, said Reggie would "give you the shirt off his back. Of course, he'd call a press conference to announce it."

Jackson was the one man who refused to be intimidated by New York. He was bright enough to understand the city, that it could be a soul-crusher or a place of magic carpets. He knew the city was demanding and skeptical, and cold and warm and loving and forgiving, that it might give you its heart or its fist, its applause or its boos. He was prepared for all eventualities. "They don't boo nobodies," he said, knowing that wherever he went and whatever he did, "I can't be ignored." He knew, too, that a slugger coming to Yankee Stadium had to contend with the granite past of Ruth, Gehrig, DiMaggio, and Mantle. So he met it head-on, announcing to the city that it wasn't getting a work-in-progress but a finished product. "I didn't come to New York to be a star," he said. "I brought my star with me." He had said if he ever played in New York they would name a candy bar after him. And when he did, they did. ("When you unwrap a Reggie bar," said Hunter, "it tells you how good it is.")

Never did Reggie Jackson's star shine higher or brighter than on the night of October 18, 1977, at Yankee Stadium. It was on this night, as the Yankees were wrapping up another World Series title against the Los Angeles Dodgers, that Reggie gilded his own portrait with three home runs, giving him a total of five in the Series and thus an achievement that out-Ruthed Ruth and everyone else in Series history. Giving the feat a special Jacksonian touch was that each bolt into the night was struck against the first pitch delivered by a different pitcher—Burt Hooton, Elias Sosa, Charlie Hough. Hough bemoaned his knuckler: "It didn't move." "Not until I hit it," said Reggie.

Because he was able to key his most spectacular performance to the most critical moments, he became known as Mr. October. He made it seem that occasions were rising to him, rather than he to they. His appetite to please was Ruthian. "I love competition," he said. "It motivate me, stimulates me, excites me. It is almost sexual.

I just love to hit that baseball in a big game." They all do, of course, but Jackson manifested it to near palpability. And on the esthetics of it: "When you take a pitch and *line* it somewhere, it's like you've thought of something and put it with beautiful clarity."

He exuded the total freedom for which Jackie Robinson had begun a lonely, dangerous fight three decades earlier. He spoke his mind on anything and everything. Once upon a time his detractors would have described him as uppity; but now he was an egotist (another small but telling measurement of progress). He spread himself over varied and successful business enterprises. He collected automobiles, antique and flashy new. He was courted by journalists, interviewed on television by Barbara Walters (a bingo status symbol in this society).

If Jackson was in many respects the eptiome of the new, incorporated hero, the equally transcendent Pete Rose represented a kind of time-honored folklore, nostalgic old values, a less gaudy stardust. While it certainly isn't true that the old-timers all hustled like Rose, it's enough that he made people think they did. He seemed a connective link to the game's origins (and, some thought, to the species' as well, so ablaze with primary bluntness was his style of play). He took the field every day and played as though he were the conscience of baseball, only accidentally of the age of the guaranteed contract and of outfielders who shied from walls or tumbling catches in their option years. He was vestigial, a throwback.

This pugnacious grass-roots hustler must be ranked among the greatest players of all time, a superstar with intangibles to match his tangibles. In an era notable for individuality, Rose demonstrated unique selflessness. In order to help his team, he moved—uncomplainingly—from his original second-base position to third base, to right field, to left field, and to first base, and did it with an enthusiasm that was part of his transmissive magic. "I'd walk through hell in a gasoline suit to keep playing baseball," he said, and it was this incorrigible love of the game, conspicuous for more than two decades without diminishment, that made him a money's worth performer.

Why Pete Rose and not Rod Carew, whom statistics proclaim as the most efficient hitter since Williams? Well, for all his excellence at home plate, you simply do not get a *sense* of Carew. Like Henry Aaron, Carew brought no dynamic to the batter's box with him. Baseball, among other things, is theater, a definition that mandates that a very small number of players will be strikingly distinctive because of productivity and "presence." In his severe crouch at home plate, the barrel-chested Rose projected a muscular determination, a life-or-death resolve that suggested he would remain as intent with that bat if he were facing a charging lion instead of a baseball. He conveyed a center-of-the-universe tension at home plate, the same kind of lust for his line drive as Jackson's for his "tater." One could sense the eruption inside of Rose when one of his liners winged to earth untouched. For all of his seven batting titles, Carew never sent the voltage through a crowd the way Rose did, and for a man to be able to do this with singles and doubles is without precedent since Cobb, whose all-time record of 4,191 hits Rose set himself in pursuit of. Accordingly, Rose watched his statistics with the same care a politician does popularity polls.

By his own admission not as naturally gifted as many of the immortals among whom he is now numbered, he milked every drop out of his talent, outhustling what he could not overpower, perhaps driven by whatever old insecurities had been seeded by once having been small for his age and considered too slight to be a candidate for professional baseball. Cincinnati-born and -bred, he yearned to play for his hometown team, and it was only through the persuasive powers of an uncle who was scouting for the Reds that he got a contract. He started in 1960 with the Geneva, New York, team in the Class D New York–Pennsylvania League. Joining the club after his high school graduation, he played half a season, batted .277 and was voted by fans as the club's most popular player. "They liked the way I hustled," he said. Even then.

In 1978 Rose did something that for thirty-seven years had been variously considered unlikely, improbable, and almost unimaginable—he hit continuously enough to get as far as the anteroom of Joe DiMaggio's 56-game hitting streak. So many of the game's priceless treasures had been pillaged and vandalized over the past few decades—Ruth's home-run records, Cobb's stolen-base records—it suddenly seemed possible that the game's heretofore inviolable "56" might also be despoiled. If Rose got 44 games toward DiMaggio's record (setting a new National League record for consecutive-game hitting) before collapsing on the slopes of this particular Olympus, he did achieve something tellingly significant—he had made, for a moment, "56" seem attainable, mortal. But only for a moment, for when he was finally stopped, the DiMaggio achievement, like some extraterrestrial body that had floated close enough to allow itself to be seen, soared off once more to its own stellar regions.

But for Rose, the streak at once bespoke the credo he lived by and the epitaph he once whimsically suggested for himself:

"Here lies the man who could hit forever."

THIRTY-ONE

THEY HAVE BECOME a mandatory part of baseball culture, a midsummer highlight in big-league ball parks. They are called Old Timer's Days, but it is a misnomer, for the men being roll-called onto the field for one more run of the applause are not old but young, and never mind the white hair and the faltering step, for they bring with them those time-shedding memories that are part of the continuity of baseball, and when these men move out onto a baseball diamond they are participating in a ritual that for a few moments allows them to trim their shadows and be as memory has set them. Within each lies an anchorage of youth, a Dorian Gray–like image etched into the minds of those who have come to applaud not old men but to renew the vigor of old memories and the young men who helped define a time long ago, who rushed in all the trappings of youth across the green grass of yesterday and set in motion evocative pendulums of remembering that have remained ceaseless.

If Americans are a generous and forgiving people, it follows that they are also sentimental, but how many occasions are there for them to unabashedly applaud their heroes, the sere leaves of another generation? Baseball's history is linear, and its past cavalcades an almost genetic part of its present. No other sport has Old Timer's Days, no other sport takes such pride in parading its living history. Anomalous America, the world's oldest democracy while still youngest of the major nations, an onrushing country of dynamic innovation, persists with odd musterings of its past. Many national occasions, once hallowed, like presidential birthdays, Memorial Day, and the Fourth of July, may have lost some of their former significance. The moment of silence on what was once Armistice Day is long gone. Cynicism has sullied large tracts of history. But Old Timer's Day provides one more wholehearted, united rousing of the past, a past that flows riverlike into the present, comforting and reassuring.

Ballplayers remain what remembering and what ageless statistics declare them to be, and herein lies one of the enchantments of Old Timer's Day; it is a glow of emotion and a feast of memory, a return to a timeless landscape. The names of lang syne big-leaguers being announced on a baseball diamond can lull the imagination into a nostalgic journey back to other times and make those times seem, unaccountably, better and more placid.

It was a bright, hot Saturday afternoon at New York's Shea Stadium. An old-time baseball afternoon, appropriate for Old Timer's Day, and some of the men waiting to be honored had been uniformed through thousands of such afternoons, going back to a time when Ruth was a rookie and Cobb the snarling lion of the basepaths. Some of them had braved Walter Johnson's fastballs and hacked at the darting curves of Grover Cleveland Alexander. They had been thrown out by Wagner, put their gloves in front of a Hornsby scorcher, and swung at swifties thrown by Grove and Dean. There were men of might and myth, like DiMaggio and Mays and Mantle, and men of moments, like Bill Wambsganss, whose unassisted triple play in the 1920 World Series had taken perhaps five seconds to execute, and who was remembered forevermore for it. Eighty-three years old now, Bill Wamby walked slowly and had trouble remembering the names of old friends, and one had to wonder how vivid in his own mind remained one of baseball's imperishable moments, whether those few seconds of time frozen in an October more than fifty-five years ago had around them some eternal light of memory, or whether they, too, were beginning to blur.

And there, too, was the man who almost never struck out, Joe Sewell, small and round-shouldered, those uncanny eyes still sharp. And Al Lopez, catcher of more games than anyone in baseball history. And Tommy Henrich, the popular Yankee, with a fine career but remembered primarily for having been the strikeout that Mickey Owen dropped in the ninth inning of the fourth game of the 1941 World Series. And Duke Snider was there, and Willie Mays and Mickey Mantle and Whitey Ford. But the unquestioned monarch of the occasion was DiMaggio, properly regal and reserved.

He is known at these affairs as the man they save for last, because there are none bigger, because the crowd prefers it that way, and because it is theatrically correct, so that the Hero of Heroes can hear the loudest applause, the longest cheers. And so after the stars and the legends and the mere men of five seconds of enduring glory had doffed their caps in the sunshine, he trotted slowly onto the field, still trim and limber, fingers touching the bill of his cap as if to hold it in place against the gales of greeting, not removing it until he had reached the center of the diamond and taken his place with the others, and then lifting it from his silver hair and holding it aloft for what seemed the precisely correct number of moments. The crowd was thunderously on its feet for this true *artiste* of the diamond, descendant of Ruth, ancestor to Mantle, progenitor of the living emotions of millions, embodiment of stirring statistics.

Left in the dugout, properly in the shade while the DiMaggio reception filled the sunshine, were the civilians—the writers, photographers, and a handful of others who had never worn a big-league uniform. Among them a conversation began. What, someone wanted to know, would the pecking order be if Yankees Ruth and Gehrig were still alive, a not unreasonable reverie, since Babe would have been eighty-two and Lou seventy-four.

"Well," asked another, "what would the pecking order be for Washington, Jefferson, and Lincoln?"

"Listen," said a more widely oriented student of American history, "what would it be if they were all here—Washington, Jefferson, Lincoln, Ruth, Gehrig, and DiMaggio?"

Now the discussion became learned and spirited. All realities were carefully considered, the American ethos studiously probed and examined. The achievement of fathering one's country was weighed against 60 home runs in a season. The Emancipation Proclamation was pitted against 2,130 consecutive games. Authorship of the Declaration of Independence was measured against a 56-game hitting streak. Legends of the baseball world were measured against those in the nation that—nominally, at least—contains it.

Finally a consensus emerged. In ascending order, it was: Gehrig, Jefferson, DiMaggio, Ruth, Washington. And the man they save for last: Lincoln.

That old Union soldier, Abner Doubleday, would approve.

Index